MORALITY, MORTALITY

Volume II

MORALITY, MORTALITY

VOLUME II

Rights, Duties, and Status

F. M. Kamm

New York   Oxford
OXFORD UNIVERSITY PRESS
1996

Oxford University Press

Oxford   New York
Athens   Auckland   Bangkok   Bombay
Calcutta   Cape Town   Dar es Salaam   Delhi
Florence   Hong Kong   Istanbul   Karachi
Kuala Lumpur   Madras   Madrid   Melbourne
Mexico City   Nairobi   Paris   Singapore
Taipei   Tokyo   Toronto

and associated companies in
Berlin   Ibadan

Published by Oxford University Press, Inc.,
198 Madison Avenue, New York, New York 10016

Oxford is a registered trademark of Oxford University Press

Library of Congress Cataloging-in-Publication Data
(Revised for vol. 2)

Kamm, F. M. (Frances Myrna)
Morality, mortality.

(Oxford ethics series)
Includes bibliographical references and indexes.
Contents: v. 1. Death and whom to save from it
—v. 2. Rights, duties, and status.
1. Terminal care—Moral and ethical aspects.
2. Death.   I. Title.
R726.K35   1993   174′.24   92-9496
ISBN 0-19-507789-X (v. 1)
ISBN 0-19-508459-4 (v. 2)

1 3 5 7 9 8 6 4 2

Printed in the United States of America
on acid-free paper

For the love of morality, another way to live

Preface

This book is concerned with the structure of non-consequentialist (deontological) ethical theories — the role of rights, duties and status therein. Chapters 1 through 3 derive from my M.I.T. doctoral dissertation, "Problems in the Morality of Killing and Letting Die," and an article "Killing and Letting Die: Methodological and Substantive Issues," in *Pacific Philosophical Quarterly*, 1983. On various drafts of these I received helpful comments from Barbara Herman, Joshua Cohen, Raziel Abelson, and Thomas Nagel. I am grateful to Joshua Cohen and, especially, to Barbara Herman, for thesis direction and subsequent editorial advice. I was first introduced to the topics dealt with in these chapters in a seminar given by Robert Nozick. Chapter 5 derives from my article "Harming, Not Aiding, and Positive Rights," in *Philosophy & Public Affairs*, Winter 1986, on which I received suggestions from members of the Society for Ethical and Legal Philosophy and the editors of that journal. Chapters 6 and 7 are related to "Harming Some to Save Others," in *Philosophical Studies*, November 1989, and "The Doctrine of Double Effect: Theoretical and Practical Issues," in *The Journal of Medicine and Philosophy*, 1991. I received helpful comments on the articles from the editors of those journals, and on the chapter from members of the Society for Ethical and Legal Philosophy and Shelly Kagan. Chapters 8, 9, and 10 derived from parts of "Harming Some to Save Others," "Non-consequentialism, the Person as an End-in-Itself and the Significance of Status," in *Philosophy and Public Affairs*, Fall 1992, and a lengthy unpublished article "Prerogatives and Restrictions," parts of which were delivered at two American Philosophical Association Meetings, Pacific Division, in 1984 and 1985. I received suggestions on the latter from the audiences and commentators at those meetings, from members of the Society for Ethical and Legal Philosophy, Thomas Scanlon, Thomas Nagel, Samuel Scheffler, and members of the New York University Law and Philosophy Group. I received suggestions on Chapter 11 from Ronald Dworkin, Thomas Nagel, and members of the N.Y.U. Colloquium in Law, Philosophy, and Social Theory. Chapter 12 is based on my article "Supererogation and Obligation," in *Journal of Philosophy*, March 1985. It benefited from suggestions made by that journal's editors and by Thomas Nagel, Mary Mothersill, Shelly Kagan, David Dolinko, and Steven Munzer. I thank the editors of the journals in which the articles appeared for permission to reprint sections.

Material in this book has been presented in my graduate ethics classes and to various audiences at New York University, M.I.T., Columbia, Princeton, Yale, Boston University Law School, the University of Arizona, and Tufts University. I am indebted to my colleagues and students who listened and offered suggestions. Over the years I have profited from the comments of Ronald Dworkin, Thomas Scanlon, Louis Kornhauser, and Larry Sager, and from discussions at the Society for Ethical and Legal Philosophy. Most recently the manuscript was presented at my graduate seminar at the University of California at Los Angeles. I am very grateful for discussion with members of that seminar, especially Michael Otsuka, David Kaplan, Barbara Herman, William Fitzpatrick, Alon Harel, Matthew Hanser, Jodie Halpern, Tim Hall, Julie Tannenbaum, Roger Florka, and Carol Voeller.

My work on this book has been financially supported by a grant from the American Council of Learned Societies, a New York University Presidential Fellowship and Research Challenge Fund Grant, an American Association of University Women Fellowship, a Silver Fellowship in Law, Science and Technology at Columbia University Law School, a Fellowship in Ethics and the Professions, Harvard University, and a Fellowship at the Center for Human Values, Princeton University. Over the years, I have also benefited from the support of Dean Ann Burton at New York University who provided funds for typing and other related services. For all this help I am very grateful.

I would like to thank the typists who went through so many drafts, Nerssa Miller, Marie Palumbo, Helen Snively, and especially Lynne Gay. I thank Leigh Cauman and Katya Rice for their editorial advice, and Lynne Gay for help in making the index.

At Oxford University Press I am indebted to many staff members for their help and patience.

While writing the material in this book, I have received support and encouragement from Mala Kamm, Samuel Kamm, Mara Alexander, Jane Cohen, Stefan Bauer-Mengelberg, Gertrude Ezorsky, Marie Friquenon, Jeffrey Gorden, Michael Otsuka, Rosamund Rhodes, Janet Radcliffe Richards, Seana Shiffrin, Maria Twarog, and Arthur Zitrin. The goodness and intelligence of my parents, Mala and Solomon Kamm, have helped me throughout my life.

I am especially grateful to Thomas Nagel for his support and for the example of his intellect. On this project, in particular, my biggest debt over the years is to Derek Parfit, for encouragement, discussion, and wonderfully detailed comments.

New York, New York   F.M.K.
July, 1993

Contents

MORALITY, MORTALITY

Volume II

Introduction

Morality, Mortality as a whole deals with certain aspects of general normative ethical theory. It also deals with moral problems that arise primarily in contexts involving life-and-death decisions. The importance of the theoretical issues and the usefulness of the discussion of them are not limited to their relevance to these decisions, however. The issues are at the heart of basic moral and political theory.

The second volume comprises three parts. We begin with five chapters discussing the question of the moral (in)equivalence of killing and letting die, harming and not aiding. Part II offers a discussion of the so-called Trolley Problem and some other closely related dilemmatic situations, for the purpose of developing a principled account of when harming some to save others is permissible and when impermissible. Part III is concerned with the further examination of the relation between restrictions on conduct and prerogatives not to make sacrifices, and how these topics relate to human rights, duties, and the existence of valuable entities and states of affairs. In addition, we are concerned with the power of agreements and of supererogatory conduct to override restrictions.

In chapter 1 we begin by considering the methodology of comparable cases used to test for the Thesis of the Moral Equivalence of Killing and Letting Die (Thesis E). We consider how to create cases that are properly *equalized* for all factors besides killing and letting die, analyzing how this is *standardly* done and also how, it might be suggested, it should be *nonstandardly* done by equalizing cases cross-definitionally as well as contextually. We argue against using nonstandardly equalized kill and let-die cases as test cases for Thesis E, and we distinguish between a strong and a weak version of that thesis. In addition, we consider whether terminating aid is killing or letting die, and we examine Joel Feinberg's views on the right to be aided.

In chapter 2 we consider a new use for nonstandardly equalized cases, comparing cross-definitionally equalized killing and non-cross-definitionally equalized killing cases to collect evidence for the truth or falsity of Thesis E. In addition we compare cross-definitionally equalized killing and letting-die cases to test for the moral significance of what we call "nonexportable" definitional properties of killing or letting die. With this as a foundation we present two arguments against Thesis E; one argument that focuses on the significance of certain definitional properties of killing and letting die, and one transitivity argument. The first argument may tell us *why* killing and letting die differ morally per se, not only *that* they do. We also focus on two methodological issues in making these arguments: the Principle of Contextual Interaction and the possible failure of transitivity.

The first section of chapter 3 is concerned with objections and alternatives to the arguments and analyses of the first two chapters. We deal with the issue of self-ownership and the negative/positive rights distinction and the issue of per se moral differences only sometimes making a difference in cases depending on contexts. We consider what relation there might be between the killing/letting-die distinction and the intention/foresight distinction (whose moral significance is described by the Doctrine of Double Effect). We pay particular attention to the objections Shelly Kagan has made to my proposals and to the alternative views on positive and negative agency that Warren Quinn developed. The second section of chapter 3 returns to examine the stronger and weaker notions of per se moral equivalence, their differential relation to the moral equivalence of cases, and what they reveal about explanation in ethics and aesthetics.

Chapter 4 presents four different tests to use on standardly equalized kill and let-die cases to determine the truth of Thesis E. We first present the Post Efforts Test (which is contrasted with the defeasibility test) and consider its results on variously varied cases, including cases where there are no wrong acts. (This is related to issues of strict liability and agent regret.) Objections to the test are also examined. Second is the Pre-Efforts Test, which requires us to forgo benefit, make sacrifices, or be imposed on to prevent behavior. After showing how this test might distinguish morally between killing and letting die, we consider objections to it raised by Bruce Russell and Joel Feinberg. We also consider what moral difference is being measured by these tests — a difference in moral objectionableness or in some other moral property — and the significance of not imposing losses on someone when he is dependent on some people but independent relative to others. The Choice Test comes third. It is in some ways more sensitive than the first two tests and may also yield different results. This is the first indication we have that there are (at least) two different measures for the stringency of prohibitions on acts — an efforts measure and a precedence measure. (This is an issue to which we pay much attention in chapter 12.) Again, the question arises whether the tests measure differences in moral objectionableness of killing and letting die or some other morally significant property (i.e., one related to how much we may require people to do). Finally, we present the Good Motive Test, which considers killing and letting-die cases in which we act either for greater good or for paternalistic reasons (e.g., in euthanasia), and consider Philippa Foot's views on the contrasting virtues of justice and charity.

Chapter 5 considers what would follow if the General Thesis (GE) of the moral equivalence of harming and not aiding were true. The possible existence of positive rights (or duties minus correlative rights) is considered, and an argument against positive rights by Judith Thomson is examined. We consider arguments that attempt to derive positive rights or duties from the existence of negative rights and warn against the failure to consider the role of independent rights or self-standing claims to things, and the significance of already having had something. We persist in seeing how far we can come, consistent with Thesis GE, to deriving the Radical Conclusion that we may have a right to something to which we have no independent right or self-standing claim if it is not permissible to take it from us.

Part II comprises two chapters. Having considered how to determine whether there is a moral difference between killing and letting die per se in Part I, we consider when it is and is not permissible to kill some to save others. First, we examine in some detail the arguments John Harris has made for a Survival Lottery and consider a very limited context in which we might install a curtailed survival lottery. The rest of the chapter is devoted to consideration of the many attempts to solve the problem of why we may not ordinarily kill one to save more (as in the Transplant Case) but may kill via redirection of threats (as in the Trolley Case). These attempts include the views of Foot, proponents of the Doctrine of Double Effect (e.g., Costa), Quinn, Montmarquet, Thomson, and Bruce Russell. We also examine in some detail whether the notion of "being already involved" is a moral notion or can be given a nonmoral description. In chapter 7 we present a new proposal (related to an earlier proposal of mine) for a Principle of Permissible Harm (PPH), one upshot of which is to show that many redirection-of-threat cases are not *sui generis* but one of a class of cases in which greater good (or its structurally equivalent component or a means that has greater good as its noncausal flip side) may permissibly cause lesser harm. We compare this PPH with the Doctrine of Double Effect and point out a morally crucial distinction concealed within the concept of "intending." The problem is to explain what important moral notions the PPH expresses; we investigate this (focusing on the maintenance of appropriate relations between victim and beneficiaries) and why the PPH does not govern omissions (even when there are positive rights). We conclude by examining the bearing of the PPH on the killing/letting-die distinction, and the problem of euthanasia, also noting how its application is limited by, among other considerations, the Principle of Secondary Permissibility and the distinction between intra- and inter-personal benefits.

The PPH represents a *right* people have not to be treated in certain ways in order to produce a greater good (e.g., increased utility); there is a *restriction* on conduct. The question now arises of whether it is morally permissible to treat people in ways ruled out by the PPH only for the sake of minimizing violations of the PPH itself, or whether there is a *constraint* on doing this. The first three chapters of Part III are concerned with this issue. In chapter 8, we first examine the arguments Samuel Scheffler presents against both restrictions and constraints, and his defense of prerogatives not to maximize good or minimize harm (his Hybrid Theory). Since Scheffler's views on prerogatives are in some ways related to those of Bernard Williams, we consider the latter's views on integrity. Our criticism of Scheffler in section one of this chapter is concerned with his view of the supposed gulf between prerogatives and restrictions. We consider whether too great an emphasis on an *active/passive* distinction (not to be confused with an act/omission distinction) does not underlie his strong opposition to restrictions and whether (by a transitivity argument) he is committed to no restrictions even in pursuing personal non-optimal projects. While we consider possible similarities between prerogatives and restrictions (or constraints), we focus on crucial differences with respect to minimizing the violation of prerogatives and restrictions, these differences giving rise to what we call the Value and Selection Problems. We consider solutions to the Selection Problem based on asymmetries in victims and differentiation between agents. In section two of chapter 8, we reexamine the foundations of a prerogative (not to maximize good or to minimize harm) which Scheffler located in the *personal point of view* (PPV). Rejecting the sufficiency of Scheffler's account, we focus on freedom of choice over entitlements in creatures who are ends-in-themselves, discussing briefly the idea of reasons generated from the PPV in such creatures. Finally, we examine the arguments Shelly Kagan has constructed for and against prerogatives, including the Negative and Positive Arguments, and the Argument from Vividness.

Chapter 9 is devoted to further examination of one approach to the Selection Problem that arises in justifying constraints, namely, agent differentiation: the fact that something would be done by me rather than by someone else. We contrast traditional (victim-focused and rights-based) views with four revisionist (agent-relative and agent-focused) views on dealing with cases in which one person is killed in order to save others from being killed. Different notions of the Self, act-scenes, negative factors to be avoided, temporal dimensions, and degrees of self-indulgence are examined in relation to the problem of justifying the constraint. One revisionist view is shown to bear a crucial similarity to the traditional view.

Having considered alternative grounds for a constraint, in chapter 10 we return to flesh out a victim-focused, agent-neutral, rights-based view founded in a strengthened PPH right (constraint), which protects against minimizing violations of the right by violating the right. We consider whether and in what sense minimizing violations of PPH rights by violating them would be both strictly irrational and also exhibit lack of concern for the right. Rejecting this as a route to founding the constraint [on grounds that strict irrationality would arise only if there were already a constraint (or an absolute right not to be killed)], we start again, generating a constraint by focusing on a concern that is at the heart of the PPH and applying it to the pursuit of any goal (utility or minimization of rights violations). We consider how the permissibility of minimization would alter every person's status and examine the distinction between eliminating a right, violating it, and infringing it, focusing on the significance of negative residues of, and compensation for, rights violations. We explore whether the structure of deontological and consequentialist theories can be brought closer together via the agent-neutral value of an inviolable status (of a certain sort), though we distinguish between the irrationality argument against minimizing the violation of constraints and support for a concept of the person as strongly inviolable. We also consider whether creatures who are inviolable are therefore more important entities whose existence makes the world a better place and whether belief in a constraint affects both how good the world is and the effect of acts done in accord with or in opposition to the constraint. We further examine the futility of permitting minimization of rights violations by violating rights ("futilitarianism") by contrasting the role of utility versus rights per se in motivating minimizing.

If it is in one way in people's interest that there be constraints (because it gives them a more sublime and elevated status), is it still possible for them to agree ex ante to alienate those rights for the sake of other interests they have? Can we do away with constraints protecting an individual not because it is for the greater good of others, but because ex ante it is in his own interest for there to be no constraints? This is the question that prompts chapter 11. Our emphasis is on victim-focused reasons against such agreements to use oneself at one time for one's own good at another time, and on the limits to a strategy of founding morality on agreements and allowing duties to be overridden by agreements. We plot the outline of the types of agreements permitted by "common-sense morality."

The concluding chapter returns to a problem first raised in chapter 8, namely, reconciling the existence of prerogatives not to maximize overall good (allowing for some such acts to be supererogatory) with restrictions on the pursuit of one's personal good. This problem becomes especially pressing since, despite our earlier emphasis on the existence of restrictions to pursuing the greater good, it is sometimes the case that greater good may permissibly take precedence over restrictions, for example, negative and positive duties or rights. If personal good may take precedence over greater good (allowing some acts for greater good to be supererogatory), and these supererogatory acts may take precedence over restrictions, why may not personal good take precedence over restrictions? Why does transitivity fail here? We attempt to prove each premise in this argument separately, arguing first that (in both weaker and stronger senses), the supererogatory may sometimes take precedence over duty. We try to deal with objections to this view. Then we argue that supererogation may even take precedence over a duty when greater personal efforts must be made to perform the duty than must be made to do the supererogatory. Here we have the reappearance of the phenomenon we first noted in chapter 4, that there are two different measures of stringency which can yield conflicting results: the efforts measure and the precedence measure. This is all we need to generate intransitivity and to produce a moral system with both prerogatives and constraints on personal pursuits. However, in dealing with an important objection we discover the need to distinguish between two types of the intransitivity, each having a pairwise and a complete form, and to focus on how any precedence that supererogation takes over large personal efforts or the pursuit of personal goals is mediated by the subordinate relation of these to duty. Having shown that the intransitivity exists, and is at the heart of a system with both prerogatives and restrictions, in section two of chapter 12 we try to find out *why* there should be this intransitivity by canvassing several possible explanations of why supererogation, but not personal good, may precede duty. Among our results are (1) the distinction between what we may require people to do for the sake of minimal versus superminimal acts, though both are parts of a morality that represents the objective worth of persons; (2) the unimportance of what we care about, how much we care being measured by our willingness to make sacrifices, in determining what we may reasonably do in dilemmatic situations; (3) the difference between a personal and various objective measures of the importance of what we do; (4) the distinction between "sacrificing for" and "losing on account of," in a complex and almost desperate attempt to avoid treating humanity (in oneself or others) as a mere means to greater good. In section three of this chapter we consider whether the intransitivity arises only because different factors account for precedence relations in each step of the argument, or rather whether our result is more general, and, indeed, another instance of the Principle of Contextual Interaction. We also consider whether our intransitivities share the cycling property characteristic of other intransitivities. We conclude by applying these results to a further discussion of those who never allow duty to be subordinated to supererogation, to Scheffler's Hybrid Theory, and to Parfit's problem of the Repugnant Conclusion.

Methodologies

Some philosophers begin with a *theory*—comprising prominent concepts, and principles or procedures—whose correctness is either immediately clear to them or has been argued for; in either case, they accept the view that the theory is logically prior to its application to specific cases. If they are convinced of the theory's correctness, they will accept any implications it might have for particular cases. For example, they may believe that happiness maximized is the most important goal, no matter how it is achieved. Although such philosophers may sometimes feel uncomfortable with the results of their theory, they do not allow their intuitive responses to cases to overrule the theory. (They may, however, expect their theory to give an account of why they have these intuitive responses which diverge from the theory. This is like the scientist who must account for our seeing a stick in water as bent, though it is straight.)

A Second Method

Other philosophers may begin in the same way, but are not so firmly committed to their initial theory. Instead, they examine its implications for various cases, and if the implications conflict with their pretheoretical judgments, they sometimes use this conflict as a reason for altering their theory. What is it about such judgments that enables them sometimes to overrule a theory? The same mind that initially accepted the theory as plausible finds the implications of that theory to be implausible. A pretheoretical response to the moral significance of general principles or ideas was necessary to accept the theory; the same type of response, only more than one, is called forth by cases.[1] It is possible to test a theory by cases because judgments about cases are often not theory driven, i.e., people who hold different theories may have the same judgments about cases. For example, an act utilitarian, may share many of the intuitions that deontologists have about cases. She just thinks these intuitions are wrong, and accepts the need to find an error theory to explain our belief in them. If an error theory is less plausible than the correctness of those intuitions, they will provide support for a nonutilitarian theory.

How a Theory May Change

How does a theory change? Consider a theorist who is committed to maximizing happiness. Suppose he is confronted with cases in which there are no actual harms (in the form of diminished utility) but he agrees nevertheless that there is wrongdoing. An example concerns someone who has been treated paternalistically. His utility may be enhanced but his will has been violated, and this is a wrong. The theorist, despite his theory, may agree that it is right that a person direct his own life, even if his utility is diminished.

Our theorist would here be conceiving of a case involving factors that he may never have thought of before, such as a case that distinguishes wrongs from harms. He then responds to this case in ways that imply that he is rejecting as a standard for evaluating its outcome the maximization of utility or the satisfaction of given desires. He may then shift to another standard for evaluating outcomes, for example, a Kantian standard or a novel theory of goods.

No doubt, the theorist already holds some views that allow him to conceive of such new factors and also to respond to them in such a way that he will judge his utilitarian theory to be inadequate. These views which he used to judge the adequacy of his theory may not change. But a rather significantly deep principle—his principle of utility maximization—has been jettisoned or revised.

A Third Method

A third philosophical method (there may be others) begins with responses to cases—either detailed practical cases or hypothetical cases with just enough detail for philosophical purposes—rather than with a total or even a tentative commitment to a theory. This procedure is attractive because it permits recognition of new factors that may be morally relevant in certain cases, factors emphasized by no theory yet developed. Philosophers using this method try to unearth the reasons for particular responses to a case and to construct more general principles from these data. They then evaluate these *principles* in three ways: Do they fit the intuitive responses? Are their basic concepts coherent and distinct from one another? Are the principles or basic concepts in them morally plausible and significant, or even rationally demanded? The attempt to determine whether the concepts and the principles are morally significant and even rationally demanded is necessary in order to understand why the principles derived from cases should be endorsed.[2]

Thomas Nagel ("The Fragmentation of Value")[3] says that, despite differences over theoretical justifications, there is a wide area of moral agreement about policies and conduct. Nagel leaves it as something of a mystery why this is true. The missing step can be provided if we see the various theorists as beginning (in their theorizing) with "commonsense judgments" about conduct, which they then seek to justify. Non-radical *consequentialist* theorists, who do not overturn such ordinary judgments about conduct and policy, will find themselves trying to generate from their theories the ordinary judgments that are more deontological than consequentialist. All this is not to say that differences in theories are not important, even when they do not lead to different policies or conduct. For some understandings of why we should do what we may all agree we should do can be right and other understandings can be wrong, first in whether they can, in fact, account for the agreed-upon judgments, and second, in the different self-conceptions with which they provide us.

The Method Used or Presupposed in This Book

The method used or presupposed in this book is closer to the third method than to the first two. We present hypothetical cases for consideration and seek judgments about what may and may not be done in them. The fact that these cases are hypothetical and often fantastic distinguishes this enterprise from straightforward applied ethics, in which the primary aim is to give definite answers to real-life dilemmas. Real-life cases often do not contain the relevant—or solely the relevant—characteristics to help in our search for principles. If our aim is to discover the relative weight of, say, two factors, we should consider cases that involve only these two factors, perhaps artificially, rather than distract ourselves with other factors and options. For example, if we wish to consider the importance of property rights relative to that of saving a life, we should not consider cases in which we have the option of avoiding violation of a property right in order to save a life.

Some people have difficulty considering cases in which the factors and alternatives are purposely limited and thus are different from those of the real world in which other alternatives are possible. This tendency may simply reflect the fear of having to make hard decisions; therefore, to test this hypothesis, one must find out whether such people are afraid to make decisions in real-life cases in which the alternatives are limited. Furthermore, the tendency in itself to introduce other options into a hypothetical case reveals something about a person's judgment concerning the relative weight of the original alternatives. For example, it is possible that it is only because someone believes to begin with that it would be wrong to violate a property right in order to save a life that he feels the need to consider ways of saving the life without violating the property right.

If cases are very unlike real cases, can we have responses to them? Or do our responses reflect carryover from real-life cases that are similar but also crucially different, with the crucial differences present only in real life being responsible for our responses? I believe we are capable of explicitly excluding certain real-life factors and conceiving of and responding to cases with only the factors we wish to attend to at the time.

Some people may claim that they have no strong, pretheoretical responses to at least some of the cases I present. This does not matter, I think, so long as enough people have definite responses. What are these responses, and why does it not matter if only a few people have them? Often in other discussions they are described in the language of vision: one is supposed to "see" something immediately. The term "intuition" is used, suggesting something mysterious.

The responses to the cases with which I am concerned are not emotional responses but are judgments about the permissibility or impermissibility of certain acts. These judgments are not guaranteed to be correct, and one must give one's reasons for making them. These reasons, in turn, are not personal emotional responses to the acts but are the properties of the acts themselves.

Even though these judgments are not guaranteed to be correct, if they are, they should fall into the realm of a priori truths. They are not like racist judgments that one race is superior to another. The reason is that the racist is claiming to have "intuitions" about empirical matters and that this is as inappropriate as having intuitions about the number of planets or the chemical structure of water. Intuitions are appropriate to ethics because ours is an a priori, not an empirical, investigation.

Responding definitively to a case does not necessarily mean responding quickly. But the fact that a response takes time to make does not mean that it is being deliberately constructed. Having responses to complex and unfamiliar cases requires that one see a whole complex landscape at once, rather than piecemeal. This often requires deep concentration. Only a few people may be able to respond to a complex case with a firm response. If "Goldilocks" is the fairy tale best associated with Aristotle's doctrine of the mean, then the "Princess and the Pea" is the fairy tale best associated with the method I describe: it tells of someone, despite much interference, who cannot ignore a slight difference in a case that others may never sense. Because even slight differences can make a moral difference, it may be necessary to consider a large variety of cases with only slight differences among them. This approach involves thoroughly working over a small area with the result of greater depth. Sometimes, however, a detail interesting in its own right is omitted for the sake of better exhibiting the final result.

Those who have definite responses are the natural sources of data from which we can isolate the reasons and principles underlying their responses. One model here is that the responses come from and reveal some underlying psychologically real structure, a structure that was always (unconsciously) part of the thought processes of some people. Such people embody the reasoning and principles (which may be thought of as an internal program) that generate these responses. The point is to make the reasons and principles explicit. Because we do not begin with an awareness of the principles, it is less likely that the responses to cases are the results of a *conscious* application of principles to which one is already committed. In this connection, one advantage of considering somewhat bizarre cases is that our responses to them are less likely to be merely the application of principles we have been taught, and the novelty of the principles we derive from them suggests that our investigation is going beyond the conventional.[4] An alternative model is that certain concepts that people have always worked with (even consciously) commit them — without their having realized it, consciously or unconsciously — to other concepts. The responses to cases reveal that one set of concepts and principles commit us to others, and these other concepts and principles can then be added on to the description of the underlying structure of the responses, but the structure was not always psychologically real.

We are not arguing that such principles are correct simply because they generate responses in some people. Rather, to be plausible, such principles must be related to morally significant ideas. It would be ideal if we could show that the concepts and principles that generate or account for the responses in cases are required by reason. Furthermore, it is not assumed that the role of principles, if they are discovered, is to help us decide cases to which our responses are not clear. It is quite possible for some people to have clear, pretheoretical judgments about every case, without being able to articulate principles. (Indeed, because the principles to be discovered are likely to be correctly formulated only if they are derived from all the types of data, using a principle based on only one type of case in order to decide another type of case may lead to the wrong answer regarding the latter case.) Still the principles may help some who lack certain intuitions.

What would be the purpose of making principles clear and explicit if we do not need them to settle cases about which we are uncertain? Perhaps it is simply to attain a greater understanding of what underlies our responses; perhaps it is to help us organize our moral thinking. Having our principles in hand may also make it easier for us to point out crucial factors in cases to those people who do not share our responses. Furthermore, it is possible to acquire a deeper understanding of our pretheoretical judgments by way of principles or theories that explain them, even though we are less certain of those principles and theories than we are of the judgments themselves. Our certainty about our pretheoretical judgments is different from, and not necessarily increased by, a deeper understanding of them.

Finally, we should not expect such principles to be simple or singular. They may be complex, in the attempt to capture results, in many cases, and many of their components may prove to be irreducibly important. We may expect, however, a continuity in content between the factors we point to in certain cases and the components of the most general principles derived from those cases. In moving from cases to principles, one is less likely to find the same discontinuity in content that marks a two-level theory whose principles are essentially utilitarian but that commends deontological responses to cases as a way of maximizing utility in the long view.

NOTES

1. In an article, "Causing and Preventing Serious Harm," in *Philosophical Studies* (65 1992: 227–255) Peter Unger has argued that our intuitions about cases are more likely to lead us astray and to be inconsistent than our intuitions about fundamental principles. He claims to have shown this by confronting us with cases that involve multiple options rather than just two, and by arguing that we will find it permissible to perform an act when it is one of several options even if we would not find it permissible to perform this act if it were one of two options. This, he thinks, should unsettle our confidence in our intuitions about the permissibility of acts. After considering Unger's cases, my own sense is, first, that my intuitions about the permissibility of an act do not alter in the varying contexts he presents and, second, that if others' responses do change as he claims, this may be through too great self-concern, e.g., if they will already perform an act judged permissible that causes harm, they may incorrectly be tempted simply to perform any act that reduces the harm they produce.

2. For more discussion of ways of relating ethical theories and judgments of cases, see my "Ethics, Applied Ethics, and Applying Applied Ethics," in D. Rosenthal and F. Shehadi (eds.), *Applied Ethics and Ethical Theory*, pp. 162–187 (Salt Lake City: University of Utah Press, 1988) and "High Theory, Low Theory, and the Demands of Morality," in I. Shapiro and J. DeCew (eds.), *Theory and Practice: NOMOS* XXXVII. New York: New York University Press, 1995.

3. In his *Mortal Questions* (Cambridge, England: Cambridge University Press, 1979).

4. Derek Parfit emphasized this point.

I

1

Killing and Letting Die:
Methodology of Comparable Cases
and Conceptions of Moral Equivalence

Make everything as simple as possible, but not simpler.   A. Einstein

It seems to matter how we die, not simply that we do. Does it matter whether we are killed or left to die, or whether we, in turn, ensure another's death by killing or by letting die? These questions have much to do with the more general issue, central to the debate between consequentialist and non-consequentialist morality, of whether there are strong constraints, for example, against killing, that limit our right to bring about the greater good, constraints by which we may be required to abide even at great personal cost. The questions also have much to do with whether there are options (i.e., morally permissible choices) about whether to bring about the greater good, for example, whether we are permitted to omit certain efforts and let someone die when this is not for the best overall. Non-consequentialists typically believe in both options and constraints. Act-consequentialists believe in neither.

Thesis E

There has been much discussion about whether killing and letting die are morally equivalent per se. Let us call the claim that they are morally equivalent per se Thesis E.

Discussions about whether Thesis E is true often make significant use of so-called comparable killing and letting die cases. These are cases in which all factors besides killing and letting die are supposed to be held constant, or in other words, are *equalized*. It is argued that factors other than killing or letting die are typically present unequally in killing and letting die cases, and these other factors produce moral differences in the cases. These differences are then mistakenly taken to show a difference between killing and letting die per se.

Proponents of Thesis E grant that certain factors are empirically associated with either killing or letting die (e.g., bad motive is frequently associated with

17

killing). However, they claim, these associations are not matters of conceptual necessity. Placing the empirically associated factors into *both* killing and letting die cases (or removing them from both) can equalize the cases. Then, the proponents say, in these equalized cases a killing and a letting die will be morally equivalent. Furthermore, it is argued, this will prove Thesis E: If we obtain judgments of moral equivalence about cases in which all factors other than killing and letting die are constant, then killing and letting die must, per se, be morally equivalent. (Indeed some seem to have assumed that all we need is *one* such case to prove Thesis E.) This argument depends on the assumption that only morally equivalent factors will yield morally equivalent cases when placed in morally equivalent contexts. (I shall raise some questions about this assumption later.)

The Methodology of Comparable Cases

What does it mean to say that killing and letting die are morally equivalent per se? What techniques can we use to find out whether Thesis E is true? Is Thesis E true? I hope to answer these questions by considering the methodology of comparable cases, and seeing whether problems in methodology shed light on substantive issues.

In the first section of this chapter, I deal with how we are to go about equalizing cases for all factors besides killing and letting die. I describe two different procedures that could be used. In the second section, I show which of the procedures for equalizing should be used if we wish to test Thesis E by using comparable cases. In doing this I make clearer what is meant by saying that behaviors are (in)equivalent per se.

Some Factors Held Equal in "Standard" Comparable Cases

How do we produce comparable killing and letting-die cases? One common procedure can be isolated by examining cases that have been judged comparable by other philosophers. A "standard" set of cases is the following "Bathtub" (B) set:

(B1): I push child under water in a tub, thereby killing him, in order to collect his inheritance. (Killing)

(B2): A child slips in the bathtub. I could easily lift him out but do not, because I want to collect his inheritance. (Letting Die)[1]

Cases (B1) and (B2) suggest a "standard" procedure for constructing comparable cases, some of whose elements are as follows.

(a) The size of the effort that must be made rather than kill or let die should be equally great or small. Not killing often requires no effort. Saving a life, however, usually requires some action, and hence effort. Therefore, in constructing standard cases a minute effort involved in aiding is taken to be equivalent to no effort in not killing. Notice that the failure to obtain the child's fortune is not counted as a sacrifice that would be made if one were to aid or to refrain from killing. However, forgoing the loss of a fortune from some other source than the child's death in order to save the child might be counted as a sacrifice made to aid.

Suppose that if I move, this will move dust particles that fall on a bomb that will then go off, killing someone. Does my standing still, making no effort at all, aid the person? Only in the sense that it stops me from killing him. In general, my standing still will count as aiding only in the sense that it prevents my killing. If my standing still is itself part of a process that provides aid, my moving will terminate assistance.

Not killing or not aiding, as well as aiding, may on occasion require much effort. For example, I may have to keep busy with something energy-consuming so that I don't pick up a gun and shoot someone *or* so that I don't give in to the temptation to save someone's life. Both killing and letting-die cases should then include such efforts.

(b) The motive of the killer and that of the person who lets die (henceforth, the nonsaver) should be the same.

(c) If the killer intends to use a victim's death as a means to an end or as an end in itself, the nonsaver should do likewise. If the nonsaver does not so intend, neither should the killer.

(d) Intending, rather than merely foreseeing, that the cause of death will occur should be equally present or absent in killing and letting-die cases.

(e) The alternatives to both killing and letting die (i.e., not killing and saving) result in the potential victim's remaining alive. This is a characteristic of standard comparable cases. This means that they do not raise the question of whether there is a moral difference per se between killing and letting die by asking whether a moral difference arises if we kill someone whom we would otherwise let die (or let die someone whom we would otherwise kill). They raise the question of the moral equivalence of killing and letting die in a context where if we do neither a further significant event occurs, namely someone lives.

I shall refer to the factors that are equalized in "standard" cases as *standard equalities*.

Further Consideration of Intending the Cause of Death

Let us consider (d) in more detail. Intending that the cause of death occur is different from intending that the person die [the factor noted in (c)], as the following "Gas" (G) cases show:

> G(1)   I turn on a gas which will save my life though I foresee that it will kill someone in the next room who would not otherwise have died. I do not intend his death.

> G(2)   I refuse to make a minimal effort to turn off a gas (which a third party set going) because the gas will save my life. However, I foresee that it will kill someone in the next room, whose death I do not intend.[2]

In these cases I do not intend the person's death, but I do intend the existence of the event that causes his death (the gas being on). Such an intention that the event that causes death exist *is not* present in the following cases:

> G(3)   I refuse to make minimal efforts to turn off a gas which I foresee will kill someone. I do this because I am busy doing something else that saves my life.

> G(4)   I refuse to make a big effort to turn off a gas which I foresee will kill someone, because it *is* a big effort.

In G(1) and G(2) I have an interest in the existence of the cause of death because it is *causally required* for my survival (i.e., either the cause of death or something else that it causes allows me to survive). This is different from my taking an interest in something happening merely because it is a *sign* of something else in whose existence I have a causal interest. A *sign* is something such that, given the way the world is, what I causally require will be present if and only if *it* is also present. In G(3) and G(4) the cause of death is only a sign of what I need. When I have an interest in the existence of the event because it is causally required, I intend it. In G(3) and G(4), there is no intention that the cause of death occur.

Consider G(5): Given the position I am in, unless I make a big effort, or take a big risk, to avoid doing so, I will fatally run into someone. If I refuse to make the big effort, do I intend the existence of the event that causes the death? My running into someone is, of course, the cause of death. My wish to avoid making the effort provides me with a reason for not avoiding running into someone. It seems, then, that I have an interest in running into someone as a sign that I have not made the effort to avoid it. But, in addition, if I intentionally do what is my running into someone, because I do not want to make the effort to avoid it, I intend the cause of death. I do not intend it as a (causal) means to anything else, nor do I intend it under the description "cause of death." But I do intend its occurrence. We would have such a case if in G(5) I had a choice of going either down a dangerous road with no one lying on it or down a safe road with someone lying on it, and I chose the latter to avoid the risk of harm to myself. There would be no intention to do what leads me to run into someone if there were no choice once I decided not to make the effort. This could occur if in G(6) the wind were blowing me to collide and I didn't make the effort to resist it. (This assumes that in G6 I kill if I do not make the effort to stop my collision. This means the case would have to differ for some reason from G(3) in which I *let die* when I do not stop a threat to someone's life. And indeed, even if I did not start the wind blowing which now makes me into a threat, there is reason to think that my moral responsibility for the location of my body makes me a killer—perhaps justified—if I do not make efforts to stop my colliding.) Another kind of case in which I kill but do not intend the cause of death (or what causes it) makes use of the fact that I can do things voluntarily without intending to do them. For example, in G(7), I wiggle my toe while working, without a prior intention to wiggle my toe, and this turns on a gas that will kill someone in the next room. In this case I kill someone without intending the cause of death or its cause.[3] Furthermore, I may know that if I start a conversation, I will voluntarily, but without a prior intention, scratch my head and this will set off a bomb killing someone. So long as starting the conversation did not cause me to scratch my head — and it need not have — I may start the conversation with a prior intention to do so without thereby intending the cause of death or its cause.

What about a case like B(1), in which we aim at the death of the child? It includes an intention that the event which causes death occur. Does the standard equalized letting-die case B(2) include such an intention? The answer to this question requires some additional distinctions. In B(2), as described, the nonsaver need not be understood as intending the cause of death *if* we identify the cause with the child's slipping. The nonsaver might have been willing to stop the initial slipping if he had seen it happen. After all, the child's slipping might represent something else more undesirable to him than the child's death is desirable. For example, it might crack the bathtub, and the bathtub might have religious significance for him. Once the slipping is over, the crack cannot be undone anyway, and then there is only the child's death to be achieved. Of course, the ordinary picture we have is that the nonsaver in B(2) *does* intend the cause of death since the cause of death is the child's lungs filling with water which results in death. He intends the cause if he would refrain from stopping it for no reason other than that he wants it to occur, perhaps because of its effect.

We have described cases in which there is and is not an intention that the cause of death occur. G(1) and G(2) are equalized for one sort of interest in the existence of the cause of death. Is there a letting-die case that is comparable to G(5) where there is an intention that the cause of death occur merely as the alternative to making a big effort? It does not *seem* so, since if I will not be killing, I need not intend the cause of death when I simply refuse to make an effort to stop it. (Then the letting-die case will be fully comparable only to a case like not making efforts to resist the wind that turns one into a lethal weapon.) But whether there is a letting-die case standardly comparable to G(5) killing case may depend on how we understand the construction of comparable cases. Let us consider this issue.

Procedures for Generating Standard Cases

If we begin with a killing case and wish to create a comparable letting-die case by using the standard procedure just described, we proceed as follows: create a case that is different from the killing insofar as it has the properties necessary to make it a letting-die case, but not a killing case. Also include all those properties of the killing case that a letting-die case can share. Since it is possible for both killing and letting-die situations to involve the intention that the event that causes death occur (either as a means or as an end in itself), we equalize for this.

By contrast, suppose we begin with a letting-die case like G(4), in which I refuse to make a big effort to turn off a gas that will kill someone, because it *is* a big effort. Then we try to construct a killing case in which killing (like letting die) occurs unavoidably if we do not make a big effort, and there is no further intention that the cause of death occur. Such a case would arise if I make no choices after choosing not to make the effort. This could occur if a force of nature impels me to kill and I refuse to make the effort to stop it because of how large the effort is. Thus my interest in the cause of death occurring is only as a sign that I have not made the effort. However, if we insist on a case in which I *choose* to do the act that kills, then the killing case will have some intention that the cause of death exist, as in G(5). Should the procedure used for equalizing in standard cases tolerate such a difference?

It may have to, if it is to equalize for the fact that I make a *choice* to let die. For do I really *choose* to do what *kills* if I do not make efforts to stop a natural force from making me a lethal weapon? An alternative is to say that I choose not to make efforts to aid (as I choose not to make efforts to resist nature's making me lethal) and it comes about then (noncausally) that I let die, that is, there is no *further* choice to let die in (G4), any more than there is a choice to kill when I do not make efforts to resist nature. These then would be the comparable cases.

Some Factors Not Held Constant in "Standardly" Equalized Cases

Factors that are not equalized by the "standard" procedure include the following.

(a′) The victim in a letting-die case (*victim-L*) need not have been killed either by the nonsaver or by any other person. He could die accidentally or of natural causes. The victim in a killing case (*victim-K*) is killed. This difference between standard comparable cases has the following significance: Suppose the letting-die case involves a natural or accidental death. Then it is possible that a moral difference between my killing and my letting die may result from a difference between a person's dying a natural rather than a person-caused death, not from a difference between my letting him die and my killing him. Killing would be shown to make a difference, but it would not necessarily mean that my killing someone was worse than my letting someone *be killed*. In refusing to equalize for the victim's being killed, the standard procedure implies that this difference makes no *moral* difference.

(b′) The standard procedure does not equalize for altering a course of events from what it would otherwise have been. This alteration could occur if the agent acted to produce either an event that causes the death *or* an event that removes a defense against it. (I am here assuming that removing a defense is not the cause of death.) I will refer to the first type of act as introducing an *original cause*. If death is bad for the person, the original cause is an *original threat*. When a defense is removed, this is a new event, but not an original cause of death. An example is when someone removes the asbestos cover surrounding a person, so that an approaching fire can consume him.[4] A killer acts to alter a causal chain; a nonsaver does not.

The nonsaver in the standardly constructed cases does not alter the course of events from what it would have been without him, so that it results in someone's death and he becomes a killer. It is possible, of course, to construct a case in which the nonsaver is also the killer—for example, when a killer stands by and does not aid his own victim-K. The point is that the standard procedure does not require this in order for killing and letting-die cases to be comparable. To suppose that the victim-L is killed by a prior act of the current nonsaver would turn the letting-die situation into a part of a killing case.

What *is* being equalized in not equalizing for (b') is that both killing and letting die stand by themselves as the agent's first encounters with the victim. The standard procedure also does not require that the killer refrain from aiding his victim as well—for example, the killer might faint immediately after shooting his victim.[5]

(c') The victim in a case of letting die was already facing a cause of death independent of any that the nonsaver produces. [This is an implication of (b').] In contrast, when a person kills in standard cases by producing an original cause, his victim does not face a cause of death produced independently of the killer.

(d') In dying, the victim-L loses only life he would have had via the agent's help.[6] By contrast, the standard victim-K, as in (B1), loses life he would have had independently of the killer. (Even if he were not self-sustaining, but dependent for life support on a third party, this would still be true.) I here assume that not killing someone does not help him have life. It does not make him dependent on the non-killer in the way he is dependent on the saver. Similarly, our lives are not sustained by the sky's not falling on us in the way they are sustained by a life-support system. We are here relying on more than a counterfactual theory of causation. Notice that losing *only* life he would have had if the agent had aided is not the same as losing life he would have had *only* if the agent had aided. The former is consistent with several people being able to aid but refusing to do so; the latter is not. A killer may introduce an original cause to someone who is (causally) independent of him, and if death is bad for the person, he introduces an original *threat* to a person who is independent of him.

Suppose the victim loses life the agent originally gave to him, e.g., the agent was his parent. Hence the victim loses something he wouldn't have had independently of the agent.[7] That is, his parent threatens his life years after his birth and then fails to aid him while he still could. Strictly speaking, in this case, the victim does not lose what he would have had independently of the agent and yet we think it just as wrong for the agent to kill and let die as in cases where the person loses what he would have had independently of the agent. Presumably this is because we think the victim had a right to his life once it was given to him and he could now retain it independently of the original donor or anyone else who helped him retain it previously. Use of "would have had independently of the agent who kills" is to be taken throughout as "would have now *retained* independently of the agent who kills," use of "would have had via the agent's help (if not let die)" is to be taken throughout as "would have now retained via the agent's help (if not let die)."

(e′) If death is bad for the victim, the victim-L in not being saved loses out on an improvement over the prospects he has without aid. I believe this is sufficient to warrant our saying that he receives a *benefit* in being aided. This is true even though in a sense he gets nothing qualitatively different from what he already had before he was faced with a threat to his life; he has merely been helped to retain his life. (Of course, he gets time alive he never had before.) By contrast, if his death is bad for him, the victim-K faces worse prospects than he would have faced without the act of the killer.

Feinberg on the Right to Be Aided

Some — for example, Joel Feinberg — refuse to use "benefit" in the way I do.[8] Feinberg thinks that we risk confusing situations in which someone is offered a gratuitous improvement over his prior condition with situations in which we help someone regain his status quo ante some interfering disaster, if we use "benefit" to refer to the latter as well as the former. He believes, furthermore, that bringing someone back to status quo ante is crucial in determining whether someone has a *human right* to be aided by a stranger (at least at small cost to the stranger). For example, he believes a small child who has fallen into a pool and is drowning has a human right to be saved by a stranger at small cost.

I have rejected Feinberg's refusal to use "benefit" for saving a life at small cost. But is Feinberg's analysis of when we have a human right to be aided correct? Suppose the child had been born to its mother while she was in the pool, so that it had never been on dry land, and it was drowning from the time it was born. Would the fact that we would not be bringing it back to status quo ante be relevant in deciding whether it had a human right to aid? Presumably Feinberg would deny that the child's right to be aided depended on whether or not it was always drowning. Again, suppose Rockefeller loses a bag with a million dollars in it. Would aid at small cost be his *human right*, just because it would bring him back to his status quo ante? I think not. Feinberg must, I believe, actually endorse, or be prepared to endorse, a theory of rights that commits us to aid (at least at small cost) individuals whose *fundamental human needs* (e.g., need for life itself, not for a million dollars) are at stake, whether this is returning them to status quo ante or not.

Other Factors Not Held Constant

There are other factors we must consider.

(f′) In letting-die cases one refuses to make efforts that would provide life to someone already under threat of death. Efforts made to avoid killing in standard cases are not efforts that would provide someone already under threat of death with continued life. Hence, the functions of the efforts refused by the nonsaver and by the killer are different.

(g′) If the same efforts had to be made to avoid killing as have to be made in order to save a life, they would be made to prevent the killer from imposing *first* on an innocent person. In contrast, the efforts made in saving would, in a sense, involve the innocent bystander being imposed on first for the dying person.

For example, contrast (i) my not killing someone, where I avoid imposing first by swerving my car into a tree, with (ii) my saving someone's life from a falling tree (my being imposed on first), again by swerving into the tree. There may admittedly be two somewhat different senses of "impose" at work here. In the first sense, one person *physically imposes* on another. In the second sense, there is imposition on one person for another just in the sense that the first person has to go out of his way in some significant respect for the other. This may or may not lead to the first person being physically imposed on by the second person. Note also that physical imposition can occur even if it is not undergone *for* the other person.

(h') In letting die in standard cases the nonsaver exercises control over something that is his (his efforts, his body, etc.), refusing to share them with someone else. By contrast, killing in standard cases is accomplished by someone exercising control over something that is not his. Another way to describe this is that in the letting die cases, A dies by B doing something with what is B's; but in the killing cases A dies by B doing something to what is not B's. He may do either something to what is A's or to what is C's, for example, if the asbestos cover protecting A from fire is C's.[9]

I shall refer to these factors which are *not* equalized in standard comparable cases as *standard inequalities*. They focus on type of death (killing or natural cause), causation, the status of the victim prior to the killer's or nonsaver's involvement with him, and the nature, function and effect of this involvement and noninvolvement.

Since there are several factors not equalized in standard comparable cases, those who use the cases in order to argue for Thesis E must be claiming more than that actively altering a course of events (b') is not a morally significant difference between killing and letting-die cases. They must be claiming that all the other differences are also morally insignificant.

Problem Cases

Some other scenarios raise questions about the factors discussed in producing standard equalized cases.

(1) Suppose A is on his way to save B's life, which would be good for B, but A is not already saving B. Without touching B or A, I stand in the way of A's reaching B. In this case I make B worse off than he would have been without me; he loses out on what he would have had without me. Is this case any different from a case in which I (i) kill B when he needs no one's aid, or (ii) disconnect a life-support system which is not mine, to which B is already attached? There does seem to be a difference among the three cases, although in all three I make B worse off than he would have been without my behavior, and may well act wrongly.

Once someone else already stands in a saving relation with B, or B is independent of my assistance and dependent on no one else, my interference takes from him something he already has. It prevents his having it from continuing into the future as it otherwise would have. When I prevent someone from initiating aid to him I do not, in the same way, prevent the continuation of some state that already existed and would continue in the future. It is in the former, not the latter, type of case that we speak of killing.

Even if interfering with the start of aid is not killing, we may condemn the act because it shares with many killings the property of causing someone to lose what he would have had independently of the agent.

(2) Suppose a man takes his child and removes it to where no one else can aid it. He then does not feed it, so it dies. Is this a killing or a letting die? If we focus simply on not giving food, we may say a letting die. But we should also focus on the fact (i) that the man actually removes the child to where no one else can aid it, thereby interfering with the beginning of others' aid by interfering with the child, and (ii) in creating the child, he foresaw the creation of the need for food which he now fails to satisfy. These two properties are "cousins" to properties found in killings. That is, (ii) is a cousin to what presenting a threat of death does, insofar as it creates a need for aid when there would otherwise have been no need, and (i) is a cousin to actively removing a barrier that protects someone from a cause of death, by, in addition, *causing* a change of the child's location. [In (i), the aid that others would provide is the barrier to death from which the man removes the child.] The child also loses life it could have had independently of the father.

(3) Suppose my behavior makes it clear that I would refuse to aid C if he were in trouble. Once others find out about this, they either stop aiding C, or kill him. Have I let him die or killed him? My aiding was necessary in order for others to aid him, or to prevent others from killing him. Therefore, when C dies, or is killed, he loses out on what he needed my help to get. In order that he live, I would first have to establish a helping relation to C, or pretend to, rather than merely avoid first imposing on him. I believe this brings the case within the fold of letting die.

What if I show up on the scene only because I know I would have this effect on others? Then the victim needs me to stay away, although I may have a right to move as I wish. But do I have the right to move where I wish if I know it will have this effect? Here it may seem that prior determination of a normative question — whether I have a right to move when there is this effect — *may* be necessary if we are to know whether I kill or let die. Ordinarily, I believe, we can characterize a killing without such prior normative decisions. Most important, the fact that decisions by others to let die or kill intervene seems decisive in my not being a killer.

Suppose the power to effect the initiation of the cause of death by others made one's behavior a killing. The killing would, nevertheless, have more of the moral quality of cases in which someone lets C die after the cause of death is already present. The fact that C loses only what he would not have had without my aid is significant.

Sometimes it is said that the difference between killing and letting die is that in letting die, but not in killing, the victim would have died anyway if I had not been around or even had not existed. The letting-die cases in (3) show this is not true of letting die, since the person in the letting-die case would not have died if I had not been around and unwilling to aid. It is also not necessarily true of killing that the person would *not* have died if I had not been around. I can kill someone at the very instant he would have died anyway. Such a killing may often be less-serious morally than other killings, but it is still a killing. (It is true, however, that the nonsaver in all the *standardly equalized* cases might not have existed at all and the victim-L would be facing the same threat, and the victim-K in standardly equalized cases would not have faced a threat of death had the killer not existed.)

Constructing Nonstandard Cases

It is possible to construct killing and letting-die cases that do equalize for some standard inequalities as well as for standard equalities. For example, the following "Support" cases modeled on cases used in some discussions of abortion [10] are so equalized:

(S1) Your body provides someone with the life support he needs in order to escape a prior threat to his life caused by someone else. You do not wish to continue supporting the person, so you directly kill him—inject him with poison—since this is the only way to stop carrying him in your body. (You do not merely disconnect him with the consequence that he dies.)

(S2) Someone is in your body receiving aid which saves him from a prior threat to his life caused by someone else. The villain now releases a new germ, which threatens your supportee's life again. You refuse to give the minute additional aid that he needs to ward off the germ because you want to stop supporting him in your body and he will be ejected only if he dies of the germ.

In these cases, if you kill or let die, the victim loses out only on life he would have had with your support, and on an improvement over the prospects he had without your help. He loses the life he would never have had if you had not begun aiding him, since he was already under a death threat when he was independent of you. Therefore, when you kill him in (S1), you do not introduce an original cause or threat to a person *independent* of you (which is not to say that you do not introduce an original cause of death as I have defined it).

In both (S1) and (S2) you are trying to avoid efforts (giving bodily support) that you have taken on as an innocent bystander, rather than efforts that are necessary to avoid your first imposing in a threatening manner on some innocent person. So these killing and letting die cases are *equalized* for prior status of the victim, the effect of efforts made, and type of death (a killing— by me or by a villain). These are factors a′, c′, d′, e′, f′, g′ which are unequal in standard cases. Therefore, we can here refer to these standard inequalities as "nonstandard" equalities. However, cases (S1) and (S2) do not equalize for causation (b'). Could one introduce this factor into a letting-die case without turning it into a killing case? [11] If so, one could equalize for this factor as well. We shall discuss this issue shortly. (S1) and (S2) also do not equalize for (h'), control over what belongs to me.

It is harder to detect the presence of a property such as "losing only what he would have had from the aider" in some cases than in others. For example, we may imagine that if I stop my ordinary movements, dust particles in the air will settle on a machine which will then kill a person. My interpretation of this case is that if I deliberately stand still, I stop aiding someone whom I was saving from death (albeit by my ordinary movements and not intentionally). After all, dust particles that would have settled on the machine were kept off because of my activity. [12] Jonathan Bennett believes that standing still in this case is killing by inaction. On my analysis, at most it would be, like (S1), a case of killing by stopping lifesaving aid already in progress, although (S1) involves a lethal poisoning which is different from standing still (a factor h' emphasizes). Another case of stopping to aid involves "ducking." [13] If you remain standing in front of someone at whom a bullet is directed, you will prevent him from being hit by being hit yourself. If you duck, he will be hit when he wouldn't otherwise have been hit. Indeed, like the killer described above who removes an asbestos blanket protecting someone from a fire, in ducking you remove a protective shield, namely *you*. The crucial difference between the two actions, however, is that the ducking—but not the removal of the asbestos shield—involves your terminating lifesaving protection you yourself were providing, by removing something that is yours (your body) and that you need not provide to save a life. So the victim, in being killed, loses only what he would have got from your protection.

Is Terminating Aid a Killing?

These cases bring us back to the issue first raised in Note 4: Is terminating aid killing or letting die, or, perhaps, sometimes both at the same time, or sometimes a killing and sometimes a letting die? Also, is the distinction between those terminations of aid that are killings and those that are lettings die drawn in a morally charged or morally neutral way? The suggestion being made here is that there is a *nonmoral* criterion for determining when a termination of aid is a killing. That is, we do not call the termination of aid a killing merely because we think it violates a moral right, or is wrong for some other reason, and call it a letting die merely because it is permissible. (This is different from claiming that no normative factor, e.g., entitlement to something, is a reason for something's being a killing.) Essentially, removing a defense against a potential cause of death—this could be a cause that had at one time already threatened the person or something entirely new—is a *killing* if the person who dies was not dependent for the defense on the person who terminates it. If an agent terminates aid and so allows a potential cause of death actually to kill someone, but it is aid that the agent himself was providing, or aid that belongs to the agent then we have a *letting die*. (This disjunctive set of conditions is meant to include cases in which A takes what is B's to help C, and B then removes it.) This will be true even though it is an act rather than an omission that removes the aid. By contrast, when there is an original cause of death, for example, the agent stabs the person he is providing with life support, there is a killing, whether the person is dependent on or independent of the agent who kills (which is not to say the killing is impermissible).

We can have a letting die even when terminating aid is morally wrong. If an agent who has a duty to save a life starts aid and then stops, he lets die but is wrong to do so. (Suppose an agent originally caused a threat of death to a person who could have survived independently of him or removed a defense against a threat of death, then aids him, and then discontinues aid. He has killed him, but only in virtue of the background to wrongly letting him die.) Furthermore, the agent need not be exactly the same person as the one who began to provide the aid. Suppose one agent of a hospital plugs someone into a life-support machine and another agent unplugs him on hospital orders. Further, imagine that the victim was originally threatened by kidney failure and will now die of a *new* infection he picks up once unplugged. (He does not die of the original threat from which the hospital was saving him.) The second agent should be seen as part of the entity (the hospital) that plugged the person in to begin with. Therefore, the case is a letting die. If, on the other hand, the unplugging itself caused the person's heart to stop, the unplugging itself would constitute an original cause of death. This would make the case a killing to terminate aid. This killing, however, would have practically the same moral weight as the letting die by actively terminating aid. It should not be taken to be analogous to killing someone who is not dependent on the killer for lifesaving aid.

Is an agent who has a *right* to terminate lifesaving aid also a killer if he was in no way connected to the provision of aid, and, in the absence of aid, an original cause kills the person whose aid is terminated? I believe he is, and that we then have a case of morally permissible killing. The agent may only unplug the person and thereby allow the eventual cause of death to intercede, but that does not mean that he lets the person die rather than kills him, on the analysis I am providing. However, if we understand his right to terminate aid as itself involving the transfer to him of the provision of aid, then if he stops aid, he will be letting die.

It is worth making two further points. Doing what is permissible certainly does not always turn a killing into a letting die, as case (S1) should indicate. Injecting the person I aid with a lethal poison, even when the victim loses only life he would have got from my aid is, I believe, a clear case of killing someone to end aid; yet it can be permissible. Furthermore, even if in some cases our moral evaluation of an act — as rightful or not — affects our application of the label "killing" or "letting die," this need not be true everywhere. There may still be cases in which a morally neutral criterion of killing versus letting die is used.

I have now argued that some instances of letting die can involve an alteration of a course of events. This means that a part of (b′) can be exported, that is, there can be an alteration of a course of events by active removal of a defense in a letting die. This does not mean that creating an original cause of death can be exported. Therefore we should designate these two components of (b′) as (b$_1$′) and (b$_2$′) respectively. So we could compare (S1) not only with (S2) but with a case (S3) in which we unplug ourselves from the person receiving life support from us, and he dies as a consequence.

Summary

I have drawn attention to the contrast between actions that bring about *original causes* of death and actions that *remove defenses* against death. I have also pointed to the moral relevance of a relation of dependence between victim and agent: A victim may be *dependent* upon the agent for life support or not so dependent (i.e., *independent* relative to this agent). The notion of dependence is a causal notion. The view being proposed here about a killing is that, in a killing, the agent's action is either (i) the original cause of death, whether the victim is dependent or independent of him, or (ii) the removal of a defense from someone independent of him (this includes independent of his defenses). The view being proposed about letting die is that, in letting die, the agent's action is (i) not the original cause of death, but may be (ii) the removal of a defense the agent provides from one dependent on him.[14] It is claimed that original-cause killings of dependents, unlike original-cause or removal-of-defense killings of people independent relative to the agent, sometimes have practically the same moral weight as cases of letting die.

Comparable Cases to Test for Thesis E

To return to (S1) and (S2) [or (S3)], if we can produce killing and letting-die cases that are equalized for standard inequalities in the way these cases are, shouldn't we use *them* as test cases to see whether Thesis E is true? If we use these nonstandard comparable cases with their nonstandard equalities, rather than cases like (B1) and (B2), don't we run less risk of having our judgment influenced by differences other than killing and letting die per se? After all, they equalize for additional differences in cases. Suppose cases like (S1) and (S2) (or S3) *were* the true test cases, and they were morally equivalent instances of killing and letting die. Then, even if standard killing and letting-die cases were not morally equivalent, Thesis E might still be true.[15]

The question then is: Are the nonstandard cases the real comparable kill/let-die cases to be used in testing Thesis E?

What Comparable Cases Should Show

There is reason to think that nonstandard cases should not be used as comparable kill/let-die test cases for Thesis E. Comparable cases are supposed to be constructed so that any judgment that they differ morally can be attributed only to a moral difference between killing and letting die per se. *But the cases should also be such that any moral difference between killing and letting die per se will result in different moral judgments about the cases.*

Cases can have the first characteristic without having the second. This is because any difference in our moral judgment might be due to the difference between killing and letting die per se, but not all differences between killing and letting die may show up in the cases. In other words, a difference in judgment may occur *only if* there is a moral difference between killing and letting die per se, but not *if and only if*. If sets of cases have the first characteristic but lack the second, they will not be good cases for comparison.

There is reason to think that nonstandard kill/let-die cases do not have the second characteristic, and so should not be used to test Thesis E. To understand this claim, we must examine the "nonstandard" equalization procedure more closely.

The Equalization of Definitional Properties and Their Moral Significance

Several of the standard inequalities dealing with absence of causation of death, the prior status of the victim, the effect of effort, and the control of what is one's own are definitional properties of letting die. That is, they are conceptual components of letting die, necessarily true of it. They are not definitional properties of killing. In particular, the following properties (which refer back to the factors listed on pp. 22–25) are conceptual components of letting die:

(b$_2$') Letting die does not itself create an original cause or an original threat of death.

(c') The victim of letting die faces a cause of death independent of any the nonsaver produces in virtue of not saving.

(d') The victim loses only life he would have had via the agent.

(f') Efforts made by the agent could have provided the victim with continued life.

(h') The nonsaver exercises control over what is his.

The remaining properties are not conceptually true of letting die. Property (a'), namely that the victim-L is killed is not true of all letting die cases. Property (e'), namely that the victim-L loses out on a *benefit* in comparison to the prospects he had (death) when independent of the nonsaver, is not a definitional property of letting die. This is because when it is in someone's interest to die, my not aiding him does not deprive him of a benefit.

Property (g'), that efforts to aid are imposed first on an innocent bystander, is also not a definitional property of aiding, since we might demand that a killer aid someone he himself had tried to kill. So, although (g') represents a standard inequality, it does not employ a definitional property of letting die; the non-aider might have imposed on the person to be aided first, by threatening his life earlier. But it is a definitional property of letting die that, at the time when efforts should be made to aid, the agent would be imposed on first (in one sense of imposed on). We could refer to this as property (g'').

Killing and letting-die cases, like (S1) and (S2), that are equalized for some standard inequalities are thereby equalized for some definitional properties of letting die. I shall term killing and letting-die cases that are nonstandardly equalized for definitional properties of letting die *or* killing, *cross-definitionally* (CD) *equalized*. "Standard" cases, such as Set (B), I shall term *only contextually* (C) *equalized*, since in these cases (roughly) only properties that lie outside of (in the context of) the definitions of killing and letting die are equalized.[16] CD cases, such as (S1) and (S2), are C-equalized as well.[17]

Ways to Equalize Cross-definitionally

It should be noted at this point that there are at least two ways in which to add definitional properties from one behavior into cases involving the other behavior. We can add them to *instances* of killing or letting die, which means that they modify what is done or not done at a particular point in time; this is what is done in (S1). Alternatively, we can add them to the background or foreground of an instance of killing or letting die. For example, if someone introduces a cause of death and also does not aid his victim, killing is in the background of an instance of letting die, or letting die is in the foreground of a killing.[18] Depending on the definitional property in question, introducing it into an instance of killing or letting die will alone be adequate to our aim, or else introducing it into the ground will be permissible. I shall continue to use the general notion of introducing a definitional property into a case, but we should keep in mind the two ways of doing this.

Using Definitional Properties to Show that Thesis E Is False

Now, definitional properties of such acts as killing and letting die could be morally significant. For example, introducing a property conceptually true of letting die into a case of killing might make the particular killing more easily justified than killing in a case that lacked the property. In fact, introducing this property might make CD-killing cases morally more like cases of letting die than non-CD-killing cases are. If the CD-killing cases were morally better than simple C-killing cases with which they shared the same "standard" equalities, and morally more like letting-die cases, then (by transivity, and barring a complication discussed later) C-killing cases should be morally worse than letting-die cases.

Suppose that letting die had a property true of it by definition that did make cases containing the property less morally objectionable, while killing did not have a definitional property with the same effect. I suggest that, other things equal between them, this would indicate that killing and letting die differ morally per se (i.e., that Thesis E is false).[19]

Different Conceptions of a Per Se Moral Difference between Conducts

It is important to realize that I am suggesting that killing and letting die can *differ morally per se* because of a definitional property true of letting die, even though that property can be exported into a killing case, indeed into an instance of killing. (It still cannot be introduced into the definition of killing per se, or, as I refer to it, into killing per se; to introduce it into killing per se would be to change the definition of killing.) This is different from claiming that killing and letting die differ in virtue of some definitional property that is unique to letting die or killing and that cannot be present in cases involving the other type of behavior. Likewise, killing and letting die could differ morally per se because of a property that is definitionally true of killing but not of letting die, and that can be introduced into cases of letting die, indeed into an instance of letting die (though not into the definition of letting die per se, or, as I refer to it, into letting die per se).

I am suggesting an alternative to what I believe is the implicit traditional view about how killing and letting die can *differ morally per se*. That implicit traditional view is that killing and letting die differ morally only if, other things equal between them, one of the terms has definitional properties that have moral significance (sometimes or always)[20] *and* these properties are never present in an instance of the other term. (The obvious factor here is creating an original cause of death, which is definitionally true of killing.)

Different Conceptions of Per Se Moral Equivalence of Conduct

Correspondingly, there are at least two different answers to the question of what it means to be *morally equivalent per se*. In *tentative* versions, one answer is that killing and letting die are morally equivalent per se, if there is no property that is both (i) conceptually required in cases of the one but *not conceptually required* in cases of the other, and (ii) that makes the cases in which it is present morally different from cases with only the conceptual properties of the other term. There is a second (tentative) answer to the question of what it means to be morally equivalent per se. It is exemplified in the claim that killing and letting die are morally equivalent per se if there is no property that is both (i) conceptually required in cases of the one but *conceptually excluded from* instances of the other, and (ii) that makes the cases in which it is present morally different from cases with only conceptual properties of the other term.[21]

Again, the first analysis of moral equivalence implies that killing and letting die are *not* morally equivalent per se if a property that is conceptually true of one of the behaviors makes a moral difference in cases that the other behavior's conceptual properties do not make. The second analysis of moral equivalence implies that killing and letting die are *not* morally equivalent per se if a property that is conceptually true of one of the behaviors but conceptually *excluded* from instances of the other behavior makes a moral difference in cases that the other behavior's conceptual properties do not make. (That is, the second notion of equivalence corresponds to the traditional view of inequivalence.)

Exportable Properties

The first analysis of moral equivalence implies that killing and letting die could be nonequivalent per se even if a *case* of killing does not differ morally from a *case* of letting die, because, for example, the case of killing contains a property, x, where x is conceptually true of letting die but not of killing. That is, *the conceptual property of letting die is "exportable."* The second analysis, however, requires for inequivalence that, for example, some conceptual property of killing that could not be present in an instance of letting die—a nonexportable property—make a moral difference between killing and letting die cases.

Since the first understanding of moral equivalence is committed to there being *no* properties of killing or letting die that have differential moral significance, I consider this the *strong* version of Thesis E. The second version is the *weaker* version of Thesis E. (I expand on other senses of "stronger" and "weaker" in relation to Thesis E in chapter 3.)

An Objection

It might be objected that letting die per se is not shown to be morally different from killing *per se*, just because one of its definitional properties sometimes has moral significance, when other things are equal. Showing that one of its definitional properties has moral significance would only show that standardly comparable killing and letting-die *cases* differ morally. (This is because the standard killing cases will lack the property in question while the letting-die cases will have it by definition.)

We might consider an analogy to illustrate this objection: Suppose that being a policewoman is better than being a fireman, but only because being a woman is, in general, better than being a man. "Woman" is a definitional property of "policewoman," and, given the supposition, we could improve the status of fireworkers by making them women. Yet it could be argued that all this does not show that being a policewoman is better than being a fireman in some deeper sense. This is because it does nothing to show that fighting crime (a property of "policewoman" that we shall assume cannot be exported to a case involving a fireperson) is better than fighting fires (a property of "fireperson" that we shall assume is nonexportable).

I believe that the answer to this objection is simply that one type of thing is morally superior to another if it has more positive properties by definition, even if they are exportable to cases involving other conduct. That is, if something has positive properties by its very nature, it is superior to something else that must rely on special circumstances, not its nature, to have those positive properties. Analogously, a person who is even-tempered by nature has a characteristic that points to his being better per se than someone who must take a drug to acquire even-temperedness. (The problem with the "policewoman/fireman" analogy is that when "woman" is exported it becomes definitional of "firewoman, and not merely a nonconceptually true component of an instance of fireperson.")

Of course, if the definitional properties that cannot be exported (for example, definitional properties of killing, such as interfering with someone, causing a death) also have moral significance, then perhaps Thesis E will be more straightforwardly proven wrong.

Why Comparable Cases Should Not Be CD-Equalized

Suppose that CD-equalized killing cases differed in objectionableness from non-CD killing cases, and this indicated that Thesis E was false. It would be the first notion of equivalence — where even a moral difference between exportable properties indicates inequivalence — that would be disproved by the difference between CD-equalized and C-equalized killing cases. We could then see why CD-equalizing would not be a sound procedure for producing comparable kill and let-die test cases. First, to create a CD-equalized killing case would mask a significant moral difference between killing and letting die per se, by compensating for its absence in killing per se. Compensating for the differences would make our reactions to the killing and letting-die cases more similar. This would make it harder for us to see that there was a morally relevant difference between killing and letting die per se.[22] In other words, we could — to answer one question with which we began — get equal responses to cases in which two factors are placed in equal contexts without this showing that morally *equal* factors had been placed in those contexts. [The contexts would be equal at least in the sense that a factor that was present in the let die case by definition was present in an instance of killing by being in the context (i.e., outside the definitional properties) of killing.]

Therefore, if the definitional properties used in CD-equalization were morally significant, it would not be correct to CD-equalize to produce comparable kill and let-die cases. On the other hand, if the definitional properties used in CD-equalization were morally *in*significant, there would be no moral difference between CD and non-CD killing (or CD and non-CD letting-die) cases, and so it wouldn't matter whether we CD-equalized or not.

Given that we might make an error when we CD-equalized if the definitional property were morally significant, and no error if we don't CD-equalize when the property is morally insignificant, we ought not to CD-equalize. How do we answer the complaint that if we do not CD-equalize we shall be unfairly judging killing and letting die in different contexts? We can say that the difference in "contexts" produced when we do not CD-equalize is just a reflection of the difference between killing and letting die per se (rather than of true contextual factors which are outside the definitional properties of both terms).

Different Notions of Equivalence and the
Construction of Comparable Cases

Therefore, if we adopt the first analysis of equivalence, we should construct comparable cases by equalizing cases only for factors outside the definitions of killing and letting die (e.g., motive, intention, efforts involved). We should only C-equalize.

However, it is important to note that, if we use the second analysis of moral equivalence, we *would* CD-equalize to produce comparable cases. Only in this way could we see whether there is moral significance in properties that *must* distinguish instances of killing from instances of letting die. These are, for example, conceptual properties true of killing that no instance of letting die could have; properties that cannot be exported into an instance of letting-die.

But note that we have described two different types of killings. *One* in which it is conceptually true that an act produces an original cause of death and a *second* in which someone removes a defense against a fatal threat when the defense does not belong to the person who removes it. (Some crucial conceptual properties of each of these types of killings will be among the conceptual properties of the other type of killing.) So when we speak of the nonexportable conceptual properties of "killing," we must be understood to have a two-pronged conception of killing with alternative conceptual conditions for each prong.

So, according to the first analysis of moral equivalence, (B1) and (B2) are comparable killing and letting-die cases if they are indeed C-equalized. According to the second analysis, they are not comparable, since the killing case could be made more like the letting-die case, while still remaining a killing (that is, it could be CD-equalized). For example, it could involve drowning a child whose life I was already saving from another threat. I have argued for the first analysis of moral equivalence.

A Particular Case

The failure to understand the difference between CD-equalized and C-equalized cases has resulted in errors. To see this, let us begin by considering (S1) again. As noted above, it seems to be conceptually true of my letting die (though not of my killing) that the person I let die loses out on life he would have had via my aid. [23] We could construct a killing case that had this property, even though the property is not conceptually true of killing. This is (S1), in which I kill (directly stab) someone who is already receiving lifesaving aid from me. This case of killing may be *almost* morally equivalent to letting the person die, to begin with, other things being equal. (At least, if I did not interfere with someone else helping the person I first helped and now kill. We assume first interaction and, hence, no background of this sort. Note, however, that I originally (p. 27) compared (S1) with (S2), which is *not* a case in which I let die to begin with. More will have to be said to explain why (S1) is almost like not aiding to begin with.)

Killing in this case may be more morally acceptable than killing someone in a second case otherwise the same except that the conceptual property of letting die is missing. Above we mentioned contrasting the CD-equalized case with the standardly equalized killing case. Let us now contrast it with a partially CD-equalized killing case. For example, it may be more acceptable than killing someone *who is imposing on me to the same degree,* but who never needed my effort, does not need the efforts his presence is forcing me to make, and in being killed loses more than life he gets by my efforts. The conceptual property of letting die — losing what he would have gotten via aid — seems to make the killing more acceptable, easier to justify than simple self-defense against someone who imposes on me, but stands to lose more than the benefit of the imposition.[24] This is true even though "the agent's being imposed on first" — a characteristic of standardly equalized letting-die cases — is equalized for in this case. (We shall discuss this case, S4, in more detail later.)

The conceptual distinction between killing and letting die taken as morally significant in these examples is not that between action and omission, or interference and noninterference. Action and interference occur both in the case of killing that has the conceptual property of letting die and in the one that lacks it. Rather, the conceptual characteristic of letting die thought to be morally significant, and introduced into one case of killing, is that the person who dies loses only life he would have had via the aid of the agent, rather than independently of his aid.[25]

Suppose my killing someone who was already dependent on me for life support and my letting him die to begin with *were* almost morally equivalent cases. The *second* analysis of moral equivalence per se, unlike the first, would then claim that killing and letting die were morally equivalent per se.[26] For properties of killing never present in instances of letting-die made no significant moral difference. However, according to the *first* analysis, the equivalence of the cases would mean that killing and letting die were *not* morally equivalent per se, in part since letting die had a conceptual property that killing per se lacks which alters the moral status of cases.

Only Almost Equivalent

We have suggested that killing to terminate lifesaving is almost morally equivalent to not saving someone to begin with. (A fuller argument for this will appear in chapter 2.) Why only almost? Several differences between the cases may be morally relevant. The first is the full responsibility for death which seems to accompany killing but not letting die. But this will be present when someone kills himself as well. There seems to be an additional difference between our cases: Though when we kill we deprive the person only of life he has via our life support, he is still a person separate from us. We are not simply killing ourself. And this "movement into" his life — even if he would not retain it without us — is a movement across the boundary between separate persons, and this may have moral significance. This is what factor (h') is concerned with. (It would also be present if we removed a defense that is not one we are providing that protected someone who we are supporting.) Furthermore, (S1) is described as involving the intention that someone die as a means to stopping support of him, while letting someone die to begin with to avoid supporting him need not involve the intention that he die (nor the intention that the cause of death occur).

Errors

Having considered this case, let us consider the errors that have been made through failure to note the differences I have been discussing. In order to prove Thesis E, Bruce Russell[27] argues that it would be all right to kill in order to stop making the same efforts that it would be all right to avoid making by letting die. The example he gives is that we may kill someone to stop providing him with life support in our bodies — this is a case like (S1) — just as we may let someone die rather than provide him with such support. The analysis I have presented should make clear why I believe Russell's argument is wrong. He compares killing and letting-die cases that compensate for a conceptual difference between killing and letting die per se. That we may kill or let die equally, to avoid the same efforts in such cases, does not support Thesis E. It rather supports the denial of Thesis E, given the first analysis of Thesis E.

Furthermore, (S1) is a case in which we kill to avoid losses that someone will first impose on us, not one in which we kill rather than make efforts to avoid imposing in the first place on someone else. The latter occurs in the standard case in which we kill rather than make efforts (e.g., I don't take a more dangerous route to avoid hitting a pedestrian). It is this sort of killing case that is "standardly" compared with letting someone die rather than make efforts to save him.

Since standard killing cases do not have the definitional properties of letting die present in (S1), Russell could not conclude that the standard kill/ let-die cases were equivalent on the basis of the CD-equalized ones, though, I believe, he wants to do this. This is true whether or not he would agree with my analysis of a per se moral difference. The failure to recognize the moral significance of properties of letting die other than that, in standard cases, it involves no action, leads one to think that if CD-equalized kill and let die cases are morally equivalent, so must the standard kill and let die cases be.

Another example that I regard as involving this type of mistake is made by Jonathan Bennett.[28] Bennett presents the following harm and not aid cases as equivalent in all respects except that one involves a not-doing (omission) and another a doing (action): (1) A man does not give up 10 percent of his income to save a village from declining economically. (2) Ten percent of a man's income would go to save a village from declining economically if he did not claim it for himself. He claims it.

Bennett notes that both cases involve not giving someone something, the first by not doing something, the second by doing something. These cases seem morally equivalent, and so, he concludes, there is no moral difference between doing and not doing per se.

The doing case, however, contains two properties that are definitionally true of not aiding but not of harming: that the victim loses out only on what he would have retained with the agent's help, and that the agent denies the use of what is his. If these *cases* are morally equivalent, it may be because harming and not aiding do differ morally *per se*, since these definitional properties of not aiding have moral significance. Note, however, that these properties do not show that it is the distinction between doing and not doing per se that has moral significance; that is, "not doing" is not the property of letting die which is being emphasized. Still, it is worth noting that the doing in this case—as well as in (S1)—may be harder for us than the not aiding to begin with. This suggests some residual difference due to doing, a definitional property of killing.

A third error that stems from CD-equalizing in test cases is made by James Rachels in his version of the "Bathtub" cases. Since the person in the killing case intends to kill, it may be thought that (B1) and (B2) will be equalized only if the nonsaver also intends to kill if this is necessary to get the inheritance. Rachels's version of (B2) does involve the nonsaver's intending to kill if necessary. But if killing and letting die did differ morally per se, intending to do one rather than the other should be worse. We would help conceal the difference between killing and letting die per se if we introduced an intention to kill into the letting-die case, since that case might become almost as bad as a killing only because it had something in it dependent on a definitional property of killing. Therefore, it is, I believe, a mistake to introduce the intention to kill in the letting-die case.[29]

NOTES

1. These cases are similar to cases in James Rachels's article, "Active and Passive Euthanasia," reprinted in *Killing and Letting Die*, edited by Bonnie Steinbock (New York: Prentice-Hall, 1981). In Rachels's cases, however, the person who lets die is also specifically described as willing to kill. I have omitted this factor for reasons that will become clear later.

2. These cases are like those discussed in Philippa Foot's article, "The Problem of Abortion and the Doctrine of Double Effect," reprinted in Steinbock, *Killing and Letting Die*, p. 163.

3. I owe this case to Timothy Hall.

4. There is much dispute whether all removals of defenses are killings and what it is about those that are that makes them killings. Suppose someone has kidney failure and lives a normal life only because he is plugged into a machine. If I, a stranger, pull his plug out, I will kill him. (It is true, however, that I do less to achieve someone's death when I remove a defense than when I also have to create the cause of death. So if it were good for him to die, perhaps I could not take all the credit for his death.) But suppose a doctor who attached a patient to a life-support system unplugs him, and the

disease he was being saved from kills the patient. We are likely to call this a letting die. I shall postpone more detailed discussion of this issue.

5. I shall not attempt to define more accurately the distinction between killing and letting die in terms of causing a threat or removing a defense, since those who argue that killing and letting die are morally equivalent per se seem to accept the intuitive distinction. They isolate cases of killing and letting die in the ordinary way, but give a different account of the moral significance of the distinction.

6. It is true that if he is helped now, he may go on to a life in which he is self-sustaining, or in which others besides the present agent will help him. If he dies now he loses out on that future life. But since none of that future life can come about without the agent's first helping him, I think it is not inappropriate to say that he will get that future life only via that agent's help. It is also true that he plays a part in his own survival even while he is being helped by the agent. Still, he would not survive without the agent. Notice that someone can lose what belongs to him or what he has a right to, and still lose only what he would have retained via an agent's help.

7. Shelly Kagan discusses such a case in *The Limits of Morality* (Oxford: Oxford University Press, 1989).

8. Joel Feinberg, *Harm to Others* (Oxford: Oxford University Press, 1984).

9. When we say that in letting die someone only exercises control over what is hers, we do not merely mean that she "touches" only what is hers. (Though this is, in a metaphorical sense, true.) For this could occur in a case of killing too. For example, if I open up my cannister of deadly gas and let the fumes kill someone, I "touch" only what is mine. The sense of "control over" we are interested in involves doing something to the person, which in turn is not captured unless we include the idea of causing the death of the person. Hence factor (h′) is dependent on factor (b′) (causation) and on factor (g′) which speaks about imposing.

10. For example, in Judith Jarvis Thomson's "A Defense of Abortion," *Philosophy and Public Affairs* 1 (Fall 1971), and my *Creation and Abortion* (New York: Oxford University Press, 1992).

11. Importantly, the cases equalize for standard equality (e) (i.e., that the alternative to killing and letting die is life). If we compared a case in which we let someone die with a case in which we kill someone who would have died anyway, we would have equalized the cases for the person having been under a threat of death already. We would also have equalized for his losing out on nothing he would have had independently of the killer or nonsaver, since he wouldn't have been alive anyway if we didn't kill him. But if we compared these cases we would not equalize for (e), since the person in the killing case would die even if *we* did not kill him, but the person in the letting-die case would have lived if not let die. Furthermore, losing out on nothing he would have had independently of the nonsaver or killer, is not quite the same as losing out on only what he would have had via the nonsaver or killer. (The former allows for his having had prospects for nothing, the latter suggests prospects for something.)

12. This case is based on one presented by Jonathan Bennett in "Morality and Consequences," *Tanner Lectures on Human Values*, Vol. 2 (Salt Lake City: University of Utah Press, 1981).

13. Discussed by Christopher Boorse and Roy Sorensen in "Ducking Harm," *The Journal of Philosophy* 115 (1988): 115–134.

14. Note that the removal of a defense that someone other than the agent provides to a person who is nevertheless dependent on the agent is *not* a case of letting die. For example, suppose someone is receiving necessary life support from my machine, but I physically cannot disconnect it. Another person's machine is providing the rest of the

necessary life support; the two machines together are sufficient for life support. If I pull the plug on the other machine because the patient's death causes my machine to disconnect, I kill him. This killing may be worse than the one in (S2) since in this case I interfere with a machine I do not provide and that would exist if I did not aid. In (S1) I interfere with another's life that would not exist if I were not aiding.

15. In chapter 4, I will argue that, in fact, cases generated by the standard procedure are not morally equivalent instances of killing and letting die.

16. I say "roughly," since some standard cases involve someone making efforts to avoid killing. But that some effort (however small) will be necessary to aid, and so is avoided in letting die, seems to be a definitional property of letting die. Therefore a killing case in which effort is required to avoid killing would be CD-equalized, strictly speaking. Of course, large efforts are not definitional to aiding, and equalizing for such large efforts would not constitute CD-equalization.

17. As will be emphasized below, there are also nonstandard cases that not only equalize for some definitional properties of killing and letting die and are C-equalized, but also equalize for some *nondefinitional* standard inequalities.

18. If we were not already using the term "contextual" for other purposes, I would describe the introduction of definitional properties into the background or foreground as introducing them into the context of the instance of killing or letting die. As it is, we can refer to it as an introduction into the "ground."

19. A more complete version of this argument is presented later.

20. However, even allowing that the property makes a difference only sometimes, not always, is nontraditional.

21. Notice that I say "conceptually excluded from instances of the other" rather than "conceptually excluded from *cases* of the other" since it may be that nothing can be excluded from the background or foreground of a case. An even stricter notion of moral equivalence requires that conceptual properties of one term do not produce a different moral outcome from the conceptual properties of the other term *because there is no difference in the role* that these conceptual properties play. This is meant to contrast with the case in which conceptual properties of one term have roles that differ from the roles of the conceptual properties of the other term, but the outcomes are the same because the different roles are functionally equivalent routes to the same outcome. My notions of moral equivalence allow for different routes to the same moral outcome overall. This includes a case in which one term has a morally significant property the other term lacks but the other term has a different property that compensates for this lack.

22. We have already inquired whether intending the existence of the cause of death (factor d) should be equalized in *standard* killing/letting-die cases (see pp. 20–24). On the basis of the discussion of CD-equalization, we might consider a reason not to: Intending the cause of death (not necessarily under that description), it may be claimed, is a definitional property of choosing to do the act that kills. That is, if we commit an act that kills, we have a reason for (i.e., an interest in) bringing about the event that kills, though not necessarily because it kills. If we equalize letting-die cases for (d) as a part of producing equal contexts for CD-equalization, we may risk masking the effect of a morally significant difference between choosing to do the act that kills and choosing to let die per se. An objection to this is that it is possible to kill because, e.g., one chooses not to pay the cost of interfering with the events that make one lethal. Then one will not intend, it may be claimed, the cause of death. This seems to imply that intending the cause of death is not definitional of *killing* and so can be equalized in standard cases.

23. It is worth repeating that I assume that refraining from killing someone cannot always be construed as aiding him, so if I kill someone he does not necessarily lose only what he would have had thanks to my "aid" of not killing him. Also, recall that "losing out on (only, no more than) life he would have had if I had aided" is not the same as "losing out on life he would have had only via my aid." The former is consistent with several people being able to aid but refusing; the latter is not.

24. I use "benefit" here in the sense of improvement over the state the person would otherwise have been in without imposing on me.

25. As noted above, abortion might be construed as a case of killing that shares a conceptual property of letting die, and in which a killing is almost as permissible as certain lettings die. That is, it is a case in which the individual killed loses only life he would have had via someone's aid. I have discussed the abortion case and the problems with such an analysis in "The Problem of Abortion," in *Ethics for Modern Life*, eds. R. Abelson and M. Friquenon (New York: St. Martin's Press, 1982) and in *Creation and Abortion* (New York: Oxford University Press, 1992). Recall that when I speak of introducing a conceptual property of letting die into a case of killing, I do not mean merely making the case one in which the killer also lets his victim die. (Consider, for example, if a killer stands by and watches his victim bleed to death when he could still save him.) We introduce the property into an instance of killing, not into its background.

26. I believe this is the way Bruce Russell argues in "Presumption, Intrinsic Relevance, and Equivalence," *Journal of Medicine and Philosophy* 4 (1979): 263–268.

27. Bruce Russell, "Presumption, Intrinsic Relevance, and Equivalence," p. 264.

28. In "Morality and Consequences," *The Tanner Lectures on Human Values*, Volume II (Salt Lake City: University of Utah Press, 1981), pp. 88–89.

29. Still, it is true that if Thesis E is false, a case in which we merely intend to, but do not actually kill, should be less bad than one in which we do kill, other things being equal.

2

Killing and Letting Die: Arguments for Inequivalence and the Problem of Contextual Interaction

In this chapter I hope to show that an *incorrect* procedure for producing comparable cases nevertheless suggests a new way to test for moral equivalence of factors, and also provides some evidence that Thesis E (in both strong and weak versions) is false. In addition, there is discussion of methodological principles.

Alternative Uses for CD-equalization

In chapter 1, I concluded that CD-equalized cases are not appropriate as kill/let-die test cases. However, in pursuing the methodological question of how to produce comparable kill/let-die cases we have come upon a new formal procedure for testing the moral equivalence of terms. This new procedure involves an alternative use for CD-equalized cases. Instead of comparing killing and letting-die cases, we *compare CD-equalized and non-CD-equalized killing cases*. (Or we could compare pairs of letting-die cases in which only one has a definitional property of killing added.) If we react more favorably to the CD-equalized killing case, this will support the denial of strong Thesis E, since it may show that letting die per se has a property that reduces moral objectionablness, a property that killing per se lacks. In this way, those who cannot see that a letting-die and a killing case differ morally may be brought to believe that Thesis E is false by seeing that the two killing cases compared are morally different.

Testing for Nonexportable Properties

However, not all the definitional properties of killing or letting die can be introduced into *instances* of the contrasting behavior[1] in cases involving the contrasting behavior. For example, the property of actively causing the event that causes death is not introducible into an instance of letting die *itself* in the way in which losing out on only what the victim would have had via the agent is introducible into an instance of killing. Producing the original cause of death, however, can be introduced as a past, background event in a let-die case. As we shall see, this makes the case overall *lose* a definitional property of letting die. (By contrast, adding letting die into the foreground of the killing case does not make the case lose a definitional property of killing.) So we may use CD-equalized *killing and letting-die* cases that do not make use of special back- or foregrounds to isolate any differential effects of the *non*exportable definitional properties, such as causing death or interfering with someone, which are definitional to killing. If there is a difference, weak Thesis E will be disproved. For example, we could compare (S1) and (S2) (or S3) (pp. 27, 30), which test these properties in a context equalized for other definitional properties.

Let us actually test to see whether an exportable definitional property of letting die is morally significant by comparing CD- and non-CD-equalized *killing* cases. To do this, we could compare (S1), in which you kill someone whom you are providing with life support, with the following case (already described):

(S4). You kill a person who is in your body but who does not get life support from being there—he is just in it through no fault of his own. You do this in order to stop making the effort of carrying him. (When this case was described earlier, we noted there that it does partially equalize for properties of standard letting die, and even a definitional property of letting die (g″). This is because the person to be killed imposes first—in both senses of impose).[2]

In (S1), someone loses only what he would get via the supporter. This is a definitional property (d′) of letting die. (S4) lacks this property.

Is killing easier to justify in Case (S1) than in (S4)? I claimed it is (p. 37). The following is an argument for believing it is:[3] If someone is dying, he has no right to be put in my body to save his life. It would be permissible to let him die rather than make the effort of supporting him. Therefore, if we kill the person in (S1) he loses out only on the results (continuing life) of efforts to which he has no right. When this person is imposing, it cannot be a reason against stopping efforts that are sufficiently large and that we had no obligation to make in order to produce a certain result, that in order to stop them we must eliminate this result. This is true even when the result of the effort is continued retention by a person of what belongs to him. If we conceive of someone's life as belonging to him (like his property), we can take it away to stop the large imposition that helps him retain it. We emphasize that the imposition is sufficiently large. This is because remaining moral differences between (S1) and (S2) (or letting someone die to begin with, which also lacks intending death) due to (S1) being a killing, mean that not every effort that we could permissibly refuse to save someone's life are efforts we could kill to stop making, even when they save his life.

However, in (S4) the person does not receive life support from you, support that he needed in order to escape a threat that he was already facing when independent of you. If you kill the person to stop making the effort, you will deprive him of life that he provides for himself independently of you, even though he imposes on you. But, more important, you will make him worse off than he would have been if he had never interacted with you.

It may seem that because the person in (S4) owes his continued life to your not killing him, if you did kill him he too would lose only life gotten via your efforts. But it is a mistake to think that whenever we refrain from killing someone we are providing him with life.

It may be that if we refrain from killing when it is *already agreed* that it is permissible to kill, he can be said to owe his life to us in a normative rather than causal sense. But then we cannot take the fact that he owes his life to us to be a *reason* for the permissibility of killing, as it is supposed to be in (S1). Furthermore, although it may be true that a consequence of your not killing in (S4) is that someone continues to impose on you, this does not mean that his continuing life is a causal "product" of that imposition, as in (S1).

In (S4), if you kill, you are taking life someone has independently of you in order to stop his imposing on you. In (S1), if you kill, you are taking what someone retains by imposing on you (his life), in order to stop the imposition caused by his continuing to have what he retains by imposing on you. This difference, I think, makes killing in (S4), which I believe is often justified, somewhat more difficult to justify than the killing in (S1). That is, a greater loss would have to be a stake to the person imposed upon for him (or his agent) to kill justifiably in (S4) than for him to kill justifiably in (S1). The line of argument that would be used to justify killing in (S4) is ordinary self-defense, and that is different from the line of argument used in (S1), which involves removing an unrightful gain. Given the means necessary to get it, continued life is an unrightful gain in (S1). Killing is justified to stop the imposition that gives rise to the unrightful gain and that continues because of it.

Innocent Beneficiaries

Suppose that what someone gets from the imposition on you, which you wish to take from him in order to stop the imposition, is not the cause of the continuing imposition. (This is compatible with his continuing survival giving his friends a *reason* to impose on you.) May you still take it? I believe you may. A case like this arises when the person to be killed is an innocent beneficiary but not an innocent threat. That is, he retains his life from the imposition on you, but does not cause the imposition. For example, his friends may tie you to a machine that provides him with needed transfusions from your body, but it is they, not he, who cause the efforts to be extracted from you and who impose on you. If the only way to stop this imposition, which you need not have incurred in order to save his life, is to kill the beneficiary, you may do so if the imposition is sufficiently large. He is still losing only what he would have had via the imposition on you in order to stop the large imposition.[4]

The Significance of Nonexportable Property

From the argument comparing (S1) and (S4), it is tempting to conclude that
we may kill someone in order to stop making any efforts that we needn't have
made to save his life, when he thereby loses only life he gets from those efforts.
By contrast, when the person imposes on us but stands to lose more than he
gets from our efforts, it is permissible to kill him only if the efforts avoided
are *larger* than what we could refuse to make to save his life to begin with.

One problem with this analysis, as noted previously, is that it seems that
we should *not* kill to end just any efforts we would not have to make to save a
life, even if the person we kill loses only what he gets from those efforts. For
example, suppose we needn't give up a thousand dollars to save someone's life.
We still should refuse to kill him if killing is necessary to get back a thousand
dollars, even though he is now protecting his life as a result of having gotten —
without our consent but through no fault of his own — our thousand dollars.
One explanation of this is that a case like (S1) indicates that the definitional
property which killing has of causing a death has some moral significance in
itself. More than this may be at work, however; for causing a death is present
if someone commits suicide or if he kills someone who will soon die anyway,
and these killings may be permissible. In (S1) someone kills another person,
and one who will not die soon anyway. Though the person retains his life via
the other's efforts, he is still a separate person who would go on living. These
are not definitional properties of killing, but causing a death may be significant in their presence. Furthermore, even if we remove a defense that is not
ours in order to stop aiding someone, we do not only exercise control over
what is ours. We run into the factor emphasized by (h′) as an additional
negative feature in (S1) not present if we let someone die to begin with.
Furthermore, we intend to kill the person in (S1), but we do not intend death
when we do not aid someone to begin work.

Standard Cases and Self-defense

Notice that if there is a difference between (S1) and (S4), there must be an
even greater difference between standard letting-die and killing cases. This is
because in the standard killing cases, unlike (S4), we do not even kill someone
who is *imposing on us first* (factor g′). Another characteristic that is at least
true of standard letting-die cases is that the person who would have to aid is
being imposed on first. Since in nonstandard cases, the agent might have been
someone who first threatened the life of the person who now needs aid, it is
not conceptually true of not aiding that the person who would aid is being
imposed on first overall. However, it is conceptually true that he is imposed
on first *at the time aid is necessary* (g″) in at least one sense of "imposed on."
The moral import of this definitional property depends on its iteration: the
absence of an earlier first-imposition by the nonsaver on the person who needs
aid now. Someone who kills in self-defense prevents his being imposed on
first, at least at the time of the killing. In some cases, a person may defend

against an attack from someone he provoked first, but this is not true in (S4). Suppose that killing someone in self-defense can be easier to justify than killing someone is not imposing first. This might indicate that g'' is a conceptual property that if iterated contributes to moral inoffensiveness. Also, that standard lettings die have a property that makes them less offensive than standard killings, i.e., being imposed on first.

The Victim in Standard Cases

This definitional property, being imposed upon first at the time efforts are needed, is also true of the victim who will be killed in standard killing cases. This suggests the following transitivity-type argument: If someone ought to do as much to save a life as to avoid killing (when not aiding does not impose first and killing does), then the victim should do as much to avoid being harmed (though he does not impose first) as the killer must do to avoid harming him (though he does impose first). One might even argue that the burden on the victim to avoid being harmed should be even greater than the burden on a potential aider to save. This is because the victim, but not the aider, will be the beneficiary of these efforts.

The conclusion of this transitivity argument seems wrong. Suppose we reject the view that the victim should do as much to prevent his being harmed as the potential killer must do to prevent himself harming. This supports the claim that the potential aider need not do as much to aid as the killer must do to avoid killing in standardly equalized cases.

This analysis by way of the "imposed on first" property also orients us toward seeing the person who is called on to aid as another victim of the person who tries to kill. He is also being imposed on first by the person who tries to kill. Just as it would be morally odd to ask the original victim to be as responsible as the killer for preventing harm, so it would be odd to ask as much of someone who will thereby become a co-victim.[5] Suppose A kills B, who is independent of this killer's lifesaving efforts, only because A does not make the large efforts necessary to avoid the lethal behavior. Our analysis depends on assuming that to require that A make the efforts rather than kill is not to impose first on him. Rather, it preemptively prevents his imposing first.

Losing Only What One Would Have Gotten From the Losses of Others

It may be that (S1) and (S4) are too close morally speaking because (S4) is already partially CD-equalized for first imposition at a given time. Perhaps, it may be said, there is no effort such that we could avoid it by killing in (S1) but not in (S4). If this were true it might suggest that it is not property (d') but rather (g'') iterated that has moral significance. To consider further whether (d') matters, we construct the Blood Cases.[6]

(Bl1). Without anyone imposing on me and just as a freak of nature, my blood seeps out of me and into the body of someone who is otherwise independent of me whose life it saves. The only way to stop this loss of blood is to kill the recipient.

(Bl2). Without anyone imposing on me and just as a freak of nature, my blood seeps out of me. The only way to stop this loss of blood is to kill an innocent bystander who is independent of me and receives no benefit from the blood.[7]

If there is some loss of blood such that its damage to me makes killing in (Bl1) to stop the damage less bad than killing in (Bl2), then (d') does morally distinguish even these cases. Nevertheless it seems clear that there is no imposition (of either sort we have described) in this case; only a loss to one person from which another benefits (through retention of what belongs to her). Factor (d') may make a moral difference, and yet the permissibility of killing by producing an original cause or removing a defense that is not mine may require that there be some imposition by or for someone (not necessarily the beneficiary of this imposition who will be killed) on me. This is because factor (h'), doing something only to what is one's own which is definitional to letting die, is not present in a killing (which also involves b' (causation) and first imposition at a time). Where only letting die is at issue, (d') alone may be sufficient for permissibility. So the person in (Bl1) may undergo surgery to stop his bleeding, rather than continue bleeding for the other person, even if this means the other person dies simply because he does not get the blood. What of a case in which the surgery that stops the bleeding would release a gas that kills two people whose lives are saved by the bleeding? Is it more permissible to do the surgery in this case than in one in which the surgery that stops the bleeding would release a gas that kills two innocent bystanders? If so, then even when (h') is not satisfied because one does something to what is not one's own, (d') makes a moral difference. It is also interesting to consider what difference the presence of (d') makes when there is no action but only an omission, that would stop the blood flow. Suppose that if the beneficiary of the blood were to die of an infection, this would stop the flow of my blood. He needs me to provide him with an easily accessible medicine to stop his infection. By contrast, consider a case in which if an innocent bystander dies of an infection, this would stop the flow of my blood. He needs me to provide him with an easily accessible medicine to stop his infection. Not helping in the first case seems more permissible than in the second, I believe, even though in both cases, aid is refused because there is an intention that the person die and the nonaider exercises control over only what is his. Only in the first case can the nonaider say that his aid would lead to the other person continuing to be benefited by his blood loss; only in the first case can he say that the person not aided loses only the benefit of the blood loss, a loss to which he has no right.[8]

Those who do not think (S1) and (S4) differ morally may use these other cases to indicate the significance of (d'). I will continue to assume that (S1) and (S4) indicate the significance of (d').

Why is it important to insist that (d') matters in cases where there is also imposition? (d') is being used to help account for why certain efforts need not be made. Suppose we begin by assuming that certain efforts involved in physical impositions are large enough to justify killing in (S4), i.e., even when the person loses life he would have had independently of interaction with us. If someone were to lose only the benefit of the physical imposition when he had no right to impose, the killing is easier to justify. This suggests that losing only the benefit of the imposition will have a role in reducing the level of effort resulting from imposition that one may justifiably end by killing. That is, one may kill to avoid a lower imposed effort if one causes only the loss of its benefit. The person who lets die in standard cases is trying to avoid first imposition [of the second, and possibly the first (physical) sort], and this will lead to the loss to someone of only what she would have had by the imposition. So these two factors should here as well have a role in justifying the permissibility of letting die rather than make certain efforts, i.e., in determining what efforts others have a right to have made on their behalf. In addition, since first imposition has not yet occurred — one is trying to avoid it by letting die — it may be significant that one only has to control what belongs to one (h') in order to let die.

First Argument for a Moral Difference between Killing and Letting Die Per Se

Suppose the argument presented above concerning (S1), (S4), and totally non–CD-equalized killing cases is correct. Then a CD-equalized killing is less morally objectionable than a non-CD killing. This suggests an argument for believing that killing is not morally equivalent to letting die per se, where "per se" means "in virtue of properties true of the term by definition."

Killing per se lacks definitional property (d') (and also g"). Suppose that letting die has no definitional properties that make it worse than killing and that killing has no definitional properties that make it better than letting die. Furthermore, suppose there is no specific reason to think that property (d') functions differently in its home ground — "letting die," the term from which it comes — than it does in a killing case. That is, suppose there is no specific reason to think that (d') is evidence for reduced objectionableness in a killing case, but not in a letting-die case. Then we can conclude that letting-die per se (by definition) has at least one more property in favor of its moral unobjectionableness than killing has. This means that killing and letting die differ morally per se. [We cannot construct a similar argument for (h') since it is not an exportable property.]

Explorations of Methodological Issues Raised by the First Argument: Exporting Definitional Properties of Killing

Notice that we can also try to introduce definitional properties of killing into letting-die cases. However, we must be careful where we do this. For example, if we introduce cause of death, we have changed the letting die into a killing.

We must also be careful not to mistakenly introduce properties that are not definitional of killing but are only standard inequalities present in standardly equalized killing and letting-die cases. For example, that the victim will lose what he would have had independently of the agent is a factor present in standard killing cases, but is not a definitional property of killing [witness (S1)].

We might note about this property, which is not a definitional property of killing, that it is the *denial* of a definitional property of letting die. This suggests comparing the moral status of (1) letting-die cases in which someone has had no prior contact with the person he lets die, with (2) letting-die cases in which someone lets a person whom he endangered die. In the latter case, we morally neutralize the definitional properties of letting die on which we have been focusing by introducing an attempted killing into the case. So the person who is let die loses what he would have had independently of the person who lets him die, though not solely *by* his letting him die. Definitional properties of letting die are *not* neutralized: The person who is let die loses only what he would have got by another's aid at the time aid was needed. But by taking a broader temporal perspective and focusing on the same type of properties, that is, on whether the person loses what he would have had independent of an earlier intervention by the person who now lets him die, we *neutralize the moral significance of the definitional properties* d′ and g″ of letting die. Importantly, we do so by emphasizing a general version of those very properties. Suppose there is not as much moral difference between (S1) and (S2) as there is between (1) and (2). Then we have reason to think that causing death [present in (S1)] is not as morally crucial as whether the victim loses what he would have had independently of imposition on the agent.

A way to construct a letting-die case with a definitional property of killing is by introducing the factor of "actively bringing about a threatening situation." Suppose I do something that endangers my life because someone else encourages me to do so. In that case, if the person who encouraged me does not aid me he will have done something that helps bring about an event that will cause my death, when I would otherwise have been under no threat. Suppose someone promises to help me, and this leads me to turn away others who would have saved me. If he does not help me, he will have done something that contributes to the removal of other barriers to my death. (This follows the model of removing a victim's fire-protectant clothing in the midst of a fire.)

Suppose these cases are still lettings die rather than killings, but letting-die cases that are CD-equalized for a property conceptually true of killing. If letting die in such cases is worse than letting die in cases without this special property, then a definitional property of killing has been shown to contribute to moral badness. If letting die has no properties that make it worse than killing and killing has no properties that compensate for the exportable property in question, and the exportable property functions on the homeground as it does when exported, then killing should be worse than letting die. A different, transitivity-type, argument could also be constructed. Suppose a letting-die case with these properties of killing is worse than a standardly equalized letting-die case, but no worse than a standardly equalized killing case. Then it is not clear how the standardly equalized letting-die case could be as bad as the comparable killing case. Of course, it might be that bringing about a cause of death by encouraging reliance is *worse* than bringing about a death by simply stabbing someone. If so, a letting die case that lacks the property of bringing about a cause of death by encouraging reliance might still be as bad as a straightforward killing. We shall consider transitivity arguments further below.

Suppose the addition of the definitional properties of killing turn the letting-die cases into *killing* cases, but also make them morally worse than the original letting-die cases. This again shows that killing has a definitional property that makes cases worse, and that is the crucial point. Such comparisons, accordingly, can be taken to be evidence that killing is morally worse than letting die per se, at least on the basis of the stronger notion of moral equivalence and inequivalence, and on the assumption that the property has the same morally significant role in its home term as when it is exported.

I have described some ways of using definitional properties to decide whether killing is morally equivalent to letting die per se. But it is also possible to use properties that are only *like* definitional properties of killing or letting die to help accomplish the same tasks. Some of the cases discussed at the end of our description of standard equalization (pp. 25–27) exemplify this. For example, if we interfere with someone's beginning aid rather than with ongoing aid, we have something close to a definitional property of a certain sort of killing. The closer the properties are to definitional properties of killing or letting die, and the more they change cases to which they are added for the worse or for the better, the more it is suggested that definitional properties of killing and letting die have differential moral significance.

Explorations of Methodological Issues Raised by the First Argument: Home Ground versus Exported Roles and the Principle of Contextual Interaction

Let us now consider another aspect of the first argument for the moral significance of definitional properties: Why does it insist on explicitly excluding the possibility that the definitional property of letting die or of killing functions differently on its home ground than it does when it is exported? This step is necessary because a factor could have a purely definitional role, making the term what it is, with no moral significance on its home ground, and yet have a moral role when exported. If this were so, we could not conclude that the term from which it came had more in favor of its moral unobjectionableness than another term has. What is crucial for deciding whether terms differ morally per se in virtue of a property, is the moral role that the property has on its home ground, not the role it has when exported. This problem is a consequence of the general fact that a property's role and, most important, its effect may differ with its context. I refer to this as the *Principle of Contextual Interaction*, and shall explore some of its implications below.[9]

It leads us to revise our first, stronger, account of moral equivalence, at least in the following way: Killing and letting die are morally equivalent per se if there is no property that is conceptually required in instances of one, but not in the other, and that alters the moral outcome on its *home ground* differently from the way that conceptual properties of the other term alter the moral outcome on their *home ground*.

(Once we become aware of the possibility that the same conceptual property might have a different effect on the outcome in different surroundings, we might even do without the reference to "conceptual properties of one term that are not conceptual properties of the other." This is because if the *same* property had *different* effects on the outcome in *different* home grounds, this could also make for a morally significant difference between behaviors. I will not dwell on this fine point.)

Difference between Exported and Home-Ground Effects Due to a Difference in Additional Factors in One Case

A definitional property could also have some — not no — moral significance in its home term, but not the *same* moral significance that it has when it is exported. In such a case it would also be a mistake to draw a conclusion about the significance of the property's impact in its home term from the change it makes when exported.

Sometimes it is hard to determine whether there is a difference in home-term versus export effect. An example may be the following: It is a definitional property of letting die that the victim-L faces a cause of death from sources other than the letting-die behavior of the nonsaver. In fact, if a nonsaver really "lets someone die" versus "just leaves someone to die," the victim-L is doomed. It could be suggested that to export this definitional property of letting die, we compare a case in which we kill someone who already faces a cause of death from other sources with a case in which we kill someone who does not face another cause of death at the time of killing. [10]

If a cause of death is a threat because death is bad for a person, it is certainly morally better to kill someone who is already facing a cause of death and whom no one (we or others) can save than to kill someone who isn't already facing such a threat. Does this show that letting die and killing differ per se because a definitional property of letting die makes a killing case morally better? It is a mistake to think so, if killing someone already under a threat of death is less bad only because the person must die anyway if we do not kill him. For in letting-die cases, someone who is already under a threat of death need not and will *not* die if we don't let him die. Our saving or not saving someone makes the difference between life and death for him, in the way our killing or not killing does not in the case we are now considering.

Another way to make the point is to notice that introducing this definitional property of letting die into a killing case may not always preserve "standard" equality (e), that is, that what we do (kill or let die) should make a difference between life and death. We cannot even be said to "let someone die," when he will die no matter what we do. That is, we doom someone when we let him die, and so we do not let someone die whom others could still help, though we may leave him to die. But the person we let die is not doomed no matter what we do. Killing someone who is doomed no matter what anyone does is probably better than letting a person die whom we could save, but then standard equality (e) is not preserved. Killing someone who is already threatened with death but who could be helped by others is as bad as other killings. (This case is more like "leaving to die" than letting-die cases, since others might aid.)

The correct sort of killing case to consider is killing someone who is *not* doomed no matter what we do, because, although he already faces a threat of death, he *could* still be aided *only* by us and would be aided by us if we do not kill. Here killing does seem morally equivalent to letting die, for if we do not aid, we kill a doomed person. Suppose we would aid, if we did not kill. Then again we kill someone who would only have lived because of our aid and would be doomed without it. This makes the case like killing to terminate life support. Even if the aid would have followed as a matter of physical necessity from not killing, it is not like killing someone who would have lived independently of us. This case is like a letting die, in that our behavior could make a difference between life and death. (If we kill someone who could have lived if we had aided him, but whom it is permissible for us not to aid and whom we definitely will not aid, then we are killing a person whom it is morally permissible for us to have doomed anyway.)

Suppose a definitional property of letting die made a great moral difference between two killing cases *only* when another property, which by definition is *not* present in letting-die cases, is present in one of those killing cases. For example, suppose the other property were "*doomed* by the threat the victim already faces" (which does not, in fact, seem necessary for the definitional property to make a difference). Then, pointing to its roles in those killing cases would be of limited usefulness in deciding about the moral significance of the definitional property on its home ground.

One way to check for the effect of an interaction with properties not present in the home ground is to compare a killing case that has the definitional property of letting die with a letting-die case. Is this killing case with the definitional property "already under a fatal threat" of letting die even *more* morally innocuous than the letting-die case? If it is, then we may suspect that the definitional property is having an effect when exported that it does not have on its home ground because of its interaction with other properties. (An alternative explanation is that the exact same property has not been exported.) On the other hand, if the killing case with the definitional property of letting die is worse than letting die, this suggests either that there is some other property of letting die that has positive moral significance or that killing itself has extra negative properties.

Errors Based on Ignoring the Principle of Contextual Interaction

James Montmarquet[11] argues that it is the fact that someone is already under a threat of death that makes letting die morally more acceptable than killing in what I have called "standard" kill/let-die cases. The evidence he gives for this view is that killing someone who is already under a threat of death is not as bad as killing someone who isn't. My discussion should show why we must be very careful in evaluating this claim. It is not just being under any threat of death already that is crucial. For if someone is already under a threat of death but others would help him, then killing him is as bad as killing someone who isn't under a threat of death. And killing someone who is under a threat of death may be better than killing someone who is not, when the person is certainly doomed anyway (no one can help him) or when doing so is part of a procedure which increases the subjective probability of his not being killed (as when we do what leads us to kill someone in a crowd who, it was reasonable to think, had an even higher probability of being killed if we hadn't done what led us to the act that killed him). But, in these cases, special contexts not present in standard letting-die cases make killing someone who is already under a threat of death better than killing someone not already under such a threat. It is when someone is under a threat of death from which only I can save him, but he is not certainly doomed, that being under a threat of death in a kill case has (at least close to) the significance of this same property in letting-die cases, and then we can see that pointing to the prior threat alone is not truly helpful in explaining why letting die may be less bad per se than killing is. For what seems to be explanatorily important is that the person will lose life he would have had only by my help if I kill him or if I let him die.

Interestingly, Montmarquet's argument may be seen as implicitly employing the technique of CD-equalization in order to test for the moral equivalence of killing and letting die. Montmarquet, however, does not recognize that this is so, or even that the property of letting die to which he points is such a definitional property. Furthermore, Montmarquet believes that if the property of already being threatened makes the crucial moral difference between killing and letting die, this indicates that killing and letting die do not differ morally per se since some killing cases have this property. I have suggested, to the contrary, that if a definitional property of letting die but not of killing improves the moral status of the cases in which it is introduced, then this may indicate that killing and letting die differ per se.

Montmarquet also points to another property of letting die. He does not clearly distinguish this other property from "already threatened," and again he does not note that it is a definitional property of letting die. This property is "not creating a threat." He notes that it is permissible to kill by redirecting an already existing threat (as when a trolley headed toward five people is redirected so that it hits only one). Killing by creating a new threat is wrong (as when we shoot one person to save five from being killed by someone else). He obviously thinks that redirecting a threat is not creating a new threat. (He also states that the single person to whom we (physically) can redirect a threat is "already threatened" even when the trolley is headed toward the five — a contentious point.) He concludes that because letting die creates no threat, it is less bad than killing in standard cases in which a threat is created.

In response, we should note that if this property of "not creating a threat" by itself did account for the difference between killing and letting die, there should be no great moral difference between the following kill and let-die cases: (1) A trolley is headed toward my thousand dollars which is tied to a track. To save my money I must do something, in the course of which (I foresee) I will, without prior intention, wiggle my foot. I know this will cause the trolley to turn onto another track, where a person sits. (2) I refuse to save someone's life from a runaway trolley because I am busy saving my thousand dollars from being destroyed by another trolley. In neither the killing nor letting-die case do I create a threat, according to Montmarquet. However, what I do in (1) seems less acceptable than what I do in (2). In (2), I do not even direct a threat (newly created or not) at anyone. This indicates that not creating a threat by itself cannot account for the moral difference between killing and letting die, at least if redirecting is an instance of not creating a threat. Of course, in letting die, I do not introduce a threat to someone whether newly created or redirected, and *this* may be significant. [12]

A Further Methodological Point about the Principle of Contextual Interaction

When we use comparable cases to test the moral equivalence of terms (and the behavior represented by them), we must be sure not only that all factors other than those we are testing are equally present, but also that they perform the same functions. Otherwise one of the terms (killing) we are testing may require that a certain factor be present in order for cases involving the term to reach a certain level of moral acceptability, but the other term (letting die) may require the same factor only for its definitional function, not for the sake of moral acceptability. If this difference existed, the two terms would differ morally per se. When we just equalize for presence of factors (which has been the standard practice) without being sure that we equalize for the function of the factors, we do not see the inner workings of the mechanisms we equalize. We might say that the cases are then like black boxes with their mechanisms hidden; we do Black-box Equalization. Avoiding this is another implication of the Principle of Contextual Interaction.

Put then more generally, the terms we are testing may interact differently with the same definitional factors *or* with the same contextual factors. If so, just equalizing for the presence of factors and getting the same judgments about such equalized cases will not ensure that the terms are morally equivalent. This is another reason why we could put terms in equal contexts, and get equal responses, though the terms are not morally equivalent.

Alternatively, the terms we are testing may interact differently with the same definitional factors *or* with the same contextual factors in *some cases but not in others*. If so, just equalizing for the presence of factors and getting the same judgments in *some* equalized cases will not ensure that the terms are morally equivalent. This is yet another reason why we could put terms in equal contexts, and get equal responses, though the terms are not morally equivalent per se. For example, we can get equal judgments because the cases are cross-definitionally equalized (introducing definitional properties of one of the terms we are testing). Then the equal judgments arise because we deliberately neutralize the moral difference between the terms per se. Relying on such special contexts to produce equal judgments masks rather than neutralizes per se difference.

If we suspect that one sort of behavior needs a certain contextual factor for an instance of it to be morally acceptable or unacceptable when the other behavior does not, we can simply create another set of comparable cases without this contextual factor, and see whether our judgment about these new cases differs. If it does, this shows that the behaviors differ morally per se even if sometimes the difference does not show up.[13] One model here, as suggested by Shelly Kagan, is that used in chemistry: Oxygen and nitrogen may react in the same way with certain chemicals. But we can differentiate their properties by showing that they interact differently with other chemicals. (However, when the behavior we are testing itself requires a definitional factor for moral acceptability, it is not so easy to change that factor, since if we change a definitional factor we will no longer be testing that behavior, but will be testing something else. We shall return to this point later.)

For example, the moral unacceptability of an instance of letting die may depend on the fact that the efforts required to save someone are very small. When the efforts required to save are great, refusing to make the effort and hence letting die may not be unacceptable. On the other hand, refusing to make such great efforts and hence killing someone in a standard killing case may be unacceptable. So we should vary the amount of effort required in cases to test for the moral equivalence of killing and letting die per se.

Cases like (B1) and (B2) are commonly taken to be examples where efforts to aid or not kill are small. For an example where they are great, contrast a case where I must go down a dangerous road to save a life with a case in which I must go down that road rather than down a safe one on which I will, without a prior intention, do something that sets off a bomb killing a person. I need not take the risk in the first case, but I should in the second. To seem wrong, letting die had to be avoidable at small cost; killing did not have to be avoidable at small cost to seem wrong.[14]

Varying and Equalizing Contexts in Medical Cases

A most interesting example of the importance of varying contexts to test for the per se equivalence of killing and letting die arises in the practice of medicine. Medicine is said to abide by the dictum, "First, do no harm." Yet doctors commonly *risk* killing (and, more generally, harming) people for the sake of saving those very people. For example, they perform surgery they hope will be corrective on someone who, if not operated upon (and left to die) would live for one year. The surgery may then cause the person to die right away. Or they vaccinate people against deadly diseases, and someone who would not otherwise have contracted a deadly disease dies from the vaccination. This seems to imply that there is no absolute priority given to not harming. Does this, in turn, mean that killing is not really considered worse then letting die even in medicine?

Not at all. For, first, the kill and let-die cases are not equalized for expected probability of death and gain. In these cases the risk of immediate death from an act that kills was small and the expected gain from the act was great. We prefer acting rather than allowing someone to have the certainty of only a small bit of life and a yet lower probability of immediate death. So in the surgery case, the very same person has a larger *expected gain* if we act than if we do not act. In the vaccination case, though we may know that someone will die needlessly, we do not know who this is at the time we vaccinate. Therefore, so far as we know at the time of action, it is in the interest of each person to be vaccinated, rather than for us not to act. Each person has a higher expected gain.

By contrast, the permissibility of letting someone die in order to help a greater number of people does not require that there be this greater expected gain to the person who eventually dies. So, we should believe at the time of vaccination that our vaccination policy, which will save the greater number of lives, is also in the interest of the person we will in fact kill. (We believe that even he has a greater chance of dying of the disease than of the vaccine. We may, in fact, be wrong about this, but we have no way of knowing.) *By contrast*, I believe, it is permissible to *let someone die* in order to go and deliver vaccine that will save many more lives, even though there never was any expected benefit to the one abandoned.

Multiplicative Effects

So far we have considered two types of possibilities suggested by the Principle of Contextual Interaction, instances in which a definitional property of a term has a different role in different contexts, and instances in which one term but not another requires that a contextual factor be present to produce a result. A third type of interaction places more emphasis on *how* a term interacts with factors in the context, that is, on whether the total effect is produced by the *addition* of term and factors or by some more interesting interaction between them, which may lead to surprising results. These results will not be predictable by considering the term in another context, where there may be another interesting interaction going on with another contextual factor. For example, harming someone *by* violating his privacy may have overall greater moral significance than merely the sum of being harmed and having one's privacy violated. There may be a *multiplicative* effect; the whole (of the wrong) may be greater than the sum of its parts because there is something especially bad about being harmed by the invasion of one's privacy.[15]

Varying Definitional Factors?

We have been discussing varying the contextual factors in order to see how terms we are testing for equivalence interact with them. Let us return to the question of the home role of definitional properties. It is harder to find out whether a definitional factor is needed to make a moral difference or merely a definitional difference than it is to find out why a contextual factor is needed. This is because the definitional property can never be removed from its home term without changing the term we are testing. So we cannot vary cases to see whether the home term does really need that factor to make instances of the behavior it represents morally acceptable. We can test the factor in this way — varying its presence — only with cases involving the contrasting term we are testing.

If we do face the problem of bridging the gap between finding that a property has a morally significant role when exported and using this as evidence for its home-ground role, the new technique of comparing C- and CD-equalized kill (or let-die) cases cannot *mechanically* help us decide whether killing and letting die per se are morally equivalent or inequivalent. It can *suggest* which properties are important, but we may just have to *see* that they have a home-ground effect as well.

Second Argument for a Moral Difference between Killing and Letting Die Per Se

The comparison of the two killing cases (S1) and (S4), one with and one without a crucial definitional property of letting die [and even more so the comparison of (S1) and a C-equalized (standard) killing case] suggests a second argument for believing that Thesis E is false. If (1) killing someone who imposes for life support is easier to justify than (2) killing someone who doesn't (other things equal), but killing in the former case is not easier to justify than (3) not attaching someone to life support to begin with, then killing and letting die differ morally per se. This is because, where $\leq$ means "as bad as or worse than," and $>$ means "better than," if (1) $\leq$ (3), and (1) $>$ (2), then (3) $>$ (2), by transitivity. (A possible problem with relying on transitivity is discussed later.)

Another way to put this point is that we may permissibly let someone die rather than make efforts of a certain size, and we may sometimes permissibly kill someone who will lose only life he would have had via those efforts rather than make them. But it is harder to justify avoiding these same efforts by killing someone who will lose more than life he would have gotten causally via those efforts. This is true even though, in (S4) and (S1), it is agreed that the efforts are such that one needn't make them in order to save a life to begin with. It might be suggested that killing someone in (S4) is worse than not aiding someone to begin with only because the former, but not the latter, involves using the person as a means and intending the cause of his death. It is not worse because it involves a killing. However, these additional factors are present in (S1) also; yet killing in (S1) is more acceptable than in (S4) — even if it is worse than not aiding to begin with because of these additional factors. Therefore, these factors alone cannot account for why (S4) is worse than not aiding to begin with to a greater degree than (S1) is. Still, to consider why

(S1) might be worse than not aiding to begin with, we could consider (S2) in which the person receiving life support will be killed by a new germ unless I make a minute additional effort to ward off the new germ. I do not do so, because I want him detached. In this case I intend his death as a means to stopping his presence in me. What this case lacks, but (S1) has, is the killing. If (S1) is worse than (S2), then this suggests that causing the death of a person different from myself and exercising control over what is not mine have an independent negative weight.

The Home-Ground Role of Definitional Properties Again

This second argument for believing that Thesis E is false bears on the view that a definitional property of letting die might have no morally significant role on its home ground. As noted, if (S1) is not better than letting die to begin with and it is better than (S4), then, it is suggested, killing without the definitional property must be worse than letting die to begin with. Now this would be true even if the definitional properties of letting die that are exported to (S1) had purely definitional roles on their home ground. If they did, it would just have to be some other definitional factor in letting die which is making letting die per se morally better than killing. This transitivity argument, unlike the attempt at CD-equalization in the first argument, therefore, does not aim to help us explain *why* killing and letting die differ; it does not attempt to home in on the specific property that is making the difference. Nevertheless, it does focus on the effect that the definitional property of letting die has when it is exported to killing cases, making the killing cases morally better. (It also assumes that it is C-equalized, rather than CD-equalized, killing and letting-die cases that are the appropriate test cases. That is why judgments about per se inequivalence are licensed by comparing letting-die with killing cases lacking [some] CD-properties and also killing cases with CD-properties.)

A similar transitivity argument applies to letting-die cases in which the moral effect of letting die has been neutralized by a killing in the background. That is, if a "neutralized" letting-die case is morally worse than a non-neutralized letting-die case, and the former is no worse than a killing case, then the killing case is worse than the non-neutralized letting die. (The transitivity here is complicated by the fact that the neutralization of the moral effect of letting die's definitional properties requires a separate killing and a separate letting die in the same case. It does not involve the modification of an instance of letting die. This may make the neutralized letting-die case seem *worse* than the simple killing case, which is untouched by a letting die as well. Yet another transitivity argument applied to letting die cases was described above.)

Problems for Transitivity Arguments

A problem may arise for all these transitivity arguments, for transitivity may fail to hold. A problem would arise if act *x* were no better than act *y*, and better than z, yet y failed to be better than z. I believe that there may be particular relations between acts that make transitivity fail. For example, suppose it is equally good to give to Charity A (act x) or to Charity B (act y). It is also morally better to give to Charity A than to Charity C (act z). Still it is possible that it is not better to give to Charity B than to Charity C. [That is, $x = y$, $x > z$, and $-(y > z)$]. This might be because Charity B is a descendent of Charity C, and it would be a slap in the "parent's" face to give the offspring money before giving to the parent. It is only if the choice between B and C is made so as to favor B, but not if the choice is made between A and C, that this insult will occur. [16]

Such intransitivities *can* occur, but there is no reason to believe that they *do* occur in the context of our second argument concerning killing and letting die. That is, there is no reason to think that letting die to avoid making efforts is no worse than killing to stop life support one is providing but that it is worse than killing someone who is not receiving life support from the person who kills.

Summary

We have focused on two definitional properties of letting die. namely that the victim will lose only what he would have had via imposing on the nonsaver. This imposing on seemed to be a morally significant factor, as shown by the fact that when it is introduced into a killing case it alters the morality of the behavior even from self-defense killings. These self-defense cases themselves illustrate the effect of one definitional property of letting die, namely that the person who kills or lets die would be imposed on first if he did not act. On the assumption of a home-ground effect of these properties, the effects of these definitional properties defeat the strong version of the equivalence thesis. The creation of an original cause of death component of killing (b'_2) and the fact that the killer exercises control over what is not his (h') seemed most significant in the absence of the first definitional property of letting die, that is when the victim would lose more than what he would gain from aid, but they have effects for other cases as well. This weighs against the weak version of the equivalence thesis (i.e., that nonexportable properties are not morally dissimilar). (The action/omission distinction has even less weight in accounting for any moral difference between killing and letting die as it appears in S3 which is a letting die that involves action but seems not much worse than not aiding to begin with, or worse only because of the intention that death occur.) Importantly, it is assumed that efforts made to avoid killing someone do not *cause* him to retain his life in the way that aid in the face of an already present threat does nor that requiring these efforts imposes on the agent first.

NOTES

1. Recall remarks on p. 32.
2. A case that lies between (S1) and (S4) would involve someone who does not

need to be in your body, but once in it becomes dependent on you for life support. If he is killed in this case, to stop the efforts of carrying him, he loses only what he would have gotten from support. However, if he had not been attached to you he would have been perfectly fine. Therefore, he did not face a threat prior to interacting with you as in the case of letting die.

3. I present this argument in greater detail in *Creation and Abortion* (New York: Oxford University Press, 1992).

4. The innocent beneficiary is also discussed in *Creation and Abortion*. Note that in the case of the innocent beneficiary, if we kill him we may impose on him before he imposes (in any sense) on someone else, but not before those helping him impose on someone else for his benefit. Note also that an imposition need not be an act of injustice in order for it to be permissible to take from the beneficiary his benefit. If someone as a morally innocent threat falls on me and this causes a big physical imposition on me that saves an innocent beneficiary, I believe that the beneficiary may be deprived of the benefit in order to stop the imposition. It is sufficient that there is an inappropriate imposition on me by another person—I have a right that others not be in certain positions relative to my body—even if it is unintentional. For more on this see *Creation and Abortion* and my M.I.T. Ph.D thesis, "Problems in the Morality of Killing and Letting Die." Suppose there is no physical imposition on me; but I am directed to do, or even voluntarily begin doing, something strenuous *for* the innocent beneficiary which I have no obligation to do, and which I cannot stop doing unless I take the benefit of my labors away. In this case, I believe, the benefit may be removed to stop this second sort of imposition. Henceforth, when I use "imposition on someone" I should be understood as referring both to physical imposition and the possibility that something weighty is being done for someone else.

5. We discuss this argument again in chapter 4.

6. Suggested by Michael Otsuka.

7. Does (Bl1) also suggest a problem with saying that (g″) is definitional of letting die? It is said that there is no physical imposition on me in (Bl1). Is it also true that I am not imposed on in any way? If so, this suggests that I can be of assistance to someone without being imposed on first in any sense. I do not think much is lost if we emphasize, instead of g″, that in letting die itself the efforts we avoid would *not be done to avoid our imposing first*. We can identify this as definitional to letting die and export it to instances of killing. I will let (g″) stand as is, but we might substitute this other phrasing. In many standard letting die cases, I believe, there is first imposition on the person who aids, and the person who lets die is avoiding first imposition on him in both senses of imposition—physical imposition and doing for another.

8. The following is another case which highlights the significance of combining in a *multiplicative* (rather than additive) way (d′) with some form of first imposition (g″ iterated): The person in the Blood Cases who receives my blood later comes to physically impose on me. In this case his getting my blood is independent of the imposition. He has his life due to my loss and he imposes, but he does not have his life as the result of an imposition (multiplicative case). If I killed him to stop the imposition, he would lose only what he gets via me in order to stop the imposition, yet the justification for killing, would not, perhaps be as strong as in the case where he would lose what he gets via an imposition itself in order to stop the imposition. Hence it is best to emphasize the multiplicative union of definitional properties (d′) and (g″) as contributing to improving a killing case. Recall also that the moral significance of (g″) occurs only if it is iterated, resulting in true first imposition by the potential victim on the agent. In

letting die cases, (d') and (g") are present as a matter of definition, and in standard cases (g") is iterated (resulting in g').

9. I first discussed this principle in "Killing and Letting Die: Methodology and Substance," *Pacific Philosophical Quarterly* 64 (Winter 1983): 297–312, and again in "Harming, Not Aiding and Positive Rights," *Philosophy & Public Affairs* 15(1) (Winter 1986): 3–32. Shelly Kagan discusses the same issue at length in "The Additive Fallacy," *Ethics* 90 (1988): 5–31.

10. Notice that facing such a cause of death at the time of the killing is different from having faced such a cause of death before being dependent on the person who kills, as in (S1). It is not true that the person in (S1) will die no matter what we do, since bodily support protects him from the previous (potential) cause of death. If we don't kill him, he will live. But in some cases someone already facing a cause of death at the time of our killing is expected to die even if we don't kill him.

11. James Montmarquet, "Doing Good: The Right and the Wrong Way," *Journal of Philosophy* 79(8) (August 1982): 439–55.

12. Further criticisms of Montmarquet can be found in chapter 5.

13. I made this point in "Killing and Letting Die," and again in "Harming, Not Aiding and Positive Rights." It is puzzling then that Warren Quinn in "Actions, Intentions, and Consequences: The Doctrine of Doing and Allowing," *The Philosophical Review* 98 (1989): 287–312, says, "And even *apart* from Kamm's point, the idea that intrinsically nonequivalent parts must always make an overall evaluation difference when embedded in identical contexts seems wrong. . . There may certainly be important intrinsic aesthetic differences between two lamp shades even though they create an equally bad overall impression when placed on a certain lamp." This *was* my point.

14. We should, however, take seriously the view that killing and letting die differ morally even when small costs are at stake. We should also take seriously the argument that the different efforts required to avoid killing and to avoid letting die do not indicate moral differences between killing and letting die per se. See chapter 4.

15. G. E. Moore discusses how a whole may be more than the sum of its parts. He calls it the principle of organic wholes. His example is consciousness of beauty whose value is greater than the value of the sum of beauty alone and consciousness alone. (Alon Harel suggests the following example: Trespass alone is not very significant nor is intending to take someone's property. The simple addition of the two is not serious. Yet trespass caused by the intention to take property is very serious.) Moore denies, however, that the intrinsic value of a part may change because of its context. See *Principia Ethica* (Cambridge: Cambridge University Press, 1903), pp. 27–36.

16. I discuss such intransitivities in chapter 12. They are further examples of the Principle of Contextual Interaction, since they say that x may be equal to y in one context and unequal to it in another context. Some differential interaction effects indicate intrinsic differences in the items tested and some do not. (The Charities Case does not, I believe.)

3

Objections and Conceptions
of Moral Equivalence

In this chapter we deal with objections and alternatives to the two arguments against Thesis E (sometimes expanding on points already made in passing) and consider further the strong and weak notions of moral equivalence.

I

The Assumption that One Should Control What Could Help Others

One objection to these two arguments against Thesis E (both strong and weak versions)[1] claims that it is insignificant whether definitional properties of letting die produce a moral difference between (S1) and (S4), since in these cases it is already assumed that it would be permissible to let someone die to begin with rather than support him. It should, therefore, be no surprise that it is almost as permissible to end support by causing someone to lose only what he gets via this imposition as it is to refuse aid to begin with. We cause him to lose what he has no right to continue to have, given the way he got it and why we want to remove it. What we want to know, this counter-argument continues, is whether the definitional properties of letting die had anything to do with *making* it the case that it was permissible to let the person die to begin with.

Response

The answer to this objection is to emphasize again that, for at least some size efforts, we may not kill rather than make them—in (S4) and in standard killing cases—though we could avoid the same effort by letting die to begin with. This itself shows that some definitional property of letting die did contribute to making it the case that letting die is permissible when killing is not. The definitional property makes it the case that there is a weaker right to aid than there is not to be killed when the victim-K would have had his life independently of imposition on us.

63

Significance of Definitional Property Depends on Self-ownership (No Prior Right to Use Others and the Prior Right of Others to Control Themselves)

Let us examine the issue raised by the first objection further. It might be argued that it would not matter to us that B will lose out on only what he would have via imposition on A and that A exercises control only over what is his own unless we first thought B had no right to A's efforts. If we thought that he had a right to these efforts or that he had a right to use A's capacities in general, the definitional properties of letting die that are in question would make little or no moral difference. Likewise, if B did not have a special claim, relative to A, to what he has independently of imposition on A, A would not have to make great efforts to avoid interfering first with or exercising control over what B has. The fact that B has something independently of A would not have moral significance if A had a valid claim to it.

We do, in fact, believe that A's efforts are not simply something B may claim as he needs them, whenever A is not made worse off by such use than B would be without aid. It is because of this that the fact that B would lose only what he would gain via A's aid is important. So, it might be agreed, this definitional property of letting die is a reason why fewer efforts are required to aid than to avoid killing in standardly equalized cases, given the ordinary context in which people are taken to have rights over themselves against the claims of those of whom they are independent in matters of life support.

There are two ways, however, to understand this: (1) the fact that *we think* the definitional properties in question makes a difference is an indication (evidence for the fact) that *we* believe that someone has a distinctive claim to his own capacities; (2) the fact that we think the definitional properties in question makes a difference is an indication (evidence for the fact) that someone *has* a distinctive right to his own capacities, and we *ought* to believe it. The latter is the stronger view that I suggest we accept.

The Relative Importance of Negative and Positive Rights

Is it true that the significance of definitional property (d') (as well as g" and h') depends totally on the assumption that someone has a distinctive right to his own capacities and that the positive right others have to his capacities is less weighty? This would not be totally correct if the violation of a positive right to aid were still considered less serious, even if wrong, than the violation of a negative right, in cases that are properly equalized.

The separateness and independence of imposition on a person (which give rise to negative rights) seem to have a force not totally dependent on the complete *moral* independence of persons (that is, where no positive rights relate them). For example, suppose a bodyguard has a duty to aid a drowning employer at effort x and fails to do so. Her reason is that effort x is great. Is this as bad as someone's failure to make effort x to avoid an act which, he foresees, will drown a stranger who is independent of him? The claim is that it is not. To support the difference between the violation of negative and positive rights, consider that if one hundred other people were drowning, it might well be permissible for the bodyguard to abandon her employer to save the hundred. However, it would still not be permissible for the bodyguard to do what she foresees will push someone into the water (causing drowning) in her rush to save the hundred. (This could be true both in the case where the person she pushes is independent of her aid, and also where the person is imposing on her. Still, I believe it is less serious in the latter case, and permissible when he is pushed because it is the only way to stop his imposition on her so that her aid may be transferred to others.) It is only when we start adding factors modeled on definitional properties of killing into the letting-die cases that they become as bad as killing. For example, the case gets worse if the bodyguard prompted the client to go into the water by promising to aid.

However, in understanding these two cases, we should also observe that when the bodyguard lets die, she *redirects* her aiding efforts from one to many even while failing in a contractual duty to aid. Comparable cases in which we redirect ourself from *killing* many to killing one are, in fact, cases where it seems to be permissible to kill one, even though we infringe on the negative right of the one. This suggests that we should not compare the killing cases which do not involve redirection with redirection-of-aid cases, in order to collect evidence that the duty not to kill someone who is independent of our lifesaving efforts is stronger than even a contractual duty to save a life. We must equalize for the *redirection structure of the case*, as well as other factors, and when we equalize for redirection we may, in fact, get equal permissibility of killing one and breaking a contractual duty to one. We should use some other sets of cases to show that positive contractual rights are weaker than negative rights.

These bodyguard cases may not be properly equalized in another way. That is, in the killing case, I intend the existence of the cause of death (even if not because it is the cause) but there is no such intention in the letting die case. Perhaps this accounts for the impermissibility of violating the negative right. To avoid this objection, we might construct a killing case that does not involve intending the cause of death.

Suppose, for example, that I break my promise to someone I have contracted to aid because it would require a big effort to aid him. On the other hand, suppose that in order to save someone (I have contracted to aid) at low cost to me, I must do something, in the course of which, I foresee, I will (without prior intention) voluntarily wiggle my foot. This sets off a bomb that kills someone. If what is done in the second case is worse than what is done in the first, then this indicates that violating a positive right is less serious than violating a negative right, other things equal. Further evidence for this would exist if I had to abandon the person I have contracted to aid because to aid him, I must do something, in the course of which, I know, I will voluntarily (but without prior intention) wiggle my foot, setting off a bomb that kills a bystander.

The suggestion is that the strength of the right that protects the life a person has independently of imposition on another is greater even than the strength of a person's strict right to get lifesaving aid from another. Perhaps this is because negative rights play a more fundamental role than positive rights in *constituting* the idea of the person itself, given that the person is conceived as a separate unit, however capable it is of relating to others or however much its development depends on relationships.[2] While *separateness* and *independence* are not the same (as I use the terms), since a separate person can be dependent (as in S1 and Bl1), independence can be seen as an ideal state, in many cases, for separate persons to be in. Sometimes separateness with independence of imposition is enough to generate a quite strong negative right (as in Bl1) but mere separateness as in (S1), is not enough.

The Significance of Separateness vs. Independence

To continue these last points, it should be noted that there may be a general resistance to the idea of a high degree of factual and moral separateness and independence of persons. One source of resistance are those who emphasize that people begin and live interconnected with others as social beings. Another source of resistance are those who believe that a basic moral structure of separate persons is unfavorably biased against those who choose to be, or need to be, connected to others. Both these opponents, I believe, fail to take seriously the distinction between a basic structure governing relations between people and the values that people pursue in their lives within that basic structure.

Suppose relating to others is a positive value. We can recognize the priority of the basic structure of separateness and independence of persons by considering whether a decision by an adult not to relate to others (who want to relate to him) will be respected, or whether he will be forced to relate to others. If his decision is often respected, that respect suggests the primacy of the individual's decision, as to whether or not to relate to others in many cases.

A second point can be made about the idea of the separateness of persons and the prior claim of each person against a given other to control life he has independently of imposition on that other. Identifying the failure to recognize separateness with what is known as a "boundary crossing," does not capture all the moral facts we are here interested in. If someone who is already receiving lifesaving aid is killed by (or at the directive of) the person aiding him, there seems to be a boundary crossing, a move violating a separate person. Yet, it has been argued, a great deal, though not all, of the negative moral significance of this crossing is eliminated if the aid need not be given and is sufficiently large and if, in being killed, the person loses only what he would get from the aid in order to stop physical imposition by him on the aider. Or, alternatively, even if there is negative moral value, it is not much greater than that of inappropriately not aiding to begin with.

Yet the fact that in these cases separateness of the person is less important than non-independence does not mean that respect for what one has independently relative to another, rather than concern for separateness itself, lies at the heart of the kill/let die distinction. For, as the Blood Cases indicate, it may be impermissible to kill someone who is not causally independent of another to end the cause of dependence when he is independent of an imposition on that other (either physical imposition or in the looser sense of something weighty being done for him by the other). The emphasis here is on the possibility of correcting the imposition. Further, since this imposition need not be on what that other person herself has independently of another, only, perhaps, independent of an inappropriate imposition on another, the concern seems to be with imposition on a separate rather than an independent person. Finally, while the idea of the separate person independent of imposition on another is crucial, the determination of when an imposition on another occurs is done first in relation to the idea of that other as a separate person, and only after this might we determine whether this imposition is on a separate person who himself meets the standards of not imposing inappropriately on yet others.

Summary

The definitional properties of letting die, (d'), (g″) and (h') have importance on the not unreasonable assumption that the fact that people are identifiable as separate gives each person a claim against another person over the life and efforts he retains independently of imposition on that other person. If someone loses only what he would have had via imposition on another person, the productive use being something to which the first person has a special claim, this is morally significant. In cases where there *is* a strict duty to aid and right to be aided, a person will lack a claim to control some of his life or efforts relative to the person he must aid. Still, this duty can weigh less than a negative duty of noninterference, other things equal, because the person not aided loses out only on what he would have had via imposition on the other, by the other exercising control of what is his. When the negative duty is violated, the person loses what he would have had independently of the aid of the violator and/or control is exercised over what is another's when there is no imposition. So, a *separate person* who is not physically independent of someone's life support may be owed such support (via a positive right, contractual or not) and then there is no *moral* independence between the persons. Still, respect for this factor of moral interdependence may be less significant for relations between any given agent and subject than respect for the moral rights stemming from separateness and independence of imposition.

A Definitional Property Doesn't Always Make a Difference

The basis of a second objection to the two arguments for the incorrectness of Thesis E is that in some circumstances the definitional properties of letting die do not seem to make a moral difference. For example, if it is in someone's interest to die, if he is of sound mind and wants to die, and if he wills that someone kill him, letting him die may not be morally better than killing him. Do definitional properties have *always* to make a moral difference, in order to prove that Thesis E is false?

The answer to this objection (which we have noted earlier, in discussing the Principle of Contextual Interaction) is just that, in some special cases, differences between killing and letting die that are morally significant may be canceled by factors that alter the usual effects of those differences. Desiring one's own killing may be such a factor. In other cases a difference may be swamped; that is, it is not canceled, only overridden. (An analogy may help explain this distinction: While having a headache may be a good reason not to perform a minor duty, it is a poor reason not to perform a major duty. In the latter case, the weight of the headache is overridden, not canceled.) The definitional property would not have to make a difference in all cases in order for Thesis E to be false, so long as it makes a difference sometimes. If a definitional property makes a difference sometimes, this gives sense to the idea that killing and letting die differ morally per se. [Analogously (to repeat), oxygen and nitrogen do not have to behave differentially always in interacting with other chemicals to be truly different per se.] Just as killing and letting die per se need not always make a difference, the definitional factors that account for their sometimes making a difference need not always make a difference. Indeed, it is one implication of the Principle of Contextual Interaction that in some contexts a property may make a difference and in others it may not.

Is the requirement that a definitional property of a term only sometimes make a difference too weak? It might be argued that at least sometimes a definitional property of killing can make a killing case morally better than the comparable letting-die case. For example, suppose someone wants to die by another person's hand, rather than by impersonal nature, and it is also in his best interest to die. Killing him may be morally better than letting him die. If we could show that Thesis E is false by showing that letting die has a definitional property that *sometimes* alters the moral status of a case for the better, then we could do this with killing also.

One answer to this objection is, I think, that it is not the nature of the definitional property of killing itself which makes the killing better in the case described above. It is someone's peculiar desire for the existence of this property that makes the killing better. Similarly, consider someone in whose interest it is to die, and who desires to be left to die of a cause already in place, even when others could save him. In this case the definitional property of letting die would make it morally better than killing. But this sort of case would not show that, intrinsically, letting die is made better by its definitional property, independent of someome's particular desire. (In another context, someone's desiring chocolate does not show it is truly better than vanilla.) I do not think that the definitional properties that I have discussed rely for their significance on such particular desires. Suppose we cannot find a property of killing that provides evidence for moral unobjectionableness in this same way in which the property of letting die provides evidence in at least some contexts. Then we shall be able to say that letting die per se has more evidence for its moral unobjectionableness per se than killing has, and hence that Thesis E is false.

Suppose killing is quicker than letting die. Is this not a definitional property which, independent of someone's desire, makes killing better *if death is a good*? But it is only *contingently*, not conceptually, true that killing is faster than letting die. Furthermore, creating an original cause of death, even if death is in someone's interest, is not, I think, as good (independent of any particular desire) as letting die, when in every other way they accomplish the same end. Other things equal, it may be better for people not to cause death.

Background to Letting Die

A third objection to the arguments given for the falsity of Thesis E is that the definitional properties of letting die seem to make little difference when the person who lets die is responsible for the fact that his victim-L needs aid. (This harks back to our discussion of the procedure for neutralizing the moral import of letting-die's definitional property in the letting-die case by introducing killing into the background.) Suppose we set in motion the events that will kill someone who would have gone on living but for our act, and we fail to do what we can to save him from our act. In this case, at the time we let the person die, he loses out on only what he would have gotten via us, by our controlling what is ours, yet it would be very wrong to let him die. If he *now* loses only whatever he can get via us, he will also thereby lose what he would have had independently of imposition on us had we not first threatened his life by doing something to what is not ours. This shows that the definitional properties of letting die, (d′, g″), can be made unimportant when the person will lose life he would have had independently of us if we had not involved ourselves with him at a previous point in time.

Therefore, the definitional property of letting die is morally significant only in a certain context. This would be just another example of contextual interaction, and also cohere with the view that a difference need not always make a moral difference to count against Thesis E. But the further important point is that this context in which the property makes a moral difference can be itself a product of the significance of the definitional property. The context in which we have not done something that threatens to deprive someone of life he would have had independently of imposition on us can be important. The definitional property of letting die has moral significance in that its *absence* — that is, our threatening someone with loss of what he would have retained independently of us — at a point in the *past* will make our conduct worse.

Intending Death or Its Cause

A fourth objection is that it is sometimes morally objectionable to intend that someone die, even if he will lose only what he would have had via our aid. This is true in case (B2), in which we do not aid the baby in the bathtub. It is also true in a variant of (S2). In this variant we let die someone for whom we are already making lifesaving efforts, only because we intend that he die as a means to our receiving a large sum of money. It is also (arguably) morally wrong to intentionally allow an event to occur when we foresee that the event will cause someone's death, simply because the event's occurrence helps us acquire the money. This is true even if we do not intend the death itself.

There are several possible responses to this objection. One is to deny that it is an objection. We need not expect that the factors that make the killing/ letting die distinction morally important are the *only* factors of moral importance. For example, the distinction between intending and foreseeing death can also be significant, at least in the case where death is bad for the person.

Letting die because we intend some intrusion on someone when we foresee it will cause death is another sort of wrong. Yet a further type of wrong may occur when we do not aid because we intend an event that causes death, though we do not intend the death *nor* any intrusion on the person. None of these factors need be related to what distinguishes killing from letting die.

A more ambitious approach to the problem suggests a specific answer to the question, What is wrong with our intending death, or an event that will cause death, or an intrusion on a person, even when the person is physically imposing and dependent for life on us, when our reason for so intending is other than that this is necessary to stop, or to avoid, giving aid? [When we intend to take life that is produced by aid in order to stop the physical imposition required to aid, there is no (or not much) negative moral significance of intending harm if we have no duty to give aid. If we have a duty to aid, then intending to take away life that the person is getting is wrong.] The ambitious suggestion is that intending death commits the agent to the further desire, that the victim have lost his life even if he *had* been living independently of the agent's aid. That is, since this agent's intention that the person die has nothing to do with the agent's already providing him with aid, she would have had the desire that the person die even if he had been independent of her. For example, it implies the agent would have refused to give lifesaving aid to begin with because she wanted the victim dead and, would have *wanted him to be threatened in the first place, when the victim would have otherwise lived independently of the agent's efforts* and though the agent was not in a position to help the victim if he were threatened. (It does not commit the agent to be willing to kill the person who was independent of his life support.) If this were true, it might be suggested that it connects the significance of intending death in these types of cases for these reasons to the significance of someone's losing life he would have retained independently of us.

Suppose the moral significance of letting die with these intentions, for reasons other than to end lifesaving efforts, were related to focusing on what one retained independently of some particular agent. Then we could see why intending versus foreseeing someone's death, or intending an intrusion on him, or intending an event that causes his death, has a more significant role in evaluating the permissibility of letting die than it has in evaluating the permissibility of killing. This is because we can deprive someone of life he would have had independently of us when we kill, whether we act with any of these intentions or not. However, letting die does not involve introducing an original cause or removing a protective barrier to the loss of what someone retains independently of us. Therefore, it is only by these intentions that we can relate ourselves in letting die to someone's losing what he would have had independently of our aid. Or at least that is the suggestion.

However, there is at least one argument against the view that the wrongness of these intentions in the absence of a desire to end or avoid efforts one is making to aid is to be connected to their relation to someone's losing life he would have had independently of the potential aider: *killings* of those who are independent of our life support, in which we have these various intentions, can be worse than ones in which we do not have the intentions, even though in cases where the intentions are absent, the person also loses out on life he would have independently of the killer. That is, *intending* that someone lose what he would have had independently of us seems to have something wrong with it besides the fact that it is linked up with someone's losing what he would have had independently of us (since foreseen killings can have that property as well). A separate objection is concerned with whether someone who intends the death of a person to whom he provides life support, for reasons other than to avoid burdens of aid, is in fact committed to desiring death if the person he aids were independent of him.

Suppose we examine the intentions of the person who refuses aid, and we find that he desires that the victim lose what he would have had independently of the aid. Suppose we then prohibit our potential non-aider from refusing aid. We would then require a connection between two people, when without the connection the victim would still, *in fact*, be losing out on only what he would have had via the aider's help. In trying to prevent something wrong, we may, depending on how much effort we are requiring, back into another wrong: interfering first with what the potential aider has independently of imposition on the person he would aid. If we take this other wrong seriously, and, therefore, do not enforce aid, we take the separateness and independence of the two persons, a basis of the killing/letting die distinction, more seriously than the bad intentions and inappropriate attitudes.

Kagan's Objections

Shelly Kagan discusses the killing/letting-die distinction as part of the theory of non-consequentialist constraints on pursuing the best consequences.[3] If it is worse to kill than to let die, as judged in separate cases, then it is possible that we should not kill one even to avoid letting many others die. Kagan asks what the specific form of the constraint based on not killing should be. He thinks there are many problems in formulating it correctly and in ensuring that it will yield the results that a non-consequentialist wants. One immense problem in using not killing to ground a constraint (independent of the intention/fore-sight distinction) is connected with statistical probability: almost anything we do has some small chance of causing a death, and we foresee this though we do not intend it. Yet we cannot prohibit all action.

But my concern in examining whether there is a moral distinction between killing and letting die is not to build a constraint on this difference alone. To make this point, consider the following contrast: Someone is in a plane that is about to crash in the water and can save himself only by doing something in the course of which (he knows) he will voluntarily (but without prior intention) press on a lever, thereby redirecting the plane toward a populated area. He risks killing many. How great must the risk be of killing how many to make his act impermissible? This may be a difficult question to answer. But suppose, by contrast, that he is about to crash in the water and can save himself only by redirecting the plane to an unpopulated area where no one will be hurt. However, if he had landed in the water (and died) his plane would have served as the life raft for several people already in the water, who would otherwise have drowned. He need not hesitate in redirecting his plane in this case, though he lets some die. This is true even though he may not know exactly what the constraint on killing is, and so may appropriately hesitate to redirect if he would thereby kill many rather than let them die.

Kagan also asks how a doctor's pulling the plug on a life support machine can be a letting die, but a nephew's pulling it because he wants to inherit would constitute a killing. Why are we permitted to turn a trolley from killing five when we thereby kill one, rather than let the five die? If the distinctions between killing and letting die are taken simply and given moral weight, there will be problems in explaining these cases. Further, given that one could formulate the distinction so that it yields the responses to cases that a nonconsequentialist thinks are right, Kagan asks what deeper justification for the distinction there is.

I have suggested that my acting to cause death will be significantly different morally from letting die by inaction when my act causes someone to lose life he would have had independently of imposition on me (though he may have it via the assistance of others). For my letting die, by definition, involves someone losing only life he would have had by my assistance by my exercising control over what is mine. But sometimes acting to cause death will also involve someone losing only life he would have had by imposition on me, as when I stab someone (or unplug him) when he is receiving life support in me. In such cases, the killing cases have added to them a definitional property of letting die, and this may alter their moral significance especially when there is physical imposition to be terminated. Explaining the distinction in this way will make it depend, at least in part, on the significance of the independence of imposition on one (separate) person relative to another person.

This analysis has some revisionist implications, which may help us explain some of the puzzles Kagan presents. It would account for why a doctor's removing aid that he provides (or that is provided by the institution whose agent he is) can have the moral significance of a letting die while a nephew's removing aid he does not provide has the moral significance of a killing. Only the first case has properties that are conceptually true of letting die and that helps make letting die permissible when killing is not, namely that the person loses only what he would have had with the help of the person who ends the aid and the person exercises control over what is his.

Recall, however, that we may still think it is worse to actually kill (e.g., shoot) someone who is receiving life support in order to stop the support than not to aid someone to begin with. This is because even if he gets life from our aid and imposes, he is a separate person and we impinge on that separateness when we kill as we do not when we let die. (In addition, such factors as intending his death and full responsibility for it may weigh in.)

The answer to why we may redirect a threat so that it kills one when we could otherwise let five die from the threat is more complex. It suggests that even if there is a moral difference between killing and letting die per se, a constraint that tells us what not to do will not simply say, "Do not kill if the alternative is to let die." (We take this issue up again in chapter 6.)

One of the ways Kagan generates puzzles for the kill/let-die (and the intend/foresee death) distinction is by interpreting those who defend the distinction as asserting that it makes a moral difference always, not only sometimes. However, many defenders of the distinction might insist that it makes a difference only sometimes, and this is enough. A distinction can make a difference only sometimes because (as Kagan elsewhere himself argues) two factors can interact with a third factor to yield the same overall result, and yet interact with a fourth factor so as to yield different results. If these two factors ever yield different results in combination with other factors, this can show they are morally different. (This is the Principle of Contextual Interaction.) The analysis I suggest of the killing/letting-die distinction goes further than this general point. It focuses on a factor other than the kill/let-die distinction — namely whether the person loses only what he would have had by imposition on me — which is nevertheless conceptually connected with letting die. This conceptual connection helps account for why we are tempted to speak in terms of the kill/let-die distinction. It also explains why the kill/let-die distinction sometimes does not make much moral difference by showing that a factor that distinguishes killing from letting die conceptually can be present in killing cases as well as in letting-die cases.

Kagan notes that causing someone to lose what he retained independently of us will be worse than his losing what he is retaining via our help, only if in the killing case he is normatively entitled to what he has independently of our assistance and in the letting die case not entitled to our resources which might aid him and which we have independently of his assistance. I have said (p. 64) that this is partially true. But part of my point is to note that a non-normative distinction — for example, that he has his life independently of imposition on a particular other person — could be the basis for such normative entitlement claims relative to that other person.

Kagan also asks, Why must we make large efforts rather than kill if we have the option not to make large efforts to save a life? and he asks why large efforts the agent must make to avoid killing are less important than the losses of the potential victim? Here are some suggested responses. If someone has something independently of imposition on me then I should make efforts to avoid imposing first on that other person, even if I needn't make efforts to provide him with what he would have via my efforts. This is, roughly put, a way to justify the existence of options not to pursue the greatest good when doing so would be burdensome, even if burdensome efforts are required in order to abide by constraints not to harm. This is one of the important implications of discussions of the killing/letting-die distinction. Furthermore, pre-

venting the potential victim from suffering a loss takes precedence over preventing the agent from suffering a loss—even a greater loss—to prevent
himself from harming the potential victim, because the goal is to prevent first
imposition on life the potential victim has independently of the agent or first
imposition on what is not the agent's when this leads to the victim's loss of
life. The relative size of losses is not all that matters in generating constraints
on action and options whether or not to give aid; what also matters, for
example, is preventing first imposition on what is had independently of the
potential imposer.

Kagan on Independence and Dependence

Kagan has further criticisms of this argument: First, he says, you do not have
your life independently of me if you depend on my not killing you. Can this
be right? Is it not analogous to saying that the building stands because the
plane did not crash into it, and the lightning did not strike it, and the millions
of other things that might have happened to destroy it did not happen? If you
would have something if I did not exist, then the fact that I prevent my
existence from being a causal threat to you is, I believe, consistent with your
having what is yours independently of me in a sense that is morally significant.

Kagan's related criticism of the proposed account of the moral distinction
between killing and letting die, and more generally between *doing* harm and
allowing harm, is that it is circular, it assumes the very distinction it is trying
to justify. We want to explain the significance of the distinction between doing
harm and allowing harm, and we explain it in terms of the distinctions between
someone's independence from versus dependence on imposition on us and/or
the distinction between doing something to what is ours versus doing something to what is not ours. These involve the ideas of *allowing* someone to keep
what he has independently of imposition on us and *allowing* what is not ours
to remain unimposed on versus the *doing* of aid.

Is this a circle, since the two sets of distinctions are not exactly alike?[4] For
example, *allowing someone to keep life he has independently of imposition on
you is not the same as allowing someone to die, and "doing" aid is not the
same as doing harm.* But if we did find ourselves needing to make use of the
do-allow distinction, or some revisionist version of it, in contexts other than
the one with which we began, does that not support the possibility that use of
the distinction is unavoidable and morally significant?

Here is an alternative circularity argument.[5] If I have a right to kill someone, and refrain from doing so, the person does owe his life to my aid, does
depend on my refraining from killing him. Therefore, the claim that someone
has his life independently of me must involve the assumption that I have no
right to take it away from him, and what right have we to assume this? Isn't
this what we are trying to prove? My answer to this is to agree that there is a
normative sense of dependence, namely that once it is shown I have a right to
kill someone, his being alive depends on my refraining. But I wish to focus on
the non-normative notion of dependence versus independence (heavily tied to

causal input or its absence), and claim that it is more difficult to argue for the existence of normative dependence, including the right to take a life on which that position relies, once we take seriously the non-normative independence of someone's survival from imposition on you.

Another Question: The Negative and the Positive

Suppose that doing harm were morally more significant than letting harm happen, at least sometimes. Kagan asks, if *doing* is so important in the context of harm, why isn't *doing* in the context of good as important? That is, why isn't doing good as morally significant as doing harm? (And, we might add, why isn't a decision to let good be done or happen without interference as morally significant as a decision to let bad happen?) If it were, why wouldn't it be a justification for doing harm that we are thereby doing good, including saving lives? Such justification would eliminate some constraints based on not killing. In other words, why is the negative weightier than the positive? First, recall that we have not said that doing harm *is* always worse than letting harm happen, nor that the *doing* element per se is what makes it worse when it is worse. (Maybe the fact that someone can lose what he has independently of us or we can exercise control over what is not ours only if we *do* something is what makes doing important, when it is.) It would also be incorrect merely to assume that when "do" modifies harm it has the same weight as when it modifies good. Doing (and intending) may interact differently with these factors, thereby producing wholes of differing moral significance.[6]

Nagel notes[7] that there is no special demand that we intend good rather than act so as to bring about good as a foreseen consequence. Presumably this is because we should not reduce the total good we produce, simply in order to intend whatever good we produce. But note that this means that, at a second level, we have adopted a policy that in some way aims at the greater good (within constraints perhaps), because it tells us not to reduce foreseen good in order to intend lesser good on a given occasion. And our reason for not switching to lesser-intended good is that we do, after all, intend that there be greater good. Still, if the intention/foresight distinction did not operate on goods in the same way as it does on harms, this might be an indication that intending does not have the same significance in relation to good as it has to harm.

More particularly, giving greater weight to the negative of harming than to the positive of benefiting represents the priority that morality gives to the inviolability of the person (insofar as we should not achieve our ends by harming or, more generally, interfering with him, at least in certain ways) over his status as recipient of benefits, emphasizing the separateness of persons.

What happens if we do not seek good? Is there insult to those not aided comparable to the insult that occurs if we harm or intend harm? I do not believe so, especially if the reason we do not seek good is that doing so will require significant harm to some. Even if only clearly permissible means are necessary to achieve the good, not seeking it may not be as insulting as harming.

If we are inviolable in a certain way it is arguable that we are more important creatures than violable ones, that we are creatures whose interests are
more worth serving. Kagan claims that the only sense in which we can show
disrespect for people is by using them in an unjustified way, and if it is
justifiable to kill one to save five, in general, we will not be showing disrespect
for the one if we use him so. But there is another sense of disrespect, according
to which we owe people more respect than animals, even though we also
should not treat animals in an unjustified way. And this other sense of disrespect is, I believe, tied to failure to heed the greater inviolability of persons.[8]

Quinn's Alternative Analysis

I have offered a somewhat revisionist view of the significance of the killing/
letting-die distinction, one that need not always group killings and lettings die
separately from a moral point of view. For example, we group someone's
killing in order to stop providing life-giving aid as often close in moral
significance to letting die in order to avoid aiding. And some lettings die have
definitional properties (or properties close to those) of killing per se which
make them close in moral status to certain killings. This revisionist view,
nevertheless, justifies the impulse to focus on killing and letting die, by showing the crucial role of their definitional properties in determining the moral
status of cases. Warren Quinn offers an alternative account of the so-called
killing/letting-die distinction that also has revisionist implications.[9] Quinn
suggests that a morally significant distinction between doing harm and allowing harm should depend upon a distinction between *positive* and *negative*
agency. This, he claims, will group cases in the morally right way, though in a
somewhat revisionist way. Positive agency involves two components: (i) causing harm by action, and (ii) allowing an event to occur with the intention that
the event occur when one foresees that the event will lead to harm, though one
doesn't intend that it lead to harm. (Note that this is not the use of intention
appealed to in the doctrine of double effect since one doesn't intend harm.)
Negative agency is simply allowing harm to occur, perhaps foreseeing but not
intending the harm or any event that will (causally) lead to harm. This analysis
is revisionist since it implies that some lettings die, where we intend the occurrence of the event that leads to death, are to be treated as morally on a par
with killings (of at least some sorts).

Criticisms

Quinn's notion of positive agency is problematic, I believe. We can consider
cases that show this and also try to explain why this analysis has problems.
First, consider a set of cases which I call the Car cases, like those Quinn uses
to explain the idea of positive agency: (1) We are rushing five dying people to
the hospital and see one person ahead on the road. We would run him over if
we continued. [If we did so, this would be positive agency (i) i.e., by action.]
(2) We are in a car rushing five dying people to the hospital. The car was set

on automatic drive by someone else before we got into it. We see someone ahead on the road. If we do nothing, the car continues; if we step on the brake, it stops. The only reason for our doing nothing is that we intend that the car pass over the spot where the person on the road stands, since passing over the spot is necessary to our getting to the hospital. [This is positive agency (ii).] (3) We are in a car set on automatic by others, which will run over one person on the road if it continues on its way. We are busy attending to five people in the car who will die if we stop attending to them. If we let the car continue on, we let the one person on the road be killed, not intending that the car pass over the spot where he is. (This is a case of negative agency.)

For Quinn, (1) and (2) are morally equivalent. But, I ask, if it would be permissible to shoot someone to stop him from driving into the one [in (1)], could we do the same to those in (2), who deliberately do not brake the car, if doing this would cause the car to brake? I think not. (This test for moral equivalence, i.e., May I stop one behavior by the same means I would use to stop another behavior? will be further examined in chapter 4.) Wherein lies the difference between (1) and (2)? Those in (1) do something to the world we all share, something that threatens harm to someone who exists independently of them. [Their behavior might be significant even if it just threatens harm to a separate person who is not independent of them (insofar as he receives a benefit from them) but does not impose on them.] Those in (2) do not do this, and this, it is suggested, is a morally significant difference, even if what is done in (2) is also wrong.

Notice that positive-agency cases of the second type *may be* said to implicitly involve CD-equalization. They import what might be said to be a definitional property of killing, intending the existence of what causes death, into a letting-die case. This may make the letting-die case morally worse than standard letting-die cases, but it is still not morally equivalent to killing cases. We have, however, denied that such an intention is definitional of killing.

We have noted (in discussing cases where we refuse to continue aid for reasons other than to avoid burdens on us) that intending someone's death or the event that causes it, even if the person loses only what he would have gotten via our aid, may be wrong in part because it indicates a further desire that an event occur that causes someone to lose life he would have had independently of our aid. This connects the wrongness of the omission with the absence of a definitional property that makes letting die morally more acceptable than killing.

The justification that Quinn ultimately offers for the distinction between killing and letting die is connected with the significance of the distinction between what is mine and what is not mine; that is, he too ties it to the self-ownership claim. Quinn claims that if we had to avoid interfering harmfully with persons only when this was for the best, then their lives would not really be theirs: they would have a right to noninterference only when this was for the greatest good. But their lives are theirs only if they have a claim that overrides utility. (Only the first form of positive agency Quinn describes can deprive someone of what is his, held independently or not. How does the second form of positive agency fit in with recognizing self-ownership? It does not interfere with what is thine, but it wills the existence of causes that interfere with what is thine.) This view is in the same spirit as the view I have proposed, except that I have attributed significance to what belongs to someone and is maintained by him independently of imposition on the person who would threaten him. For if it is *his* life but he needs life-saving aid from us, what it is permissible to do to him or what it is permissible to do to us for him, could differ from what is true of killing in other cases.

Quinn on the Trolley Problem

Consider another problematic implication of Quinn's account of positive agency. He claims that it offers an explanation of the Trolley Problem. This is a case in which many non-consequentialists think it would be permissible to kill an innocent bystander in order to help others. If we turn a trolley headed toward five away from them onto a track where it will kill one, we are engaged in positive agency (i) (via action) that results in harm. If we let the trolley go to the five, Quinn says, it can only be because we intend to save the one. This means that we intend that the trolley *not* head in his direction. The trolley can only go in two directions, to the one or to the five. Quinn seems to think that intending that it not go to the one involves intending that it go where it will harm the five. (This does not involve intending the death of the five, or even intending the event of the trolley going over the spot where the five are. It involves intending that the trolley go away from the one, from where, we foresee, it is causally necessitated to hit the five.) This then is the other form of positive agency (ii), allowing an event with the intention that it occur, foreseeing that it will by causal necessity lead to harm. Quinn concludes that, since we are involved in positive agency whether we turn the trolley to the one or don't turn the trolley from the five, we might as well see to it that the smaller number of people is killed.[10]

Criticisms

One question to ask about this analysis of the trolley case is whether, if we do not turn the trolley away from the five, we are intending that the one not be hit. We may only be intending that we not do the hitting, whether or not we think it morally wrong to do so, and this is not to intend an event that leads to harm to the five. Suppose, however, that Quinn's analysis of what we intend is correct. Then we have a choice between positive agency either way we go, according to Quinn. But consider a rather striking implication of Quinn's analysis. Suppose a trolley is headed to one person (not five) and can be redirected to five. On Quinn's mode of analysis, turning the trolley to the five is positive agency by action. Suppose positive agency by inaction is morally equivalent to that by action. (Quinn's solution to the Trolley Problem depends on this supposition, as well as on his analysis of what we would do in not turning the trolley from five to one.) *Then turning the trolley from one toward five is morally equivalent to refusing to turn the trolley from five toward one.* (In the latter case we would, according to Quinn, intend that the trolley be away from the one, foreseeing it will by causal necessity hit the five.)

Yet, I believe, these behaviors are not morally equivalent. It is our duty not to turn the trolley from one to five; it would be permissible to shoot someone who was going to do it. It is not, however, obligatory to turn the trolley from five to one, it is only permissible, and we could hardly damage someone severely if this alone would cause him to turn the trolley from five to one. These cases, therefore, suggest that there is a moral difference between altering the world we all share so that it presents a threat to another innocent, non-threatening person, who exists independently of us, and allowing threats to proceed, even if we intend an event that is part of their proceeding.

Suppose Quinn is wrong when he says that not turning from five to one involves intending an event that harms the five. Then I would still rely on my earlier discussion of the Car cases to make my point about the moral difference between the two types of positive agency. I conclude that Quinn offers no solution to the Trolley Problem, either because his theory of positive agency is wrong or because he misdescribes what occurs in the case, and his attempt to assimilate positive agency (i) and (ii) for moral purposes is incorrect. So the fact that someone loses only what he would have gotten via our aid as we act on only what is ours creates a significant difference even in a context where we intend an event that we foresee will of causal necessity lead to harm.[11]

II

The Two Conceptions of Moral Equivalence

At the expense of some repetition and for the sake of emphasis, let us consider again the significance of the two different notions of moral equivalence we have analyzed. Suppose that we accepted the first analysis of moral equivalence (i.e., no definitional properties of killing or letting die have differential moral significance), and we used cases like (B1) and (B2) as comparable kill/let-die cases. Suppose further that we concluded from them that killing and letting die were morally equivalent per se. The implications of this conclusion would be much more significant than the same conclusion reached by using both the second analysis of moral equivalence (that is, no nonexportable definitional properties of killing and letting die make a moral difference) and comparable killing and letting-die cases that are CD-equalized for definitional properties. This is because if there were moral equivalence per se of the first type, this would mean that no conceptual properties of letting die differ in moral significance from the conceptual properties of killing. There may be more types of cases in which *a* killing and *a* letting die will be morally equivalent; there will be C-equalized, as well as CD-equalized cases. For example, letting-die cases could be morally equivalent to C-equalized cases in which we kill someone who would have lived without aid, as well as to cases in which we kill someone whose life we were already saving. By contrast, the conclusion for moral equivalence per se that used the second analysis of moral equivalence could be compatible with the conclusion that (B1) and (B2) are not morally equivalent *instances* of killing and letting die. Killing and letting die might be morally equivalent in a smaller number of types of cases.[12]

Making the Insignificant Difference Significant

We have noted, however, that even terms (and the behaviors to which they refer) that fulfill the strong first notion of per se moral equivalence may have different effects in some contexts. So the fact that terms behave differently in some contexts, although necessary to show that the terms differ morally, is not sufficient. This is *not* because the terms must always behave differently, but rather because contexts differ, and behaving differently in some contexts does not indicate that there is a per se moral difference. For example, a conceptual property, unique to one of the terms, which in itself had no moral significance, might interact in some cases with a contextual factor, such as desire, to produce a moral difference. Then whether we kill or let die could make a moral difference without these two being morally different per se. Analogously, even if there is no moral difference between chocolate and vanilla, the fact that everybody at a party prefers chocolate might make it wrong for us to serve vanilla. (I suggested that only such contextual factors as people's attitudes, desires, or beliefs could make features intrinsically of no moral significance have different moral effects.)

Two Notions of Inequivalence and "Being Worse Than"

The other side to the greater significance of the first notion of equivalence is the reduced significance of its corresponding notion of inequivalence. Killing and letting die would be morally different per se if any conceptual property of one made a difference on its home ground that properties of the other did not make on its home ground, even if it was a property for which instances involving the contrasting behavior could be equalized. This implies (as we have seen above) that CD-equalized killing and letting-die cases could be very close morally (perhaps even equivalent). This could happen even though killing and letting die differ morally per se, if only exportable definitional properties of each term made a difference. The difference per se might make no difference in these cases. Indeed, the comparison of CD- and non–CD-equalized killing cases with a case of letting someone die to begin with shows that in the very process of making a case of killing—the CD-equalized killing—more morally similar to a case of ordinary letting die, we can collect evidence for the moral difference between killing and letting die per se.

Suppose that the per se moral differences did not show up in many cases. The fact that sometimes killing and letting die did make a difference in virtue of conceptual properties that had a moral effect in the home-ground term would be enough to ground the first notion of *inequivalence*. Therefore, the first notion of *equivalence* should emphasize that conceptual properties *never* have differential home-ground effects.

The first notion of equivalence is, therefore, very liberal in tolerating the same overall responses to cases, consistent with per se *inequivalence*. The first notion of moral inequivalence can tolerate even the possibility that some conceptual property of killing has the same moral significance in some cases that a property of letting die has, only in different cases. Killing and letting die would still be morally inequivalent per se because they would *not be substitutable for each other in every non-opaque context (i.e., contexts not a function of intentional states) salva moral value* on all possible dimensions. (I am here analogizing the notion of moral equivalence to the idea of synonymous expressions which preserve truth value in all non-opaque contexts.) Suppose that killing has a conceptual property that letting die lacks and whose moral effect always compensates for that of a conceptual property that killing lacks but letting die has. Then killing and letting die are not identical tout court, but they could still be *morally* equivalent in the strong sense of the first notion of equivalence, since they would be substitutable without *moral* difference in *all* non-opaque contexts.

It is important to see that the associated strong idea of *moral inequivalence per se* is, therefore, compatible with killing being *no worse than* letting die per se. For if some conceptual property of killing has the same moral significance in some cases that a property of letting die has, only in different cases, then while killing and letting die would be morally inequivalent per se, this would not imply that one was intrinsically better than the other. So being "*no* worse than" does not imply being morally equivalent, though being morally equivalent does imply being no worse than. Those who discuss the issue of the moral equivalence of letting die and killing per se may really be interested in another question, of whether one is per se worse than the other; and the answers to these two different questions are not necessarily the same. (We shall discuss this point again in Chapter 4.)[13] How could one retain the idea that letting die per se is intrinsically better than killing, and at the same time acknowledge that in some equalized cases a killing may even be better than a letting-die? A proponent of the first notion of inequivalence would have to somehow distinguish the claim that special (e.g., opaque) contexts cancel or make a virtue of killing's negative features from the claim that killing has features that are intrinsically morally as acceptable or unacceptable as those of letting die, only in different contexts.

If conceptual properties unique to each behavior and not exportable to instances of the other behavior only sometimes made a moral difference (in the right sort of contexts, e.g., not dependent on desire), this would be enough to ground the second notion of *inequivalence*. Since the absence of these properties cannot be compensated for, the second notion of equivalence is not so liberal in tolerating the same overall responses to cases, consistent with per se moral inequivalence. If there are no cases in which nonexportable properties make a difference, and exportable properties do not differ morally or can be compensated for, the second notion of equivalence will be fulfilled.

The Role of Contexts

Having the same responses to cases while retaining the idea of per se inequivalence bears on another question with which we began: Would only moral equals produce equal responses in equal contexts? Unequals might yield equal results in the same context if the equal context involves CD-equalization of morally significant properties. (Although here, strictly speaking, a factor that appears in the context of one term will appear in the definition of another.) But it is important to note that unequals may also produce equal responses in other ways. As suggested by the Principle of Contextual Interaction, the different moral significance of conceptual properties may be totally canceled (as well as merely overridden) in some contexts even without the introduction of definitional properties of the contrasting behavior. For example, if a person desires to die and it is in his interest to die, it may make no difference whether we kill him or let him die. If someone is doomed to die no matter what we do, it may matter much less whether we kill or let die. If we have a right to see to it that an aggressor dies, it may also not matter whether we kill him or let him die. We may kill as well as let die even innocents who could have survived independently of us, if we do so in a morally permitted manner, for example, by redirecting a threat.

Just as the effect of properties may be canceled, so may they be multiplied by special contexts. For example, it may be that the seriousness of harming someone by or in the course of invading his property is more than the sum of harming him and invading his property taken separately. The seriousness of each act is multiplied to some degree by the other. [Notice that here the multiplication seems to go in both directions (symmetry). For example, it is worse to invade if we invade to harm, and worse to harm if this is by invasion.]

In general, two factors might interact in the same way with one context, yet interact differently with a changed context, and sometimes this shows that the factors were not morally equivalent per se. For example, when the costs needed to aid or not kill are low, a killing and a letting die might be equally wrong. (We shall raise some questions about this in chapter 4.) However, when we raise equally the cost required to avoid killing and the cost to avoid letting die, we might find that a killing is worse than a letting die.

Further, morally different factors may yield the same overall (macro) response by different routes. There might be functionally equivalent but not identical routes (at the micro-level) to the same moral response. Simple equalizing for the presence of all factors other than the terms whose equivalence we are testing and getting the same responses will not ensure that the operations accounting for the equal responses are the same. (I described this as the problem of Black-box Equalization.) If the operations are different, this may increase the likelihood that responses will differ in *other* cases with other kinds of equal contexts.

Since equal responses might come even with unequal factors in equal contexts, we will not necessarily be able to predict that comparable kill and let-die cases will differ morally, even if we agree that there is a moral difference between killing and letting die per se.

One final point: Suppose killing and letting die per se were morally equivalent in the strong sense, so that they were morally equivalent in standardly equalized cases. This would not necessarily imply that they were equivalent in *cross definitionally* equalized cases.[14] If they were equivalent in standardized cases, this would mean that neither exportable nor nonexportable properties made a moral difference. But in creating cross definitionally equalized cases, we may export a property of letting die that contributes to its being permissible into a case of killing, making the killing case better, but be unable to export a property of killing which contributes to its being permissible into a CD-letting die case. Then the CD-killing case will have more characteristics in favor of permissibility than the comparable letting die case (assuming the characteristics do not cancel each other out in a burst of contextual interaction). If we start off with per se equals and CD-equalize we may wind up with morally different cases.

Types of Moral Explanations

Sometimes our moral reasoning may seem much like a type of reasoning discussed in aesthetics.[15] We point to a factor (for example, the blue in a painting) and say that it plays a role in making this painting beautiful, but don't therefore conclude that it will have the same effect (or any effect) in a different painting. So we might point to a killing and say that its being a killing makes a moral difference in one context, and not expect to find the same difference in another. However, the reason this would be so, it seems to me, is still different from what prevails in aesthetics. For in ethics, I think, if a factor made a difference sometimes, it could be overridden or canceled by another contextual factor, but should still retain weight that had to be canceled or overridden. (This is like the idea of a prima facie or pro tanto reason, which can be overridden.) In aesthetics, by contrast, a property may truly not have any constant merit-weight that needs to be overridden. On another model, we are like chemists. We say that chemical x caused the fire in the case, knowing full well that in another environment where its fire-causing properties are neutralized it will not cause a fire, but instead have the same innocuous effect as another chemical y. These are examples of the Principle of Contextual Interaction.

An alternative to this approach to explanation in ethics is to characterize carefully a more complicated property than killing or letting die that defines when killing and letting die do or do not make a moral difference and that *will* be predictive in all cases, or to isolate types of contexts that wipe out moral differences in less complicated properties. (These may be two sides of the same coin.) This approach isolates principles of permissible killing; most aestheticians claim that we cannot isolate analogous principles (rules) of good art. A more complicated property that predicted when killing was wrong, it might be suggested, is one property we have emphasized, that we cause someone to lose life he would have had independently of imposition on us. This, however, would have to be further refined, for sometimes it is permissible to cause someone such a loss. (We make the effort to offer a more refined principle in chapter 7.) But it is important to recognize that much is lost if we do not see how this more complex property connects with conceptual distinctions between killing and letting die. That someone loses out on only what we could have caused him to have is definitional to letting die. Furthermore, it is because of the conceptual properties that killing has (e.g., interfering with an ongoing course of events by an original cause of death) that it is possible for *it*, but not letting die (which allows a course of events to continue or actively causes one's own aid to end), to cause someone to lose what he would have had independently of our efforts. [16]

NOTES

1. Recall that arguments against the weak (second) version of Thesis E rely on the differential moral effect of *nonexportable* definitional properties (for example, of causing death).

2. Suppose this were true. Then requiring those who are better off to aid the worse off, when the worse off are not required to aid, will give the better off more positive duties and may also thereby leave them with fewer protected negative rights than the worse off. This may be contingent on the positive duties being enforceable by coercive means. If they were enforceable in this way, the better off would have a weaker sense of themselves as separate persons. But do not those who benefit from positive rights thereby lose the sense of themselves as separate units, because additions are made to their welfare? Perhaps taking away (even permissibly) destroys the unit in a way that giving to it does not, because one can permissibly refuse what is given to one, but not as legitimately fail a duty to give, or resist permissible enforcement of it.

3. Shelly Kagan, *The Limits of Morality* (Oxford: Oxford University Press, 1989), pp. 116–21. A large part of this discussion of Kagan, and the subsequent discussion of Quinn, are from "Non-consequentialism, the Person as an End-in-Itself, and the Significance of Status," *Philosophy & Public Affairs* 21(4) (Fall 1992): 354–89.

4. I owe this point to Thomas Nagel.

5. Originally mentioned in my "Killing and Letting Die: Methodology and Substance," *Pacific Philosophical Quarterly* 64 (Winter 1983): 297–312. Thomas Nagel reminded me of the argument.

6. The Principle of Contextual Interaction suggests this.

7. In *The View from Nowhere* (New York: Oxford University Press, 1986).

8. We shall return to the topic of inviolability and the significance with which inviolability endows a person, as well as Kagan's challenge to this claim, in chapter 10.

9. In "Actions, Intentions, and Consequences: The Doctrine of Doing and Allowing," *Philosophical Review* 98 (1989): 287–312.

10. Notice that this proposed solution to the Trolley Problem resembles in one respect the solution Philippa Foot offered in "The Problem of Abortion and the Doc-

trine of Double Effect," reprinted in B. Steinbock, ed. *Killing and Letting Die* (Engle-wood Cliffs: Prentice Hall, 1979): It sees us as having to do the same type of thing no matter what we do, and this is the reason we may maximize lives saved. Foot said that a trolley driver on a runaway trolley headed to five faced a choice, *killing* five or *killing* one, and therefore should kill the fewer. Judith Thomson's variation on Foot's original trolley case (in "The Trolley Problem," *The Yale Law Journal* 94 [Spring 1986]: 1395–1415) involved a bystander, rather than a trolley driver, who must decide whether to let the trolley kill the five or turn the trolley so that it kills one. For him, if not for the trolley driver, it is a choice between *killing* one and *letting five die*, Thomson thought; two different types of behavior. Quinn's account of positive agency analyzes this case of Thomson's on the model of a choice between the same types of behavior once again, only this time it is *positive agency* (i) in turning the trolley to one versus *positive agency* (ii) in not turning the trolley from five.

11. Quinn responds to some of these criticisms in "Reply to Boyle's 'Who is Entitled to Double Effect?'", p. 197, reprinted in Quinn's *Morality and Action* (Cambridge: Cambridge University Press, 1993). The primary points he makes there are, first that we might shoot the person who refuses to turn a trolley from five to one if he does so intentionally so that it is a case of positive agency. This I deny. Second, he says someone might blamelessly disagree with his theory, and for that reason, refuse to turn, and then, Quinn says this person shouldn't be shot. My response to this is that if Quinn conceives of this person as still intending that the trolley be going toward the five, but blameless (though incorrect) in thinking this is not wrong, it is not clear why Quinn thinks this person may not be shot. We often attack people who are morally excusable but nevertheless doing the wrong thing (e.g., an insane person about to murder someone). Third, Quinn says it is not part of his view to morally equate true negative agency in not turning the trolley from the five and positive agency in turning the trolley to five. In this case, he agrees we may not shoot the person who does not turn. With this I agree. Quinn does not respond to the point that refusing to turn does not involve an intention that the trolley head on the track to the five. (I am grateful to Matthew Hanser for helping to clarify the points Quinn makes in response.)

12. See p. 83 for limits on this. As already noted, those who support the moral equivalence of killing and letting die per se seem to appeal to the equivalence of killing and letting die in *both* C-equalized and CD-equalized killing and letting-die cases. For example, Bruce Russell cites killing and letting-die cases that are only C-equalized in "On the Relative Strictness of Positive and Negative Duties," reprinted in *Killing and Letting Die*, pp. 215–31, and CD-equalized ones in his "Presumption, Intrinsic Relevance, and Equivalence," *Journal of Medicine and Philosophy* 4(1979): 263–68 I believe the original supporters of Thesis E (such as Rachels) want cases that are only C-equalized (like B1 and B2) also to be morally equivalent instances of killing and letting die.

13. I am grateful to David Kaplan and Roger Florka for forcing me to get clearer on this issue.

14. I owe this point to Julie Tannenbaum.

15. For example, by Arnold Isenberg in "Critical Communication" reprinted in *Art and Philosophy*, ed. Kennick (New York: St. Martin's Press, 1979).

16. As described earlier, we can neutralize much of the bad moral import of this last property of killing by adding a definitional property of letting die to killing cases. (Then we interfere with aid we are giving.) Causing death, which is definitional of killing, may, however, introduce negative weight even when the person killed loses only

what he would have had via the killer's support. This remaining negative is due, in part, to the greater responsibility we have for worsening a state of affairs if we cause an outcome rather than merely allow it to occur. The same full responsibility is present if we cause a *good* event, rather than merely allow it to be caused by something else, or even removing barriers to its occurring. The negative is also due to interference with what is not ours, even if it only exists through our aid.

4

Killing and Letting Die in
Standardly Equalized Cases

Using Standardly Equalized Cases

In earlier chapters, we considered standard and nonstandard procedures for equalizing killing and letting-die cases. We focused on how nonstandard equalization could be useful in helping us see *whether* Thesis E is false and also in highlighting *why* it is false (if it is). It did this by helping us see which definitional properties make a moral difference.

In this chapter we shall return to the use of standardly equalized cases in discussing Thesis E. My aim is to use this procedure, which is employed by many who think killing *is* morally equivalent to letting die per se, but to see whether in fact it indicates the opposite of what they have claimed. I shall examine some of the very cases often considered to be instances in which a killing is morally equivalent to a letting die, and ask whether we really do think this is true. Like the second (Transitivity) argument given in chapter 2 for the inequivalence of killing and letting die, checking our reactions to standardly equalized cases will not directly tell us why the cases differ, only that they do. It is one of the merits of cross-definitional equalization and the first argument for inequivalence, that they try to help us answer the why question.

Since we are testing our reactions to standardly equalized cases, any criticisms we make of Thesis E based on these reactions would pertain to the strong version of Thesis E. This is the claim that no definitional properties of killing or letting die have differential moral significance per se. Henceforth in this chapter, all references to Thesis E will be to this strong version, unless otherwise noted.

> Case B1: I push a child under water in a tub, thereby killing him, in order to collect his inheritance. (Killing)
>
> Case B2: A child slips in the bathtub. I could easily lift him out but do not, because I want to collect his inheritance. (Letting Die)

As discussed earlier, it has been claimed[1] that we judge what is done in these cases to be equally objectionable morally. It has also been claimed that all factors other than killing and letting die have been equalized in these cases and, implicitly, that equals results given equal contexts are possible only if killing and letting die are per se equivalent. Therefore, it has been concluded, these cases show that killing and letting die are morally equivalent per se.

Post Efforts Test

Let us assume that these are properly equalized cases. One way to deny that they support Thesis E is to argue that we evaluate them as equally bad, even though killing and letting die differ per se, because bad intention to have the child die swamps differences in other factors. This is to argue that this one case represents a specific context, which hides the true difference between killing and letting die per se. Let us put this argument to one side, and consider whether we really do think these cases are equally objectionable. Rather than rely on our direct intuitions about the (B) set, consider a further test that may tell us whether we really do think that these cases are equally objectionable.[2] Consider how much of a loss we would think ourselves justified in imposing on someone, or how great an effort we could require of him, if his suffering it at t_2 would help save the life of the child he tried to kill at t_1 in B1 or failed to aid at t_1 in B2.

This test requires that the act not yet have succeeded in causing death, and that the omission not yet have made further aid impossible. We also assume that if the loss is not imposed at t_2, the child will die.[3] (We could run the same test in a purely hypothetical fashion by assuming that the child had died. We then ask how much of an effort could permissibly be demanded of the killer and the nonsaver if only this would resurrect the child.)

I call this the *Post-efforts Test*, since what is involved is deciding about efforts to be made (or loss imposed) *after* someone has done something that is considered wrong, here, attempting to let die or to kill. Bruce Russell[4] realizes that efforts that should be required to avoid an act that will kill might be different from efforts that should be required after the act has been done in order to prevent its consequences. The upper limit on efforts required to avoid the act might be lower than the limit on efforts required to make up for the consequences of failure to avoid the act when doing so required minimal effort. Russell makes use of the distinction between pre- and post-act efforts to argue that efforts morally required to avoid an act of killing are smaller than is commonly thought. He also agrees that someone who has been negligent in acting should be chosen to aid the victim of his act, over an innocent bystander. But, he argues, this is because the person who acted negligently has already done something wrong. He also argues that endangering someone's life without fault makes one no more liable to aid one's victim than an innocent bystander is.

Post-efforts for Omissions

In saying this, Russell may well underrate the responsibility we should take for correcting the consequences of any causal chain of which we are a part, even when we are not a fault.[5] That is a complex issue. But, in addition, Russell fails to apply the *pre- and post-effort distinction* to omissions. He does not test to see whether the efforts morally requirable of one who has already acted to kill are also requirable of one who has *already* failed to aid. He fails to consider what happens when there is no innocent bystander, but only two people who have both done something wrong already, one having acted wrongly, the other having omitted aid wrongly.

What answer shall we give to the question posed by the Post-efforts Test? It would be right to require the agent who tried to kill (for example, in B1) to suffer to save his victim a loss equivalent to (or greater than) the loss he threatened to impose on his victim. I believe it would not be right to require such high-post efforts of the person who let die (for example, in B2). So even cases like B1 and B2, which seem equally objectionable at first, do not seem to merit equal post-efforts. One possible explanation for the difference in post-efforts is that Thesis E is false; there is some morally significant difference between the killing and letting die. If the killing and letting die in B1 and B2 are morally equivalent, shouldn't it be permissible to prevent the consequences of one behavior by the same means it is permissible to use to prevent the consequences of the other, provided that the cases are properly equalized? I believe it is permissible (if necessary) to kill the person who pushes the baby into the water in order to achieve the good consequences of the baby's not drowning (even if not by preventing the act; suppose, for example, I shoot the agent, he topples into the water, and the baby pops out). But I do not think it is permissible for me to force the person in B2, who I am certain has omitted to aid and who would not otherwise aid, to aid the baby by shooting off his own arm so that he reaches out with the other arm. Nor may I kill him so that he topples into the water and the baby pops out. Therefore, perhaps even in these cases, there is a morally relevant difference between the killing and the letting die. Does this mean the two cases are not equally morally objectionable, and that we needed some further test besides our intuitions about the original cases to decide on their objectionableness? Perhaps not, for the moral difference may not have anything to do with what makes us feel outraged at the behavior, and it is this outrage which is a measure of objectionableness. So Thesis E may not be supported by cases (B1) and (B2) even if they are equally objectionable.

Philippa Foot has argued that letting die is contrary to charity but often not to justice (then letting die is not a matter of violating rights).[6] But killing is a matter of violating rights (at least in cases like B1). This could account for the difference in what we are required to do by the Post-efforts Test, if violating rights were morally subject to a different level of compensatory behavior than wrong acts that do not violate rights. Alternatively, suppose there were a positive *right* to aid in B2. Post-efforts for letting die might still be different from post-efforts for attempting to kill, because violating positive rights counts for less than violating negative ones, other things equal. This could be true when killing, but not letting die, takes from someone a life he would have had independently of imposition on the agent.

Two Tests for Stringency of Duties

If the post-efforts requirable do differ for killing and letting die in standardly equalized cases, then it is not true that what we mean by unequally stringent duties is only that one is more easily defeasible than the other. The idea of easier defeasibility is exemplified by the fact that when the efforts to be made or losses (to oneself or others) to be endured in order to aid or not kill someone increase, we may have no duty to aid but we still have a duty not to kill. The duty is defeated (hence more easily defeasible) in one case but not in the other. Warren Quinn argues[7] that killing impermissibly may not be worse than letting die impermissibly (as in B1 and B2), but there are still different defeasibility standards for killing and letting die. Compare (1) rushing to the hospital to save five, thereby foreseeably letting one die, with (2) rushing to the hospital to save five, thereby foreseeably running over and killing one person standing in the road. The first is permissible; the second is not.[8] On the basis of these cases we might conclude that saving five lives is enough to defeat a claim to be aided (the claim is defeasible to this degree), but it does not defeat a claim not to be killed. This would show that killing is not morally equivalent per se to letting die. As we noted earlier, this may not be the ideal example to make the point about the defeasibility of not killing and letting die. One reason might be that if we let one die on our way to saving five we will have discharged our duty to save life (given that we could not save all six), so this is not an example in which we have defeated a claim to be aided in order to do something other than meet claims to be aided. Indeed, it can be analyzed as a case of directing a benefit to five versus to one. The killing case, however, is not a case in which we refuse to direct a threat to five from its going to one, nor a case in which we direct a threat to one rather than let five be killed by it. But in a true redirection case, we *may* kill one rather than let five die. We must create cases that equalize for a redirection structure to use them as test cases. In addition, the killing in (2) but not the letting die in (1) involves intending the causes of death, another unequalizing factor. A better set of cases to show differential defeasibility, therefore, may involve the contrast between having to swerve into a tree to avoiding killing someone, but not having to swerve into a tree when doing so would save someone's life.

The Defeasibility Test is not sensitive enough if it does not reveal a moral difference that exists between B1 and B2. For as already noted, if the killing and letting die in cases B1 and B2 are morally on a par, shouldn't it be permissible to stop the consequences of one behavior by the same means it is permissible to use to stop the consequences of the other? I have said it is permissible (if necessary) to kill the person who pushed the baby into the water to achieve the good consequences of the baby's not drowning (even if not by preventing the bad act, e.g., I shoot the agent, he topples into the water, and the baby pops out). But I had said it is not permissible for me to get the person in B2, whom I am certain has omitted to aid, to aid the baby by shooting off his arm so that he reaches out with the other arm. Nor may I kill him so that he topples into the water and the baby pops out. Therefore, perhaps even in these cases, there is a morally relevant difference between the killing and the letting die.

But again note that the moral difference may have nothing to do with what makes us feel outraged at the behavior; not all morally significant differences show up in this way. Another example of this: We may be more horrified at what is done in B2 than at what is done when someone rushes five people to a hospital foreseeing that he will run over one person who is in the way. Yet we might permissibly impose greater post-efforts on someone in the second case than in the first if this would prevent permanent bad consequences. (We might also do more to prevent the driver's act — what I call a pre-effort — than to stop the other person from maliciously not aiding.)

Equalizing Backgrounds

It will now be useful to consider an interesting derivative of the Post-efforts Test. It equalizes for standard inequalities, in particular for some definitional properties, by equalizing backgrounds and foregrounds. Suppose we know that John maliciously let Mary die, and that Jim maliciously killed Jane (in standardly equalized cases). Knowing this, we then find out that Jim also maliciously let his victim die. (For example, we originally thought that Jim fainted right after shooting Jane, but then find out we were wrong; he stood by and did not aid her for malicious reasons.)[9]

Would we increase the post-efforts required of Jim or losses it is permissible to impose on him to make up for or prevent the consequence of what he did, once we find out he also let Jane die? I think not. The efforts would be at their high point already just due to his having done the act of killing. Indeed, if someone had a change of heart and tried to help the person he had endangered (that is, he did not intend to let die) he would still have to make the maximum efforts to make things up to his victim, I believe. (However, we would think better of him than of the unrepentant person.)

But suppose we found out that John, who we already knew had maliciously let Mary die, also maliciously caused Mary's death. Would not the post-efforts demandable of John go up? I believe they would. If so, it would be because efforts morally demandable were not at their maximum already. A possible explanation of this contrast with the previous case is that Thesis E is false.

After the additions to our knowledge, the cases involving Jim and John both present us with cases of someone who killed and let die. Yet, I believe, the order of discovery changes our decision about post-efforts. Letting die added to a known killing brings no change in post-efforts, because killing already, by itself, calls forth maximum efforts. Killing added to a known letting die, however, increases the post-efforts, because letting die by itself does not call forth the maximum post-efforts. One thing we do in what was originally the let-die case, is to neutralize in the case as a whole a definitional property of letting die (the victim's losing out on only what he would have had via imposition). Put in other words, we have equalized for a standard inequality between killing and letting-die cases. We have done this by making the person who is let die also lose out on life he would have had, considering the case as a whole, if the person who lets die hadn't also caused his death. (We have also equalized for causation with first imposition. Discussion of S1 and S2 and the Blood Cases considered these factors.)

Equalizing with Approximate Definitional Properties

It has already been noted (chapter 1) that properties that approximate to the definitional properties of killing or letting die could also be exported. An example is an approximation to causation that does not turn the letting-die case into one that also has a killing in it, but does still neutralize the import of a definitional property of letting die in the case as a whole. For example, I tell someone to jump into the water when he wouldn't otherwise have done so, foreseeing that he will drown, and do not aid him when he needs my help. Furthermore, we can add what is perhaps missing in ordinary standard let-die cases, namely, a right to aid on the victim's part. [This is a form of equalizing standard inequalities, if we assume that in standard killing cases someone's (negative) *right* is violated. This is because we explicitly add a (positive) right to the let-die case.] Such a case might involve my not aiding someone after I prompt him to go into the water by promising him that I will aid him, when I am a bodyguard specifically paid to aid. I believe the Post-efforts Test says that efforts demandable are greater here than in standard letting-die cases. This suggests that as cases have more properties like those present in standard killings, letting die gets worse. Do they get worse than killings? I believe not.

A Transitivity Argument

At this point it is appropriate to reintroduce a *transitivity argument*[10] against the claim that standardly equalized cases involve a killing and a letting die that are morally equivalent: Suppose the Post-efforts Test shows that a letting-die case to which we add both causation (or its cousin) and an explicit right, becomes morally worse than a standard letting-die case. However, it does not become worse than a standardly equalized killing case. Then does this not suggest that a standard case of letting die is not morally as bad as a standard case of killing? If *a* is worse than *b*, and *a* is no worse than *c*, isn't it a good bet that *c* will be worse than *b*? [Here we argue that, if one sort of letting die is (close to) morally equivalent to a standard killing, this suggests that a less bad sort of letting die isn't. In another transitivity argument in chapter 2, we argued that if one sort of killing was (close to) morally equivalent to standard letting die, then this suggests that a worse form of killing isn't morally equivalent to a standard letting die.]

Criticisms of the Post-efforts Test: Accomplices and Temporal Location

Criticisms could be made of the Post-efforts Test. Some might claim that unequal post-efforts are not explained by the fact that letting die differs morally per se from killing. Rather, unequal post-efforts are explained by the fact that in all standard letting-die cases, necessarily, the person who lets die has an accomplice. When the person who lets die did not also perform the act that endangers the other person, there must have been someone or something (nature) that caused the danger. When there are two "sources" of a person's death, it might be claimed, post-efforts should be divided. Therefore, it is no wonder that the person who only lets die has lower efforts demandable of him post-omission. When the person who let die is also the one who killed, the post-efforts should jump up. But this is not because Thesis E is false; it is only because there is now one factor (one person) instead of two factors morally responsible for the death. In the standard killing case there is either one person who both causes death and lets die, or one person who causes death and no one else who lets die. There is then no one or thing with whom to share responsibility. (One might argue, though, that where the killer does not let die, nature "failed" to rescue.)

Furthermore, it might be said, the person who lets die must do so *after* the operation of the cause that will kill. It is not that he does anything intrinsically different, only that he does it after. This, it is suggested, makes what he does count for less.

Responses to Temporal Location

This two-part objection can be answered, I believe. Take the last part first. The fact that the non-aider's role comes after the occurrence of the threat does not show that it is less bad per se. Furthermore, if Thesis E were true, then the same argument should apply to killing. If two people were jointly involved in killing (so that each one's act is necessary but not sufficient to result in death), then the one who sticks his dagger in last should be less morally responsible for the death than the one who sticks his dagger in first. But this seems incorrect. In fact, one might argue in this killing case that the person last in line, the one who ensures the death, is morally more responsible for it.

If this were so, and if it were correct to treat letting die as equivalent to killing, then the person who lets die should have greater moral responsibility for the death than the person who caused the danger, because the person who lets die is last. So, in a sense, if letting die were morally equivalent to killing, it would be worse than killing.

Creating a Need for Aid and Making an Act Dangerous

It might be counter-argued that because it comes later, letting die did not create the need for aid. This, however, seems like an argument *for* a moral difference between standard killing and letting die, since endangering creates a need for aid. However, the person who endangered someone might complain that, if not for the person who lets die, or for nature which did not "come to the rescue," his own act would have been innocuous. (The probability that an act will cause a death could be determined by taking into consideration whether other people will help protect a victim from the consequences of the act. If no one will help, an act is dangerous; otherwise it is not. The person who is needed to save would determine the probability that any act is dangerous.)[11]

So, unless letting die were morally different from killing, there are reasons to think that the "after" factor (which is conceptually true of letting die) would make it morally worse than doing the act that introduces the cause of death, rather than merely equivalent to it. On the other hand, suppose that coming *after* did make conduct less bad, and coming *after* were *conceptually true* of letting die. Then it might be evidence, other things equal, for letting die being less bad than killing *per se*. The feature of "afterness," because it is conceptually intrinsic to letting die, would reflect on the moral status of letting die *per se*. One couldn't simply say that letting die and killing were morally equivalent *per se*, but "afterness" made letting die less bad, because the factor that made letting die less bad would be one that was conceptually true of it.

Responses to the Presence of an Accomplice

Now we can turn to the first part of the objection to the Post-efforts Test. This is the claim that letting die accrues lower post-efforts because there is an accomplice. If Thesis E were true and if the intuitive judgment supporting a difference in post-efforts held, then what is said of letting die should also be true of killing. Suppose that two killers are jointly responsible for a death. However, only one is available to make efforts to prevent the ultimate bad consequences for the victim. Then the effort demandable of the one should be, at most, one half of what could be demanded of the two together. In addition, suppose we found out that someone had let die the victim of a known killer (who fainted after his act). Since the killer had a letting-die accomplice, the killer's post-effort should go down. Indeed, as noted above, it might be said that killers also have unhelpful nature as a later accomplice, just as those who let someone die from natural causes.

Both these results seem incorrect. The efforts required may be shared if two killers are available. But each one is morally responsible for the death, and this gives him responsibility for making the maximum post-effort demandable *if the other killer is not present with whom to share it*.[12] So if killing and letting die were morally equivalent, in the absence of a person who was an "accomplice," the person who lets die should also have to make the maximum effort demandable.

Burdening Victims

An oddity in holding the person who lets die equally (or even more) responsible for the death along with the killer and therefore demanding great post-efforts of him has already been noted in chapter 2: It burdens *another victim of the killer*. When a person is called upon to save a life, it might be said that there are really two victims of an endangering event, not one.[13] The person who is called upon to aid does not deserve to have his life interfered with any more than the person whose life is endangered. Yet like the latter, he will be interfered with. Can a victim of the situation be as morally responsible for post-efforts if he fails to aid as the perpetrator is (assuming same motive and intention) once he acts or omits?

If the victim who must aid is as morally responsible for preventing harm as the person who could prevent harm by not killing, then presumably the victim of the act of killing is also as morally responsible for preventing his death as the potential killer would be. This means (keeping the post-effort test in mind) that the victim should have to do as much to keep himself from dying, if he has first done nothing when he could have done something to ward off an attack, as the would-be killer should do to save the person he has attacked (holding all factors, including motivation, equal). This seems incorrect.

We could also ask whether a potential victim should do as much to prevent the initial act of the killer as the killer should, or do as much to avoid being attacked in the first place as the killer should do rather than attack. (These are what I call Pre-efforts Tests. They are discussed in more detail below.) If he failed to make these efforts, should his post-efforts be as high as those of a killer?

Viewing the bystander called on to aid as a co-victim also makes it possible to analyze the lifesaving situation as one in which one person is asked to share victim status with another. We have then to ask whether and to what degree the initial *victim* has the right to require another person to share in his misfortunes in this way?

There are other criticisms that could be made of the Post-efforts Test, but since these also apply to the tests I will discuss below, I shall postpone dealing with them.

Post-efforts Required without a Prior Wrong Act: A Moral Defense of Strict Liability

In concluding this section, it is worth noting a problem about whether post-efforts might be required for circumstances where no one is at fault for a wrongful act or omission. This is the issue of strict liability. Suppose the efforts needed to prevent a harmful act — pre-efforts, we shall call them — are greater than we could require of someone. Or suppose we do not know for sure that an act will cause harm and the efforts required to protect against the *chance* that it will are too large given the low probability that they will actually be preventing a harm. Then it is not wrong to do the act. Suppose that on an occasion the act does cause harm; but the harm can still be undone or the victim can be compensated for the harm. Should the agent who acted permissibly be obliged to aid now? One claim is that, if the efforts required to undo or compensate are no larger than the agent would have been required to make (or we would have been permitted to impose) in order that he avoid the act had it been known that it would harm, then the agent should make the post-efforts. This depends on the following claim: Efforts are required so that an agent's act not leave a victim with a certain harm. This aim can be achieved either by making the efforts pre-act, or if this would be inefficient, post-act. Further, the post-act efforts could be made to prevent the consequences or to undo them. If we may impose efforts to stop an agent from acting solely to prevent the consequences of her act, the theory is that we may impose the efforts post-act just to stop the consequences. This analysis could have much to do with giving an account according to which strict liability is a *morally* acceptable policy. It therefore bears on the extended debate between defenders of strict liability and defenders of negligence.[14]

A more radical claim, it could be argued, follows from all this. Even in situations where an agent has no choice but to do what will harm another, shouldn't he be required to compensate his victim if the efforts required to do so are no greater than he would have had to make to avoid the act if it had been avoidable? This also means that when agents do not *act* but are made into threatening entities, even by forces of nature, they could be liable for post-efforts so long as *we* might permissibly have harmed them to prevent their posing a threat.

For example, suppose you are turned into a threatening missile by a freak of nature. If you land on someone they will be killed. Suppose you have a little device in your hands that could redirect you away from your potential victim and into a brick wall. The impact would break your leg. It seems to me you would be morally required to use the device, if you had it, though you were not responsible for being a missile. But you do not, in fact, have such a device. Why may *we* not redirect you into the wall, if you should have redirected if you could have, though you can't in fact? Suppose it is permissible for us to do this, but, in fact, we cannot. You fall on your victim, but it is still possible to save him from death by doing what will cause you a broken leg. Why is this not permissible?[15]

An alternative view emphasizes the distinction between making efforts to avoid *the act* that will cause harm, and making efforts to avoid *having caused permanent harm*. One might be required to make a certain effort to avoid an act and its foreseen consequences without being required to make that same effort to avoid the consequences of the act occurring. This leaves open an "in-between" position: The efforts required of someone to prevent the consequences of his non-negligent act could be greater than what would be required of any bystander, but not as great as would be required to avoid an act that is known to cause the harmful consequences. So although I should swerve my car to avoid running into someone, and I should do more than a bystander is required to do to help someone I have nonnegligently run into, I need not swerve my car if this alone will get the victim of my non-negligent act to the hospital in time to save his life.

Further Specifications: The Doctor's Mistake and Williams's Agent Regret

This "in-between" position may still call for different approaches to the following different cases: (a) One is made into a threat by nature—rather than by one's own act—and there was no way to avoid presenting a threat. (b) One is made into a threat by nature. There were means to eliminate this threatening status, but their cost to oneself made them not morally requirable in view of the low probability that the harm would occur. (c) One's own chosen act made one into a threat, but there were no means (pre-act) to avoid being a threat. (d) One's own chosen act made one into a threat. There were means to ensure that one was not a threat, but their cost to oneself made them not morally requirable in view of the low probability that the harm would occur. The post-efforts for non-wrong *acts* might increase depending on whether or not there was a possibility (even if one morally need not have made use of the possibility) of making the pre-efforts to prevent harm. (One problem with this suggestion, however, is that sometimes one does an act only *because* it has so low a probability of harm that the big efforts to ensure its being harm-free are not required. Suppose one does an act only if it has a low probability of harm and one would have avoided it if one had known it would certainly cause harm in case large preventive efforts were not made. Then one might also not have done the act if one had known one was committed to making such big post-efforts if harm occurred. Yet it may be socially useful that such acts with low probability of harm be done.)

The analysis that explains why post-efforts could be required even if there was no fault in the cause of an action can help explain why a physician whose harmful conduct is non-negligent, but an *avoidable* cause of injury, should bear costs for compensating the victim. The following case, presented at a Harvard Medical School Symposium, falls into class (d): The doctor is non-negligent because he has followed the standard of care in the community. However, his cutting of a ureter was avoidable. Why then was it not avoided? The act that will actually harm occurs so infrequently that consistently applying the super precautions necessary to avoid it will be wasteful. However, if the doctor had known that on this occasion his act was going to harm, he would have been obliged to expend cost X (i.e., some cost) to avoid the act *rather than decide not to do the operation at all*. We could use the fact that he would not have been permitted to avoid the act to explain why he should, after the avoidable harm has occurred, expend cost X, or perhaps at least close to cost X, to make up for the harm. (Suppose the hospital, not the doctor, would have had to pay cost X to stop the harm. Then the hospital's insurance should pay post-costs.)

Note also that requiring consent to a surgical procedure from someone who is fully informed of possible risks, avoidable or not, does not necessarily relieve a physician of responsibility for harm. For suppose the person consenting had "no real choice" but to have the surgery, for example, if he would die without it. It would no longer be a free choice to bear the cost of harm from surgery.

Bernard Williams[16] discusses cases in which someone non-negligently injures another by choosing to perform an act that could, I believe, theoretically, have been performed so as not to injure. His case is that of someone who drives non-negligently but hits a child. In this case the standard of due care has been observed; only if what are considered "excessive" precautions are taken could the accident have been avoided. Williams believes that the agent cannot behave as a mere bystander, though he did nothing wrong. It is appropriate for him to—he would exhibit a bad character if he didn't—feel what Williams calls agent regret. He may act on agent regret by compensating his victim. We could agree with this and still think that he (unlike the doctor) need not do as much post-act as he would have had to do pre-act if he had known he was driving a certainly deadly machine. This is because he would have been permitted to refrain from doing the act of driving altogether at such cost, and may wish to omit it if he even risks such costs. By contrast, the doctor would have had to go ahead with surgery. Therefore, if we wish people to engage in driving rather than avoid it, we should not require such large post-efforts costs for non-negligent behavior. (However, we shall have to consider separately the role of various dutiful acts in connection with post-efforts.)

How does our account of the ground for making amends when there was no faulty act compare with Williams's own account? Perhaps it is a substitute for, or fuller explanation of, it, making it less mysterious. [17]

Dutiful Acts

We have argued that being permitted to avoid an act if the cost (pre or post) to make it non-harmful is too great may lead us to reduce these costs *if* we want to encourage people to do the acts. If someone is not permitted to avoid an act known to be harmful but would have to make pre-efforts to make it harmless (a doctor performing surgery might be in this position), post-efforts may be as high as pre-efforts. But what of other acts we are duty-bound to do (not just acts we have an option of doing and which we do in a morally appropriate way, such as non-obligatory driving done non-negligently)? If we perform a duty that causes harm, then perhaps we should not be responsible for the harm that occurs; doing our duty relieves us of responsibility at least for unforeseen harms since we *had* to be doing what we were doing, given whatever probability of harm was expected and so factored into our still having a duty to act. (This seems to have been Kant's view when he says that we are not responsible for harm to a victim if he dies because we do not lie to save him.) By contrast, agent regret will prompt the provision of more help than a bystander would have to give, in situations in which we act non-negligently but with no duty to act. Here the efforts we would have to make if we knew the act would certainly be harmful are reflected in diminished form in our duty to make post-efforts.

The exception that threatens the Kantian view on duty is our previous analysis of the doctor who also had a duty. We could achieve synthesis, perhaps, by noting that the doctor would not have been relieved of his duty by the need to take large preventive measures, when it was known that the act would harm without them. But in other cases large pre-act costs could relieve us of our duty or else would not be required. It is in these cases that there will be no *post-efforts* required.

Social Post-efforts

In cases in which the compensation that would make up for a loss to the victim is very costly, or in cases where no choice of act was possible for the agent, we may think it right to spread the cost of compensating the victim across society. The primary idea here is that the victim does not deserve his loss, and from behind a veil of ignorance we would, as rational constructors of our society, choose to have each member of society lose a small amount so that a great burden of loss does not fall on the agent whose act (or movement) non-negligently causes damage to his victim.

We have considered post-efforts to a wrong act or omission. We have also considered post-efforts to an act that is permitted because pre-efforts to prevent it are too great; that is, we have now (briefly) investigated a *relation between pre- and post-efforts*. Now let us consider pre-efforts in detail.

II

Pre-efforts Test

If the strong version of Thesis E were true, then it seems that the efforts that one could be required to make or the losses one could be required to suffer *rather than* do what kills or lets die should be equivalent. If the efforts or losses differ, an explanation for this might be that killing differs from letting die *per se*. This is a test for *Pre-* (Act or Omission) *efforts*, directed at preventing the act or omission before it occurs.

If we follow the model of standardly equalized cases, then cases to illustrate this test seem to be as follows:

> F(oot)1: I know I will voluntarily wiggle my foot without a prior intention to do so, and because of the context I am in this will set off a bomb that kills someone. I must make a big effort to avoid being in this situation.

> F2: I must make a big effort to save someone's life.

> N(ature's Threat)1: I am a human missile hurtled by the wind. I do not make the great efforts necessary to stop my fatally crashing into someone.

> N2: I do not make the great efforts necessary to go and save someone's life.

> T(arget)1: Someone will pay me a thousand dollars if I shoot at a certain bull's-eye. I foresee, though I do not intend, that if I do shoot at it, my bullet will go through a person standing behind the target.

> T2: If I let someone else shoot at a bull's-eye, a thousand dollars will be paid to me. However, I know there is a person standing behind the bull's-eye who will be killed by the shot. No effort to speak of is required to stop the shooting.

Notice that it would not equalize properly for intending the existence of the cause of death (which T1 and T2 do) to compare T1 with T3, which follows.

T3: Someone will pay me a thousand dollars if I shoot at a certain bull's-eye behind which no one is standing. Doing this means that I won't be able to save someone who is drowning.

In F and N sets the person who must pay a price to avoid acting or omitting will thereby become worse off than he already is and would have been. In the T set, the person who suffers the loss is asked to forego an improvement in his current status or the status of others over what it otherwise would have been. In T3 the person is also asked to forego an improvement, yet the case is structurally like N2; there is no interest in the cause of death. In T_1 and T_2, the cause of death is causally necessary to achieve the agent's gain; the deaths are foreseen but not intended. In the following cases the deaths are intended:

I(ntend): You will kill someone because you intend that he die. Still, not to kill would cost you $10,000. This is because you can avoid killing him only by driving on a rocky road that will smash your $10,000 car. You don't care about losing the money per se. You don't take the alternative route just because you want the person dead.

I2: You will let someone die because you intend his death. If you were to save his life it would cost you $10,000 because you would have to drive on a rocky road which would smash your $10,000 car. You don't care about the money per se. You don't save him just because you want the person dead.

The claim is that in all the killing cases described, the person would have to make the effort to avoid killing or suffer the loss of what could be gained by the cause of death or the death itself. In the letting-die cases, he would not have to make the efforts or suffer the loss (as in T3) rather than let die. However, he should suffer the loss of what he would get via the cause of death (as in T2) or via the death itself, *unless* doing so involves him having to make large efforts to aid (as in I2). One possible explanation of the wrongness of not aiding in T2 was suggested in chapter 3: Intending the death or its cause in these cases indicates a desire that someone lose what he would have had independently of imposition on the person whose aid is in question. However, this does not mean we may extract the same pre- or post-efforts to stop the omission or its consequences as we may extract to stop the killing. This suggests that the *wrong of intending harm is structurally less significant for non-consequentialism than is the wrong of doing harm*. The difference in efforts requirable also suggests that we do not *determine* what our duties are merely by seeing what we can accomplish at small cost to ourselves.

Ex-ante Pre-efforts

Most of the cases described above in which making an effort or suffering losses are necessary to avoid killing or letting die involved someone *on the spot* avoiding killing or letting die by these efforts or losses. There are other types of "avoiding" cases. In these, efforts must be made or losses suffered in order to avoid being placed in a situation at a later time when one will *unavoidably* kill or let die. For example, what cost should one incur to put a safety device on one's machine so that it will not dangerously misperform (thereby killing someone)? What cost should one incur to set up a device that will let one know (when one would not know otherwise) that someone is in need of lifesaving assistance as a result of a cause unrelated to one's own behavior?

Preemptive Strike

Yet another version of the Pre-efforts Test measures what it would be permissible for *us* to do to prevent someone else's killing or letting die, rather than the efforts that other person must undertake. It seems permissible to kill the person in B1 or I1 to stop him from killing. It is certainly not true that we could do this to the person in B2 or I2, or even T2, even though he is doing something we condemn.

For example, could we carry out a threat to kill someone to stop him from killing or to force him to aid (where the aid required is intrinsically minimal)? To equalize these cases, we must imagine that if we carry out our threat in the killing case, no one will be killed, and if we carry it out in the letting-die case, no one will be let die. To envision the latter we must imagine that carrying out our threat on the potential non-aider (killing him) will cause him to fall onto a device that saves a life. (He could have saved the life by stepping on the device.) My claim is that the threat it is permissible to carry out[18] is less for letting die than for killing, standard contexts held equal. (In chapter 3, we have already seen how this test could be employed to decide whether cases in which we let die intending the cause of death are to be morally equated with cases in which we actively cause death, as Quinn's theory of positive agency claims.)

The cases in set I are interesting because, as in B1 and B2, bad intent and motivation are present. If the person may let die it is only because of what this alternative involves, that is, requiring him to suffer a large loss for the sake of someone else. The fact that he would very willingly have sacrificed a great deal to aid were it not for his bad intention and the fact that he also would have sacrificed a great deal to prevent himself from aiding, given his bad intention, still does not make it permissible to require him to aid by imposing a large cost. Because he need not have suffered a loss had he objected to it for its own sake, given its large size he cannot be forced to give when he would refuse for a bad reason.

It is also important to see that what matters in deciding whether pre-efforts can be required is not simply the size of loss involved, but what the efforts would be for. For example, we can imagine that the person in I2 has a natural tendency to save lives at great expense to himself. To make it impossible for himself to aid, he must spend even more than what he would spend in aiding. Therefore, if we require or force him to aid, *he* will be better off than if he does not aid. Yet it is suggested that this is not a sufficient reason to require or force him to suffer the large loss in order to aid, if he doesn't want to. Once the loss or efforts involved in aid are large enough, it is up to the agent to decide whether he will aid or lose more in preventing himself from aiding.

Notice also that if the *pre-efforts* or losses it is permissible to require or impose in standard killing cases are greater than the *post-efforts* it is permissible to require or impose in letting-die cases, this is, perhaps, an even clearer indication of per se moral difference between killing and letting die. This is because having already done something wrong (e.g., not making minimal efforts to avoid killing or letting die) might be thought to be morally worse than refusing to avoid a harmful act at great cost. Yet the pre-act great costs would be appropriately demanded in the case of killing, making their omission wrong. Finally, I repeat a point made in the discussion of post-efforts: the fact that greater pre-efforts can be imposed in killing than in letting-die cases can indicate a morally significant difference in the behaviors without this correlating with the degree of outrage or horror we feel at the behaviors in question. Not all significant moral differences are connected with "wickedness" revealed in conduct. We can see this by comparing B2 with a case in which I intend only the cause of death. For example, Fr(iends)1: My friends must be rushed to the hospital or they will die. As I go over the route to the hospital, I see a person on the road whom I will run over unless I stop. I keep on going. Greater outrage at B2 is consistent with higher pre-efforts in Fr(1).

Russell's Criticisms of the Pre-efforts Test

What criticisms could be raised of this Pre-efforts test (in its three varieties: self-imposed efforts, ex ante efforts, and other-imposed efforts)?

Bruce Russell[19] has suggested that if efforts required to avoid killing are larger than those required to avoid letting die, this has nothing to do with Thesis E being false. It is due to the fact that, for both killing *and* letting die, there is an upper limit to the amount of pre-efforts required of us.[20] This upper limit, Russell claims, is the same for killing and letting die. But we must be fair in distributing our efforts, that is, we must treat all relevantly similar persons alike. If a great number of people would benefit from our effort of a certain size, the total efforts required of us could go over the upper limit. But we should not be required to go over the upper limit. Since we must treat all fairly, if we cannot make this effort for everyone, we should not be required to make it for anyone who is relevantly the same. Now, as a matter of empirical fact there are many people who could be saved by my giving up $1,000 (so the number of people × $1,000 > upper limit); therefore I needn't give even one person $1,000 to save his life (i.e., to avoid omitting to save his life). As a matter of empirical fact, there are few people whose lives could be saved by my giving $1 (number of people × $1 < upper limit); therefore I must give each person who needs it $1 to save his life. There are few people who are such that if I am not to kill them, I must give up $1,000. Therefore, I must give up the $1,000 rather than kill. But all this has nothing to do with whether Thesis E is false. Russell also claims that his analysis explains why Kant said that the duty to aid is an imperfect duty, that is, not owed to everyone; if it were owed to all, it would put us over the upper limit.

Criticisms of Russell

Suppose Russell's analysis of differentiated pre-efforts is correct. Then also suppose that I would have to suffer a broken leg to avoid an act that would kill someone, if she were the only person in the world who required this. Then if there were only one person in the world whose life could be saved by my doing what breaks my leg, I should have just as strong a duty to do what breaks it rather than let him die. But is this so?

Furthermore, Russell's view that fairness (universalization) prohibits us from treating one person in a way we cannot treat relevantly similar people seems to have odd consequences. For example, if I cannot avoid killing *everyone* in a group of people by making the maximum effort required of me to avoid killing, Russell's conclusion seems to be that I shouldn't make the effort to avoid killing anyone. Furthermore, it seems correct to *help* one poor person, even though one knows that one won't help relevantly similar people. In fact it is because we may have a duty to save some and not all relevantly similar people, that Russell's claim to have explained Kant's notion of an imperfect duty is questionable. Kant said that imperfect duties are duties that it is permissible sometimes to choose when to fulfill, but we are not relieved from ever carrying them out simply because we need not always carry them out. According to Kant, it just is a mark of imperfect duties that we have a duty to help some, but not all of the relevantly similar candidates. (Universalization requires only that it is permissible to treat everyone who is in similar circumstances in the same way; it does not require that we do so, though it might sometimes require that we select in a fair way among similarly situated people.)

Further, suppose we were sometimes required to lose our life rather than kill someone. Would any size sacrifice to save a life, multiplied by any number of people who needed the sacrifice, impose a greater burden on us than dying? If not, then Russell's analysis implies that large efforts to aid many people will be required, if it is required of us to die rather than kill.

Further Criticism

It is also worth considering the views of another critic — Joel Feinberg — of a Pre-efforts Test. Feinberg offers an alternative explanation of the differential pre-efforts morally required for not killing and not letting die.[21] Requiring an individual to pay greater costs to avoid killing than to save someone's life is consistent with the per se moral equivalence of killing and letting die because (1) *as a society* we do incur large costs to save life, as we do to avoid destroying it, and (2) it makes sense to make saving a function of the society as a whole and ask only a small portion of the cost from each individual. I find at least two problems with Feinberg's explanation. The fact that *society* will incur large costs to save life does not mean it should not incur even larger costs to avoid actually killing (for example, by spending more to prevent some social project from introducing poisonous chemicals into the water than to save lives from disease). What of cases in which society cannot assign to individuals a small portion of the cost necessary to avoid a *killing*? For example, suppose only the person who would do the act that will kill is physically in a position to pay the large cost necessary to avoid the act. Then the large cost seems to be assigned to the individual. If killing and letting die were morally equivalent, then in situations in which a large cost for saving someone could *only* be borne by a single bystander rather than by society's agent (for example, a fire-fighter), why would there not be a social rule assigning the single bystander that duty?

Pre- and Post-efforts as Measures of Duty?

Another criticism of the Pre-efforts Test could also have been raised in connection with the Post-efforts Test, but has been postponed until now. One way of phrasing this objection is that the efforts required in both tests may measure not the differential moral objectionableness of killing and letting die, but rather the fact that the former is actually prohibited but the latter is not actually prohibited. That is, it may be our duty to avoid what is not morally worse than what it is not our duty to avoid. And extra efforts are required of us to do our duty. In other words, the moral difference per se that is measured is merely the existence of a duty. Since our duties may not correlate directly with what is morally objectionable, it is not differential moral objectionable-ness of the acts per se that the two tests measures. [22]

This view depends on the possibility that two behaviors can be equally objectionable morally and yet only one be prohibited. In actuality, there are two versions of this view. The first is that simply as a matter of fact (not necessarily morally justified) we have a stronger duty not to kill than not to let die. (If there is no moral justification here, it must be legal or customary duty that is meant.) The second theory is that it *ought* to be the case that certain types of acts are prohibited or enforceably prohibited though they are not morally worse (and are even morally less bad) than other acts which should not be prohibited or enforceably prohibited. ("Prohibited" means that we should not do them, are obligated not to do them; "enforceably prohibited" means that society or some agent may permissibly force people to do what they are obligated to do. It may be morally permissible to enforceably prohibit only certain categories of bad acts.)

Responses

One problem with this objection is that if there morally *should* be a duty or an enforceable duty not to kill, but morally there should not be an (equally strong) duty or enforceable duty to aid, this could itself signify a real moral difference between killing and letting die *per se*. Another way to put this point is that killings in standard cases could have some morally significant property other than objectionableness which letting die in standard cases lacked, that made it correct for us to prohibit the act and to require large efforts to avoid such behavior.

A second possible answer to the objection is that it wouldn't be our duty to avoid doing one thing at a certain effort but not our duty to avoid doing another thing at that effort unless the former were morally more objectionable behavior. As I have emphasized before, I suspect this answer is wrong. For example, letting die in I2 seems more morally objectionable than killing because one decides to run over someone as one rushes five people to the hospital. Yet we could enforce efforts not to kill in the latter case, when we could not enforce them in I2. This does not mean there is no moral inequivalence between killing and letting die in these cases; only that the moral inequivalence that is being measured by the differential pre- and post-efforts is not the moral objectionableness that, for example, triggers a response of outrage or horror.

A third response is that in many cases we are released from duties if the effort to carry them out is too great. It is only if the content of the duty is serious that we are not released. So just being a duty is not enough to account for the requirement to make large pre- and post-efforts. On the other hand, failing to perform a non-duty could still be very objectionable. It does seem objectionable of someone in F1 not to take measures to avoid killing. He is not released from the duty not to kill because of the effort this involves. It does not seem as objectionable for the person in F2 not to make the sacrifice to save the life. This would lead one to believe that, in these cases at least, the relative badness of the content of the act and of the omission is what contributes to the fact that avoiding one and not the other is a duty, and accounts for the difference in pre-efforts.

Fourth, suppose letting die were prohibited or enforceably prohibited as killing is, for example, by Good Samaritan Laws demanding large sacrifice. Then, if saving were a strict duty in B2, and yet post-efforts for B1 were higher than for B2, this might suggest that there was real differential moral objectionableness at stake. At the very least, it would suggest some morally significant difference between killing and letting die—whether or not that is describable as moral objectionableness or as the factor that gives rise to duties—in standardly equalized cases, that makes it morally permissible for even third parties to impose losses in one case and not the other.

Can a Moral Difference Be Swamped?

Let us consider further the issue of pre- and post-efforts as a measure of moral objectionableness from a slightly different point of view. It might be said that killing and letting die in cases like B1 and B2 are equally bad because the intention to harm someone or the small size of the efforts required swamps any difference that killing makes in other standardly equalized cases. But how can one both say that the bad intentions override any remaining differences introduced by killing or letting die, and also say that post-efforts requirable are larger for the killing case? This, however, leaves it open that the moral difference indicated is not moral objectionableness. Furthermore, the objectionableness of what is done in the let-die case is not really a function of how small the aid would be. For example, in case I2, the aid required is large, and yet just in virtue of the motive and intent the omission strikes us, I believe, as just as bad as in B2. Yet we don't require the large pre-efforts here that we would require for the agent in I1 or B1.

One answer to this puzzle is simply that B2 is not morally as objectionable as B1, so there is no reason to suspect that efforts demandable post-act (or omission) are not a function of how objectionable the act (or omission) is. Another answer is that there is a morally significant difference other than objectionableness that efforts tests measure.

Reasons to Think the Killing Case Is Worse

The following could be offered as reasons for thinking that B1 is morally more objectionable than B2:

(1) Above we considered that when we introduce into B2 the fact that the person who let die also caused the threat, the case gets worse. But if the measure being employed was the Post-efforts Test, and post-efforts went up with the addition, this may indicate merely that a significant difference has been introduced but not that this difference consisted of "objectionableness." Furthermore B2 with killing added to the background might be *worse* than B1 alone. The fact that post-efforts did not go up when we added letting die to the foreground of B1 need not indicate that this case is no more objectionable than B1. If it is more objectionable than B1 and equivalent to the modified B2, then the unmodified B2 may be as bad as B1.

(2) What is so bad in B2 is that someone intends great harm to someone else. That is present in B1 too plus a violation of a negative right. So B1 is worse.

In connection with this it could be argued that someone might have very strong respect for negative rights, combined with extreme hatred of those whom he recognizes as having negative rights. (Indeed, he might hate them because they have negative rights that limit how he may act.) This person recognizes full well the special status of persons, but he intensely dislikes them.

If this is the sort of person who lets die in B2, are he and his behavior morally different from the person and act in B1? The person in B1 acts against both someone's best interests and rights. The agent in B2 acts against his victim's best interests (though we have suggested that he might be exhibiting a preference that a threat *be instituted* against someone independent of him as well). The person in B1 achieves his evil intent *by* making use of what belongs to the other person (his body), which that person has independently of the agent. The person in B2 does not.

(3) Even if there were a positive right to aid in B2, violating a positive right may not be as serious as violating a negative one, other things equal. (At least, when there was no responsibility for endangering the victim in the letting-die case.) But what do we mean by "not as serious" here: not as offensive or

rather a sort of disrespect that threatens a person in a way that can be guarded against? Positive rights represent links between people, but the separateness of persons represented by negative rights is conceptually at the core of the idea of a person.

While these are factors to be considered, it is not clear that they support the claim of differential objectionableness, rather than some other morally significant difference between B1 and B2.

Case Where Letting Die Is Morally Worse than Killing

Suppose we believe that B2 is not as morally objectionable as B1, and that pre- and post-efforts tests show this. There may be cases of letting die that *are* morally worse than killing where the pre-efforts required to avoid killing are greater than those to avoid letting die. To repeat, compare what we could require of someone to save a person whom he would otherwise intend to let die for purely malicious reasons (I2), with what we could require of someone rather than let him save many people by doing what he foresees will kill a person. Suppose the person performed the act that killed rather than pay some large cost. I believe that even if his act is wrong, it would be less morally objectionable than the behavior of the person who does not aid because he intends someone's death. So there may be a morally relevant distinction between this killing and letting die, even if it doesn't lead us to conclude that the killing, or the person who does it, is morally more objectionable than the letting die or the person who does it.

The following general proposal and two more specific proposals might be made about these sorts of cases.

General

Types of behavior that it is morally permissible to require at (great) effort are not necessarily the behaviors that produce the most good or avoid the most evil. Types of behavior whose avoidance we can require at great effort are not necessarily the behaviors that are morally worse.

Specific (1)

Requiring extraordinary efforts from A to do or to avoid doing certain things in standard cases involves taking from him what he would have had independently of us or those for whom he would make efforts. This can only be done to prevent him from doing the same to others, that is, taking from others what the others would have had independently of imposition on him. We can condemn someone who does not aid because he intends that another be harmed, but when imposing on him is in question, we can do nothing, because he does not impose on what another has. (If he promises to aid and this promise leads someone to act in reliance on him, he is subject to being imposed on.)

This is one proposal for delimiting the sorts of behavior it is permissible to prevent by enforcing pre-efforts. It would imply that we could not force *any* degree of pre- or post-effort from the person in B2 to aid, let alone as much as to stop the killing in B1. Yet, I think we believe we may force some efforts from the person in B2. A second specific proposal, which we shall now consider, speaks to this point.

Specific (2)

Whatever efforts we believe it would be morally objectionable for someone not to make to save some person's life when he alone can save it, are efforts that are only somewhat greater than we think it would be permissible for us to force him to make. Still, the efforts may be lower than those it is morally objectionable not to make rather than kill in standard comparable cases. This conclusion is based on weighing whether someone deprives another of what he would have had independently of imposition on him. Efforts can be lower to avoid letting die, even when the letting die is more morally objectionable than the killing. The efforts we believe it objectionable to refuse as aid do, further, differ from those requirable to avoid killing as follows:

The Post-efforts Test considers how much can be required of someone after he has already done something wrong. Though pre-efforts to avoid killing (it has been claimed) are higher than those to be made rather than let die, they may be lower than the post-efforts demandable if those efforts required to avoid a killing are not made. That is, the post-effort demandable in the case of killing can go up as a form of punishment. But the same is not true, I believe, of pre- and post-efforts to be made rather than let die. Suppose someone behaves objectionably in failing to aid and we step in to extract post-omission efforts which can still save the victim. We cannot require more of him than we could require as aid to begin with. We cannot, furthermore, require more of someone who would omit to aid from morally vicious reasons than of someone who would omit from less objectionable reasons. While we can say of someone who refuses to give a large amount of aid on account of having an intention to harm that his behavior is morally objectionable, we cannot force him to give that aid. This is some indication that what he ought to have done was not requirable in the same sense as efforts to avoid killing, and that harmful intention counts differently from harmful acts..

The Demandingness of Morality

I conclude that the Pre- and Post-efforts Tests do measure a morally significant property, though this may sometimes not be overall moral objectionableness. Similarly, whether something is our duty (and enforceable duty) or not may indicate the presence of a morally significant factor other than objectionableness (or the degree to which something promotes good or diminishes bad). We shall reconsider this point and what makes certain acts liable to being required in chapter 12.

It will suffice at this point to make certain remarks connecting our discussion of pre- and post-efforts with the issue of the demandingness of morality. It is sometimes thought that consequentialism cannot be the correct theory of morality because it is very demanding. This criterion suggests that any theory that is very demanding could not be correct and that we could object to a theory on the grounds that it is very demanding. But what our discussion of pre- and post-efforts suggests is that those who believe there is a moral difference between killing and letting die in standard cases do *not* think the correct morality is never very demanding. They demand a great deal to avoid violation of negative rights, not so much to avoid letting die, even when being saved is a positive right. The question for them, it may seem, is not whether morality is very demanding, but demanding *for what*. On their view, the demandingness question essentially involves a two-place predicate: demand *x* for purpose *y*.

On the other hand, it is misleading to say that those who deny the strong version of Thesis E could not make use of the "demandingness objection" to consequentialism, even if the world were such as to make mere respect for negative rights a very demanding business (e.g., in times when not killing innocents brings death upon one). Consider an analogy: Suppose I want to buy a VCR, but simply because of the high price being asked for them, I decide not to buy. I say the VCR is too *costly*, so I don't buy. But then I go out and spend what was being asked for the VCR on a car. Someone accuses me of not really objecting to the *cost* in the case of the VCR, since I was eventually willing to pay out that very same amount. But presumably this accusation is inappropriate, even if I was willing to pay the amount for some item. What I objected to in buying a VCR *was* its cost. So, similarly, even if one holds that morality may charge cost x for act y, that does not mean one isn't objecting to cost x (but to something else) when one rejects paying cost x for act z.

III

Choice Test

A third way to test for the moral equivalence or inequivalence of standard cases could be called the Choice Test. It asks us to decide which of the two situations in a set we would prefer to avoid if we could not avoid both. If we prefer to avoid the killing this would indicate, given that these are comparable killing and letting-die cases, that Thesis E is false.

This test procedure has an advantage over the first two. It is conceivable that we would be required to make the same pre- and post-efforts for two different acts, when they are each considered in isolation. This could be true even though they differ morally. Not killing and not torturing may be such a set. The way to distinguish the members of this set would be to see which we would sooner avoid given a choice between them. In constructing choices it is, I believe, best to choose between two separate standard cases of killing and letting die. For example, we decide whether we would prefer (1) not to have avoided an act that kills or (2) not to have saved a life.

The Wrong Way to Run a Choice Test

If we run the Choice Test using killing and letting die combined in *one* case, the problem arises that there is often some other property that distinguishes the killing part from the letting-die part. For example, suppose I must choose whether to let someone die *or* kill another person to save him. I will be using someone as a means if I kill, but not if I let die. Or suppose that I must decide whether to let a trolley headed to one person kill him — I thereby let him die — or divert the trolley to another person, whereby I kill him. An unwillingness to kill would make it impossible to give the two people an equal chance to survive. This is a difference in addition to letting die versus killing in these cases.

Philippa Foot thinks she uses the Choice Test when she says that the strong duty to aid his child which a parent has does not make it all right to kill someone to save the child.[23] So, in the choice between killing and letting die, the child must be let die. But this is not a pure test to show that not killing takes precedence over aiding, because the letting die and killing cases do not equalize for morally relevant differences between the two. For example, the killing case involves using someone as a means to save the child, whereas the letting-die case does not involve using anyone as a means. The child dies because we may not kill someone else, not as a means to save someone else.[24]

Furthermore, Foot might also agree that the parent should not refuse minimal assistance to a dying person just because the latter's death will make it possible for the parent to feed his child. This means that in a choice between letting someone die *because* his death will save one's child or letting one's child die, we should do the latter. The two cases would then both involve lettings die, but only one would involve using someone as a means. The fact that we should not refuse minimal assistance because we intend death, even when giving minimal aid has a very costly consequence for us, suggests that the fact that we should refuse to kill (in the kill/let-die set) was no indication of the greater weight of not killing over aiding.

A Properly Constructed Choice Set

The following is a suggestion for a correct choice set.

> C1: A fatal trolley is headed toward five people, and we can redirect it, killing one on another track.
>
> C2: A fatal trolley is headed toward five people, a wind comes up, and we can let the wind turn it toward killing one on another track.

If we would prefer that C2 be the case rather than that C1 be the case, we would prefer letting die to killing in a standardly equalized comparable case set. But is this a standardly equalized case? The alternative to killing one in C1 is letting five die. The alternative to letting one die in C2 is my interfering with the wind which would result in my *killing* the five. Possibly it might be said that the case in which we let die is to be preferred to one in which we kill because of how bad the alternative to it is. Furthermore, in C1 we intend the cause of death when we kill, but do not when we let die. A better set would be the following:

> C3: I must send a fatal trolley toward five or direct it to a track with no one on it, foreseeing that in the course of doing this I will, without a prior intention, voluntarily wiggle my foot, thereby setting off a bomb that will kill one person.

> C4: A fatal trolley is headed toward one. I could let it go or redirect it toward five.

In C3 and C4, I do not intend the cause of death of one person (nor any event that causes the cause of death, assuming my wiggling need not be caused by my directing the trolley). In C3 I choose between killing one and killing five; in C4 I choose between letting one die and killing five. If the C4 world is better, it is due to the difference between killing and letting die, per se.

A different type of case for the Choice Test: You see someone walking along a wall, balancing precariously. You know that if he falls, he will crash to his death on the rocks below. You believe, correctly, that there is a fifty percent chance that he will fall if you do nothing and a fifty percent chance that he will survive if you do nothing. If you call out to him, warning him of the drop below, there is a fifty percent chance that he will lose his balance and fall, and a fifty percent chance that he will be saved from falling. The expected utility of not interfering and of interfering are the same.

Suppose there is a preference for not interfering over interfering. We thereby indicate we care more not to have killed someone than to have saved him, other things equal. But in this case (unlike C1 and C2), the alternative to killing is not that someone will certainly live, nor is the alternative to letting die that the person is certainly saved. For if the act that may kill is not done, the person may die, and if the behavior that may let die is not done, the person may be killed. The fact that, *in this one case*, there is no difference in probability of death for the same person whether we act or omit action reduces the significance of the choice between killing and letting die.

As noted above, in medical contexts, if we took seriously the injunction "above all do no harm," we would never perform surgery that might harm someone for the sake of possibly saving him. We do not in fact take that injunction seriously, because at least when the probability of harming (specifically killing) is less than the probability of saving by a certain procedure, we do actions that may cause death. But in these medical cases, not everything is equal, that is, there is a higher expected chance of life if we perform the procedure. In these last two choice cases, the same act is either the killing or the saving, depending on what actually happens.

Pre-efforts Test and Choice Test

It is very important to note that an act or omission may be less stringently required than another act or omission as measured by the Efforts Tests, and be more stringently required as measured by the Choice Test. That is, it may be permitted or required that we perform the act or omission less stringently required by the Efforts Tests, given a choice between it and the act or omission more stringently required by the efforts measure. This could be an indication that there is a morally significant difference between the behaviors which accounts for the permissibility of requi_ing big efforts only for one, and yet where efforts are not in question simple objectionableness can determine choice. For example, I may be required to make great efforts to keep my obligations in a business deal, but not such great efforts to save a life. Yet I may (or should) choose to save a life rather than carry out my business obligations when the two conflict. It is for this reason that we cannot directly prove the impermissibility of choosing to kill one rather than let five die (e.g., when we had to run over one to get the five to a hospital) from the fact that more efforts are required to avoid such a killing than to save a life. Notice that these choice situations may not be the ones which it is appropriate to use in testing for the per se moral equivalence of killing and letting die. This is because they contain, for example, intending the cause of death in the killing but not in the letting die case. However, this is not crucial to the conflict between acts to which I am pointing now. For the claim about conflict is only that a certain behavior (whatever it involves) merits being avoided at certain pre- and post-efforts whereas another behavior (whatever it involves) does not, and yet we may choose to do the latter rather than the former.

The possible conflict in results of the Efforts and Choice Tests suggests a complexity in the structure of non-consequentialism that we shall investigate further in chapter 12. I do not believe, however, that there are cases involving killing people and letting people die where there is, in fact, a conflict in the results of the two tests.

Conflicting Results and Equivalence

Suppose, for the sake of argument, however, that the results of some of the tests discussed in this chapter conflicted with the results of other tests. That is, some indicated that letting die was per se morally superior to killing, and others indicated that killing was per se morally superior to letting die. What would this imply for the moral equivalence of killing and letting die? The first, stronger notion of moral equivalence says that if letting die has a conceptual property which killing lacks and that makes a moral difference on its home-ground, which a (different) conceptual property of killing does not make on its homeground, then killing and letting die differ per se morally. If killing had a conceptual property (or groups of these) that had the same effects as the properties of letting die, killing and letting die would be morally equivalent per se because they would be substitutable for each other in all (properly equalized) contexts without change in moral value (on any dimension). But the fact that different conceptual properties in killing and letting die could compensate for each other in this way should not be taken to imply that performing equally well overall but on *different tests* would compensate in such a way as to produce *moral equivalence*. Killing and letting die would still be morally inequivalent if there was just one properly equalized context where they behaved morally differently (in such dimensions as objectionableness, permissibility, post-efforts or pre-efforts test, choice test, etc.). But (as noted above p. 81) this moral inequivalence is compatible with killing being no morally worse than letting die if it had characteristics that made it as good as letting die only in different contexts. Similarly, if it had characteristics that made it score better on some dimensions of moral value while letting die scored better on other dimensions of moral value, if these dimensions balanced each other out. We must, therefore, be careful to keep separate the question of moral equivalence per se from the question of whether one is morally worse than the other per se. We may, of course, be answering both questions.

If *all* tests that measure the intrinsic characteristics of killing and letting die (in non-opaque, properly equalized contexts) concur that letting die is better to do than killing, then letting die is better to do than killing, per se. They are also morally inequivalent. (Of course, even less than this may be sufficient to show that letting die is better to do per se than killing; for example, if it scores higher on the more or the most important tests.)[25]

IV

Good-motive Test

The fourth test for the moral equivalence of killing and letting die in standard cases involves focusing on cases in which there is a benevolent motive for both killing and letting die.[26] Call this the Good-motive Test. Consider the following cases:

> E1: Someone is suffering from a disease that makes his life truly worse than death. He does not want to die for fear of Hell, however. We kill him for his own good (euthanasia), knowing (suppose) that there is no Hell after death.

> E2: Someone is suffering from a disease that makes his life truly worse than death. He does not want to die, however, for fear of Hell. He requests medication we own that will keep him alive. For his own good, we refuse to give it to him, and he dies.

The *intention* in both cases is that the person die, and the *motive* in both cases is the good of the sick person. Sometimes when people oppose a state of affairs, a motive in not aiding is that *they* not be the one to help bring about the state of affairs. If this were the motive in E2, the case would not be comparable to E1. We have constructed E2 so that it involves a true *paternalistic* motive.

Foot argues that the killing in E1 is morally objectionable, but letting die in E2 is not (as) objectionable, if the person who lets die in E2 has made no prior commitment to help the person. A doctor, by contrast, might have made such a commitment. (Is it clear that a doctor can be committed to render aid when it is not in his/her patient's best interest?) If killing and letting die are morally equivalent *per se*, why are not the act and omission in E1 and E2 morally equivalent?[27] If killing in (E1) is wrong this shows that we cannot account for the moral distinction between killing and letting die by saying that killing makes things go worse while letting die only does not make them go better. For killing can be wrong even when it would make things go better (and letting die can also make things go better.)[28]

Charity versus Justice

Foot claims that not aiding is not necessarily less objectionable than killing. For example, in cases B1 and B2 she says "It is not that (the) killing is worse than (the) letting die."[29] However, she says, when the not aiding in B2 is wrong, it is contrary to the virtue of charity (which tells us to seek the good of others), whereas when killing is wrong it is contrary to the virtue of justice. She holds that one has a right not to be killed, but no right to aid in this case, and justice is a matter of rights. When we let die in E2 we act *for the sake* of charity and we violate no right to be given aid. When we kill in E1 we also act for the sake of charity, but we would violate a right not to be killed against one's wishes. Presumably, Foot thinks that not violating the right takes precedence over acting charitably, and it is, therefore, wrong to kill in E1. Notice that if one respects rights in E1, one need not *aim* against the best interests of a person. One is not aiming to be uncharitable if one doesn't kill; one only *foresees* that one will not be able to promote someone's interests because rights stand in the way.

Problems

One seeming problem with Foot's account is that there are cases in which it *is* permissible to interfere with negative rights (not to be interfered with) for the sake of doing the charitable act. For example, we stop suicides when we believe that death is not in the person's interest. Charitable motivation that is *in favor of life*, at least sometimes, seems to override a negative right. Yet charitable motivation that leads us to be *against life* does not override the negative right. This is explicable if we say that killing someone takes away something significant that he has independently of us (his life), and not doing this takes precedence over charity. But interfering with a suicide only takes away liberty temporarily, and the achievement of significant benefit for the person can override this interference.

There is a second possible problem with Foot's analysis. If the root difference between killing and letting die in B1 and B2 were that between there being a right and there being no right, it would be just as wrong for someone to refuse to give lifesaving aid he had contracted to give (violating a positive right) as to kill a person. But it could be argued that even if we die as a consequence, being denied aid to which we have a right is not to suffer as great a wrong as (or perhaps it is to suffer a significantly different wrong from) being deprived of life we could have had independently of any first imposition on another. When the former happens, our links to other people are in jeopardy. (Consequentially, of course, we die.) When the latter happens our separateness and, often, independence from others is in jeopardy. This may be more important (or at least the sort of offense we have a right to more protection against), because independence supports the boundaries of our separateness, and there must first be *separate* entities, before they are linked. (When having been promised aid prompts us to put ourselves in jeopardy, the failure to aid comes closer to being as wrong as killing. This is because someone else comes close to having caused us to lose what we would have had independently of imposition on him. Further, intending that someone be faced with a threat and so not helping may involve the hope that someone will lose what he now has independently of imposition on you. Still, given that he needs aid, he loses only what he would have gotten via your aid.)

A third problem is whether Foot's account of cases E1 and E2 is consistent with her view that killing is not worse than letting die in B1 and B2. If not violating a right takes precedence over acting charitably in E1, why isn't violating a right in B1 a more serious offense than simply being uncharitable in B2? If it is more important to respect the right than to render charity when there is a conflict between the two, why isn't violating the right a more serious offense than offending charity when they appear in separate cases like B1/B2?

Responses

One possible answer[30] to the last query is that we may have a more stringent duty not to kill than to save life, but this may mean only that one behavior is more easily defeated than the other. For example, the need to make efforts defeats the duty to aid more easily than it defeats the duty not to kill. Therefore, that the duty not to kill some particular person is more stringent than the duty to aid some particular person in the sense that it is less defeasible does not, it may be claimed, imply that a violation of one duty *when it is present* is more grave than a violation of another. There may be more occasions in which the duty to aid is permissibly defeated. But that does not mean that when we let die *im*permissibly we have done anything less serious than when we kill impermissibly.

However, the Post-efforts Test was intended to suggest that this view is not correct. When the less stringent (by the defeasibility standard) duty is violated, it is still a less serious matter than when the more serious duty is violated; hence (B1) is morally different from (B2).

Another response to the last objection to Foot's account is analogous to a suggestion made in the context of the Choice Test: Independently we could judge two behaviors to be morally equal, given that one did not have to do one in order to avoid doing the other. (The example given when discussing the Choice Test was murder versus torture.) Yet if they are in conflict, one may be preferable to the other. So violating a right and having an uncharitable intention could be as seriously wrong independently, but given a choice we should not violate a right. The problem with this account is that although murder and torture independently may elicit equally great pre- and post-efforts, this does *not* mean that independently they are equally morally objectionable. Indeed, preferring to do one rather than the other suggests that they are not. The less bad act may just be so bad that it elicits the highest efforts we are (morally) able to impose.

Another possible explanation of why we may hold that violating justice is equivalent to offending charity in B1 and B2, yet deny that we may violate justice for the sake of charity, focuses on the fact that in B1 and B2 we contrast violating a right with *aiming against* someone's welfare. By contrast, in E1 if we do not kill, we will not be aiming against someone's welfare. We will *foreseeably not* promote someone's welfare. We do not aim at what is bad for him. So if killing is worse than this foreseen failure to promote someone's welfare, this need not mean that killing is worse than intending someone harm.

However, what of cases in which someone respects a right because he aims at the person's harm, that is, the consequence of not killing involves intended harm? For example, someone might be glad there is a strong anti-paternalistic theory of negative rights because he knows that most people, left to their own devices, will do harm to themselves. This reduces the numbers who can successfully compete with him. We still cannot permit violations of someone's significant negative right, merely to prevent his being the victim of an agent's aiming against his welfare. Protecting the negative right takes precedence over preventing behavior on a bad intention.

Justice at Issue in B2

Foot herself may have come to think that her view that B2 is as bad or in other respects morally as significant as B1 was inconsistent with the position that rights dominate charity. This is because, in another article,[31] she suggests that B2 may be as bad as B1 because it is assumed that there is a strict right to aid in B2. This position, however, faces the question of whether violating a positive right is as significant as violating a negative right. It also raises problems for E2. For if someone has a *positive right from even a stranger* (i.e., independent of contract) to a small amount of lifesaving aid, why should we be permitted to refuse it from a charitable motive?

Perhaps someone has a right to lifesaving aid only when it is in his interest to get it, as in B2. Then we would not have to aid in E2 (where there is no contract for aid), though we would have to aid in B2 on grounds of a right. However, *if* Thesis E were true, it should then also be true that someone has a right not to be killed only when it is in his interest not to be killed. This means it would be permissible to kill someone against his will in E1, contrary to what Foot claims. Foot, however, need not be worried by this since she is not arguing for Thesis E. She could claim that there is a right to aid only when it is in someone's interest but not when it is against someone's interest, unless there is a contractual obligation to give aid. That is, unless there was an explicit agreement for aid no matter what. (This could be consistent with the view that some rights need not be derived from interests; so, for example, there could be a right not to be treated paternalistically.) Foot can still claim that there is a serious right not to be killed, even when being killed is in one's interests, unless one has waived (or forfeited) the right. (Notice that the addition of a contract could strengthen a right to aid, so that we had to give aid even when it was against someone's interests. By contrast, there is no need for such a special contract in the case of the right not to be killed. This should worry a proponent of Thesis E, but not Foot.) Another possibility is that if the aid desired in E2 were like the aid desired in B2, i.e., a helping hand rather than medicine, one could not deny it even if it were against the interests of the victim to go on living.

Again note that positing a positive right in B2 to account for the supposed equivalence of B1 and B2 is useless, if violating a positive right is morally not equivalent to violating a negative right.

Objecting to Motives

What is so interesting about the dominance of the right not to be killed in all this, is that someone will probably be more revolted, morally speaking, at being left without minimal aid for *malicious* reasons (whether he has a right to the aid or not), than at being killed against his will for his own interest. The malicious motive may be most significant in causing outrage; yet the moral ground for interfering with the killer is more straightforward than for forcing aid.

Furthermore, the "victim" will probably object almost as much to another's paternalistic refusal to promote his *autonomy* by refusing to give minimal aid when the "victim" wishes to remain alive, as he will object to being killed for paternalistic reasons. Yet requiring aid from the agent who refuses to give it is less easily justified than preventing the agent who would kill from killing. The killer, but not the non-aider, will interfere with what someone would have retained independently of an imposition on him, and this, I believe, is the ground of enforceable prohibitions on his behavior. Again, I emphasize the *relational element* of this prohibition: A may not interfere with B's life held independently of imposition on A even if B is dependent for life on C; B does not lose rights vis-à-vis A simply because he is weaker relative to C.

Conclusion

We have applied four tests to standardly equalized killing and letting-die cases: Post-efforts, Pre-efforts, Choice, and Good-motive. My claim is that these tests suggest there is a morally significant difference between killing and letting die. This may or may not be a difference in moral objectionableness, but it does show up as a difference in what we may permissibly require of people. Hence, the tests suggests that the strong version of Thesis E is false.

NOTES

1. By James Rachels in "Active and Passive Euthanasia," reprinted in Bonnie Steinbock (ed.), *Killing and Letting Die* (Englewood Cliffs, N.J.: Prentice-Hall, 1981).

2. To say two cases are equally morally objectionable may or may not be the same as saying they are morally equivalent. It is possible that in considering this further test we are testing for moral equivalence rather than moral objectionableness because these differ. I shall return to this point.

3. In response to my proposing this test, Raziel Abelson has commented on the problem of individuating omissions. Would we say that someone had done something wrong if he fails to aid at t_1 but does aid at t_2? It is hard to tell whether the wrong omission for which someone must make up has occurred, or whether aid has just been put off. This difficulty can be overcome in at least two ways: (a) assume for purposes of argument that we know that the agent's delay was due to the intention never to aid, or (b) accept behavioral criteria of no intention to aid, constructing the case so that someone went away from where he could be of assistance, and must be brought back.

4. In "On the Relative Strictness of Positive and Negative Duties," reprinted in Bonnie Steinbock (ed.), *Killing and Letting Die* (Englewood Cliffs, N.J.: Prentice-Hall, 1979).

5. On this issue, see Bernard Williams' discussion of agent regret in "Moral Luck," in *Moral Luck* (Cambridge: Cambridge University Press, 1981); my "The Insanity Defense, Innocent Threats, and Limited Alternatives," in *Criminal Justice Ethics* (Summer 1987), pp. 61–76 and *Creation and Abortion* (New York: Oxford University Press, 1992) and pp. 95–98 below.

6. In "Euthanasia," *Philosophy & Public Affairs* 6(2) (Winter 1977): 85–112.

7. In "Actions, Intentions, and Consequences: The Doctrine of Doing and Allowing," *Philosophical Review*, 98 (1989), pp. 151–152.

8. These are like Foot's Rescue Cases from "Killing and Letting Die," in T. Garfield and P. Hennessey, eds., *Abortion; Moral and Legal Perspectives* (Amherst, Mass.: University of Massachusetts Press, 1984), pp. 178–185.

9. Thomson imagines a killing case like this in "Rights and Deaths," *Philosophy & Public Affairs* 2(2) (Winter 1973): 146–59. In response to a case like this, Raziel Abelson suggested that *all* killings include lettings die, even ones in which the killer dies after performing the act that kills. This is because, he says, the person who kills *lets himself* do the act. Presumably, this is supposed to be comparable to my letting *someone else* kill a person. This latter case would indeed involve a letting die. I believe it would be strained to say that in letting ourselves kill someone we let him die, or even let him die from an attack. It is even an oddity to think that one lets oneself kill. Such a view involves a faulty theory of action, since it treats a person's act as though it were a compulsion with which he could have interfered, but didn't. In a case of compulsion, the doing is oddly passive and automatic; the active part of the person seems relegated to making the decision about whether to *let* what is happening to him (the compulsion) have its way. But in deciding to do the act that kills, unless the "act" is compulsive, one is totally involved with the doing. There is no separate letting happen. So it does not seem that every killing also involves a letting die. Suppose, however, that every killing also involved a letting die, and the killing and letting-die components were morally equivalent. Then someone would be doing twice, rather than once, the same bad thing. But then, if killing and letting die were morally equivalent, someone who decides to let die and re-commits himself to this decision would *also* be doing something as bad. Suppose we still reject the moral equivalence of cases in which there is (1) a killing and a letting die and (2) a letting die and a letting die. Then the view that "double commitment" alone makes a case of killing and letting die worse than a case with a single letting die would be wrong. For the double letting die would have "double commitment" too, and yet not be as bad.

10. This argument type was used in chapter 2 also.

11. The agreement between two people for one to do something potentially (or actually) harmful whose harm the other either prevents or undoes, is not innocuous, and not only because the aid may fail to appear. Being the object of aid tends to make one beholden to an aider, and the agreement may, therefore, have the structure of a "protection racket" whose aim is to benefit from someone's dependence. The person who had the aiding role in one protection racket can easily be the harmer in another; though in real life some who cannot avoid participating in the structure reduce their immorality by playing only the aider role ("the knight in shining armor").

12. However, suppose there were an *agreement* for me to endanger and for another person to *rescue* rather than to let die, and I wouldn't have endangered without believing the other would rescue. If the other does not rescue, post-efforts should go down for me since the non-aider failed in what is here agreed to be his duty to aid. This assumes that my reliance on him was permitted.

13. Some might object to this on the grounds that it is a blessing to be in a position to save a life. Both claims may be true.

14. As discussed in, for example, George Fletcher, "Fairness and Utility in Tort Theory," 85 Harvard Law Rev. 537 (1972).

15. I first presented these cases and discussed the issues raised here in "The Insanity Defense, Innocent Threats, and Limited Alternatives," *Criminal Justice Ethics*, Summer 1987, pp. 61–76. For further discussion see that article, and also *Creation and Abortion* (New York: Oxford University Press, 1992).

16. In Williams, "Moral Luck," in *Moral Luck*.

17. Note that among the different types of cases we have discussed in connection with post-efforts are: (1) an act or omission (deliberate refraining) which is avoidable at reasonable cost and which it is therefore wrong not to refrain from; (2) no act or omission, but an event that one cannot avoid being involved in that causes harm; and (3) an act (or omission) one could have avoided only by efforts excessive at the time they were relevant.

18. This may differ from what it is permissible to simply threaten to carry out.

19. In "On the Relative Strictness of Positive and Negative Duties."

20. As noted in discussing the Post-efforts Test, Russell distinguishes between those who have already improperly done an act and those who must choose whether to do an act or make a sacrifice to avoid it. (Doing the act rather than making the sacrifice cannot automatically be assumed to be improper.)

21. In *Harm to Others* (Oxford: Oxford University Press, 1984).

22. The fact that being a duty can add extra weight, all by itself, can be seen by considering cases in which the same act is a duty for one person and not for another. For example, if I promised to play a game with someone, I ought to make greater effort to play the game than someone who hasn't promised (where all other factors are equal).

23. In "The Problem of Abortion and the Doctrine of Double Effect," reprinted in Bonnie Steinbock (ed.), *Killing and Letting Die*, (Englewood Cliffs, N.J.: Prentice-Hall, 1979).

24. Foot refers to Ross's view that the duty of non-malfeasance is more stringent than the duty to aid. But Ross also makes the same mistake: As evidence for the relative stringency of the duties, he says we may not kill to acquire money to aid. See *The Right and the Good* (Oxford: Oxford University Press, 1930).

25. The question of whether and how to weigh different tests is complex and important, but I shall not discuss it in detail here. I will note only that the fact that the Choice Test was introduced as being more sensitive than the Efforts Test does not imply that when the two conflict the Choice Test should be seen as the dominant indication of

moral value. The Choice Test may have been more sensitive than the Efforts Test in that it picked up better on a difference in the *same* property that the Efforts Test measured, but to which the Efforts Test was unable to respond further because the test had reached *its* maximal sensitivity level. By contrast, when the two tests conflict, they may be measuring *different* morally relevant properties, and this does not necessarily mean one property is morally weightier than the other.

26. These sorts of cases were first employed to discuss the difference between killing and letting die by Phillipa Foot, in "Euthanasia."

27. Some may find E2 objectionable because it involves a paternalistic motive. We might, then, consider cases in which we must harm or not aid someone who is morally bad, for the sake of the greater good rather than for his own good. For example, if someone is a Nazi and his death is in the best interests of the world, might it be permissible (even obligatory) not to aid him, intending his death? Yet might it not be impermissible to kill him.

28. The "makes worse/not makes better" explanation of the greater wrongness of killing is offered by Michael Moore in *Act and Crime: The Philosophy of Action and Its Implications for Criminal Law* (Oxford: Oxford University Press, 1993), pp. 25, 54, 58.

29. "Euthanasia," p. 101.

30. The one Quinn gives, as noted above.

31. "Killing and Letting Die," in *Abortion: Moral and Legal Perspectives*, p. 182, Jay Garfield and Patricia Hennessy, eds., 1984.

5

Harming, Not Aiding,
and Positive Rights

In previous chapters we have considered reasons why killing and letting die might not be morally equivalent, and tests that may indicate this. We said that killing might not be morally equivalent to letting die per se, even if some cases involving them were morally as objectionable. We also said that even if some letting-die cases were more objectionable than some killings, there could still be some moral difference, other than objectionableness, that accounted for differences in Pre- and Post-efforts Tests. In this chapter I wish to assume, for the sake of argument, that killing and letting die *are* morally equivalent in order to examine how broad the implications of this would be. (We have already considered one aspect of this issue in distinguishing between the weak and strong versions of Thesis E.) Given this aim, for purposes of the discussion that follows I will employ the first, stronger notion of per se moral equivalence. Hence, I shall begin with the assumption that cases that are only C-equalized are the correct comparable killing and letting-die cases, and that (contrary to what chapter 4 suggested) killing and letting die in such cases are morally equivalent.

I

The General Equivalence Thesis

It might be thought that if killing and letting die are morally equivalent per se (Thesis E), then so are harming and not aiding in cases in which less than life is at stake. We can refer to this as the General Equivalence Thesis, or Thesis GE.[1] (The distinction between harming and not aiding is drawn analogously to the killing/letting-die distinction previously described on pp. 70–73.) In keeping with my treatment of Thesis E, I shall investigate the implications of a strong version of Thesis GE. I shall assume that the claim that harming and not aiding are morally equivalent per se commits one to the view that instances of harming and not aiding in cases that are only C-equalized are morally equivalent.[2]

The supporters of Thesis GE could see it playing a part in moving us beyond Robert Nozick's minimal state,[3] where people have strong negative rights (rights not to be harmed) but weak or nonexistent positive rights (rights to be aided). If it is as wrong to refuse to aid as it is to harm, per se, then if people have rights not to be harmed, they may well also have rights to be aided (positive rights), and it may be a state's duty to provide that aid when it is needed.[4]

Does General Equivalence Imply Rights?

As noted in chapter 4, Philippa Foot has argued against such a form of reasoning, claiming that a case of not aiding can be morally as bad as a case of harming without this implying that there is a right to aid if there is a right not to be harmed. This is because, she claims, not aiding and harming can be contrary to two different virtues, harming to the virtue of justice, not aiding to the virtue of charity. Only matters of justice are matters of rights. Presumably this could be true even if all comparable cases of harming and not aiding were equally morally objectionable. But if harming and not aiding were contrary to *different* virtues they would be, at least to this extent, morally inequivalent. We, by contrast, are assuming moral equivalence. We have also asked whether being contrary to justice and rights does not call forth greater pre- and post-efforts, and so indicate a significant moral difference.

Hence, I wish to put Foot's criticism to one side in the following discussion. Note, further, that even if it were not possible to derive a positive right from the equal moral objectionableness of harming and not aiding (as I have also suggested), it might be thought possible to derive a duty to aid (without a correlative right) just as strong as a duty to refrain from harming. We could consider how far the moral-equivalence theses would take us toward such duties. In addition, it may be that some will not want to distinguish as strictly as Foot does between justice and charity, or will not want to distinguish between justice and charity in the way Foot does. They will want to derive rights in a way that parallels their views on the equal moral objectionableness of harming and not aiding. (I have suggested, however, that such rights might be unequally stringent, if killing and letting die are not morally equivalent per se.)

Thomson's Argument against Positive Rights

Judith Thomson gives an argument[5] for there being no right to be aided. She says: (1) The stringency of a claim (right) is a function of how badly off someone will be if his or her claim is not met; (2) Where equally stringent claims are in conflict, the greater number should be satisfied; (3) If (1) and (2) are correct, and if there were a claim to have one's life saved, then it would, in general, be permissible to kill one person to save five lives; (4) However, this conclusion is wrong, and therefore, there is no claim to have one's life saved.

Whether or not Thomson is right about one's having no right to be aided, there seems to be a problem with this argument for that conclusion. The problem, I think, is with (1); for if stringency is not *merely* a function of how badly off someone will be if his right is not accorded him, then we cannot reach the counterintuitive (3). In fact, it has been argued that the right not to be killed is more stringent than a right to have one's life saved, because the bad state comes about in a different way. The origin of a right may also affect how stringent it is — for example, did the king give me my right, or the prince? If, in an emergency, I must choose whether to take the property of someone whose property I have promised not to take or that of someone else, who simply has an ordinary property right, I believe the former has a stronger claim on me, even if I know that the first owner will not have any of his expectations defeated since he will never discover the loss. If stringency is affected by things other than how badly off someone will be, there may be a right to have one's life saved, but it would be a less stringent right than the right not to be killed. (This, of course, would be contrary to Thesis E.) If so, it could still be impermissible to kill one to save five, in general.

Consider an additional point: In some cases we know that there are rights to be aided (e.g., contractual rights of a patient vis-à-vis his doctor). Yet even in such a case the doctor may not kill the one to save his five patients. It would seem that this is not because the five have no right to be aided, but because their rights are not as stringent as the one's right not to be killed. It might be suggested that a patient has no right to be aided by a doctor, only a right that the doctor use specific means (e.g., medication) to help the patient. But is this attempt to specify the right misdirected? Thomson herself has rejected the idea that there is no right not to be killed, only a right not to be killed in circumstances *x*, *y*, and *z*. Furthermore, even if we specify a right to be aided by medication, we shall have to say, for example, that the patient has a right to be aided by the medication only if the doctor need not kill someone to get it. If we must even specify the right to be given medication, why may we not just rest where we began, with the right to be aided?

It is useful to note once again, however, that the fact that the duty not to kill is more stringent than the duty not to let die, by the measure of the amount of personal and other *cost* that we must tolerate rather than kill or let die, does not prove that we may not kill someone rather than let others die. For a duty may be more stringent according to the measure of effort or other cost and not according to the measure of precedence. For example, I may have to do more to avoid failing in my business responsibilities than I have to do to save a life, and yet I may drop my business responsibilities to save a life.[6]

Still, if Thesis E were true, it should be the case (I believe) that the right not to be killed and the right to be aided would be equally stringent. On this assumption, would Thomson's argument imply (3)? But suppose we kill one to save five, intending the death of the one, but only foreseeing the death of five if we let them die. Then it may be that a prohibition on intending the death of nonthreatening innocents who are independent of imposition on us (at least in such cases as this) takes precedence over satisfying the greater number of claims. Thomson's argument suggests that she does not believe that the intention/foresight distinction matters. Still there are cases where what we would need to do in order to satisfy the greater number of claims would involve our doing something we only foresee will cause a death; that is, we would not be intending the death as a means nor even intending the cause of death. An example is a case in which we decide to continue driving on a road, in order to take five dying people to a hospital, even though we foresee that in the course of driving we will without prior intention wiggle our foot and this will set off a bomb killing one. In such cases Thomson's argument, including (2) and the truth of Thesis E, will imply that we may kill one to save five. If this is the wrong conclusion, her argument provides reason to think that Thesis E is false, and even if there are positive rights to lifesaving aid these rights are not as stringent as rights not to be killed.

I shall now examine some ways in which we might attempt to derive positive rights or duties to aid, assuming Thesis E is true.

II

The Derivation of Strong Rights and Duties

Those who accept Thesis E and, on the basis of it, GE might be tempted to derive very strong *rights* (that is, rights that have negative and positive components) to have certain things or to be in certain states in the following way:

Assume that Theses E and GE are correct. They imply that if (a) someone has the right not to be harmed by being deprived of his piece of property of type x, then (b) another person has the right to be aided in keeping or getting an instance of x. If he has this right, he will, presumably, have a right that we not take x away. Therefore, anybody can be said to have the right to have an x, in the sense that we must actively see to it that he has got it, and not take it away once he has it. This right to an x is derived from the right to be aided. which is, in turn, derived via Thesis GE from the right not to be harmed. (This derivation assumes that the amount of aid required does not exceed the sacrifice we could be required to make rather than deprive someone of his x.)

Likewise, someone might derive a strong *duty* to provide certain things in the following way:

Assume that Theses E and GE are correct. They imply that if (a′) someone has the duty not to harm someone else by depriving him of his piece of property of type x, then (b′) he has the duty to aid yet another person in getting or keeping an instance of x. If he has the duty to provide the x, he will presumably have the duty not to take it away. These duties to see to it that someone has x are derived from the duty to aid someone in getting x, which is derived via Thesis GE from the duty not to harm. (This derivation assumes that the amount of aid required does not exceed the sacrifice we could be required to make rather than deprive someone of his x.)

I do not think this is a correct procedure for deriving rights to have things, or duties or rights to aid. (Notice that for purposes of brevity I use "right to aid" as synonymous with "right to be aided" rather than with "right to give aid," and use "duty to aid" as synonymous with "duty to give aid.")

The Error in the Derivation: Ignoring Independent Rights

Given that we assume Theses E and GE, the error comes in the move from (a) to (b) and from (a') to (b'). Those moves fail to distinguish between two types of situation in which we are called upon to aid: those in which we help someone get or retain something that is his, and those in which we provide him with what is not his. A way to draw this distinction is to separate cases in which the people we would aid thereby get or keep something to which they are assumed to have a right regardless of whether they have a right to aid — I shall refer to this as having an *independent right* to something — from cases in which we help people get or keep something that is not already recognized as something to which they have such an independent right. Having an independent right to something should be distinguished from what I, in previous chapters, referred to as having something independently of our aid. Someone may not be able to retain that to which he has an independent right independently of us, and hence he may need our aid.

If Thesis GE is true, it implies that not aiding someone will have the same moral status as harming someone only when all factors in the harming and not-aiding cases other than harming and not aiding are the same. All other factors may be the same when we deprive someone of his piece of property x and when we do not help him retain his piece of property x. So, if it is wrong to take away his x, and Thesis GE is true, it will be wrong not to aid him in getting or keeping his x, other things being equal. But all other factors are not equal if we deprive someone of what is his independently of a right to aid, but fail to help someone get what is not accepted as his independently of a right to aid. Therefore, we cannot show that it is wrong to refuse to help someone get some x that is not already accepted as his, just because Thesis GE is true and it is wrong to deprive someone of some x that is accepted as his. "The right to have x," in the sense of the right to get it and keep it cannot be derived using only Thesis GE and a claim about the right not to have things taken from us that are recognized as ours independently of a right to aid, unless x is such a thing.[7]

Likewise, the *duty* to help someone get an x to which he has no independent right cannot be derived using Thesis GE and a claim about the duty not to take away things recognized as belonging to someone.

Examples

To make clearer the distinction between these cases consider the following Election (E) cases [and also the Grocery (G) cases on p. 129]:

> (E1) I steal the thousand dollars that belongs to my opponent in a political campaign because I believe that the absence of these funds will cause him to lose the election. (I do not keep the thousand dollars.)

(E2) I refuse to give my opponent the minute aid he needs to regain a thousand dollars of his that is accidentally falling over a cliff. I do this because I believe that without the thousand dollars he will lose the election.

(E3) I refuse to give my opponent in a political campaign the minute aid that I know he will use as seed money in order to overcome an obstacle to collecting a thousand dollars for his campaign. I do this because I believe that without the money he will lose the election.

It might seem that if Thesis GE is true, and there are no further distinctions of which to take account, then what is done in both (E3) and (E2) should be as bad as what is done in (E1).[8] Some may think (E2) is not as bad as (E1). This would imply a rejection of Thesis GE. Let us ignore this for now, since I believe that there is a moral difference between (E2) and (E3) that does not depend on the falsity of Thesis E or GE. Even if my opponent is an ordinary (i.e., not particularly evil) politician, it seems worse to refuse aid in (E2) than in (E3).

The source of this moral difference is that in (E2), but not in (E3), we help someone regain something that we recognize as his. The fact that it is his thousand dollars is not derived from any right he has to our minimal aid. He is recognized as having a right to the thousand dollars regardless of whether he has any right to aid. In general, aiding someone can involve either helping him get or keep something to which he has an independent right or helping him get or keep something to which he does not have an independent right.[9] (E2) exemplifies the former and (E3) the latter.[10]

Conclusion

Therefore, we cannot derive a person's right to something (e.g., a thousand dollars) or our duty to provide it, by arguing: Someone has a negative right not to be deprived of his thousand dollars. Thesis GE is true. Therefore, someone has a positive right to the aid (or we have the duty to provide the aid) necessary to get him the thousand dollars not already specified as his. (This derivation assumes that the amount of aid required does not exceed the sacrifice we could be required to make rather than deprive someone of his thousand dollars.) Therefore, he has a right to the thousand dollars (within the limits on requirable aid). We cannot argue in this way because there may be no right or duty to aid (via Thesis GE) unless there is first an independent right to the thousand dollars.

Using Thesis GE and Case (E1), we can conclude only that a harming and a not aiding are equally wrong when the thousand dollars is already recognized as his. And, of course, if we knew that he had an independent right to the thousand dollars, we would not need to derive his right to have it from the right to aid. If we have to assume that he has an independent right to something before we can derive his right to it, the argument for a right to it is circular.

I emphasize that if one used Thesis GE and a case like (E1) to derive only a right or duty to help someone get or keep his *x*, this problem would not arise. But I am suggesting that by forgetting to apply Thesis GE only to cases that are properly equalized for all factors besides harming and not aiding, there may be an incorrect attempt to show that one has to help someone get something that is not independently recognized as his. It may, of course, be possible to prove without Thesis GE that someone has an independent right to something, and then use Thesis GE to argue for the right to aid or duty to aid to acquire that thing. The point is that this proof will have to be carried out; there is no shortcut via the Equivalence Theses and harming cases involving things to which someone has an independent right.

Notice also that the general point I have made is not dependent on my being correct about that to which someone has an independent right. For example, in the Election cases I have assumed that my opponent has an independent right to his thousand dollars in (E2) but not to the thousand dollars (E3). These assumptions may be wrong, but this would not affect the general point I am making. Regardless of what we assume someone has an independent right to, we can ask whether we can derive rights to have things (or duties to give things) to which there is no independent right, by using Thesis GE and harming cases involving that to which there is an independent right.[11]

An Objection

Perhaps there is a flaw in this argument concerning the significance of independent rights. When we harm someone by taking that to which he has an independent right, at least *two* things are going on. First, we interfere with an item to which he has an independent right; second, we take from him *what he already has*. It is possible that both these factors are of moral importance. Then the failure to equalize aiding cases for either factor would be a mistake. This is consistent with its being a mistake not to equalize for independent right, and so does not call into question our emphasis on this factor. However, if the fact that we caused someone to lose what he already had were also of significance and should be equalized, the second clause of the second sentence of the derivation at the beginning of this section (p. 124) would have to be modified. That sentence claimed that "if (a) someone has the right not to be harmed by being deprived of his piece of property of type *x*, then (b) another person has the right to be aided in keeping or getting an instance of *x*." (b) could be modified either by deleting "or getting" in which case it strictly applies to things the person already *has*. It might also be acceptable (if broader) to replace "or getting" with "or arranging the return of," in which case we are dealing with what the person already *had*. Let us focus on the latter revision. Getting something to which someone had an independent right but which he never previously had, would fail to equalize for a significant factor.

It is also possible that one of these factors is of moral importance and *not* the other. If the factor that is crucial is having an independent right, then nothing we have said above need be changed. But *if* it were only the "already had" factor that was crucial, then clause (b) of the derivation should speak of "aid to keep" only, and would apply even if the person were to retain that to which he had no independent right.

But, of course, if we are concerned about not slipping up in equalizing, and are not convinced to begin with which of the two factors is significant, thinking either or both might be, we should reach conclusions only about cases with both. In fact, I do not believe the "already had" factor is of much moral significance, though it is worth pointing out that clause (b) as originally formulated does not attend to it. Independent right, however, does seem to be a morally significant factor. Therefore, I shall not alter the previous discussion, though I will specifically argue against the significance of "already had" when conjoined with having an independent right and will return to consider the significance of "already had" in cases where we are concerned about the loss of something to which someone had no independent right.

Self-standing Claims

Now, there may well be things to which we have a claim, and of which it would be wrong to deprive us, even though strictly speaking they do not belong to us in the sense of being our property. These would be things that we simply "ought to have." The claim to these things differs from an independent right in that the claim seems conceptually connected to the idea that someone should be helped to have the things (even if not by just anyone). An example might be minimal clothing and shelter. (The independent right by itself is not in any way connected to the idea of a right to get or duty to give aid.) Even someone who denied Theses E and GE could still believe that there were certain things that people simply "ought to have," and that this notion was conceptually tied to that of receiving aid. She might, however, believe that the efforts required to avoid depriving people of these things is greater than the effort required to help them get it. (This would involve rejecting strong Thesis GE.)

The claim to these things and the claim to aid in getting and keeping them, however, is not derived from its being wrong to take these things away, combined with Thesis GE. We simply identify a class of things that we think people ought to have, independently of Thesis GE. (I shall refer to such claims as self-standing *claims*.)

Therefore we have not used Thesis GE to *derive* rights or claims to have things not otherwise thought to be ours, or duties to provide these things, either from cases in which we have a right not to be deprived of what is ours or from cases in which we have a right not to be deprived of something "we ought to have." These results diminish the significance of the Equivalence Theses.

III

The Relation of Thesis GE to Thesis E

I believe that the difference between helping someone to get or keep that to which he has an independent right and that to which he has no independent right may be especially easy to overlook if Thesis GE is derived from Thesis E or adhered to against a background of attending to Thesis E. In killing and letting-die cases, someone's life may be viewed as something to which he has an independent right, almost as if it were a piece of property to which he had a right. So a case of letting die is one in which someone loses out on something to which he has an independent right. (Also, someone's life will be something that he has already had at some point, so saving a life will not involve providing someone with something he has never had. It is not clear that this is a morally significant point in its own right, however. We return to it in Section IV.)[12]

If there were no letting-die case analogous to (E3) (where (E3) involves refusing to help someone get that to which he has no independent right), the most that could be derived from the truth of Thesis E via Thesis GE is the moral equivalence of cases like (E1) and (E2). In fact, there are cases where someone may lose his independent right to his life (at least relative to some others). For example, it is permissible to kill a malicious aggressor in self-defense and permissible to not aid him in self-defense. But suppose they forget either that killing and letting-die cases both involve someone's retaining something to which he has an independent right or that in the absence of the independent right killing and letting die are permissible. Then proponents of Thesis GE who are influenced by Thesis E may apply Thesis GE to a harming case in which there is no independent right and treat it like a case with an independent right. Indeed, it may be their point to do just this, since it would be a very important result to use Thesis GE to derive rights to have new things, or duties to provide them. The implications of Thesis GE are not nearly so broad if they are limited to helping people retain (or regain) that to which they have an independent right or a self-standing claim.

Examples

To further clarify this point, consider the following three "Grocery" (G) cases, which share all factors except the noted differences:

> (G1) I take someone's food, because I want him not to have it.

> (G2) I refuse to give minimal aid to help someone regain his food that has been lost, because I want him not to have it.

> (G3) I refuse to give minimal aid in order to provide someone with food that was never his, because I want him not to have it.

Suppose the food is necessary to keep the person alive, and staying alive is viewed as something to which he has a self-standing claim at certain costs. Then if Thesis E were true, and even if it were not, harming and not aiding in all three cases might be morally equivalent. (It is possible that a self-standing claim to food supplemented by a property right might be stronger than a self-standing claim alone.) If the food is not necessary for life, but is only a delicacy that provides a person with pleasure, then even someone committed to Theses E and GE should distinguish between (G2) and (G3). If any of the not-aiding cases is equivalent to the harming case (G1), it will be (G2) and not (G3). In (G3), nothing to which someone has an independent right or self-standing claim would be involved.

In fact, most people would probably balk at the equivalence of even (G1) and (G2) when they involve delicacies, and this could be used as evidence that Thesis GE is false. In cases typically used to convince us of the truth of Thesis E, the loss someone would suffer if harmed or not aided is very significant, for example, his life. But if Thesis GE were true, then harming and not aiding should be morally equivalent even when the loss would be insignificant. However, when confronted with versions of Grocery Cases (G1) and (G2) in which the food is a mere delicacy, it may be that the supporter of Thesis GE will want to abandon his position. This is because he may think it is sometimes wrong to take away even a trivial delicacy that belongs to someone else (that is, something to which the person has an independent right), although it is not as wrong to refuse to help someone retain a delicacy to which he also has an independent right in otherwise comparable circumstances. If (G1) and (G2) were still morally equivalent when food for life was at stake, then it would not be because Thesis E is true.

IV

Emergencies

An implication one *might* be tempted to draw from the distinction between helping someone get or keep that to which he has an independent right, and helping him get or keep that to which he has no independent right, concerns the handling of emergencies. It is sometimes thought peculiar that more energy is spent on saving people from "crises" than on saving people whose ordinary lives keep them in as bad a state as that produced by a crisis. A crisis is usually an event that disrupts the person's life as it was prior to the moment of crisis; so aid would bring a person back to his state before the crisis, helping him retain or regain what he had in the past. Usually these are things to which he is also thought to have an independent right. By contrast, if we aid people who ordinarily live in situations no better than a crisis, we make them better off than they have ever been or would have been without the aid; our aid brings them to a state of well-being that has never and would never have been theirs otherwise.

The distinction I have drawn between helping someone to keep that to which he has an independent right and helping him to get that to which he has no independent right *might be thought* to account for the greater efforts made in emergencies. However, I believe it would be wrong to say that it is appropriate to make more effort in crises merely because they are cases of helping someone to *get back* what he already had. What is important is that he had an independent right (or self-standing claim) to what he had. But people can have independent rights or self-standing claims to what they have never had. For example, things can be theirs, and be recognized as theirs, and yet they may not be in possession of what is theirs. This means that the urgency of putting some people in the condition they were in before a crisis and would have been in but for the crisis, should not necessarily be greater than the urgency with which we improve the ordinary condition of others who do have independent rights or self-standing claims to things they have never had.[13]

Returning to the Status Quo Ante, Rights, and Self-standing Claims

It should not be thought, furthermore, that everything one has had ex ante is something to which one has an independent right or a self-standing claim. As already noted in chapter 1 (p. 24), Joel Feinberg argues that rights to aid arise only if we must return people to the condition they were in or would have been in but for a bad turn of events. I questioned Feinberg's point by considering the case in which a child has always, since birth, been drowning in a pool. Presumably Feinberg would not want to argue that any right it has to be aided is weakened by the fact that it did not fall into the pool after it was on dry land. Further, I argued that we would not have a stronger duty to provide someone with a luxury simply because she had had it previously and lost it. I believe that something other than the return of what someone once had and would have had but for a bad turn of affairs, lies behind the view that people have a right to aid. This other ground is probably some sort of view about what we have a self-standing claim to, for example, the necessities of life, at least at moderate cost to others.

V

Harming When There Is No Independent Right or Claim

It might be suggested that if we could show that harming is impermissible in situations in which no independent right or self-standing claim is involved, then Thesis GE would be used to show that not aiding will be equally impermissible in a comparable case. This is indeed a possibility, but it will not succeed if harming is permissible (or does not exist) in the absence of an independent right or self-standing claim. [In discussing this point we may face basic problems about the use of the term "harm," for if depriving someone of that to which he has no independent right (or self-standing claim) is not even a harm, Thesis GE will not apply at all. In case this is true, let me both deliberately extend the scope of Thesis GE and create an extension of the term "harm," calling it "harm′" to cover these other cases.]

To consider this issue let us examine the "Position" (P) cases:

(P1) John holds first place in his field. He has a right to the position only so long as he proves himself the best in his field, but no right to it otherwise. Jane enters in another competition in the course of which she freely does something, without a prior intention, which distracts John. Because of this he loses his position, though Jane herself does not win it.

(P2) John holds first place in his field. Jane doesn't give him the minute aid he needs to train against competition because she is busy competing in another competition. [(P1) like (P2) should not involve any intention that the event which causes John to lose occur.] So he loses his position to his competitor.

Permissible Harm'

As noted above, some might argue that we can harm someone only if we violate his rights in some way. If this were so, then Jane would not harm John in case (P1), since he has no independent right or self-standing claim to the position, and no right not to be competed with. If Jane does not harm John in (P1), then Thesis GE could not imply that aiding in (P2) was required.

However, it seems to me that if Jane has not harmed John, strictly speaking, in (P1), she at least makes him worse off than he would otherwise have been, through causing him to lose what he already had and would have continued to have but for her actions. Let us, therefore, say that she harms' John. Nevertheless, it is not impermissible for Jane to harm' in (P1), so we cannot use an extension of Thesis GE to conclude that Jane must aid in (P2).

Harming' Worse than Not Aiding

In some cases harming' may also be worse than not aiding, even though it is permissible, and does not interfere with any independent rights or self-standing claims. This involves a denial of extended-Thesis GE. For example:

(P3) Jim is Jane's best friend. She enters race A while Jim enters race B. She foresees that in racing she will voluntarily do something, without prior intention, that will distract John and cause him to lose.

(P4) John is Jane's best friend. She enters race A, and is busy training for it, so she cannot help John train for race B. She knows he will therefore lose race B.

Putting oneself in a position that harms a friend seems to involve doing a worse thing than not aiding him in (P4), even though it is not impermissible. If P3 is an instance of harming', then an instance of harming' can be worse than an instance of not aiding, when its being worse is neither dependent on anyone's rights or self-standing claims being violated, nor tied to the impermissibility of harming'.

If it is sometimes permissible to harm' when there is no independent right or self-standing claim to the thing lost, is it always permissible? A clue to the answer to this question comes from considering whether it is always wrong to deprive someone of something to which he *has* an independent right.

Loss of That to Which One Has an Independent Right

For example, suppose someone owns a restaurant and this gives him an independent right to it. If I enter into business competition with him as a result of which he loses his restaurant, and he is worse off than he would have been, have I harmed him? I have harmed him because I caused him to lose something to which he *had* an independent right. I did this by causing him to lose his independent right to the restaurant.[14] Yet it is (commonly thought) to be permissible to do this by competition. So, even when an independent right to something exists, it is possible that harming will not always be wrong. We could not, therefore, use Thesis GE to derive my competitor's right to have me aid him when he is about to lose the independent right to his restaurant through competition with someone else.

I might also permissibly do something that caused someone to lose that to which he continued to have an independent right. For example, I could, by mutual consent, engage in a rope-cutting contest with my competitor during which I cut the rope that holds his floating restaurant to shore. (He did not consent to my doing this particular act, but it was a side-effect of my doing that to which he did consent.) Here again I could be said to have harmed him.

Incorrect Means of Causing the Loss

I could not, however, set fire to my competitor's restaurant. That is, certain means of depriving him of that to which he has an independent right are prohibited. This leads us to note that even in cases in which there is no independent right to the thing lost, it is commonly thought to be wrong to make use of certain means to get the thing away. For example, if an apple has been dropped into my lap by the wind and I am not nutritionally needy, it seems that I have no independent right or self-standing claim to the apple. (If it rolls out of my lap onto the ground, I could not say to someone who goes to pick it up that it belongs to me because it first fell in my lap.) Yet for you to grab it away from me when it is in my lap would commonly be thought to be wrong (even if I have no great need for the apple when you have no great need for it). It is thought to be wrong because it is thought to violate my right against physical interference.

Likewise, sometimes we can harm′ someone by depriving him of what is important to him (as opposed to the apple), but to which he has no independent right or self-standing claim. This can be wrong because it violates an independent right not to be physically interfered with; for example, if we grabbed away a fortune that had fallen into someone's lap.

But we do not transgress this right not to be physically interfered with in not aiding. Yet, if Thesis GE were true, it may seem that physically interfering with someone should not have significance in itself. The claim that it has significance in itself seems to be part of what Thesis E and Thesis GE (insofar as it is derived from Thesis E) must deny.

Deriving a Radical Implication: The Right to Be Given That to Which One Has No Independent Right or Self-standing Claim

Suppose Thesis GE did entail this denial, but Thesis GE's supporters still thought it wrong to grab away something valuable that has fallen into my lap.

Then Thesis GE might be taken to imply, at minimum, that it is equally wrong not to help someone *retain* a valuable thing to which he has no independent right or self-standing claim, at least if the costs involved in doing so are no greater than are required to avoid interfering with him so that he loses what he has (in equalized contexts). We might go further than this: If already having or having had something is of no significance, then Thesis GE might be taken to imply that it is equally wrong not to give someone a valuable thing to which he has no independent right or self-standing claim, at least if the costs involved in doing so are no greater than are required to avoid interfering with him so that he loses what he has.

Here, at last, we seem to have derived a very radical implication from Thesis GE, one that could not be derived by using the Election or Grocery cases. It amounts to the claim that it would be wrong not to give me the same sort of thing that it would be wrong to take away by interfering with someone. For it would seem that if it is often wrong to cause someone to lose that to which he has no independent right or self-standing claim, if Thesis GE is true *and* implies that physical interference is not a crucial difference between harming and not aiding, *and* if already having had something does not matter, it follows that we will be morally required to give or help someone retain that to which he has no independent right or self-standing claim.

Factoring In Physical Intrusion

This apparent implication of Thesis GE is radical, since it amounts to the right to be given or the duty to give almost anything at all. I do not believe we can accept such a view. If we do not accept it, does this mean that Theses GE and E are false? One route to saving the theses while still rejecting the "radical conclusion" begins by agreeing that physical interference is not a separate negative factor when the loss at stake is life itself (or any physical loss much larger than interference alone). However, with lesser harms', physical interference does indeed stand out as a separate negative factor. In such cases, harming' and not aiding are only morally equivalent per se when harm' does not come about through physical interference. For example, harm' comes about through computer transfer of "manna from Heaven," supposing the manna to have "fallen into" my bank account rather than my lap,[15] to someone else's account. Then the claim based on Thesis GE, which avoids the radical conclusion, would be as follows: harming' someone by depriving him of something to which he has no independent right or self-standing claim without violating his independent right not to be physically interfered with is *not* wrong. Therefore, the comparable case of not aiding is also *not* wrong.

This claim, however, does not seem to be true in all cases. For example, even if we factor out physical intrusion, maliciously or even thoughtlessly doing what will deprive someone of a benefit to which he has no independent right or self-standing claim will often be morally wrong.[16] If Thesis GE is true, therefore, there should be comparable cases in which refusing to give someone things to which he has no independent right or self-standing claim will be wrong. The same effort will have to be made to provide these things as would be necessary to avoid taking them away. This means that Thesis GE *has* been used to derive at least some moral pressure to provide some goods to which there was no independent right or self-standing claim.

This implication, however, is less radical than the implications derived from a *refusal* to take account of physical interference as a separate negative element. This is because *more effort* would probably be required of us to avoid such physical interference than to avoid nonintrusive harming' (other things equal). Therefore, more effort would be required to aid in comparable cases, assuming the truth of Thesis GE. Still, many cases of nonintrusive removal of goods to which someone has no independent right or self-standing claim will be permissible, and so, likewise, should the refusal to aid in comparable cases.

Denying the Radical Conclusion without Factoring in Physical Interference

Is there a way to retain Theses E and GE without deriving the right to be given everything that it would be wrong to take from someone by physical interference, *but without taking special account of physical interference in harming'* when it itself is greater than the loss sustained by way of it? One way is to emphasize the distinction between (1) a victim's being harmed' by suffering a loss through another person's physical interference, and (2) a victim's suffering the same loss without another's physical interference, rather than emphasizing the distinction between (3) an agent's interfering with someone and (4) his not interfering. Someone could suffer the loss of a fortune that fell into his lap either by someone else's taking it or by its blowing away. [This is the distinction between (1) and (2).] He could suffer the first loss if *we* take his fortune away or if we do not help prevent *someone else* from taking his fortune away. [This is the distinction between (3) and (4).]

The version of Thesis GE that denies that it ever matters whether we physically interfere cannot take seriously the distinction between (3) and (4), but it might allow for a distinction between (1) and (2). That is, it could be considered worse for a victim to be harmed by a person's interference than to be harmed by natural causes, but not worse for an agent to interfere with someone than to let him be interfered with. There is a distinction in the locus of the problem: in the victim or in the agent.

Emphasizing the first distinction would lead proponents of Thesis GE to claim that, *if* it is impermissible to take away a fortune that has fallen into someone's lap, then we must help someone against an aggressor who will take away the fortune that has fallen into his lap. Proponents of Thesis GE would not be committed to the more far-reaching conclusion that one had to help someone get or retain a fortune to which he had no independent right (or self-standing claim) and that the wind was blowing away from him. This analysis would seem to reconnect the wrongness of harming with the violation of a right. Not aiding, like harming, would be wrong only *when the indepen-*

dent right not to be physically interfered with was being violated by someone. (There would be a harming, not merely a harming'.) Harmings or harmings' where there is no intrusion on the victim would still be equivalent to not aiding, involving nonintrusive loss of entities to which the victim had no independent right or self-standing claim. (Im)permissibility of the first would imply (im)permissibility of the latter.

Helping Prevent Physical Interference versus Simple Losses

Notice, however, that such a view is in some conflict with the original analysis given of cases (B1)/(B2) (in chapters 1 and 2), (E1)/(E2), and (G1)/(G2), and further reduces the significance of Thesis GE. For example, we shall be driven to the conclusion that intrusively taking away money in (E1) is morally equivalent to not giving minute aid to help my opponent regain his thousand dollars *if* someone else took it from him, but not if a natural disaster caused its loss. This further reduces the significance of Thesis GE, since it reduces the number of cases in which a harming and not aiding are morally equivalent. (Further, if Thesis GE has the same structure as Thesis E, killing someone would be morally equivalent only to letting a person be *killed*, not to letting him die of natural causes. This conclusion could be avoided if intrusion had independent significance only when losses less than it were at stake.)

Denying the Radical Conclusion by Extending Independent Rights

There is a third alternative for those supporters of Theses E and GE who do not want to abandon the theses but also refuse to accept the radical conclusion. It is to claim that once a person has something, he has an independent right to it. Therefore, all cases of depriving someone who already has something involve infringing independent rights to the object that would be lost. Then the fortune dropped into someone's lap by the wind is something to which the person has an independent right once it is in his lap. The fortune lying on the ground that you fail to give to someone, however, is not one to which he has an independent right. So, its being wrong to do what causes the loss of the fortune would not imply that it was wrong to fail to give someone a fortune lying on the ground.

Such an account of the origin of an independent right, however, seems dubious. This solution, furthermore, would commit proponents of Thesis GE to the view that when it is wrong to do what causes the loss of the fortune, it is just as wrong to refuse to help someone *retain* such a fortune about to be blown out of his lap by the wind. For in this last case, there would also be an independent right to the fortune.

We could reach the same results for cases by resurrecting the significance of "already had something": Instead of saying that one acquires an independent right to whatever one has, one simply attributes significance to having (or having had) something already. Then we should not take it away, but need only be committed by Thesis GE to helping someone retain (or get back) what he already had.

However, attributing this significance to "already had" still seems dubious, especially since nonintrusive taking (e.g., by computer) of such items often seems permissible.

Summary

In summary, none of the plausible alternatives to the radical implication of Theses E and GE seems to involve the impermissibility of harming in the absence of an independent right or self-standing claim of some sort, nor to plausibly imply the derivation via Thesis GE of a right or duty to aid in the absence of an independent right or self-standing claim. However, some new duties (or more weakly, moral pressure) to provide goods to which there was no independent right or self-standing claim do seem derivable via Thesis GE. This is so if we either consider interference per se to be a negative factor which we must both not produce and not allow to be produced, or agree that nonintrusively depriving someone of goods to which he has no independent right or self-standing claim is sometimes wrong.

VI

Other Factors to Equalize: Responsibility for Harm and Capacity for Self-help

I have considered one type of problem with deriving rights and duties from the supposed truth of Theses E and GE. I now wish to briefly point out another problem that might arise in deriving such rights and duties. This problem again stems from failing to apply Thesis GE to properly C-equalized cases. This failure may sometimes be due to focusing too much on cases typically used in the discussion of Thesis E.

In the typical case of letting die [e.g., (B2)], help is needed by someone who cannot help himself, and who is not himself responsible for his predicament. But it is also possible to be called on to save the life of someone who could help himself, or even could help himself but has chosen not to. Furthermore, one could be called on to aid someone who is responsible for endangering his own life. Likewise, in non–life-and-death aiding cases, you may be called on to aid someone who cannot help himself or someone who can, someone who is or is not responsible for his needing aid. So it is a mistake to argue from the (supposed) truth of Thesis GE to the equivalence of depriving someone of something and not helping someone get something that he could have got by himself, chose not to, and was even responsible for not having.

Yet some might be eager to use Thesis GE to argue for duties to provide people with certain things quite independently of first finding out whether people could provide themselves with these things. Many demands for social rights seem to be phrased in a similar way. For example, a universal right to health care would imply that even the very rich who could afford to pay for themselves have a right to other's (or the state's) assistance. The emphasis in these proposals is on there being certain things that people should not even have to think about providing for themselves. (I do not wish to deny that this might be true. Just that we cannot discover this by using Thesis GE and C-equalized cases.) An alternative to such a view is to have conditional rights that take the form: If you can't provide for yourself, and (possibly) have not caused a loss to yourself, then you have a right to aid.

The possibility that at least sometimes people should try to help themselves before acquiring a right to help from others, raises an additional point. The responsibility that people might have to help themselves before relying on the efforts of bystanders, even when their predicament was not their own fault, does not seem matched by an equal responsibility to protect themselves from being harmed by agents. It is the potentially harmful agents who must carry more of the responsibility for protecting people from being harmed. In other words, a person who can, might be obliged to pay the price for an improvement in his prospects, even when this only involves return to his ex ante condition, but a potential harmer in C-equalized cases must pay the price to avoid making someone's condition worse than it would have been without the agent's involvement. Suppose this is so not merely because it is more convenient or effective for the respective first parties to watch over themselves. Then it would indicate that our duties to avoid harming and not aiding in C-equalized cases differ relative to the measure of what the victim of each of these must do in comparison with the harmer and non-aider. (That is, we measure the strength of x and y by seeing how they compare with z.) This, in turn, would mean that Thesis GE is wrong.

NOTES

1. Bruce Russell has said in "On the Relative Strictness of Positive and Negative Duties," reprinted in Bonnie Steinbock (ed.), *Killing and Letting Die* (Englewood Cliffs, N.J.: Prentice-Hall, 1979): "Given the above account of the distinction between killing and letting die, I will argue that the distinction has no moral significance in itself . . . If the above account is broadened by replacing 'killed,' 'dies,' etc. by appropriate versions of 'harmed,' 'is harmed,' etc., an account of the distinction between *harming* and *allowing harm* will result" (p. 217). I am not sure that this commits Russell to the claim that *harming* and *not* aiding are morally equivalent. This is because, as will be emphasized in the text, there may be a difference between not aiding someone to get or keep something and not aiding someone who will be harmed if we do not aid. (As noted in chapter 1, the killing/letting-die distinction is different from the killing/letting be killed distinction, since the person we let die may not be killed but die of natural causes.) Though the thesis about harming/not aiding and even harming/allowing harm are in some ways broader than Thesis E, they are in one respect narrower. The moral equivalence of killing and letting die applies even to cases in which being killed or let

die is not bad for one; the other theses apply only to cases where it is bad for a person not to be aided or (by definition) to be harmed.

2. I shall speak of Thesis E and Thesis GE, with the understanding that I am interested in the strong varieties of these, unless otherwise noted.

3. Robert Nozick, *Anarchy, State and Utopia* (New York: Basic Books, 1974).

4. Russell ("On the Relative Strictness . . . ") who, as noted, speaks of the moral equivalence of harming and allowing harm to occur (rather than harming and not aiding), says, p. 231, n. 24: "These considerations can form the basis of an argument for moving beyond what Robert Nozick has called 'the minimal state.' If individuals have positive as well as negative rights . . . then there is no reason the state should not protect those as well."

5. In *The Realm of Rights* (Cambridge, Mass.: Harvard University Press, 1990), p. 161. My discussion of Thomson here borrows from my "Non-consequentialism, the Person as an End-in-Itself and the Significance of Status," *Philosophy & Public Affairs* 21(4) (Fall 1992): 354–89.

6. For more on this, see chapter 12.

7. Cases in which we do not help someone get or retain what is independently his (but not ones in which we do not help someone get or retain what is *not* independently his) may coincide with ones in which we let someone be harmed. That is, it may be that it is only if someone loses something to which he has an independent right that he is harmed, rather than merely made worse off. If this is true, it supports Russell's use of words described in note 1, that if Thesis E is true then harming and allowing harm (rather than not aiding) are the potentially morally equivalent pair. On the other hand "harm" may connote only the involvement of an agent, not accident.

8. It might be said that these are special cases involving an opponent, and so we should not expect the equivalence of harming and not aiding. But if the strong version of Thesis GE is really true, it should be so in all standardly equalized cases (except those involving particular desires or attitudes), as described in earlier chapters. If Thesis GE is false, by contrast, this does not mean all standardly equalized harm and not-aid cases must be morally unequal, though they may be, as (B1) and (B2) may be.

9. The "or" is not exclusive. There may well be in-between cases. For example, suppose my opponent needs to have my minute aid to collect pledges that have been made to him. Is the money pledged his or not his, and is this case closer to (E2) or to (E3)? The point I am concerned to make is that some not-aiding cases clearly involve something to which someone is thought to have an independent right and some clearly do not. The fact that unclear cases exist does not mean that clear cases will not differ morally.

10. In cases typically used to convince us of the truth of Thesis E, those who harm or don't aid do so to promote bad ends, for example, the death of an innocent child in (B1) and (B2). But it is possible that those who harm and don't aid are promoting good causes or at least seeking to defeat a bad one. For example, suppose that my political opponent is a Nazi. I would refuse to aid his bad cause, a cause of which I disapprove, at least if it is not a question of helping him to get that to which he has an independent right. It is not clear, however, that I may steal his campaign funds. In such cases, the derivation of a right to new campaign funds based on a right not to have his funds stolen seems especially dubious. (Notice that we might well consider it impermissible to refuse lifesaving aid to the Nazi politician, just as we would think it wrong to kill him. This would be in keeping with the view that the to-be-pledged campaign funds are not his, but his life is, and we might refuse aid so that he loses the former but not the latter. It may, of course, just depend on our thinking that it is very

important to him that he go on living and this, if not his Nazi political goal, is a legitimate desire.) Furthermore, if we need not even help the Nazi get back funds to which he has an independent right, though we cannot take the same thing away (even by nonintrusive means), we would seem to have a counterexample to the truth of Thesis GE.

It was suggested by an editor of *Philosophy & Public Affairs* that the derivation of the right or duty to aid even when there is no independent right is not more dubious in the Nazi case. It is only that how we ought to respond to the right (e.g., whether we must respect it or whether infringement is justified) differs from those cases in which bad ends are not involved. I, on the contrary, believe that the Nazi has no right to aid helping him get that to which he has no independent right, and I have no duty to give it. However, suppose this were not true. If the right or duty to aid would be more easily infringeable than his right not to be harmed (and my duty not to harm), then some distinction between the strenuousness of these rights (or duties) based on the distinction between harming and not aiding or between that to which we have an independent right and that to which we have no independent right would still remain.

11. For the most part, I believe proponents of Theses E and GE do not deny ordinary views about that to which one has an independent right. Indeed, they typically use these ordinary views about what it is wrong to take away from people (in the harming cases) in order to derive rights to aid necessary to keep these things.

12. It is true that he will never have had the time alive that he will have if he is saved. But in this sense helping someone regain his $1,000 would also involve giving him something he has never had, since he will then have the $1,000 for a time period in which he has never had it before.

13. This assumes that we ignore any additional pain that comes from being without things to which they have become habituated.

14. The distinction between losing one's right to something and losing that to which one has a right was emphasized to me by an editor of *Philosophy & Public Affairs*.

15. I owe this example to Bruce Ackerman.

16. This point was emphasized to me by Derek Parfit. He believes it is true when depriving someone of the benefit will serve neither the agent's nor others' interests.

II

6

The Trolley Problem

Having considered differences between killing and letting die, I will now consider in more detail when it is permitted to kill and when it is not, and what principle describes these conditions of permissibility. In particular, I shall be concerned with whether and when it is permissible to kill some, who are innocent, nonthreatening individuals, rather than let others die.[1] So we continue our discussion of killing and letting die in another guise. I will first consider a case in which non-consequentialists commonly hold that we may not kill. I will then consider some proposals that non-consequentialists have made for the permissibility of killing some to save others in another type of case.

In preface, let me make two points. First, in discussing the issues of this chapter I will *assume* that it is morally preferable that a greater rather than a smaller number of people survive, even when the greater and smaller groups consist of totally different members.[2] Second, in this chapter my aim is to account for what I take to be "common sense" moral intuitions, putting to one side for the time being the question of whether these intuitions are ultimately correct. (Of course, how we account for the intuitions may play a part in deciding whether they are correct.)

A Non-consequentialist Position

It is a common view of those who criticize pure consequentialism in ethics that ordinarily it is impermissible to kill one person in order to save others. (It is common to refer to those who do not think best consequences alone determine the right act as non-consequentialists.) For example, a non-consequentialist will typically think that we may not chop up one innocent, nonthreatening person, who would not otherwise die, in order to transplant his organs into a greater number of people merely because this alone will save their lives. (Call this the Transplant Case.) I believe, as a non-consequentialist, that we may not do this even if *we* were responsible for the five being in danger. For example, suppose we set a bomb that will kill the five people and then we have a change of heart. If the only way to save our five victims and avoid our becoming their killer is to do the transplant from an innocent bystander, we may not do so.[3]

Killing in the Transplant Case

John Harris has argued *for* the permissibility of killing the one person in the Transplant Case.[4] (Indeed, he argues for the permissibility of killing one to save two, not merely a great number.) I wish to consider Harris' arguments, in part, because some of them are closely connected to the topic of earlier chapters—whether there is a moral difference between killing and letting die. In addition, I wish to consider whether even a non-consequentialist should endorse killing in some variations of the Transplant Case.[5]

Harris presents several arguments to support killing in the Transplant Case. First, the scheme that involves doing so would, he says, maximize utility. We can also see that if each person were ignorant of who would need a transplant and who would be used to save others, each would maximize his expected probability of living if we used a system that permitted killing. Such a scheme would be rational for each from an insurance point of view. In addition, Harris argues, there are important symmetries in the positions of any one who will be killed to save others and the people they will be used to save. For example, he claims, we cannot say that the one would be killed, but the many would only be let die if we do not act. For it is only if we beg the question of the permissibility of killing the one (by assuming it is impermissible), that we can say we will have *only let the others die*. This is because if someone, or more precisely a doctor, fails to do what it is permissible for her to do to save patients, she will have, at least morally speaking, "as good as killed them."

Harris's Symmetries

Putting to one side for later discussion the problem of a self-interested insurance scheme, let us consider the argument from symmetry. I believe it rests on a confusion between the moral and non-moral sense of "killing." Suppose it were true that if it were permissible to kill the one person, and we did not, we would, morally speaking, have "as good as killed" the others. But we could call not helping the larger number killing, in this moral sense, only if we had already agreed that it was permissible to kill the one to save them. There is a different, non-moral sense of killing which does not depend on any view of what is morally permissible. This allows us to say that we would be killing the single person if we chopped him up, whether this is permissible or not. In a comparable non-moral sense, we would let the others die if we did not kill the one to save them. Then, there would be an asymmetry in the position of the one and the position of the many.

We might further argue that there is moral significance to the non-moral difference between killing and letting die. We might argue—as we have in earlier chapters—that where these terms are used in a sense that does not presuppose a pro or con position on whether the letting die is morally speaking a "killing," the difference between killing and letting die makes a moral difference. If there were such a moral difference, then *this* might lead to the conclusion that it was morally wrong to kill the one. This conclusion, in turn, would block the claim that letting the others die was, morally speaking, a killing.

Other Symmetries

Harris argues for other symmetries in the position of the one and the many; for example, he argues that if the one acts in self-defense as he repels our attack on him, the many would also act in self-defense if they kill the one to save themselves. But here again it seems there is an asymmetry: The one would repel those who attack him, but the many would not be under attack from the one they kill. This is because he does not make their situation worse than it would have been given the working out of the illness that already confronted them (and which he did not give them). He just does not make their situation better. The same is not true if they attack him; they do make him worse off than he would have been just through the working out of events independently of them.

Harris claims that if the one would be killed to save the many, the many would be sacrificed *to save* him if we do not kill him. Several responses are available here. First, the one, unlike the many, is facing no fatal threat already (unless we decide to kill him) from which he must be saved. Leaving him alone results in his being alive, but that is not *saving* him from anything. So, *a fortiori*, the five are not sacrificed *to save* him.

However, we can imagine cases in which the one *is* already under a fatal threat, and needs organs to survive. If we do not kill him (or deliberately let him die by omitting some simple act) in order to save the many, the organs of the many will become available after they die to save the one. This is because the one is in need of organs, but *unaided* he will die a bit later in time than the many if they are not aided.[6] (Call this Transplant II.) About this case, it can be argued that if we do not kill the one because it is morally impermissible to kill him, then we do not let the many die merely *in order* to save the one. This will be true even if we use their organs to save him after their death. By contrast, if we killed the one, we would be killing him (or letting him die with the intent that he die) merely in order to save the many. Therefore, even in this case, there is an asymmetry that may help justify our not killing the one.

The Permissibility of Killing to Ensure Equal Chances for Life

However, I wish to disagree that this argument shows we may not kill the one in Transplant II. I suggest that it is impermissible to kill the one *only if* he would have gone on living for a significant period of time without the organs of the many. This is because killing would then deprive him of something significant that he would have had independently of imposing on the many, solely to save them. (This is true in the original Transplant Case.) By contrast, if the five die unaided, they would not die solely to save him, and they would not lose something significant that they would have independently of his aid, since without his aid they will have no life. (We here emphasize the definitional properties of letting die emphasized in earlier chapters.)

In Transplant II (and variants), however, it may be consistent with overall nonconsequentialist views to kill the one. This may be a case in which, speaking generally, *fairness* should override the considerations based on separateness and independence of persons that motivate the prohibition on killing. For example, imagine a case involving only two people (Transplant III). Suppose Smith will die in four hours unless he receives the organs of Jones who will die in two hours.[7] My suggestion for this case[8] is that the distinction between killing Smith and letting Jones die, and between intending Smith's death and merely foreseeing Jones's death, are *not* the morally determining factors in this case.

Smith, independently of aid from Jones's organs, will live only two hours past Jones. Suppose this is an *intrinsically* insignificant time period (except perhaps as a buffer to death) and insignificant to Smith.[9] It is also insignificant *relative* to the total years Jones or Smith might live if he got the other's organs. The two hours are (suppose) valuable to Smith only *instrumentally*, as a way of outliving Jones, so that he may get Jones's organs. I suggest the following: If the large advantage brought to one person by an intrinsically insignificant period of time involves benefiting from losses incurred by another person who could himself greatly benefit from losses to the first person if there were no such advantage to having the intrinsically insignificant period of time, then equal concern for each should lead us to toss a coin to see whether Jones will be left to die or Smith will be killed.

The same result might be achieved if we recognized Jones's right to determine whether his organs shall be used by Smith after Jones's death. He might refuse to let them be used, in order to make it in Smith's interest to agree to a coin toss. For with the coin toss, Smith will have at least some chance of getting a significant additional life span. However, Jones might want to do this even if Smith could live a year independently of Jones's organs, and Jones's organs could be preserved and given to Smith at the end of the year. It is not clear that it would be morally permissible of Jones to strike such a bargain in these circumstances. This is because a year is an intrinsically significant period of life. It is only when the intrinsic worth of what Smith stands to lose if he is killed, what he would have had independently of the use of Jones's organs, is small, that this policy of tossing a coin could be morally appropriate. For suppose Smith could live another five years before needing the organs Jones will lose in two hours. (Let us assume we could keep the organs for five years before use.) Then if Smith *lost* the coin toss with Jones, we would, in killing him, be depriving him of a significant period of life that he would have had independently of any benefit from Jones's organs. This would be wrong. (An exception to this moral inappropriateness could arise if, while not under pressure of any threat from Jones not to let Smith use his organs, Smith voluntarily wishes to equalize his and Jones's chances by permitting us to kill him if he loses a coin toss.)

The Survival Lottery

This policy, permitting killing in cases like Transplant III, makes use of a crucial notion introduced in our discussion of killing and letting die, that is, the distinction between what is had independently of imposing versus what is had only by imposing on others. It strikes a balance between a prohibition on killing Smith and a survival lottery between two people. In the survival lottery, we may select from among healthy people the one who will die to save another or who will share a fair risk of death with another. Here, even people who would lose significant periods of life that they would have had independently of the assistance of organs, are involved in decisions about who lives and dies. Indeed, Harris would object to using only the sick who would die shortly without aid anyway to save others. This is because he thinks that excluding the healthy from those who could be killed to save others would favor the lucky (healthy) over the unlucky (already sick). The position I describe distinguishes between the luck of those who can turn an intrinsically insignificant advantage of a few hours into the possibility of benefiting greatly from the loss of others (who themselves might otherwise benefit), and the luck of those who can have an intrinsically significant advantage independently of such others. On the view I propose, the latter should *not* be killed to obtain organs for the sick, while it might be permissible to kill the former. Furthermore, it might be permissible to kill them even if this does not maximize lives saved but only represents giving equal chances for survival to two different people. (Although here, the understandable reluctance to cause death when no additional lives are saved may stand in the way of giving any equal chances other than "Nature" gave in her lottery as to who dies sooner.)

Killing to Save a Greater Number

Suppose we return to cases like Transplant II which involve a difference in numbers; there are five Joneses (who, unaided, will die sooner) and one Smith. At the very least, my proposal suggests that we should toss a coin to decide whether to kill Smith to save the several Joneses. One additional question is whether we should give the side with the greater number a greater chance to win than the single Smith has. I suggest that we should not, when the use of Smith's own organs are at stake. This contrasts with what we should do when organs not belonging to him stand to be distributed in order to aid either the Joneses or Smith. This is because our proposal which permits some killing aims to eliminate one sort of inequality which stems from luck, when the question is who will benefit from whose organs. The aim is not to save the maximum number of lives. Giving each person an equal chance to benefit from the other side (by tossing a coin between the side with the five and the side with one) seems correct, therefore. So if the Joneses win, Smith is killed, and if Smith wins, he gets the Joneses' organs after their deaths.

Suppose that there was one Jones and five Smiths, that is, one person whose organs could service five people each of whom will live slightly longer than he will, but five whose organs could also benefit the one person. Here, I believe, counting numbers of lives that can be saved is permitted. In this case, the desire to eliminate natural luck would not override a killing/letting-die distinction. So a coin toss would not be in order. This is true even where the five Smiths will each live only two hours longer than Jones independently of Jones's organs. That is, suppose we would have to kill all five—perhaps Jones needs one organ from each Smith—if we are to save Jones. The moral weight against killing can combine with the numbers of lives at stake to make us refuse to correct for the Smiths' luck in having an extra two hours. If Jones needed only one Smith organ (and so only one would have to be killed), the fact that more lives will be lost if Jones wins combined with the negative weight of killing would still argue against a coin toss.

Respect

Finally, I return to another of Harris's arguments for the Transplant Case. Harris claims that there is no sense to saying that we may not kill Smith because we respect persons, since we show disrespect for even more people if we do *not* save the lives of a greater number. Again, he argues, the one and the many will be in symmetrical positions, either the one or the many will be disrespected.

One way to answer this point, I believe, is by showing that if we do *not* kill the one the five will still be respected, rather than disrespected. One way to argue this is to say that the same respect shown to the one in not permitting him to be killed is, by the very denial of permission, shown to the five. The reason for this is that insofar as we do not kill the one in this case because we think a person is the sort of entity that may not be used in such a way, the five persons are also recognized as the sort of entity that may not be so used. Of course they will die because they and the one are all creatures of this sort, but this does not alter the fact that refusing to kill the one shows respect for *all* the people. (We shall return to discuss this type of argument in greater detail in chapter 10.)[10]

Redirection Cases

I have argued that it is sometimes permissible to kill an innocent as a means to saving others (or perhaps even to save another), even though this involves no redirection of a threat. That is not a commonly accepted view. However, a case which is commonly accepted by non-consequentialists as an exception to the impermissibility of killing one innocent person to save others was first discussed by Philippa Foot as the Trolley Case.[11] In her case a conductor is in charge of a runaway trolley headed toward killing five people on the right-hand track, but he is physically able to redirect the trolley onto the left-hand track, foreseeing with certainty that it will kill one person (call him Joe) immovably seated there.

If a non-consequentialist believes that it is morally permissible to switch the trolley in this case (and variants of it), she will need a justification that distinguishes what is done here from what would be impermissible in the Transplant Case. That is, she will have to reconcile the apparently conflicting intuitions that it is permissible to redirect fatal threats away from a greater number of people to a lesser number of people, but that it is not morally permissible to kill one innocent healthy person in order to transplant his organs into a greater number of people when this alone will save their lives. Otherwise, she will fall victim to the claim that non-consequentialism is incoherent.

One of my aims in the next chapter is to offer a proposal that accounts for the distinction a non-consequentialist may draw between the (original) Transplant and Trolley Cases, as well as for distinctions between impermissible and permissible harming in other cases I will describe. Although this proposal will, I hope, account for the distinctions in that it points out on what general lines the distinctions are made, this is not necessarily the same as justifying our drawing the lines in this way. However, I shall *also* canvas some possible justifications.

In addition, I hope to show that this proposal makes clear that cases (like the Trolley Case) in which we redirect threats share a fundamental moral structure with cases that do *not* involve redirection of threats at all. I also hope to show that my proposal groups together cases that are ordinarily distinguished on grounds emphasized by the Doctrine of Double Effect (henceforth DDE). Indeed, I will argue that the account that gives a consistent interpretation of cases considered in this chapter suggests that the DDE draws the boundaries of permissible harming too narrowly in one respect and too broadly in another. We will, therefore, discuss the DDE in greater detail.

The order of discussion will be as follows: In the remaining part of this chapter, I will try to show how previous proposals on the Trolley Problem fail, in order to motivate presentation of a new proposal. Doing this will involve presenting a series of cases that are intimately related to those already described. These cases, however, will be important not only as counterexamples to previous proposals. Intuitive responses to the cases will form the basis for the new proposal. Therefore, although the rest of the chapter may seem entirely critical, it is in fact part of the development of a positive proposal. In the next chapter I will present the positive proposal that claims to account for the intuitive responses to all these cases.

OTHER PROPOSALS

Foot's Proposal

Philippa Foot argues[12] that a Transplant Case involves *killing* one (whom we assume faces no threat to the life he has independently of the potential transplanter and those he would be killed to save) to *save* five. So this is a choice between *killing* and *letting die*. By contrast the Trolley Case involves a choice between *killing* one and *killing* five. These cases help show, she claims, that the duty not to kill is stronger than the duty to aid, but that when we face a choice between killing many and killing fewer, we should kill the fewer.

Judith Thomson criticized Foot's solution by noting[13] that *any bystander* may choose to turn a runaway trolley to save the five, even though *he* would not kill the five if he failed to turn the trolley. (Call this the Bystander Case.) This shows that we may redirect the trolley and thereby *kill* someone rather than *let* the five *die*.

This need not show, I believe, that we are indifferent as between killing and letting die, since we might not be indifferent between turning the trolley to one, or letting it go on when it will hit only *one*. Likewise we may prefer that a very strong wind turn the trolley away from the five, and toward the one rather than ourselves redirecting it. It is also worth noting that Foot's version of the Trolley Case, in which the trolley is *already* headed to the five and must be redirected, involves *the conductor* himself choosing between *letting the five die* and *killing* the one. This is true even though if he lets the five die he will be the killer of the five (given that he started the trolley toward them). It is only when the trolley is at a crosspoint (Crosspoint Case) and the conductor must direct it toward one or five that we have a true case of his killing one versus killing five.[14]

Doctrine of Double Effect

Foot emphasized the distinction between killing and letting die as an alternative to placing the sole non-consequentialist emphasis where the DDE places it, that is, on the distinction between intending harm and only foreseeing harm. The DDE says that it is impermissible to bring about lesser harm as an end in itself or as a means to a greater good, but that it is morally permitted (or required) to do a neutral or good act as a means to a greater good, though we foresee lesser harm as a side effect. The DDE is a major principle that has been suggested to account for restrictions on pursuing overall good, the other major principle being the harm/not-aid distinction. (It is also the only type of principle that could, though it needn't, serve as an absolute restriction, since any act has a small probability of causing harm, but one either intends a harm or does not.)

I shall simply assume that if we wanted to defend the DDE it would be in its non-absolutist version allowing for the permissibility of intending harm to the guilty and in self- or other-defense against even moral innocents who are threats. This will eliminate many of the problems of fitting the principle to intuitive responses to cases. I do not deny that work needs to be done to justify these exceptions.

As Shelly Kagan notes[15], it is likely that a correct non-consequentialist theory will require both a harm/not-aid distinction (of some form) and an intention/foresight distinction (of some form). For without the former, the DDE might be taken to imply that I may *omit* to aid, foreseeing a harm to others, *only* if what I wish to do produces a greater good. This implies that I cannot leave someone to die in order to save my child from going blind. (We reach these conclusions by assuming that we are obliged to promote greater good if there is no intended harm.) I should note that the DDE, as I understand it, does not locate what is wrong in the actions it prohibits simply in an agent's state of mind or simply in the fact that harm to a person leads causally to an end. The DDE, I believe, is concerned with whether an agent's being in a certain state of mind will result in his harming or allowing harm as a means or an end.

Some versions of the Trolley Problem help make this clear. We can imagine a case[16]—call it Track Trolley—in which the trolley is headed toward killing five people and it can be redirected toward one, but the mechanism that redirects it works as follows: We can now push a button that will direct the trolley, when it later gets to a crosspoint, toward where one person now sits. This button also controls the track on which the one person sits and has the effect of moving the track so that the one person is pushed into the path of the trolley as it heads toward the five *before* the trolley reaches the crosspoint. The weight of the one person is in fact what stops the trolley, though we know that if he weren't there to stop it, the trolley would be redirected, once it gets to the crosspoint, onto the track away from the five. In this case, it is permissible to turn the trolley and, I believe, we do so without even running afoul of the DDE. For, though we foresee that the person will, in fact, be the cause of the trolley's stopping on account of what we do, we do not intend this.

In the Transplant Case, the DDE would emphasize that we intend the one person's death as a means to saving the five, but in the Trolley Case we only foresee it as a side effect of saving the five. Foot argued against the adequacy of the DDE by showing that, contrary to what it claims, it is *not* always permissible to produce the best overall outcome when we do so without intending lesser harm as a means or end. She claimed it would be impermissible to use a gas in an operation to save five lives if we knew the gas would seep into a neighboring room killing one, even though we didn't intend harm to the one (Operation Case). Her position on this point, I believe, is confirmed by a case in which a runaway trolley will kill five people unless we explode a grenade that (we foresee) will kill an innocent bystander as a side effect. (Call this the Grenade Case.) I believe non-consequentialists should agree that it is impermissible to explode the grenade. This means that the DDE is not sufficient to explain the Trolley Case.

Furthermore, merely foreseen, but not intended, involvements that produce unintended harm can be wrong. Suppose I merely foresee that I will lightly bump into someone on my way to rescue five people, but I also foresee that this bump will cause a bruise that causes him to bleed to death, since he is a hemophiliac. It seems impermissible for me to proceed.

Nevertheless, many foreseen harms will be permissible—for example, bombing the munitions plant in time of war even if it results in bruising hemophiliac children next door. But notice that it may make a difference whether the children die (or are involved in a way that leads to their death) as a direct result of our goal being achieved (the munitions plant blowing up) or as a direct result of our means to this end (our exploding bombs). The latter may be harder to justify than the former.

It is possible that with all the attention given to the intention–foresight distinction, the distinction between harm as the foreseen side effect of the means to our end and harm as the foreseen side effect of our end itself has been incorrectly ignored. For example, Foot argues against the DDE by insisting that it is not permissible to use a gas in surgery to save five people when it will seep next door, causing a merely foreseen death of one. However, Foot does not notice that it *is* permissible to use a gas to perform surgery on the five when the result is that the five once again breathe normally, even though their breathing now changes the movement of air so that fatal germs that previously were safely closeted reach a person in the next room (Operation II). That is, when the lesser harm is the result of a greater good (the five breathing), it is permissible to bring it about, but not when it is itself a means to a good or the side effect of a means to the good. (But note that if the five themselves breathe out the germs, and so are innocent threats to those who are not abnormally susceptible to disease, it will not be permissible to save them, I believe.) These distinctions must be accounted for by a correct principle of permissible and impermissible killing.

Additional problems for the analysis that the DDE offers are presented by the following case, which shows that the DDE is not necessary to an explanation of the Trolley Case. Suppose that a trolley that we redirect away from five people will come rolling back to kill them anyway (because of the slope of the land) unless it crushes and so sticks to Joe (Prevented Return Case). In this case we *foresee* that the trolley will kill and crush Joe, but we *also intend* its killing and crushing him as a means to saving the five, for we would not turn the trolley at all unless we believed this would happen.

Judith Thomson presents a similar case. Her Loop Case involves a trolley headed toward five being redirected to a branch that itself also leads to the five. What stops the redirected trolley from hitting the five anyway is the presence of a fat man on that branch whose great weight stops the trolley. Thomson believes it is permissible to turn the trolley in this case, though we here require the impact on the fat man as the means to stopping the trolley.[17]

Revisionism and the DDE (I)

Notice the difference between the Prevented Return and the Loop Cases: In the former, only the person on the track to which we redirect keeps the trolley from hitting the five; the five do not similarly keep the trolley from hitting the one. In the Loop Case, the five's being hit would keep the trolley from hitting the fat man just as he keeps it from hitting them, for if they were not there the trolley would eventually hit him. I believe redirection is permissible in both cases, but it is interesting to note that Michael Costa, who bases his analysis of the Trolley Problem on a modified version of the DDE,[18] believes that redirection is permissible only in the Loop Case. This is because, he thinks, we are permitted to intend harm to the one when harm to the five would save the one otherwise.

Costa presents a revision of the traditional DDE in that (1) he claims that not intending harm as a means or end is part of a sufficient condition for a permissible act, but not a necessary one, and (2) he describes cases traditionally thought to involve intending neutral means as involving intending intrinsically bad means to a good end. It is (1) that accounts for his view on Loop versus Prevented Return. He contends that we do intend harm (or use) of the one in Loop to save the five, but this is permissible because harm to the five is what would help save the one. This position diverges from DDE not only in permitting intending harm sometimes, but also because it permits intending harm when the one would be the beneficiary of even *unintended* harm to (or use of) the five. [This is like the view that we may kill someone who then loses only life he is getting from the loss others suffer, in order that we may rescue them from suffering losses that threaten them.] But note that it will not always be permissible to kill the one when the five have the unintended effect of helping save him. Recall the Blood Case (p. 47). Also, if five people shield one by standing in front of an oncoming bullet, it may be permissible for them to move but not to take the one and move him in front of the bullet. (May they shoot him while he is still behind them if this is necessary for them to move?) So it might still be that redirection has some significance for permissibility that putting the one in front of the threat does not have. Furthermore, since in the Loop Case this special significance is present even when intending harm *also* seems to be present, the special significance of redirection in the more basic types of redirection cases is perhaps not merely a matter of *not* intending harm as a means, contrary to what Costa suggests.

In addition, I have suggested that redirection is permissible even in the Prevented Return Case, where the five would not protect the one, so the person we would harm is not the beneficiary of harm to the others.

Costa's second revision of the DDE, as noted, concerns what is in itself a bad rather than a neutral means. This revision is relevant to the view that the DDE is a sufficient condition for permissibility. For if it were sufficient, would it not be permissible, as Foot argued, to set off a gas to save five even though, as a side effect of the gas, one person would be killed? And yet this is morally wrong. The DDE, as traditionally understood, claims that setting off a gas is a neutral event in itself that can have good and bad consequences, as in the Operation Case. (Likewise, dropping bombs is a neutral event that can have good and bad consequences. It supposedly contrasts with dropping bombs on innocents, which is intrinsically bad, though it may have good consequences.) Turning a trolley may also be seen as in itself neutral with good and bad consequences.

By contrast, Costa argues that starting the gas is to introduce a new threat in the world and this is an intrinsically bad means, even to a good result. However, redirecting an already existent threat for good reason is *not*, he

claims, an intrinsically bad means to a good end. Hence, the DDE, reinter-
preted, is sufficient to rule out the Operation Case. Let us consider this proposal.

First, Costa speaks of the incorrectness of starting a new threat as a means
(or end). But consider the Lazy Susan Case: The five are seated on a Lazy
Susan Device toward which the trolley is headed. We push the Lazy Susan as
the means of getting them away from a trolley which cannot itself be redirected; this causes the Lazy Susan to ram into a bystander, killing him. In this
case, turning the Lazy Susan has a bad effect, and it seems that it is as much a
new threat, introduced because we wish to save the five, as the gas is in the
Operation Case. Yet it is permissible, I believe, to turn the Lazy Susan. (This
case is important because it shows we may save the five by means other
than redirection.) Why is creating a new threat sometimes permissible and
sometimes not permissible?

Costa says that turning the trolley for sufficient reasons (i.e., when it leads
to greater good) is not in itself a bad. Here the judgment of (the supposed)
intrinsic badness of a means is made to depend on an evaluation of *both* the
good and evil it produces. If we turned the trolley to five when it posed a
threat to only one, that is, when it did not lead to greater good, presumably
Costa would say that turning the trolley is in itself bad. Here again the judgment of the intrinsic badness of the means is made to rest on an evaluation of
the good versus the bad that the means produces. One question this prompts
is why the means that involve a new threat are evaluated only by reference to
their bad and not also by reference to their good effects, whereas the redirection of threats, which is not always in itself considered all right, seems to be
judged by both its good *and* bad effects. A second, even more basic, question
is how this revisionist procedure of judging the *intrinsic* nature of the means
by its effect(s) is correct at all for judging by effects is the denial of intrinsic
(dis)value.

Despite these problems, I believe that one proposed solution to the Trolley
Problem,[19] which bears some resemblance to Costa's proposal, may be correct. Two of its major components are that (1) harm may permissibly come
about as a result of greater good (in particular, intended greater good), and
that (2) there are fine dividing line(s) between what is intrinsically neutral and
what is intrinsically good, in virtue of the difference between describing events
in terms of causal effects and independent of such effects. The first point leads
to the conclusion that turning the Lazy Susan with the five on it that kills the
one involves a means to saving five which is perceived as so closely connected
with the good of saving the five people, that the fact that it is also a new threat
is tolerable. The second point leads to the conclusion that turning the trolley,
which is a threat because of the causal effect it would have on the five, is very
intimately connected to the good of five being saved because their being safe
is *not* a causal effect of the turning. That is, their being safe is not another
event from the turning away of the trolley that would have killed the five. By
contrast, the good effect of the gas in the Operation Case is a causal effect.
Hence, the bad effect of the trolley (and the Lazy Susan) is seen as the result

of something very close to being an intrinsically good means, whereas the bad effect of the gas is not seen as the bad effect of what is (seen as) being very close to an intrinsic good.

My hypothesis is that Costa sees the gas and its bad effect as an intrinsic evil in part because he groups the bad effect with a neutral event, but the bad effect of the trolley is grouped with something that is close to a good in itself (when the trolley moves away from the five). The good effect of the gas is not included in the evaluation of the "intrinsic" quality of the means, unlike the good effect of the redirected trolley, because the good effect of the gas (but not of the trolley) is a causal effect. (I shall elaborate on these points in chapter 7).

Revisionism and the DDE (II)

Jonathan Bennett has argued that a common test for the distinction between intending and foreseeing harm fails to distinguish accurately between cases we think are morally different.[20] Consider a particular case: In waging a war, we supposedly intend the deaths that result from terror bombing. However, when we bomb a munitions plant, we only foresee the unavoidable deaths of children next door in a hospital. The distinction between intending harm and foreseeing it is supposed to account for a moral difference between the cases. A test of whether the deaths are intended or foreseen is whether we would proceed with the bombing anyway if we knew that the deaths would *not* occur. The test says that we do not proceed if we intend the deaths. The standard answer, therefore, is that we would proceed with munitions bombing, not with terror bombing, if the deaths did not occur. But, Bennett notes, the aim we have in terror bombing is achieved even if the people only seem to be dead until the war is over. Therefore, we will continue to bomb if the people seem to be dead, even if they remain alive. Hence, we may intend only that death seems to be present in terror bombing even when we foresee that the people will really die. If we only foresee the death in both munitions and terror bombings, the distinction between intending harm and foreseeing harm cannot account for the supposed moral difference between the cases.

One response to Bennett[21] is to argue that we intend death as a means to "seeming dead." Or we might revise the DDE so that it prohibits intending any intrusion on a person that one foresees will lead to serious harm to him. Warren Quinn goes further, arguing against Bennett by revising the DDE to prohibit intending any involvement (intrusive or not) that leads to harm.[22] In terror, not munitions, bombing we intend such involvement.

One problem with both these revisions is that they do not capture what, I believe, was the original point of the DDE: that we not *intend* the serious harm (something evil) itself. Nevertheless, how do these revisions relate to the Trolley Problem? It is true we do not intend involvement with or intrusion on the single person to whom we redirect the trolley, but neither do we intend these on the bystander in the Operation Case, and yet action there is prohibited. Why, then, is turning the Trolley not prohibited?

Quinn on the Trolley

We have already considered Quinn's views specifically directed to the Trolley Problem, but it is worth repeating them at this point. Warren Quinn offers what might be considered a version of Foot's proposal.[23] He believes that in the Trolley Case we face a choice between what he calls positive agency in the death of the five or positive agency in the death of the one, and so it is best to minimize the numbers of deaths. Most crucially, he claims that this is true even in Thomson's Bystander Case. In the Transplant Case we would face positive agency in the death of the one versus negative agency in the death of the five, and avoiding positive agency takes precedence.

According to Quinn, there are two different conditions for positive agency in the death of someone: (i) performing an action that harms, and (ii) omitting to perform an act that could save a life, because we intend an event that we foresee will cause death. (This does not mean that we intend that harm or death come to the person. We need not even intend his involvement in our purposes when we foresee harm to him as a result.) Negative agency is allowing an event that harms another to occur without an intention that the event occur.

Since the Bystander Case is a permissible trolley turning, it is crucial to see how Quinn's analysis works for this case. If the case is, in fact, a case where not turning would involve negative versus positive agency, and avoiding positive agency takes precedence over negative agency, then we will need some theory besides the permissibility of minimizing deaths from positive agency to account for the permissibility of turning the trolley.

If we turn a trolley headed toward five from them onto a track where it will kill one, we are engaged in positive agency via action [positive agency (i)] that results in harm. Quinn believes that if we allow the trolley to go toward the five, it can only be because we intend to save the one (from the trolley we would otherwise turn). This means that we intend that the trolley *not* head in his direction. The trolley can go in only two directions: toward the one or toward the five. Quinn seems to think that intending that it not go toward the one involves intending that it go toward the five, thus harming them. This does not involve intending the death of the five, or even intending the event of the trolley going over the spot where the five are. But it does involve intending that the trolley be at least away from the one whence we foresee that it will head toward the five. This would be positive agency (ii), since we would be intentionally allowing an event to occur (the trolley moving away from the one), foreseeing that it will lead to harm. Quinn concludes that since we would be involved in positive agency whatever we did, we might as well see to it that the smaller number of people are killed.

One question to ask about Quinn's analysis of the Trolley Problem is whether, if we do not turn the trolley from the five, we are intending that the one not be hit. We may only be intending that we not do the hitting, whether or not we think it morally wrong to do so, and this is not to intend an event that leads to harm to the five. But suppose that Quinn's analysis of what we intend is correct. Then, on his account of it, we would be involved in positive agency either way we go. But there is a rather striking implication of this analysis. Suppose a trolley is headed toward one person (not five) and can be redirected toward five. On Quinn's mode of analysis, turning the trolley toward the five would be positive agency by action. Suppose positive agency by inaction—positive agency (ii)—is morally equivalent to positive agency by action. (Quinn's solution to the Trolley Problem depends on this supposition, as well as on his analysis of what we do in not turning the trolley from five to one.) *Then, turning the trolley from one toward five is morally equivalent to refusing to turn the trolley from five toward one.*

I believe that these behaviors are clearly not morally equivalent. It is our duty not to turn the trolley from one toward five; it would be permissible to shoot someone who was going to do it. It is not, however, obligatory to turn the trolley from five toward one; it is only permissible. Further, we could hardly damage someone severely if this alone would cause him to turn the trolley from five toward one. I believe that these cases again suggest that there is a moral difference between altering the world we all share so that it presents a threat—positive agency (i)—to an innocent, nonthreatening person who exists independently of imposition on us, and allowing threats already in place to proceed, even if we intend an event that is part of their proceeding.

I conclude that Quinn offers no solution to the Trolley Problem, either because his theory of positive agency is wrong or because he misdescribes what occurs in the case.[24]

Montmarquet

James Montmarquet suggests[25] that it is permissible to redirect the trolley (a) when we thereby maximize overall good, (b) because the person to whom we redirect is already under a threat of death, and (c) we redirect an already existent threat, we do not create a new one. According to Montmarquet, (b) is true because one person is already threatened by X if either (1) he will die of X if we do nothing to interfere or (2) X can be redirected so as to kill him. I have described Montmarquet's proposal using his notion of "already threatened," but he sometimes speaks of the permissibility of turning the trolley because the single person is "co-threatened." The latter, but not the former, notion requires that the single person already be threatened by the *same* threat as threatens the five. Notice that (b) does not say that the single person will necessarily *die* of the threat that already exists to him. Montmarquet also argues that once someone is under a threat, it is permissible to create a *new threat* to him that is no worse than the one he faces already, in order to promote the greater good.

Contra Montmarquet's Condition (a)

I believe each element of Montmarquet's proposal is incorrect. Contra (a): Maximizing overall good will not always justify redirection [even if (b) and

(c) are true]. For example, suppose a trolley is headed toward killing Joe. We can redirect it onto another track where it will kill *five* people; so according to Montmarquet, these five are already threatened by the trolley. If we redirect to the five, the vibrations through the earth will divert a fatal bomb away from *twenty* people one mile away, thus maximizing overall good. (Call this the Stop-the-Bomb Case.) I believe that a non-consequentialist who has intuitions that killing in the Trolley Case is permissible should nevertheless find killing in the Stop-the-Bomb case *impermissible*.

Likewise, suppose a trolley is headed toward a surgeon who, if not hit by the trolley, can and will save the lives of seven other people dying of a disease. We are physically able to redirect this trolley so that it kills five people instead of the surgeon. If we do so we will help save the greater number of lives. (Notice that this would be true even if the trolley would only cause the surgeon, toward whom it is originally headed, a headache which prevents him from operating.) I believe turning the trolley in this case (call it the Surgeon Trolley Case) is impermissible.

Next, suppose the fatal trolley is headed toward the five. If redirected, it will kill Joe and, despite anything we do, come rolling back to kill the five anyway. However, miraculously, the trolley's passing back over the track on which Joe is has an effect on the earth beneath, turning it into a serum that can bring the five (but not Joe) back to life (call this the Miracle Case). I do not believe turning the trolley is permitted in this case (which serves as a useful contrast to the Prevented Return Case).

Suppose the trolley is headed toward five people and can be redirected toward one. If it is redirected it will cause vibrations that stop a bomb about to kill another twenty people a mile away. However, a second trolley is headed toward the original five, so that even if we redirect the first trolley, the second will kill them (the Double Threat Case). Redirecting is impermissible in this case, I believe, even though it would maximize the numbers saved.

As a final point against (a), suppose we may choose whether to send the trolley toward one person on the left track or toward one person on the right track. Either way one person will die, but if we send the trolley to the right track some beautiful flowers that give many people pleasure will also be destroyed (Flower Case). I claim that increasing overall good by saving the flowers should play no role in deciding along which track to send the trolley. The extra utility is irrelevant; so I refer to a Principle of Irrelevant Utility as operating in such cases. [26]

Suppose, however, that the trolley is already headed toward one person. If it hits him, he will fall over a ledge, crushing twenty people beneath (Ledge Case). In this case, it is permissible to turn the trolley toward the five. In the Ledge Case the trolley does not *directly* threaten the twenty (that is, they will not die of *it*), but the trolley will cause the event that causes their death. They will be *killed* as a result of the trolley's movement and their number should be counted against those who will be killed by the trolley's redirection.

Contra Montmarquet's Condition (b)

It is not true that when the trolley is headed to the five, Joe is already threatened by it. In general, if a threat can be redirected to someone this does not mean he is *already* threatened by it. (So clause (2) of Montmarquet's analysis of "already threatened" is wrong.) If he were already threatened by it, then if I am in New York, I am already threatened by a plane headed toward five people in New Jersey, because the plane could be redirected toward me (and not other people in many other places).[27] If it were permissible to redirect to Joe, or I was seriously tempted to redirect to him, he might be said to be under a threat that I would redirect the trolley. But this does not mean he is already under a threat of the trolley itself. Furthermore if the *permissibility* of redirecting made it true that he *is* already threatened, it would be impossible to *derive* the permissibility of redirecting from the fact that he is already threatened. Only clause (1) of Montmarquet's analysis of "already threatened" correctly represents our ordinary understanding of this concept. In sum, the fact that if the trolley is redirected, Joe will die of a threat that *already existed* does not mean that Joe was already threatened by that threat.

Even if the single person were already under a threat of death, would this mean it was permissible to kill him? Suppose Joe were dying of a disease, but we could easily cure it. (In this case Joe is already threatened, but he is not co-threatened by the same threat.) Would it be permissible in this case to turn the trolley on him only because he had the disease? I believe not. Suppose someone is already threatened (in the ordinary, non-Montmarquetian sense) with a deadly disease, but we cannot redirect the trolley toward him. Montmarquet's analysis implies that we could kill this one person (by creating a new threat to him) rather than give him the simple cure for his disease, if this would maximize lives saved. (Suppose, for example, that only the weight of his dead body falling on a button will stop the trolley, so we shoot him.) Furthermore, using Montmarquet's unique sense of "already threatened," it would be permissible to kill, by a newly created threat, *two people* in New York to whom it would be possible to redirect a trolley now heading toward one person in New Jersey, if this would save the lives of five people who will be the victims of a totally different fatal threat. (This is because the two are already threatened with death on his view, and we maximize the number of lives saved if we harm them.) Yet killing, in both these cases, in fact, seems impermissible.

Already Threatened versus Already Doomed

In deciding whether it is permissible to kill someone because he is already threatened with death, it is crucial, I believe, to consider whether the person is already *doomed* to die by the threat to him. If he is doomed, killing him to save others is more likely to be permissible than when he is already threatened but need not die unless we do not aid him or kill him. Yet, there are also cases in which many people are already co-threatened (that is, threatened by the same threat coming toward them), but not all are certainly doomed. Suppose, for example, someone will either kill all six people *or* five of six people, but no one knows which five. None of the six people is doomed so far as we know. Yet here we may also doom a lesser number, even with a new threat, to save one or more. This is because either (a) those who will then die are no worse off than they would have been anyway, or (b) the (subjective) probability of each person's dying was reduced by our plan which, in fact, killed someone who would not otherwise have died. (Likewise, if we kill one person of a group of six to stop a threat that would have killed five of the six, the person who dies had a 5/6 chance originally of dying, so far as we know, which we reduced to 1/6 assuming we randomly chose whether to kill him or another.) In these cases, the only way to diminish one threat is to introduce another. This is also true if someone is dying of a disease and we have a chance of eliminating it only by giving him a drug that runs a lesser risk of killing him.

However, as argued above, Joe on one trolley track is *not* already threatened or co-threatened with the five in any ordinary senses of these notions. If we may, nevertheless, redirect the trolley to him, Montmarquet's claim that we may not make things worse for people than they already were, is not true.

Already Involved

While not a component of Montmarquet's views, a view related to his is (in my experience) a frequent response of those who first come across the trolley problem. That view is that the difference between the Trolley and Transplant Cases with respect to the permissibility of killing rests on the (supposed) fact that the one in Trolley is *already involved* while the one in Transplant is a mere bystander, uninvolved. One must not drag in the uninvolved. Sometimes the focus is on the fact that the one is on a track like the five, and this means he is involved. But this cannot be right, since if the trolley could be redirected onto a bridge where one stands, this too would be permissible, and if a plane headed to five in New Jersey could only be redirected so that it was foreseen that it would kill one person in California, this too would be permissible. One is tempted to say, therefore, that we cannot deduce what is permissible from a prior, non-moral criterion of involvement, but rather, anyone is involved to whom it is permissible to redirect a trolley. That is, there is no non-moral notion of involvement which can serve as grounds for permissibility.

One reason for criticizing this view and investigating further the notions of involved/uninvolved is suggested by the following case: A trolley headed toward five can physically be redirected toward one, but if it hits the one it will travel onto a track where two more will be killed, *unless* we redirect it again so that it only kills another one. (Call this the Tree–Trolley Case.)[28] (We could

construct more complex versions of the same idea — more branches upon the tree, where we can continue to maximize total numbers of lives saved by further acts of redirection.)

My view is that it is correct to sense a difference in the positions of 1_A and 1_B. In some way (which I would hope to clarify) 1_B is more of an uninvolved bystander than is 1_A, and there is, appropriately, greater reluctance to turn the trolley onto 1_B than onto 1_A. A possible analysis of this case is as follows: Whatever conditions make it permissible to redirect onto 1_A (but not to kill in Transplant) can be described independently of the idea that 1_A is involved versus uninvolved. This will not be a crucial notion in the explanation of the permissibility of redirection of threats. That 1_A is involved will be the *conclusion* of an explanation of why it is permissible to redirect to him. But we, as agents who did not initiate the trolley threat by our acts, have not made it the case that 1_A is the legitimate victim of a permissible redirection which he is. 1_B (unlike 1_A), before we act to redirect away from the five, is not physically in a position to be the legitimate object of a permissible redirection. Whatever relation 1_A bears to the five such that we may redirect toward him, he stands in that relation independent of any act of ours, though, of course, he is not threatened actively without an act of ours. But 1_B comes to stand in that same relation to the two people on the second set of branches only after we have redirected the trolley away from the five. In that sense, he, but not 1_A, was originally uninvolved; that is, *without our act 1_A, but not 1_B, was in a position such that a permissible redirection would harm him*. Notice that the two on the second branch are in the same situation as 1_A, "involved," as I have analyzed this notion. Because of our act the two will be harmed as the (foreseen) consequence of one particular redirection which is permitted. We do not need an additional *permissibility link* — the permissibility of another redirection — to justify their being killed. Why then the greater reluctance to say merely that whatever relation justifies the first redirection also justifies the second one? The proposed short answer is that an agent should not involve those originally uninvolved, in this heavily theoretical sense of uninvolved.

Consider an analogy: If I *permissibly* leave my door unlocked, the consequences of this is that someone is likely to be tempted to break in and then I may *permissibly* shoot him. I have had something to do with making someone who was, without my act, not eligible for being killed, eligible. If even permissibly killing someone is a bad relation to be in, then one might want to review (a) whether it is in fact permissible to leave one's door open, or (b) if one does leave one's door open, whether one should be permitted to kill the burglar. One might, I believe, understand if an agent refused to turn the trolley from the two to the one on the second branch, since he will then harm someone whom *he would be responsible* for having made into an involved party (i.e., someone toward whom it is permissible to redirect), even though it is only through permissible acts that 1_B becomes involved.

Notice that this analysis of the Tree-Trolley Case does not focus on the fact that the agent would be called upon to *act* more than once or on the burden of this when each act will kill. For it is possible to imagine a case in which the trolley is programmed at once both to go toward the one and, if it proceeds further, take every further turn that minimizes deaths. The qualms for an agent of engaging in such deliberate programming (i.e., when the lay of the land would require deliberate redirection to minimize lives lost) would be the same as the qualms at redirecting by a separate act onto a person eligible for redirection (i.e., the object of a new permissibility link that comes about) only because of our prior act. The conclusion of this argument is that a person is involved if (it has been first shown that) it is permissible to harm him; and the permissibility of harming him may just be a matter of (a) the *relation in which he stands to others or the type of acts one would have to perform in harming him, and (b) whether he stands in such a relation or is susceptible to such acts independently of the acts (even permissible ones) of the agent.*

There are problems with this proposal, however. First, there are cases in which the agent who would permissibly turn the trolley *is* responsible for 1_A being susceptible to a redirection. Most notably this is true of someone who started the trolley onto the five and who like a bystander, may permissibly turn the trolley. But consider also the following Construction Case. I am a bystander and see a trolley headed to the five. I see another person also watching. There is no track onto which to redirect the trolley. But I am an engineer and very quickly I construct a side track in the only way possible. Unforunately, it leads right toward that other bystander. I redirect the trolley. It seems permissible for me to build the track and redirect the trolley, even though the bystander could not have been the victim of a redirection without my actions. Why may I redirect here but not toward 1_B in Tree-Trolley?

It is possible that someone responsible for impermissibly creating a threat may have an obligation to keep on redirecting though someone who enters the story by permissibly making possible a redirection bears a different relation to each subsequent person who thereby becomes susceptible to redirection. I leave the Tree-Trolley case for future discussion.

Contra Montmarquet's Condition (c): Creating New Threats to Unthreatened People

I have argued that a person is not already threatened simply because a trolley can be redirected to him, and yet we can kill him by redirecting the trolley. But it is also true that we may kill someone to whom it is not possible to redirect the trolley, and who is facing *no* other threat. This means that, contra Montmarquet's (c), it is permissible to *create a totally new threat* that will kill someone to whom we could not have redirected the trolley or any other threat.

For example, suppose a fatal trolley is headed toward five people. It cannot be redirected, but we can stop it by means that harm no one. However, its stopping alters the air pressure in the area, causing an avalanche of heretofore stable rocks to fall on an innocent bystander (Rockslide Case). I believe we may stop the trolley. It might be objected to the Rockslide Case that because the rockslide is an effect of the trolley's stopping, it is part of the trolley threat and hence not totally new.[29]

We can imagine other cases, however. For example, in Rockslide II five are seated on a (publicly owned) Lazy Susan that is threatened by a trolley which cannot be redirected. We can save the five by turning the Lazy Susan, but this creates a rockslide, killing a bystander. In another case (already discussed), a fatal trolley is headed toward five people and *cannot* be redirected. However, the five are located on one side of a large (publicly owned) Lazy Susan device which could be turned so that the five are out of harm's way. The Lazy Susan is turned and it rams into a bystander. In another variant, the five who are threatened by the trolley sit on the Lazy Susan and on the other side of the Lazy Susan sits Joe. There is no threat on its way to him and none that can be redirected from the threatening path it already follows. When we move the Lazy Susan, Joe will unavoidably be pushed into a brick wall and die (Lazy Susan Case II). Alternatively, he might be pushed into the trolley and die of the same threat the five were threatened with (Lazy Susan III). I suggest that, in the last two cases, it may be permissible to turn the Lazy Susan. In the last two cases, notice, we move a person into a threat rather than a threat into a person, but it makes no moral difference. Furthermore, if it is permissible to turn the Lazy Susan, it is so for the same reasons that make it permissible to redirect the trolley; this helps us see that redirection *is not morally crucial to redirection cases*. Redirection cases can be seen as part of a larger class not necessarily involving redirection of a threat. Among cases in this class, I believe, are cases in which we must choose between sending threat A to person X or threat B to person Y, where sending one threat just is the flip side of not sending the other threat. These cases are like squeezing a closed tube of paint — pushing down in one area (on one threat) causes paint (threats new or old) to pop up in another area.

Lazy Susan Cases II and III also serve as answers to those who think it is permissible to turn the trolley only because we are doing something to the threat itself; here we do something to the Lazy Susan rather than to the threat. As noted we also send a person to the threat rather than vice versa.[30]

We could make the same point *less* controversially by recalling that turning the Lazy Susan with only the five on it can cause a rockslide that kills the bystander a mile away (Rockslide Case II). Or, alternatively, that the turning Lazy Susan itself, with only the five on it, smashes Joe, who is a bystander (Lazy Susan Case). If there is any doubt that it is permissible to turn in Lazy Susan II and III — because we must move Joe rather than move something into him — there is none in these cases.

However, it does seem impermissible to press a switch that turns the trolley headed toward the five onto a track where no one sits, if the switch also controls another trolley that has been inactive till now.[31] When the switch is pressed it not only turns the first trolley away from the five, but also turns the second trolley toward one person on another track (Switch Case). In this case, the switch action (a means to turning the trolley), not the first trolley, produces a new threat; I suggest it is not permissible to redirect the first trolley.

It seems then that, contra Montmarquet's condition (c), we may sometimes harm someone previously unthreatened with a *newly created threat*, and not only by the redirection of an old threat nor by the redirection of people into the old threat [as would happen if the turning Lazy Susan moved Joe into the position formerly occupied by the five and so facing the trolley (Lazy Susan III)].

Thomson's Proposals

Judith Thomson has made three proposals for the Trolley Problem. I shall comment only briefly on her earlier work and discuss her two latest positions in detail. [32] Her first proposal was, essentially, that it is permissible to *redistribute* a threat from a greater to a lesser number, if we are doing something *to* the threat, not to a person (even if a person dies as a consequence). In the Lazy Susan Case, however, we do not *redistribute* a threat. The one does not die of it, as the five would have; he dies of the Lazy Susan. In Lazy Susan III, we do redistribute the threat, but in neither case do we prevent deaths by doing something *to* the threat, rather we do something to the Lazy Susan. What may remain true is that we minimize the number of lives lost, and do not do something to the person who dies. But, as Thomson herself asks, [33] if we kill someone do we not do something *to* him?

Thomson's second proposal also, essentially, has two parts: It is permissible for even a bystander to redirect the trolley from killing five to killing one (Joe) because he makes what threatens the greater number threaten the lesser number (redistribution claim), and not *by* means which in themselves infringe on serious rights of the one person. Therefore, it is not permissible to kill in the Transplant Case because we would have to save the greater number *by* violating a significant right of the one. We save the many *by* chopping one man up. Likewise, it is not permissible to throw someone off a bridge so that his body will fall in the way of the trolley and stop it in its path (Bridge Case). This is because we would stop the trolley *by* violating the right of the person not to be toppled in front of trains. But killing in the Trolley Case is permissible because (1) Joe dies of the same (redistributed) threat that would have killed the five and (2) we bring about the better state *by* redirecting a trolley, and this in itself does not violate Joe's significant rights. Joe dies *as a result* of the redirection of the trolley, and we do something *to* him (kill him) not just *to* the trolley, but we do not save the five *by* (killing) doing this to him. Thomson further suggests a test for the permissibility of what we do: If it would have been permissible for us to do what we are doing had Joe not been present, this indicates that we act permissibly in doing the same thing even if he is present.

Criticisms of the Second Proposal

Contrary to Thomson's first claim, it is permissible to direct a threat away from the greater number even when the one that is killed as a result dies of a totally different threat from the one that threatened the five. Thomson's insistence that the one be threatened by what threatened the five conflicts with the permissibility of redirecting in the Rockslide I and II and with turning the Lazy Susan in Lazy Susan Cases I and II. These cases emphasize, contra Thomson, the non-redistributive character of permissible redirection and non-redirection.

Whether the few and the many would die from the *same* threat is not decisive, so that part of Thomson's proposal is wrong. Let us, therefore, consider the second part of her claim, that we not save the many by infringing on someone else's serious rights.

Several questions can be raised for this claim, I believe. Suppose the trolley is a very valuable antique that *belongs to Joe* (Owned-Trolley Case). Ordinarily it would be a significant violation of Joe's rights to do something to *his* trolley, but, presumably, if it is a threat to five people, it *is* permissible to redirect it, even toward Joe himself, and this even if he and it will be destroyed in the process. Here we save the five *by* turning Joe's trolley and so *by* infringing on a significant right of his. How does this gibe with Thomson's theory? Perhaps it is enough to say that where one's property is a threat, there is no infringement in manipulating it.

Thomson herself introduces another case and asks why, by her criterion, it is not permissible to wiggle a publicly owned bridge—this in itself violates no right of Joe's—in order to topple Joe off it so that he will fall before the trolley, stopping it from reaching the five (Wiggle-the-Bridge Case I). Thomson argues that this is not permissible because we *require* Joe's being in front of the trolley (a serious infringement of his rights) in order to stop the trolley, and this amounts to stopping the trolley *by* violating his rights. However, in another case that we have considered, the Prevented Return Case, harm to Joe is similarly *required* in order to save the five. Yet it was permissible to turn the trolley. (Recall that the same was true of Thomson's Loop Case.) There also seem to be cases in which it is impermissible to help the five though we would not help them *by* infringing on the significant rights of others. Suppose wiggling the bridge itself stopped the trolley headed to the five. However, wiggling had the foreseen side effect of toppling Joe to his death. This effect is not required to stop the trolley. Wiggling the bridge seems impermissible (Wiggle-the-Bridge II). Likewise, it would be impermissible to set off a grenade in the Grenade Case (p. 151).

Thomson's first solution to the Trolley Problem avoided some of these problems by arguing that we may distribute the trolley threat by doing something *to* the trolley, rather than to anything else (e.g., a grenade or a bridge). Likewise the proposal that we may not create new threats excludes wiggling the bridge or using the grenade. But these proposals exclude too many permissible cases, for example, turning the Lazy Susan that starts a rockslide.

Finally, suppose infringement of a *minor* right of Joe's is required to stop the trolley. For example, suppose the Lazy Susan on which the five are seated belongs to Joe. Ordinarily, moving it to save the five, even against Joe's wishes, would it itself be a permissible minor infringement of his rights. But when the foreseen consequence of this is that Joe will be smashed by his own turning Lazy Susan, I believe turning becomes impermissible (Lazy Susan IV).

This contrasts with its permissibility when the Lazy Susan is not Joe's and with the permissibility of manipulating *a threat* owned by Joe (Owned Trolley Case). There is what I call a multiplicative, rather than an additive, effect of the fact that the Lazy Susan is Joe's and the fact that it will kill him. It is not that the infringement of his property rights is added to his being killed to make for a total so great that turning becomes impermissible. It is that the death comes about *by* way of the infringement which makes for the impermissibility of turning. The offensiveness is in what is yours, when it is not a threat, being used against your best interests.

In general, I believe, an in-itself minor infringement of a right *can* be a barrier to action when we know that the infringement would lead to greater harm to the person infringed upon. For example, if I know that patting someone on the shoulder very lightly will cause him, because of his rare medical condition, to bleed to death, I may not deliberately pat him.

We seem, therefore, to have cases where we do not stop the trolley "by" significant infringement of someone's rights — either there is no infringement (Grenade Case) or it is minor — and yet it is *impermissible* to stop the trolley. We also have cases where we do stop the trolley by significant infringement of someone's rights (Owned Trolley and Prevented Return Cases) and yet it is permissible to do so.

Even the Lazy Susan Case II may present problems for Thomson's analyses. For, I have argued, a minor infringement of Joe can be a barrier to our acting, if we foresee that it will harm Joe significantly, and moving Joe is a minor infringement. It may be suggested that in Lazy Susan Case II any minor infringement in moving Joe is only foreseen as a consequence of turning the Lazy Susan. By contrast, such an infringement is intended if we push the Lazy Susan Joe owns. Hence, turning is permissible in the former and impermissible in the latter case. This difference may make a moral difference. However, suppose we foresaw that a grenade that would move the trolley would also send out shrapnel that lightly tapped a hemophiliac, causing his death. Here, only a minor intrusion is foreseen, yet its further bad consequences rule out using the grenade, I believe. Why then don't they when we move the Lazy Susan in Lazy Susan II?

Finally, Joe might be under the Lazy Susan, and we know that if we move it, thereby moving the five away from the trolley, we would, *in doing this*, crush him (Crush Case). I believe this is permissible. Crushing him is itself a significant, not a minor, infringement. If turning is crushing and we save by turning, do we save by crushing? (But it may be that we crush him *as a consequence* of turning.)

Thomson and Ex Ante Rationality

In her very important book *The Realm of Rights*, Thomson offers an ex ante rationality account of the permissibility of turning the trolley. She claims that if it is permissible to turn the trolley, this is because there was a time prior to the time when the trolley must be turned to save the five such that it was to the advantage of each of the six at that earlier time that the trolley be turned away from the five at the later time. It was to their advantage because (a) turning the trolley would maximize the survival chances of each, given that each had an equal chance of being in any of the positions on the two tracks and hence a greater chance of being one of the five than of being the one alone, and, furthermore, (b) the death the single person faces is not a worse death than the death the five would face — for example, no more violent or sudden — and (c) there are no other factors — for example, deeply held beliefs about how they should be treated that would, on balance, make it not to the advantage of each to have the trolley turned. Thomson also claims that if these same conditions also held true of a case in which we could cut up one for his organs to save five (the Transplant Case), then it would be permissible to cut up the one to save the five. In our world, it just happens that it is not true that each person does maximize his chances of survival ex ante if we cut up someone for the greater number, since different people are known to have different risks of being in the position of needing such assistance. For example, we know that the presence of disease is affected by lifestyle. The death from being cut up may also be worse than death from natural causes, because it is more sudden, and this makes it overall not to the advantage of each to have a policy of cutting up one to save more. At least, this is what Thomson claims. (It is worth noting that not too long ago we did not know that lifestyle affected the presence of disease, an anesthetized death for transplants is still probably pleasanter than sudden death of the one by trolley, and natural causes may produce as sudden a death as a trolley.)

One of my qualms about Thomson's solution to the Trolley Problem is just that it *does* justify cutting up people in transplant cases in other worlds on the same grounds that turning a trolley is sometimes justified in this world. Thomson does not believe there is necessarily a further morally significant difference between killing the one in a Transplant Case in that other world and what is done to the one in the Trolley Case. A related concern is that Thomson's solution could justify killing in many types of trolley cases in which she herself has argued[34] that killing is impermissible. For example, if an innocent bystander is standing on a bridge over the trolley as it heads toward the five, is it permissible to topple him over in front of the trolley to stop it? The answer seems to be no, even if there was no known greater probability of any given person being on the bridge than being one of the five on the track, and even if being toppled suddenly and hit by the trolley would be no worse a death than being hit by the trolley through redirection of it.

I suggest that the structure of action in the Transplant and Bridge Cases is different from that in the Trolley Problem in a way that would make killing in these cases impermissible even in a world where they shared other features that Thomson thinks made turning a trolley permissible. This means that the correct description of a non-consequentialist constraint on killing will have to make reference to more complex factors than not killing or not intending harm to an innocent person independent of us. Strictly speaking, it is possible that Thomson's account could accommodate this result, because the more complex structure of action could be interpreted as making impermissible killings not to the advantage of each person in a way not noticed by Thomson. [That we would not turn a trolley from killing one person to killing another person, even though the structure of action will be the same as in cases where we turn from five to one, may only show that the distinction between killing and letting die (or between intending the cause of death and not intending it) weighs more than the fact about the structure of action, when no additional lives can be saved. It does not show that an ex ante rationality argument, which depends on the difference in numbers of people, is correct.] This difference in structure shows up in relation to consent. When Thomson's conditions are met, she thinks turning the trolley is permissible without actual consent to an ex ante agreement by the people involved. But my sense is that, at the very least, actual ex ante consent of the potential victim would be required to make killing her permissible in a Transplant Case in any world. Indeed, it may be that if each person understood what was involved in someone's being killed in the manner required in a Transplant Case, when the victim does not *consent at the time* of the killing to being killed, each should not consent ex ante to its being done. Even actual ex ante consent would not validate the killing.

Russell's Proposal

Bruce Russell has offered another proposal[35] in some respects similar to Thomson's second proposal, and comparison of the two may prove useful at this point. As I understand it, Russell has suggested that we may not save lives by *illegitimate plans*. An illegitimate plan is a plan that involves means for saving those lives that either require deaths as causally necessary or involve deaths that are merely side effects of the means we use. Russell's idea of an illegitimate plan for saving people is broader than Thomson's proposal, at least insofar as he disallows also foreseen, not causally required, deaths. Thomson restricts herself to the impermissibility of significant direct intrusions on someone (or something of his) and the impermissibility of indirectly requiring serious infringement of someone's rights as a means to stopping a threat to others. (This is achieving good "by" the significant infringement.)

Employing his criterion, Russell could argue that it is permissible to kill neither in the Transplant Case nor in the Grenade Case. (Thomson's second proposal rules out only the former.) But how then will it be permissible to kill in the Trolley Case? For our plan is to redirect a trolley, foreseeing Joe's death as an absolutely certain side effect. Furthermore, Russell also believes that there is no intrinsic moral difference between killing and letting die. Therefore, if actively *causing* a death without intending the cause of death or the death is not permissible, it would follow that just passing a dying person on the way to saving the five should also be impermissible. But this makes it impossible ever to save some rather than others in situations where we cannot save everyone; there will always be an illegitimate plan. For if we do not rush off to save five, leaving one to die, but instead save the one, we shall be letting the five die as a foreseen side effect instead.[36]

We have now examined various proposals meant to reconcile apparently conflicting intuitions, and found them wanting. In the next chapter I shall offer a new proposal.

NOTES

1. I deal with the issue of when we may kill those who are morally innocent but threats (as well as those who are not threats but innocent beneficiaries of threats) in *Creation and Abortion* (New York: Oxford University Press, 1992).

2. I deal with whether this assumption is justified in *Morality, Mortality*, Vol. 1 (New York: Oxford University Press, 1993).

3. I discuss this sort of case in more detail in chapter 9. The type of case in which the person who would harm the one also will have harmed those he seeks to save was, I believe, first discussed by Alan Zaitchik in "Trammel on Positive and Negative Duties," *Personalist*, 58, Ja '77, pp. 93–96. Judith Thomson also discusses such a case in "The Trolley Problem," *Yale Law Journal* 94 (Spring 1985): 1395–1415.

4. In "The Survival Lottery," reprinted in Bonnie Steinbock (ed.), *Killing and Letting Die* (Englewood Cliffs, N.J.: Prentice-Hall, 1979).

5. This discussion also appears in *Morality, Mortality*, Volume I.

6. Daniel Dinello offers a case in which the one, Jones, would be saved by the sacrifice of *one other* person, Smith. If Smith is not sacrificed, he will be saved by the use of Jones' organs, since Jones will die before Smith does if we do not interfere. See Dinello article, "On Killing and Letting Die," in Steinbock (pp. 128–131).

7. This is Dinello's case.

8. Contrary to Dinello's recommendation.

9. For discussion of buffers to death, see *Morality, Mortality*, Vol. 1.

10. I have also discussed it in "Harming Some to Save Others," *Philosophical Studies* 57(3) (November 1989): 227–60 and in "Non-consequentialism, the Person as an End-in-Itself and the Significance of Status," *Philosophy & Public Affairs* 21(4) (Fall 1992): 354–89.

11. In "The Problem of Abortion and the Doctrine of Double Effect," reprinted in Bonnie Steinbock (ed.), *Killing and Letting Die* (Englewood Cliffs, N.J.: Prentice-Hall, 1979).

12. In "The Problem of Abortion and the Doctrine of Double Effect." We have already described her position in the course of discussing Quinn, in chapter 3, note 10.

13. In "Killing, Letting Die and the Trolley Problem," *The Monist* 59 (1976): 204–17.

14. Judith Thomson also makes this point in "The Trolley Problem."

15. In *The Limits of Morality* (Oxford: Oxford University Press, 1989).

16. The case, but not its interpretation, is owed to Keith De Rose.

17. Thomson's case is in "The Trolley Problem." It might be suggested that in the Prevented Return and Loop Cases we do not intend the death of the one when we turn the trolley, for the following reason: If the single person escapes and so does not stop the trolley, the five will die despite the fact that we turned the trolley. But this is no worse than what would have happened if we had done nothing. So we have no strong interest in the one being hit. If the one does get fatally hit and stops the trolley this is, so to speak, frosting on the cake. At most, we might intend that, if he gets fatally hit, then he should be crushed so that once already dead he serves a useful purpose. This contrasts, it may be said, with what is true in the case which is like Prevented Return

except that, if the trolley is turned away from the five but the single person escapes, two more people will be hurtled in the track to which the trolley will return. In this case, if we turn the trolley and the death of the one does not stop the trolley, seven people will die instead of five. Here we have an interest in the one being hit when we turn the trolley. But, I would argue, despite what has just been said, we also have an interest — if not as strong — in the one being hit in the original Loop and Prevented Return Cases. That we lose nothing if he escapes, does not mean that we are not turning the trolley because we think he will be hit and would refuse to spend the energy to do so if we thought he would not be hit. This at least seems like intending that he be used by being hit. Furthermore, we would not turn the trolley merely foreseeing with certainty that he will be hit without intending that the trolley also stick to and crush him, for if it did not six people would die instead of five.

18. See "The Trolley Problem Revisited," and "Another Trip on the Trolley," in J. M. Fischer and Mark Ravizza (eds.), *Ethics: Problems and Principles* (Harcourt Brace Jovanovich, 1992).

19. Which I first presented in "Harming Some to Save Others."

20. Bennett's discussion is in his "Morality and Consequences." For a further way in which a test for the distinction between intention and foresight fails to distinguish morally different cases, see chapter 7.

21. I suggested such a revision in unpublished work (1982).

22. In "Actions, Intentions, and Consequences: The Doctrine of Double Effect," *Philosophy & Public Affairs*, 18 (Fall 1989): 334–351.

23. In "Actions, Intentions, and Consequences: The Doctrine of Doing and Allowing," *Philosophical Review* 98 (1989): 287–312.

24. Quinn responds to these criticisms in "Reply to Boyle's 'Who is Entitled to Double Effect?'", p. 197 reprinted in Quinn's *Morality and Action* (Cambridge: Cambridge University Press, 1993). The primary points he makes there are, first, that we might shoot the person who refuses to turn a trolley from five to one if he does so intentionally so that it is a case of positive agency. This I deny. Second, he says someone might blamelessly disagree with his theory, and for that reason, refuse to turn, and then, Quinn says, this person shouldn't be shot. But I suggest that if Quinn conceives of this person as still intending that the trolley be going toward the five, but blameless (though incorrect) in thinking this is not wrong, it is not clear why this person may not be shot. We often attack people who are morally excusable but nevertheless doing the wrong thing (e.g., an insane person about to murder someone). Third, Quinn says it is not part of his view to morally equate true negative agency in not turning the trolley from the five and positive agency in turning the trolley to five. In this case, he agrees that we may not shoot the person who does not turn. With this I agree. Quinn does not respond to the point that refusing to turn does not involve an intention that the trolley head on the track to the five.

25. In "Doing Good: The Right and the Wrong Way," *The Journal of Philosophy* (August 1982): 439–55.

26. For further discussion of this principle see *Morality, Mortality*, Vol. 1.

27. Strictly, that I am the only one to whom redirection is possible should not be relevant, since (b) says you are already threatened if a threat can be redirected to you; it does not exclude the possibility that the threat can also be redirected to others in many other directions.

28. This type of case was first presented to me by Professor Robert Bone at Boston University Law School.

29. The question does also arise about Rockslide whether *we* can still be said to *kill* the single person in doing what we do, or whether we can only be said to have caused his death.

30. Warren Quinn suggested that being on or near a Lazy Susan is itself to be already threatened. This result is too broad; it would imply that any area that contains something that could be transformed into a threat is already dangerous, but most areas are like this.

31. I owe this case to an NYU graduate student whose name I have forgotten.

32. The first proposal is in "Killing, Letting Die, and the Trolley Problem," the second is in "The Trolley Problem," and the third is in *The Realm of Rights* (Cambridge, Mass.: Harvard University Press, 1990).

33. In "The Trolley Problem."

34. In "The Trolley Problem."

35. In "On the Relative Strictness of Positive and Negative Duties," reprinted in Bonnie Steinbock (ed.), *Killing and Letting Die* (Englewood Cliffs, N.J.: Prentice-Hall, 1979).

36. Suppose now that Russell tells us that if, no matter what we do, saving some will involve a plan that involves the death of others, it will *then* be permissible to save the greater number. The problem with this is that he would then have no way to distinguish morally between our chopping up one to save five and our spending our time and resources on saving the five at the expense of letting one die. It might be suggested that a reason why we might permissibly do the latter, but not the former, is that, if we spent our resources on the one rather than the five, we would save him by a plan that costs five lives, but, if we merely do not chop up one person, we do *not* have a plan to save his life that costs five lives—after all, he was not under any threat (but ours potentially) from which he needed saving. So there is a moral difference after all. But this difference would disappear if the single person who is not chopped up *is* in need of the organs of the five and will get them if they die. Then Russell's analysis, revised as I have suggested, will again imply that it is indifferent whether we chop the one up to save the five, or use our resources to save the five and let the one die. (Notice that if Russell, in order to deal with these problems, emphasized the wrongness of intending a death rather than merely foreseeing it, but did not reintroduce the moral distinction between killing and letting die, he would not be able to account for its being wrong to kill in the Grenade Case where we only foresee the death of the one.)

7

Harming Some to Save Others

A New Proposal

Let me now present a new proposal—a Principle of Permissible Harm (PPH)—for dealing with the Trolley Problem and related cases. I will describe it first tentatively and as briefly as possible and then elaborate on it. The explanation I propose, to account for the various permissible and impermissible killings we have so far considered (and others as well), is based on the idea that it is permissible for greater good to produce lesser evil.[1] Starting with this idea, we will find it necessary to introduce variations on it, and even suggest a more general principle which encompasses the original idea.

The Principle of Permissible Harm is intended to cover cases involving harm to morally innocent individuals who will not soon die and who are not threats or parts of threats. Its restrictions on harm do not apply to those who are either guilty aggressors or innocent threats or shields. The PPH is being presented as a sufficient condition for permissibility, and as a requirement that, if not met, will result in prima facie impermissibility. We may however be able to justify acts that do not abide by PPH's restrictions by pointing to overriding considerations.[2] Since the core idea has variations, we will come to understand the proposal better by considering its application to cases.

Application to Cases

First, the original Trolley Case: When we turn the trolley away from the five, I believe we conceive of a threat to them being thereby reduced. Insofar as the trolley is already a threat to them, its movement away from the five does not cause another event, which is the five's being saved. Rather the trolley's being further from the five just is their being saved, or their being saved is the flip side of the trolley's being away, given the other facts in the case. This means that the turning of the trolley is conceived of as a good event in itself, or one very intimately and noncausally related to the greater good, which causes the lesser evil of the one being killed. The conclusion is that the redirection is permissible. (This analysis does depend on our conceiving things in this way, but this is not problematic, I think, if we do tend to conceive things in this way.)

The redirection of a trolley already on its way to the five has the same structure, for moral purposes, as the direction of a trolley that is at a crosspoint and must be directed either to the one or to five. In both cases the turning to the one has the noncausal effect of saving the five. This similarity in *moral* structure may account for Montmarquet's view that the one is already under a threat even when the trolley is already headed to the five, since he is as much (or as little) under a threat (relative to the five), *morally* speaking, as the one is (relative to the five) in the other case when we must decide what to do with a trolley that is at a crosspoint. The preferable view in the Crosspoint Case may be that neither the five nor the one is already under the trolley threat, but each side is already under the threat of having that trolley threat directed to it.

Suppose we have a choice, at a crosspoint, between sending one trolley to the five and sending *another* trolley to the one, and must send at least one of the two different threats. In this case, sending one threat to one person *is* not sending the other to the five. What we do, therefore, is as intimately related to the greater good as turning a trolley away from the five was said to be: There is no further event necessary for the five's being free of a threat given the facts of the case, other than our sending one threat to the single person.

Notice that it does not suffice to say that it is permissible to redirect the trolley because we have not created a new threat and there is sufficient reason for turning it. For suppose a trolley is headed to one but if redirected to two it will defuse a bomb threatening five different people. It is not permissible to turn in this case, which is more like a case in which we start a grenade to stop a trolley, foreseeing it will kill bystanders. The difference between the Grenade Case and this one is that removing a threat to one person is a good in itself; setting a grenade is not. However, the effect of the threat's being removed is bad — two die — and a greater bad than the good. This redirection, which has overall *bad* consequences when considered as a redirection, is what further causes the bomb to be defused. The greater good (or what is intimately related to it, like a threat moved away) does not here produce a lesser harm. Another way of putting this is that the proposed sufficient reason for turning the threat must lie in what we are doing, that is, redirecting to a lesser number, not in some causal aftereffect (e.g., five saved from a bomb).[3]

In the Lazy Susan Case, the greater good seems to be an *aspect* of the turning of the Lazy Susan, since the five sit on it. The Lazy Susan does not remove a threat to the five, it removes the five from the threat. This good which is the turning Lazy Susan eventually rams into Joe. This is permissible.

We have noted another case in which the ultimate good of five people actually being saved, rather than the good of a threat being removed from them, causes harm: We save the lives of five patients whose normal breathing then causes a shift in air patterns which leads fatal germs, hitherto safely closeted, to kill bystander Joe (Operation Case II). This again is permissible.

Application to a Straightforward Impermissible Case

What about cases in which it would be *impermissible* to act? It was said that if a grenade that we set off to stop the trolley would itself kill one person, it would be *impermissible* to use it. According to the PPH this is because the grenade, whose existence is not a good, kills the bystander. When a good event (e.g., five saved) is an *effect* (i.e., a separate caused event) of the grenade going off, rather than the *flip side* of an event such as the trolley being turned in the original Trolley Case, or an *aspect* of an event such as the Lazy Susan turning, then the lesser harm is associated with the in-itself neutral event of a grenade explosion. The lesser harm is not seen as the effect of the greater good (or of what is non-causally related to it) as in the Trolley Case.

Cases in which what we do is justifiable only as a means to the greater good but involves as a direct effect the lesser harm, have the same structure as the Grenade Case. These include the following: (1) In the Double Threat Case (p. 158), we redirect a trolley from the five and to the one because this will cause a bomb to shift away from twenty people a mile away, but the five from whom we redirect the trolley will die anyway of a second threat coming at them. The redirection of the trolley in this case would not be a good in itself or have good as its flip side, since the five will die of another threat. It is only a means to the saving of the twenty. Hence, the harm to the one would not be the effect of a greater good or what is so intimately related to it. (To use a notion which will be explained later, saving the five from one threat does not even produce a structurally equivalent component of the greater good, since a second threat still faces the five.) (2) In the Stop-the-Bomb Case (p. 158), we shift a trolley from one to five because this causes movements in the earth that defuse a bomb that was threatening twenty. In this case too, a lesser harm does not come about as the result of a greater good, since turning the trolley has the direct effect of saving one while producing a threat to five.

Suppose the grenade's going off under the five lifted them into the air (and away from the trolley), as well as directly killing Joe. *Insofar as we conceive* of this as a case like the Lazy Susan, that is, as one in which the good of the five being moved to safety is an aspect of the grenade's going off, we may permit the lesser harm it also causes.[4]

Foot, as already described, argued that our duty not to kill is stronger than our duty not to let die. In particular, she argued that we may not use a gas in performing surgery to save five if we foresee that this gas will seep next door and kill one innocent bystander. The PPH endorses this conclusion if the gas causes both the greater good and the lesser harm. This is so, for example, if the gas runs a machine that helps save the five patients and kills a bystander because it is poisonous to him. But an objection to Foot's general claim that not harming takes precedence over aiding is provided by the cases in which the greater good itself causes the harm. If we know that successful surgery on five will cause them to breathe normally and this, in turn, will change air currents so that germs closeted up to now will kill one person, it is permissible to help the five.

The Impermissibility of Requiring Harm

In the Bridge Case, we throw a bystander off a bridge to stop the trolley in its tracks. Throwing him off the bridge and having him be in front of the trolley is causally required to stop the trolley. Here some intrusion on a person leading to great harm to him, or even great harm itself, is intended as a means. The good does not cause the bad, the bad causes the good. Hence it is impermissible to use the bystander in the Bridge Case.

Suppose we wiggled the bridge and this alone causes the trolley to stop, but we also foresee that it will topple the bystander to his death (the Bridge Case II). If we understand this to be a case in which what is not itself a greater good, but what causes the five to be saved, also causes lesser harm, then it is impermissible to wiggle the bridge.

The Permissibility of Requiring Harm and Refinement of the DDE

It might be argued that sometimes it is permissible to intend significant infringement of rights as a means to the greater good. For sometimes in such cases an event that helps bring about the greater good and lesser harm is caused by a structurally equivalent component of the greater good. The Prevented Return Case is one example. Suppose that an event that looks like a greater good begins a chain of events which causes the lesser harm and this lesser harm helps sustain the greater good. Then it may be permissible to act to produce a state of affairs that *would be* the greater good if it were maintained, with the intention that the lesser harm that this state causes occur as a way of *maintaining* this state. Notice that this is different from the less controversial course of events in which we intend that a *foreseen* harmful side effect of a completed and self-sustaining greater good be used to achieve a totally different good. In this case we would proceed to produce the first good even if its harmful side effect had no further good effect. This is not so in the Prevented Return Case, since if the harmful side effect (death) of turning the trolley did not *keep* the trolley away, we would not turn the trolley at all, given that all six people would then die.

Several factors may be helpful to us in understanding the Prevented Return Case and distinguishing it from others. One way to understand this case is as follows: (1) The five's being free of *one threat* (i.e., free of the trolley originally coming at them) is an intrinsically good state of affairs. It would be a greater good in comparison to its bad side effect (the one's being hit) if it could be maintained. (2) However, we would not be justified in turning the trolley if a *second threat,* the trolley's coming back at the five, occurred. Nevertheless, the good of the five's being free of the first threat *is* a structurally equivalent component of the greater good that would justify us in turning the trolley. This is because when the first threat is away the five face no other threats, at least temporarily, and are in the same situation they will find themselves in if the threat is kept away permanently. Suppose that what produces the lesser harm which is causally useful in keeping the trolley away is either this state which is structurally equivalent to the greater good or means that are closely (noncausally) tied to it, in the way a threat moving away from the five is. Then the fact that the lesser harm is causally necessary to maintain the greater good is not a reason against acting.

This analysis may be rejected because we have achieved the greater good *by* harm, where the true greater good is seen as the *continued safety* of the five. This true greater good (or an event that is noncausally related to the true greater good) will *not* be the cause of the harm. But I believe we should accept that it is permissible for a structurally equivalent component of greater good, which is, in itself, something that if not wiped out would be a greater good than the harm it causes, to cause lesser harm. This does not mean that *any* component of the greater good may be brought about when it would cause harm that brings about the greater good. For example, consider the Wheel Case. Suppose we cannot redirect most of the trolley, but we can redirect one of its wheels. If we detach the wheel and turn it toward the one, the rest of the trolley will still continue toward killing the five. However, we know that the wheel will crash into the one and its impact as it crushes him will reverberate through the tracks, causing the rest of the trolley to jolt to a stop before it hits the five. May we redirect the wheel? I do not think so. The five are not free of the threat that faced them when we turned the wheel, so a state that is structurally equivalent to the greater good has not caused the lesser evil.

We can supplement this analysis of the Prevented Return Case by noticing that it is the initial movement away of the trolley itself which both raises the possibility of the second threat (its own return) and creates the lesser harm (Joe crushed) that stops that second threat. *It is only because we get rid of the initial trolley threat that the threat of the returning trolley appears.* This has at least two implications. First, it suggests why, when the trolley is away from them, the five are in a state structurally equivalent to the greater good. That is, they seem to be in an unthreatened state which, if sustained, is identical with a good greater than the harm produced. (So it differs from the Double Threat Case.) Second, it also accounts for the fact that, although we seem to intend harm to Joe as a means of stopping the trolley from returning, it is not correct to say that we turn the trolley or intend his harm *in order* to stop the second threat. If it is true that we intend harm to the one person, for we turn the trolley *because* (we think) this harm will happen and we would not turn if (we thought) it would not happen, this does not imply that we turn the trolley *in order* to harm the person as a means. We have a reason to turn it that is *completely* satisfactory in itself (*in order* to get it away from the five and leaving them threat-free), and nothing we do is undertaken in order to hit the one, even if we turn the trolley *in order* to help the five only *because* we think that he will be hit.

This is a difference from cases to which the DDE is usually applied. Insofar as the test for whether one intends rather than merely foresees an event is whether one would continue to act (or omit) if it didn't occur, the test fails to distinguish between acting *because* the harmful event will occur, and acting *in order* that the harmful event occur. Dealing with the first type of case, as exemplified by the Prevented Return Case, will be important, therefore, for understanding the DDE better. The Prevented Return Case involves acting *because* a harmful event will have a causal effect, but it does not involve acting *in order* that it and its effect occur, nor does it involve being prepared to do things other than what one is doing to turn the trolley away from the five to bring about the harmful event.

We shall return to examine the significance of this second implication for the DDE later. At this point, it is useful to note only that we could never be absolutely certain that the one person's death will cause the trolley to stop (i.e., whenever a causal relation is introduced there is no longer certainty). Therefore, if the Prevented Return Case involves a permissible redirecting, it is wrong to justify our principle, to the effect that it is permissible for greater good to bring about lesser evil, by arguing that it avoids the possibility, ever present in consequentialist theories, that harm will be brought about in vain, with no greater good as a consequence.

Let us contrast the Prevented Return Case with other cases, for example, the Tractor Case. In this case, not only is the trolley threatening the five but, prior to the existence of the trolley threat, a runaway tractor was and is about to crash into them. This is a second threat, which, unlike the one in Prevented Return, exists independently of the movement of the trolley away from the five. The only thing that would have stopped the tractor from crashing into the five was throwing Joe at it. This, however, was impermissible. Now we find that if we turn the new trolley threat away from the five it will hit and kill Joe and move him into the path of the tractor, thereby stopping its movement. We certainly would not bother to turn the trolley from the five, thereby killing Joe, if this did not stop the tractor, for the five would be doomed anyway. If we turn, it is because (we believe) Joe will be dragged.

It might be argued that in this case turning the trolley is *impermissible*, even though a sufficiently large component of the greater good—that is, the removal of one threat from the five—occurs when we move the trolley. In this case, unlike Prevented Return, the component cannot be identified as the state of affairs that if not undone, would be a greater good than the lesser harm, because as the trolley moves away the five are still not free of the tractor threat hovering over them. *This state of affairs, of one threat gone and another facing them, is not such that, if not undone, it is a greater good.* It is not *structurally equivalent* to a greater good, that is, sufficient and complete in itself if only sustained. This is a consequence of the fact that the second threat is not a by-product of removing the first threat, even temporarily; some factor independent of the trolley already is (or will be) producing the tractor threat. Our removing the trolley does not remove this other threat that is already facing the five.

The problem that exists in the Tractor Case, which does not exist in Prevented Return, is that a threat exists that is not a product of a greater good (or what is noncausally related to it, or its structurally equivalent component) and we would take advantage of reducing one threat (the trolley) in order to use Joe to eliminate another independent threat. Taking advantage of the bad side effect of our reducing one threat, in order to save people from another independently existing threat, seems problematic; the removal of the trolley threat seems like an excuse for doing what it was impermissible to do in order to get rid of the first (tractor) threat. By contrast, in the Prevented Return Case, the removal of the trolley threat is our sole aim, and we remove it initially knowing that the removal will itself have the effect of sustaining itself, and we intend this and the means to it.

In terms of the contrast, turning *because* this will remove the second threat versus turning *in order* to remove the second threat, the Tractor Case is a difficult call. Certainly it is a good in itself to remove one threat from five, and we could say that we do this because we foresee the second threat will be dealt with as a result of our doing only what is necessary to move the first threat away. Yet, I believe, we do so in *order to* cause a harm that eliminates the second threat, even though we would not do anything other than what we do in turning the trolley to cause the harm. (If we did additional acts or omissions matters would be perfectly clear.)

Being Saved From Threats Already Facing People

Could the analysis available for the Prevented Return Case also account for Thomson's Loop Case? But how can we say that the greater good of the five being free of all deadly threats occurs (even temporarily) when we turn a trolley along another track that also leads to the five, as it does in her case? We might say that we do, in fact, conceive of the initial redirection of the trolley in Thomson's Loop Case as reducing one threat to the five, since we eliminate a trolley from being a threat from one direction which is a component in eliminating its being a threat from two directions. But this would not distinguish the Loop Case sufficiently from the Tractor Case, where we eliminate one threat by turning the trolley as well. What places the Loop Case with the Prevented Return case morally is that the second threat (the trolley going down the second side of the loop) is caused by the removal of the first threat, and therefore the trolley headed to the five from one direction was the only threat facing the five originally at the time we had to act. But, can we conceive in the Loop Case of the trolley's initial removal as creating a state of affairs structurally equivalent to the final good? It seems odd to say that when we turn the trolley from the five and onto another track also headed to the five that there is a state in existence which, if not undone, is the greater good. This is so, in part, because there is no possibility that what has been done will be undone, that is, the trolley is not going to go back on its old path, but is headed at the five in a new direction. (But perhaps we can think there is a structural equivalent because we expect, and turn the trolley because we expect, that the one person will stop the trolley from becoming a second threat. But in the Prevented Return Case we thought there was a structural equivalent without considering that hitting the one would stop the trolley from going back.)

Suppose that we cannot argue that it is permissible to turn the trolley in the Loop Case because lesser harm is the result of the structural equivalent of greater good. If it is nevertheless plausible to turn the trolley it is because there is an even more general way of describing a principle of permissible harm, one which incorporates greater good (or what is noncausally related to it, or its structural equivalent) as the cause of lesser harm.

The Loop Case, Prevented Return, and all the other cases in which redirecting threats and redirecting people from threats are permissible are cases in which *the greater number of people being saved from all fatal threat(s) they already faced (at the time we must act) causes lesser evil but also results in those very people being saved from all threats*. They are cases in which people being saved from threats already facing them occurs neither by harming someone nor by way of means which have the side effect of harming someone but do not have saving people from all threats initially facing them as an aspect or flip side. We turn the trolley or the Lazy Susan, and as an *effect* of this saving of the five from a threat they already faced, someone else gets harmed. If there is a second threat to the five—for example, the trolley coming at them from another direction in the Loop Case—it is also produced by removing all the threats they faced when we acted. Notice that we identify separate threats in part by distinguishing the direction of the threat. The trolley coming at the five from the right is not the same threat as the same trolley coming from the left. The second threat does not exist until the first is removed. (A Lazy Susan-type case could also involve a second threat which is produced by the saving of five from threat(s) they already faced. For example, when we turn the Lazy Susan away from the trolley, the Lazy Susan would swing into the same trolley from a different direction unless it crashes into the one person it hits so that it sticks to him.) The people are saved from the second threat, not the one(s) they were already facing when we had to act, by means which involve harm to someone, and these means are themselves produced by their being saved from all the threats they already faced. I believe that whenever greater good, what is noncausally related to it, or its structurally equivalent component causes lesser harm, we shall also have a case where saving people from the threat(s) they already faced caused lesser harm. (This assumes the focus is on cases where greater good comes by reducing threats.) So, the greater good formulation of the PPH implies the saved-from-what-already-threatens-them formulation. The question is whether the second formulation implies the first also.

Rather than settle this issue, I will hereafter think of the PPH as having two versions PPH(1) and PPH(2), the seond possibly more general than, and inclusive of, the first.

Implications

Do results in the Prevented Return Case apply to a case that is a variant of a case well known in discussions of the Doctrine of Double Effect? In the well-known case, we foresee that if we bomb a crucial munitions plant during a just war, children next door will die from the plant exploding. This, it is said, is permissible. However, it is impermissible to terror-bomb the children in order to produce grieving parents who will surrender. My variant is that the bombed-out munitions plant would be rebuilt immediately by the parents, if they were not consumed by grief over the deaths of their children next door (Munitions Grief Case). In this case, we would not expend effort to bomb the plant unless we believed the children next door would be killed and the parents' grief thereby was caused, for this alone sustains the damage to the plant. Yet, I believe, it is permissible to bomb in this case consistent with its being impermissible to terror bomb. Here we bomb *in order to* destroy the munitions plant *because* (we believe) the children will die and grief will ensue, but not *in order* to bring about death and grief.

Suppose, by contrast, that our bombs can only burn up one stick of dynamite in the munitions plants, but not destroy the plant (which could not be destroyed by the stick's burning). This dynamite stick, however, is on the side near some children. It would set them on fire, and the conflagration spreading from them would be large enough to set the rest of the munitions factory afire (Component Case). In this case, a component (one dynamite destroyed) of the end state (the total munitions plant destroyed) causes the twenty deaths which in turn are the means to the end state. The component by itself, if not undone, would *not* be the structural equivalent of the end that is said to justify harm to children, unlike the bombed out munitions plant in Munitions Grief Case. Dropping the bomb, in this case, and relying on the causal effects of the foreseen side effect (the children's burning) to finish the job is, I believe, impermissible. This, like the Tractor Case, involves bombing *in order* to bring about further effects that deal with a threat (munitions plant left standing). But if the distinction between doing "in order that" and "because of" serves us in the bombing cases, does PPH(1) serve us? Is destruction of the munitions plant a greater good or only the means to a greater good of ending the war? The PPH(2) would apply only if we assume that the munitions plant's remaining in existence threatens more people than will be killed if it explodes. If this is not true, we may have to move to an even more general formulation of the PPH or see Munitions Bombing as an exception to the PPH.

Notice also that the PPH may imply that there is a moral difference between the children dying as a side effect of the munitions plant blowing up and their dying as a direct effect of the bombs themselves. This is so, if the munitions plant blowing up is conceived of as having greater good as a flip side, but the bombs falling is a mere means to the greater good. This point is connected to a general problem with harms that result from mere means. Suppose we are permitted by the PPH to turn the trolley in the Prevented Return Case, although we would not do so unless we believed the trolley would kill and crush the bystander. It is very important to understand that this does not mean that we may cause the trolley to stick to the bystander, when it would otherwise not reach him at all, by an act (or aspect of an act) *not needed* in order to turn the trolley temporarily away from the five. For example, we may not give the trolley an extra-hard push (Extra Push Case) so that it hits and sticks to the bystander when it would not otherwise have done so.

(This, of course, means that if the extra push were needed for a hit, we should not bother to turn the trolley at all when sticking to the bystander is needed to prevent return.) The cause of the trolley's hitting the bystander (i.e., the extra push) is not part of the greater good (or what is structurally equivalent to it), nor part of what is intimately, noncausally related to the greater good, that is, removing the threat from the five. This is because it is *not* causally necessary to give the extra push to get the trolley temporarily away from the five to begin with. We would give the extra push in order to get the trolley to hit and stick to the one. The harm to the one which results from the extra push then causes the greater good of the five being saved, but this is the impermissible relation in which something that is not the greater good or intimately related to it (or its structural equivalent, or the removal of all fatal threats facing someone at time we act) causes the lesser harm.[5]

Suppose that for there to be a case of intending an event E (versus merely foreseeing it) as an end or means we require *all* the following conditions to hold: (1) Someone must do an act (or omission), A, because E will occur and would not do A if E would not occur; (2) someone must be willing to do acts (or omissions) other than A to bring about E if A fails (as in Extra-Push Case); (3) someone must do an act (or omission) A in order that E occur either as an end or a means; (4) E may be an effect of something that is or is not the greater good or its structural equivalent.[6] If these conditions were all required, then the killing of the one person in the Prevented Return Case would not be an instance of intending a death, and this case would not show that the DDE fails to be a necessary condition for permissible action against innocent non-threats. (The Operation Case shows that the DDE is not a sufficient condition for permissibility, so the PPH would still be necessary to fully explain the permissibility of redirection.) However, I shall continue to use a notion of "intend" which only requires that condition (1) be satisfied, and I assume that the traditional DDE would find acts which satisfy only condition (1) to be morally unsatisfactory if E were the occurrence of a lesser harm. (Even revised versions of the DDE (such as Quinn's) that condemn intending the involvement of a person when we merely foresee harm coming to them seem to require only (1). That is, Quinn's account would condemn doing an act A *because* an involvement of someone will occur, though we don't intend the foreseen harm. If only (1) were necessary for the DDE's notion of intention, the permissibility of turning in Prevented Return would undermine the DDE as a necessary condition of permissibility, while supporting the PPH.[7]

A final point about components and structural equivalents: In the Miracle Case we turn the trolley from the five toward the one whom it kills, and then it turns back and kills the five. However, we know that its trip back to the five will produce a miracle drug not otherwise in existence that can resurrect only the five. In this case the five's being initially saved from the threat of the trolley is not any sort of component in the final good of the five's surviving (let alone a component structurally equivalent to the greater good), since it is wiped out by the return of the trolley. Turning the trolley, then, would merely be a means via lesser harm to the greater good; it would have greater good as a separate causal effect, and so is not permitted.

The Person-as-Enclosure

There is yet another distinction that we might be tempted to draw. The threats in the Prevented Return and Tractor Cases would be coming to the five from outside them. But suppose one of the independent threats facing the five is *already theirs*, that is, they are ill and were going to die of organ failure in a few hours. The only thing that would save them is taking organs from healthy Joe, but this is not permitted. However, the trolley now threatens the five, and if we redirect it, it will kill Joe, whose organs can then be used to save the five (Failed Organs Case). We would not redirect if there were no way to save the five from organ failure, for they would be saved from the trolley threat only to die soon from another threat. I believe it would be wrong to redirect in the case just described in which the five can live. The distinction drawn between the Prevented Return and Tractor Cases explains this, since the five are still under a second threat (disease) when we would turn the trolley. Hence, the trolley turned, although it diminishes a threat, does not diminish all threats and does not produce (in a noncausal fashion, as the flip side of turning away) even the structural equivalent of the greater good. The lesser harm is, therefore, not the result of a greater good or of what is intimately related to it. But *if* it were permissible to redirect in both the Prevented Return *and* Tractor Cases — on the supposition that the difference emphasized above to distinguish these cases is not morally significant after all — it might still make a difference that the organ failure (unlike the tractor threat) is *in* the five already.

Another case that points to this factor involves five people who have a fatal transmissible disease, which they can rid themselves of by breathing out. Their breath will transmit the germs to Joe who will die (Diseased Breath Case). Is it permissible for them to breathe out? Their breathing out seems to be a good — carrying away disease — and causes lesser harm. Yet, I believe, it is impermissible for the five to breathe out. Is this perhaps because they themselves ought not to turn a *trolley*, if it were external and headed to them, though it is permissible for a third party to do so? Then consider whether a third party is permitted to pump out their germs when the germs will then be breathed in by Joe. May a third party ignore the fact that the threat is in these people already? I suggest that the third party is not permitted to do this and that this case is different from the Operation Case II in which five people breathe out normal air, thereby pushing germs elsewhere in the environment in Joe's direction. If a threat we wish to eliminate is already part of a person, it seems that, as much as a good that belongs to a person may not be taken from him, a bad that already belongs to a person should not be imposed on others. (We might redirect a benefit headed to one person in the direction of five instead, but, once the benefit has got to the one, we ought not take it away from him.) The idea of the *person-as-enclosure* seems to work in both ways — for good and for bad.

The PPH and Appropriate Victim-Beneficiary Relations

Having considered its application to some cases, let us return to a more general discussion of the PPH. For purposes of the following discussion, I will assume that case results support the following components of the PPH(1), which summarize many of our intuitions concerning sufficient and (overrideable) necessary conditions for the permissibility of causing the deaths of nonthreatening innocents who would not die shortly anyway so that others may benefit in particular cases:

1. It is permissible that greater good (or its structurally equivalent component) have lesser harm as one of its aspects or as its direct or indirect effect, even when this harm sustains that greater good.[8]
2. It is permissible that a mere means to a greater good have lesser harm as an effect, if and only if the greater good (or its structurally equivalent component) is an aspect of the means or noncausally its flipside, even when this harm sustains the greater good.

Even more of our intentions may be captured by PPH(2).

1. It is permissible that a greater number of people being saved from all death threats already facing them have lesser harm as one of its aspects or as its direct or indirect effect if and only if their being saved from all death threats already facing them is aimed to accomplish the greater good of saving those very same people.
2. It is permissible that a means to saving a greater number of people from all death threats already facing them have lesser harm as an effect if and only if (a) saving those people from the threats already facing them is an aspect of the means or its noncausal flipside, and (b) this saving is aimed to accomplish the greater good of saving those very same people.

Note that those who think killing in Prevented Return and the Loop Case is impermissible, will reject PPH(2) and may settle on a version of PPH(1) which drops the reference to "or a structurally equivalent component."

The PPH has been discussed in the context of our acts. I suspect that we may use its standards even in making judgments, analogous to moral judgments, about natural events. For example, suppose that nature were organized along purely consequentialist lines, so that when five people became ill, their being ill always caused another person to die, making his organs available, which would then be used to save the five. I suggest that we would think that such a course of nature offended our conception of appropriate relations between people. This is a case in which a bad state of affairs (the illness of five) causes a lesser harm (the death of one), which then causes the greater good (preventing the death of five). It is also a case, given that it occurs frequently, in which we read in something like an intent-without-an-agent;

that is, we read in a function or purposive structure to the death of the one. (Though we needn't think the five get sick so that the one shall die.)

Since there is no agent here who acts to save five by using one person, the primary immorality is not an inappropriate relation between an agent and his victim, or a sullying of an agent; the primary immorality, it may be suggested, is the potential for an inappropriate relation established between victim and beneficiaries. When there is an agent and he acts contrary to the PPH, the PPH focuses on the fact that he may (barring special justifications) establish an inappropriate relation between his victim and those who are saved.

If this is true, the PPH seems to contrast with theories that locate what is wrong with harming nonthreatening innocents to help others in the special relation established between agent and victim that involves intending a victim's death. It would be victim- not agent-focused

On this understanding of the PPH, what is its point? Let us consider PPH(1). It seems to offer a revision of the DDE in the following ways: Lesser evil may come about as a consequence of greater good or what is intimately related to it but not (as the DDE permits) as a consequence of the mere means to the greater good. In this respect the PPH suggests that the DDE is too broad. The PPH suggests that the DDE is also too restrictive, insofar as it would rule out using harm in the Prevented Return Case; for the PPH distinguishes, within the class of seeming intentional harms, between acting *in order* to harm and acting *because* there will be harm. Certainly, my acts or omissions not undertaken as necessary for removing the threat to the five are considered as done "in order" that the lesser harm come about; but even if nothing extra is done, as in the Tractor or Failed Organs Case, it may be that the act is done in order that harm come about, and this the PPH rules out.

Though the PPH condemns both lesser harm that is the side effect of mere means to greater good and the lesser harm that is brought about in order that greater good comes about (*one* type of case in which the harm is itself a means to the greater good), it is not clear that a moral theory that incorporates the PPH must condemn equally both these cases in which lesser harm arises. But if it does not, we shall have three issues to resolve. *First*, what view of persons and their appropriate relations to other persons who are potential beneficiaries of harm does the first part of the PPH capture? It seems that the part of the principle concerned with the greater good as cause insists that if good is happening to a greater number—something intrinsically legitimate—it may have the further effect of interfering with the like or lesser good of a lesser number. This lesser number cannot complain that they are interfered with; they cannot demand that the intrinsic good not occur, though they can demand that certain means not be used to bring about that good. [In some ways an agent- rather than victim-focused analysis of the PPH may seem more attractive. It might be said in explanation of the PPH that so long as an agent is directly involved with something good, he will feel more comfortable bringing about harm. This sounds like a literal version of the "no dirty hands" thesis].

The *second* issue concerns what view of persons is reflected in the claim that we may act in order to redirect a threat from the greater number of people (or the greater number of people from a threat) *because* a harm to another person will occur that sustains the greater good, but not *in order* that harm to another person produce the greater good. The latter is ruled out even when nothing more is done than is necessary to redirect a threat (or those threatened), for example, in the Tractor Case. The PPH certainly does not insist that we should not do what makes use of persons as means. (It permits us to do what we foresee will lead to a person being a means to the good we are pursuing; I have suggested this is a form of intending that use, and a certain form of reliance on it.)

The *third* issue is whether and why the impermissible form of intending harm is a more serious wrong than the impermissible form of acting with mere foresight to harm. (Warren Quinn answers this question by emphasizing the distinction between treating someone as a means by intending harm to him impermissibly, and failing to treat him as an end by impermissibly failing to take his interests seriously enough when harm to him is foreseen.)[9]

One approach to answering these questions suggests that the PPH exhibits an extremely pure form of concern for nonsubordinated relations between potential victims and beneficiaries. It tells us that to understand redirection cases, one must see them as having the same basic structure as "pure choice" cases, like the Crosspoint Case in which the trolley would be sent down one way or the other, it not yet being in a position where it will kill unless we redirect. In pure choice cases, which are kill versus kill cases involving Joe versus the five, the harm, or increase in probability of harm, to one is an effect of the good of the others not being harmed. If a trolley is *redirected* it involves harming someone as a result of aiding others already threatened (a kill versus let-die case). But, the claim is, as in pure choice cases, the harm is an effect of the good or a means intimately related to the good, and this makes the fact that we are killing rather than letting die morally less significant, at least when we can thereby save a greater number.

Similarly, it is claimed, cases in which we remove a threat from five, thereby causing another entity to threaten Joe (e.g., the Rockslide Case), have the same basic structure as another sort of pure-choice case; one in which we have to send threat A to Joe or threat B to the five. Again, where two threats are involved, the good is the flip side of the threat going to Joe in the pure-choice case, and likewise in the case where removal of threat B from the five causes threat A to Joe. (In both, either the five get B, or Joe gets A.)

The morally attractive feature in the structure stated by all these cases, it is claimed, is that Joe's status as an equal person is respected, in the sense that he, need not feel *subordinated* or sacrificed to the five, though he is *substituted* for them in a slot of danger. The *reason* Joe is harmed is that we want to save the five, but, like a soldier who is sent on a dangerous mission instead of five soldiers, he is sent to face a threat instead of the five, but not to serve the five. (This leaves it open that the position he is sent into instead of the five has as one of its functions *to* serve others.)

Another way of understanding the structure of pure choice (whose important component, it is claimed, is that harm is an aspect of or caused by the greater good or what is intimately noncausally related to it) is to see the greater good that causes harm to a person as an *end in itself* confronting another *end in itself* (a person). Given what a person is, only a greater good may defeat his claim to noninterference.

What does this victim-focused explanatory proposal for the PPH say about cases in which harm to Joe is caused by the mere means to redirecting the trolley? Since it tells us that the structure of "pure choice" situations applies, it seems to yield the following conclusion: First, allowing Joe to be killed by the effect of a mere means to the better end state would have the same moral structure as a *pure choice* case in which we would choose to send threat A to Joe, rather than send threat A to what could be *the means* of saving five lives (thereby preventing the means from saving the five). For example, we would send a trolley to Joe instead of toward a canister of gas that can be used to save the lives of five people. In both the pure choice and the redirection cases the person confronts a mere means.

The analysis suggests the most intimate connection (identity) between the reason why we may not harm as an effect of the mere means to a better end state, and the reason why we may not preserve a mere means that leads to a greater good rather than preserve Joe's life when deciding between them in distributing threats. So, the same reason why we may not send a trolley at a crossroads toward two people and away from one surgeon, who is the means to helping twenty, is a reason for not using means that will have the causal effect of saving twenty when it will harm two as a side effect. Equality between potential victims is disturbed by choosing means over Joe in a pure choice situation, and by confronting Joe with a mere means to the greater good as the cause of his death.

We can also understand what is at stake when a mere means threatens direct or indirect harm, by using the related perspectives introduced above: When a mere means causes harm, something that is not an end (i.e., something not worthwhile in itself) confronts something that is worthwhile in itself (Joe's being alive); its functioning in itself cannot outweigh Joe's living. If the good end (the five living) that the means is to produce is allowed to give the means enough weight to override Joe's weight, equality between Joe and the five is destroyed. The five now are not merely permitted to confront Joe with their own moral weight, but they are allowed to transmit their moral weight to intrinsically less weighty items in the world (the mere means). In a sense, they are allowed to take over the world we all share for their own interests. If harm to Joe himself (or his involvement leading to his being harmed) becomes a means to the greater good then those five will have transmitted their weight so that they come, in a sense, to own that other person, not only the world we all share.

If the means confront Joe, he is being *sacrificed* for the five, rather than being merely substituted for them, because their survival is not just a *reason* for sending a threat to Joe; it alters the weight of entities (means) in the world vis-à-vis Joe. To be sacrificed for others on this interpretation, then, is either to be harmed as the effect of the mere means to those others' benefit, or to be harmed as the mere means. It is only being harmed as the aspect and direct or indirect effect of (a) the greater good (or sometimes its structural equivalent) or of (b) means which have greater good (or sometimes its structural equivalent) as an aspect or flip side that is morally acceptable.

When the five's surviving is the flip side of what harms Joe, the five are only doing what Joe was doing, that is, surviving, and this harms Joe. (However, Joe's surviving, though it would have made impossible the five's surviving, would not *cause harm* to the five; the trolley was already a threat to them. There is this asymmetry between the five and Joe. But the permissibility of turning the trolley indicates that it is not always a morally significant asymmetry.) If a means which causes the five's survival is what harms Joe, then the five achieve their survival in a way Joe did not achieve his survival. If Joe's surviving had originally been based on a means that harmed the five, the parity between Joe and the five would be reintroduced. (Costa's justification for redirection in the Loop Case makes use of this (p. 153).) But parity (or reciprocity) in the use of *incorrect* means to survival is not as good as parity of *correct* means. So it is not simply the lack of parity on both sides that makes it wrong to employ means that harm in order to save the five.

Problems

While I find this defense of PPH(1) attractive, I think that it goes wrong, though in interesting and revealing ways. The clue to the problem lies in the *purity* of the result. If we cannot accept this pure result, we must argue that the structure of cases of redirection (of threats or potential victims) and of cases in which stopping one threat creates another threat is not given by the structure of pure choice of threat cases. The outstanding examples here are the Prevented Return Case and others where involvement of a person or actual harm is used; for here a person is not just made to substitute for another; we do something because he will be a means to help another. Such cases can be mapped onto the following choice case: Send a threat toward the five or send the threat toward Joe when Joe's being hit alone keeps the threat from coming back to the five. As a result of substituting for the five, the one helps preserve their being free of a threat, and he would not become a substitute were it not for this. Is it consistent with treating a person as an end-in-itself that sometimes we take advantage of the fact that she will be a means, as in Prevented Return? Is equality between persons preserved here, since we turn *because* he will be harmed, rather than *in order* to harm him? This I have claimed, is a crucial question. Perhaps it is only if we turn the trolley in order to harm him that using him is our *reason* for turning. (This notion of "a reason" is different from "any factor that played a role in our deciding whether to act or not.") It here seems especially hard to defend an account of the PPH which focuses on the victim or victim-beneficiary relationship. This is because it seems that the difference between someone's being harmed because he will be a means, rather than in order that he be a means, lies in the agent's attitude, rather than in a difference in the victim's status. Finally, even if what we have presented is a successful defense of PPH(1), what does it do for PPH(2), if this also deals with cases where no greater good or its structural equivalent confronts the person? It does, in fact, seem to me that there is a morally significant similarity between lesser harm being caused by a greater good (or its structural equivalent) and lesser harm being caused by the greater number being saved from everything that fatally threatened them. More needs to be said about this, however. An additional problem with the defense of the PPH will be discussed below (p. 190).

Killing, Letting Die, and Positive Rights

What do the Trolley Case and the PPH tell us about the killing–letting-die issue? We can make several points, including some comments on what others have said.

If the PPH is correct, it implies that one may sometimes kill rather than let die, and it specifies the conditions when this is so. Then killing will not be morally worse than letting die in these cases.

This should not be taken to imply that there is no per se difference between killing and letting-die; for letting die, unlike killing, may be permissible without having to meet the requirements of the PPH. For example, if a trolley is headed toward my valuable property, perhaps I may permissibly busy myself taking care to remove it, thereby not having the time to help someone else toward whom a second trolley is headed, even though I foresee his death. But it is not permissible for me to save my property when I foresee that I will, without prior intention, do something that causes a trolley to be redirected from a track where it damages property to one where it kills a person.

Furthermore, as also noted above, if the person I kill is someone whose life I am already saving at the cost of efforts he has no right that I make, killing may abide by rules more similar to those (non-PPH rules) by which letting die abides. I have suggested that the way to understand this is not that killing per se is not morally worse than letting die once we have equalized for all factors in killing and letting-die cases, but rather to see that a conceptual property of letting die is added to a case of killing, thereby altering its moral status in the direction of acceptability. This itself shows that letting die and killing differ per se, if letting die has conceptual components active on its homeground that made it morally more acceptable than killing (when killing also lacks other, comparable "acceptability"-making properties).

Letting-die cases and killings that are like letting-die cases can be treated outside the PPH constraints even when the person who loses out has a strict right to be aided. For example, suppose each of six people (Joe plus the five) has a contracted right to my aid to save his life. The five need a drug which takes much time for me to prepare in my lab. Joe needs only for me to sit with him. If I decide to save the five, Joe will die because I go to my lab to prepare the drug instead of staying with him, not because the five will be saved; I preserve means to saving the five rather than help Joe. (Of course, I do not cause his death, but the omission is significant in being the "but for which" he would have lived.) I believe it is permissible for me to go to the lab. Suppose Joe has always been attached to me for life support and indeed has a right to be attached, and I cannot move freely to save the five, who also have a right to my aid, unless I kill Joe to detach him. I believe it is permissible to do this, though Joe will thereby die so that I can prepare the means to the five being alive.

In these cases we have imagined that all six people have a strict right to my aid. How is it that the interference with a claim on me that, for example, Joe has, and even one that he is already having met, does not function in the same way as a claim he has to his life when I do not help provide him with it? The answer to this seems to be that when the five, as well as Joe, have a claim on me, I stand in relation to each of these claims (including Joe's) as something like a stock that has been sold to too many buyers. Each has an equal claim and each must confront each of his opponents for the use of the oversold item. Because there is legitimate conflict over the use of *my* resources to help each of the six, the loss of life that comes from the denial of a certain use of these resources can be the result of preserving a mere means to saving the five. The means, after all, involves a certain distribution of *my resources, control over which is in dispute*, not resources that are Joe's, and the resources do not cause the loss of what he has independently of imposition on me (as they would if *my* grenade caused Joe's death when he lived independently of me).

Suppose the five do not have as strict a claim as Joe has to my aid. It may still be permissible to infringe his right to my help in order to save many lives. However, in this case, unlike a case in which there is no right to my aid, when Joe has such a right, only stronger or more numerous rights to my aid, or a much greater good, can override his right. Also, not aiding or terminating aid for the *sake of* freeing my resources for others' use is different from doing these things with the primary intention of making available Joe's own resources to save the five. The latter may be impermissible when the former is permissible. We see life Joe has independently of imposition on me (or the five) not as contested stock so far as I (and the five) are concerned, but as stock to which only Joe has a claim. There is no need for him to meet challenges to its use from others, at least when its use is important to him, and the standards for how its loss can come about are therefore stiffer.

A further conclusion can be derived from this discussion: One theory of rights is that they are constraints on action rather than components of goals, and therefore we may not violate someone's right in order to maximize respect for the same rights of others. But the above discussion suggests that although this may be true of negative rights (rights to noninterference) when the conditions of the PPH are not met, it is not true of at least some positive rights (rights to aid): One person's positive right may often be denied for the sake of maximally according comparable positive rights even though the conditions of the PPH are not met.

If we consider the Trolley Case itself we can get further evidence (some of which has been pointed to earlier) of the distinction between killing (someone who is independent of imposition on us) and letting die. Suppose the trolley is headed toward Joe. Would we be indifferent between letting it go to him and doing something without prior intention that results in the trolley turning another track where it will kill Jim? The PPH does not condone killing in this case (since no greater good leads to lesser harm), and if we are *not* indifferent, this suggests that killing differs morally from letting die. If we *would* be willing to toss a coin to decide whether to kill Jim or let Joe die, it would be because this is the way to give equal chances to Jim and to Joe. Having the greater good of equal chances will require us to overcome our resistance to turning the trolley (a killing which also involves intending the cause of death (or its cause)). We do not turn the trolley when it is a choice between one and one (unless we are concerned with giving fair chances), because no greater good causes the lesser harm. Furthermore, in all cases involving a greater number and a smaller number, if we do not take advantage of the permissibility of having a greater good cause a lesser harm, it is probably because we will still be killing rather than letting die. The fact that turning is just permissible, not obligatory, implies that there is a sufficiently weighty alternative factor on which we may choose to act.

In imagining how this would happen we may have to consider a case with the following properties. Because I do not want to kill, I let the five die. Suppose we think (as Quinn does) that this means I intend the cause (of the cause) of their death—that the trolley be headed to them rather than the one. Then we should contrast this with turning the trolley so that I am intending the cause (of the cause) of the one's death. Suppose we think letting the five die because we do not want to kill does not involve intending that the trolley be going to the five. Then we should contrast the letting die with our doing what we (mistakenly) think might help the five, and in the course of this, without prior intention, doing what turns the trolley to the one. If we would prefer to let die than kill in this way, we have evidence that killing in itself matters.

It was noted previously that in order for us to consider redirecting the trolley headed to the five, the trolley must be a potential cause of harm (direct or indirect) to them, rather than merely something (e.g., in the Surgeon Trolley Case) that interferes with someone or some*thing* (e.g., a machine) that *will* aid the five. When it is said that in the original Trolley Case it is permissible to kill one to help five, we do not mean that we may kill one to help five *be aided*, but only to ensure they not be killed. So, we may sometimes, in accord with PPH, kill to prevent others losing what (in a loose sense) aid they already had, but not to prevent people losing out on getting more. Let us consider specific cases in this connection.

Imagine *two* cases, in one of which the trolley is headed toward destroying one electric power plant that provides energy to run machines that will save five lives, and in the other, it will destroy one surgeon who will save five lives in operations tomorrow. In each of these cases, I believe, it is not permissible to redirect the trolley to kill Joe, the single person. Suppose the trolley is headed toward mowing down five power stations, each of which will help run one machine that will save someone's life (a total of five lives). It is not permissible to redirect the trolley to the single person in this case.

Suppose the trolley is headed toward one power plant that is *already* running five machines that are keeping five people alive. In this case it is permissible to redirect the trolley toward Joe, for the trolley would otherwise destroy a lifesaving connection that is already in place. Likewise, suppose the trolley is headed toward one person who is keeping alive five people. In this case the trolley would interrupt the ongoing connection between the one and five by killing one person. Interfering with such life support that individuals have already would cause them harm, and so it is permissible to redirect the trolley to Joe (or any lesser number of people). In these two cases, a power plant and a person are protected at the expense of Joe because we are protecting the five from interference with their ongoing life line. (None of this means the aider herself could not choose to break the connection to the five she aids.)

Recall the Ledge Case, in which a trolley was headed toward a single person who is *not* supporting the lives of five others but who, if hit by the trolley, will fall over a ledge and crush the machines at the bottom, machines that are providing life support for five people. In this case it is also permissible to redirect the trolley to Joe (who is not involved with any others).

Notice that these cases do indicate a problem with the analysis (given above, pp. 185–7) for the PPH by contrast with "pure choice" cases. For in that analysis it was said that there was a connection between our refusal to choose to send a threat to one person rather than to a mere means to greater good, and our refusal to allow a mere means to cause lesser harm. It was said that both cases showed that ends-in-themselves must not confront mere means and lose, that we must not allow the five people to transmit their weight to mere means. But it seems we now have counterexamples. That is, in a pure choice case if five people are *already* being aided by a machine, we *would* send a trolley to one person rather than toward the machine. (The pure choice cases, in which a means not yet helping the greater number *is* destroyed rather than harm the one, suggest some moral difference between preventing aid from starting and interfering with aid already going on. There is this difference even if we are the ones who started the aid, and even if we could stop aid without a direct attack on the persons aided.) Yet suppose a gas were *already* saving five people and one person (rightfully) came along where the gas was drifting and was fatally threatened by it. We should stop the gas. The difference between these cases is that the machine in the pure choice case does not truly *harm* the one person (even though interfering with its operation is the alternative to threatening the one person), but the gas does harm the one person.

In conclusion, let us return to the issue of per se equivalence of killing and letting die. Montmarquet (whose work we discussed in chapter 6) suggests that the permissibility of killing to save in the Trolley Case shows that it is not killing versus letting die per se that is morally important, but rather certain properties that letting die always has, and only some killings (e.g., Trolley-type killings) have. When killings have these properties they will be as permissible as comparable letting-die cases. The properties he believes important have already been described in the previous discussion of Montmarquet's views, namely, that the victim is already threatened with death, and that we as agents do not create a new threat. In addition, he believes that letting-die cases (as well as Trolley-type killings) are permissible when they maximize utility.

I have argued before (pp. 157–164) that the factors to which Montmarquet points are not, in fact, the reasons for the permissibility of redirecting threats. I also do not believe that the factors to which Montmarquet points account for the permissibility of letting die, or that what makes letting die permissible when killing is not accounts for why killing in the Trolley Case is permissible. That is, I do not believe that the PPH accounts for the permissibility of letting die. I do not believe that letting die is permissible only if it maximizes utility or maximizes lives saved. One may refuse to save someone's life because the sacrifice to oneself would be too great, though this does not maximize utility or lives saved. The facts that the victim is already being threatened and that we do not create a threat in letting-die cases are important because they mean that if we do not aid, the victim will lose out on only what he would have had with our assistance by our controlling what is ours. In many cases of killing, the victim loses what he would have had independently of imposition on the killer (since he was not already under a threat for which he needed the killer's assistance) and the agent imposes on him.

It is worth recalling how the "already threatened" factor, in particular, is misleading. One reaction I have already described to the claim that one may kill (at least by redirecting a threat) someone who is already threatened with death, was that the person on the track to which the threat may be redirected is not, in virtue of this physical possibility of redirection, therefore, already threatened. But we also imagined that he *was* already threatened with death, and asked why that should contribute to the permissibility of killing him. One reaction to Montmarquet's claim was that he confused "being already threatened with death" with "being already certainly doomed," for if someone will definitely die no matter what we do, it may well be easier to justify killing him, by redirection or otherwise, for a good cause. But if *we* doom someone already threatened by letting him die, he loses only what he would have had from the aid, for our capacity to doom in this way arises from the fact that no one else could help him. Nevertheless, he was not already certainly doomed, since we could have saved him.

However, when we are responsible for dooming someone already under a threat of death by *killing* him, this means that others would have come to his assistance or that he could have helped himself had we not interfered, and so we are responsible for his losing out on what he would have had independently of us (even if not independently of others). If he is *already* doomed, he does not lose out on anything he could have had if we kill him. If we kill someone whose life only we could have saved, once we refuse to save it, then we kill someone who we have already doomed.

Killing would also be impermissible even if the victim would lose out on only what he would get via our aid if it would be wrong for us not to aid him.

For example, suppose Joe has pneumonia and will die without our penicillin. This will not increase the permissibility of turning the trolley from what it would be if he were healthy, if we ought to give him penicillin to save him from pneumonia. We may not refuse aid with the sole intention of making the person doomed so that it will be permissible to kill him.

I have been suggesting that Montmarquet's conditions are not *sufficient* to account for the permissibility of killing or to fully explain the permissibility of letting die. I also suggest that the factors to which Montmarquet has pointed are not necessary to account for the permissibility of killing. Killings whose permissibility is based on grounds similar to those for the permissibility of letting die need not have the factors Montmarquet emphasizes. Suppose an agent directly kills a victim (e.g., stabs him) who has *always* been receiving high-cost life support in that agent, life support to which the victim had no right. In this case the agent creates a new threat (in Montmarquet's sense of new threat), and the victim has never been under a threat of death. (To say that someone whose need for life support has always been met *was* once under a threat of death would imply that anyone who needs food to survive and has never been without it *was* once already under threat of starvation.) And yet this case, but not the Trolley Case, is one in which killing is permissible because killing shares with letting die morally significant properties that most killing cases do not share.

Practical Issues, the DDE, and the PPH

If the PPH is correct might it help us understand certain puzzling features of cases traditionally discussed in connection with the DDE? For example, the Catholic view on abortion includes the claim that we may remove a cancerous womb though this causes the fetus to die as a side effect of not being attached to its support system, but we may not crush a fetus' skull in order to remove it to save the life of a woman who carries it, though in neither case (by hypothesis) do we intend the fetus' death. Because intention to kill is lacking in both cases, it is puzzling that the DDE should be involved at all, and instead the appeal is often made to the impermissibility of a direct attack on the fetus in the second case.

The PPH might tell us that in the first case, the death of the fetus is the side effect of a *good end* (the removal of the cancerous womb). In the second case, the death is the effect of a mere means to that good end. However, recall that on some revisionist views of the DDE, it is intending involvement of a person that can be wrong, not just intending harm. In crushing a skull, an involvement will be intended which leads to harm; this, rather than a mere neutral means (e.g., one that does not intend involvement of the fetus) leads to harm. This would make the case run afoul of the DDE.

Quinn notes that we may be able to distinguish between (a) cases in which we intentionally involve someone and thereby reap a benefit we would not have been able to reap without that person's presence, and (b) cases in which we intentionally involve someone and thereby accomplish no more than we would have been able to accomplish had the person not been present.[10] Crushing the skull satisfied (b) because all that is accomplished is the woman's being free of a threat she would not have faced if the fetus had not been present. This distinction is, therefore, related to the fact that the fetus is in the position of a morally innocent threat to the woman. It may be permissible, I believe, to intend not only involvement but also the death of such threats in order to make the woman no better off than she would have been had the fetus not been present. I would also emphasize that in being killed the fetus loses the life that is a benefit it is receiving from the use of the woman's body, something not true of all innocent threats. Therefore, the PPH is irrelevant to the justification of abortion if the fetus is imagined to be a person who imposes on the woman and also benefits from the imposition.[11]

Note also that the PPH and the DDE would apply to these cases at all only if the death of the fetus were considered the lesser harm in comparison to the death of a woman, and it isn't clear that this is so, given the Catholic view that the fetus is, or should be treated as, a person. It is puzzling, therefore, why the Catholic Church would approve even the foreseen death of the fetus, since only one life will be saved no matter what we do; the DDE speaks only to producing a *greater* good at the expense of foreseen lesser evil.

Does the analysis provided by the PPH bear on discussions of euthanasia that employ the DDE? According to the DDE, it is impermissible to intentionally kill even a terminally ill patient who will die soon anyway in order to put him out of excruciating, unrelievable pain. (We may imagine we could kill him with morphine, whose painkilling properties are here ineffective.) However, according to Catholic moralists using the DDE, it would be permissible to give a dose of morphine if it were sufficient to knock out the pain, although as a direct, foreseen effect it also caused the patient's death. This must be because *death is viewed as the lesser harm* and eliminating pain as the greater good for this person.

There are alternative interpretations of this case. J. Boyle[12] thinks that it is permissible to give the painkiller, foreseeing the death, and that, if we do not, we are responsible for causing pain as a side effect of letting live. Either way we do harm of some sort. But we might counterargue to this that, if we accept an action-omission distinction as crucial to an analysis of doing, then in not giving a painkiller we do not do anything that causes pain as a side effect. We merely allow pain to occur. (We also avoid causing death.) This assumes that we merely allow the person to continue alive, and do not engage in activity to prolong his life when he would otherwise die. (If we actively resuscitate him, we may well do harm by *causing* pain as a side effect of resuscitation.) Therefore, if it is permissible to give the painkiller and cause death as a side effect — as I believe it is — it is for some reason other than that if we do not do this, we will have caused some other harm (pain) as a side effect. The principle of *do* no harm would be satisfied if we merely did not give the painkiller and *allowed the pain* as a side effect, though that does not mean that this is the right way to act.

Alan Donagan[13] objects to Boyle's reasoning on other grounds. He claims that death is not a side effect if we give the painkiller, nor is pain a side effect of allowing someone to live. Rather, they would each be intended costs of the pursuit of, as the case may be, relief of pain or life. This, I believe, is not correct. Pain would be intended for staying alive only if, for example, causing someone pain were necessary to keep him from falling into a comatose state and thence dying. Dying would be intended to avoid pain in the case where we gave the morphine merely to stop life processes when the morphine had no painkilling properties.

Let us, therefore, assume that the interpretation I have offered of the Painkiller Case is correct. Additional problems remain for the DDE analysis. First, it is worth pointing out that the fact that both the lesser evil (death) and greater good (no pain) are happening to the same person plays a role (even) in the DDE's yielding the "right" answer in the case where morphine is given only as a painkiller. For, according to the PPH, it would not necessarily be permissible to give person A a painkiller if, by some chain of events, this would, as a foreseen side effect, shorten the life of some *other* terminally ill patient B. (This is just another example of the insufficiency of the DDE in accounting for constraints on conduct, like its failure to explain the impermissibility of running over one person on the way to saving five others.) The fact that it is permissible to cause foreseen lesser harm in one person for his own greater good is an indication that there is something special about the context where only one person is involved.

Therefore, with respect to the case in which we intend death, those who apply the PPH, unlike those who apply the DDE, draw a distinction between intending a lesser harm to *one person* as a means to helping *another* and intending a lesser harm to *oneself* as a means to benefiting *oneself*. We draw a distinction in applying the PPH between inter- and intrapersonal intended harms, often prohibiting the former and permitting the latter.[14] In this the application of the PPH is supported by many of our practices. For example, it is permissible to deliberately crush a person's own healthy organ (a lesser evil) if that is the only way to save his life (the greater good). If this is so, then why may we not intend someone's death in order to relieve his pain as well, if it is assumed that death is the lesser evil and avoiding pain the greater good? This is an assumption that the DDE itself must make—that death is the lesser evil in some cases—in order to conclude that it is permissible to inject a painkiller that we foresee will cause someone's death. If we may sometimes intend a lesser harm (amputate a leg) to save someone's life, why should we not be permitted to kill someone with a drug that does *not* also reduce pain, intending the death as the means of eliminating the pain?

An alternative analysis of these cases is that death is not a lesser harm; it is a comparative *good* because the life is so bad. This makes taking life comparable to crushing a *diseased* (not a healthy) organ, but one in which there is some residual function (analogous to any good that life for the ill person still retains). This we may certainly do to achieve a greater good for the person, even a merely greater comparative (not intrinsic) good such as no more pain. It is possible that some wavering about whether death is the lesser harm or a comparative good may account for some people allowing it as a foreseen caused effect but not allowing it as an intended means.

It is certainly a mistake to think that death is a greater harm for the person than suffering pain when he is intentionally killed, but it is a lesser harm than suffering pain when it is a foreseen effect of the painkilling injection. (There may, of course, be social concern about the harmful consequences of giving doctors a right to kill as a means of alleviating pain; perhaps these *harmful* consequences to society would be *greater* than the benefit to the patient. But that question and not the question of the significance for the patient alone of intending rather than foreseeing, seems to be of significance in the case of the terminal patient.)

A key objection to this argument for euthanasia, however, might be constructed by considering analogies. A small lie will cause less harm than the disaster it avoids; a small degree of psychological self-manipulation (of the sort that violates respect for rational humanity) will cause less harm than the greater harm it helps us avoid. Yet it may be *wrong* to lie and to self-manipulate, since right and wrong are not necessarily a function of lesser and greater harm (in a deontological, non-consequentialist theory). It can be intrinsically wrong to do something to oneself, though it diminishes the amount of harm that will befall one.

Further, there are cases in which what is granted to be the lesser evil may permissibly be brought about as a side effect, yet not be intended. For example, in the course of giving a lecture, along with many new true beliefs that come to be had by the hearers, I can foresee that some new false beliefs will also arise as a side effect. These false beliefs as a side effect are a price worth paying for the greater good of more true beliefs. Now suppose that on one occasion the only way for me to achieve the goal of giving an audience many new true beliefs is to tell a lie which in fact involves a piece of misinformation. [15] It may well be morally impermissible for me to tell the lie to achieve the greater good, even though it would be permissible to tolerate the generation of the false belief as a side effect of the informative lecture. Intending that the false belief come about makes a moral difference.

If killing a person for his admitted greater good were like self-manipulation or telling a lie rather than like amputation of a diseased or even healthy organ, we would have an argument against euthanasia. Note, however, that if the greater good becomes great enough, even a means that has something intrinsically wrong about it, like a lie, may come to be justified. So, if the lie may sometimes be justified, we must decide whether intentionally depriving someone who is terminally ill and in pain of some life (or intentionally attacking Life itself, as I believe some people see this) at his request could be significantly worse than a lie.

Is there a reason to think that killing is so significant a wrong when done for someone's own greater good at his own request when competent? Kant offered at least one reason: [16] Human happiness has value only because it is the happiness of a rational being. To treat the rational being as a means to happiness by sacrificing him to the pursuit of his own happiness is to sacrifice what grounds the value of happiness to the thing it grounds. This argument seems to apply well against the use of certain drugs, which cause us to lose reason in order to feel pleasure. (Though the argument is contentious insofar as it implies that happiness is important only in a rational being when it seems to have value even in an animal.) But if a rational being will not retain his rationality even if he goes on living, euthanasia would not be ruled out by this objection of Kant's; someone does not sacrifice what he would lose anyway. Note further that if a rational being will suffer greatly, he would be sacrificing his rational humanity to avoid pain, rather than to achieve happiness. Is it true that avoiding pain has worth only if it leaves a rational being in a nonpainful state (rather than nonexistent), as Kant's argument would seem to imply? The question is whether avoiding pain could be worth more than maintaining one's rational existence. Here there are two types of circumstances to imagine: we eliminate pain by existing in a nonrational (undignified) state; and we eliminate pain by dying, avoiding indignity, and pain as well. The latter possibility, that is, ranking avoiding great pain over maintaining rational life, but without loss of dignity, does not seem out of spirit with a Kantian conception of the person.

These pro-euthanasia arguments may appear not to require us to get consent of the person to be killed. They rely only on showing that we would do him a greater good. But, of course, this would be to incorrectly endorse paternalistic action. It may well be permissible not to aid someone when we control what they need—though perhaps even this is not permissible for doctors who have a duty to aid—if we believe it is in their best interest not to receive what we control. Yet it may not be permissible to intrude upon what is theirs (e.g., their body) to achieve their own greater good when they do not wish this to be done. But when the DDE endorses giving the painkiller which will, as a side effect, cause death, is that argument also meant to work without requiring consent from the patient? Patient consent seems to be required both when death will be a side effect and when it is intended if there is intrusion into someone's body.

But what shall we do when competent consent is not possible? In the cases of adults who are no longer competent and whose view on euthanasia were never expressed, our decision for nonvoluntary euthanasia might be contrary to views they actively held the last time they were competent. (We need not worry that they have changed their minds since they became incompetent because, by hypothesis, their minds were not functioning properly from then on.) On the other hand, if an individual in great pain expresses the view that he wishes to die at a time when he is in great pain, it might be argued that the pain makes his decision not freely chosen or makes him incapable of deciding. But being in such a painful state permanently seems like an objective reason for dying as well as a cause of a decision to die. This argues in favor of heeding such a request, but also for considering it as a ground for *nonvoluntary active euthanasia* as well. (Nonvoluntary does not mean involuntary; it is done without consent, not despite refusal.)

However, people may act *against reason* without being incompetent, and we must often respect these decisions. How then can we impose an objective rational decision on someone who is not able to decide when he might have decided nonrationally and had a right to do so? It may be that in the absence of a known competent decision favoring a *nonrational* policy, we should impose a rational policy. This involves our switching from a hypothetical substituted-judgment standard—what would he have decided—to a best-interests standard. The argument for nonvoluntary active euthanasia is especially strong in the case of children, since we have an especially strong duty to act in their best interests and weak obligations to heed their voluntary decisions.

Limits on the PPH

We have already noted that the PPH applies to inter- rather than intrapersonal harms. It also speaks of "innocents," but it should be restricted to nonthreatening innocents who are independent of life support from imposition on the agent who acts or on the greater number who will be saved. It does not apply to morally innocent threats, that is, individuals who, through no fault of their own, will pose a threat to others. It also does not apply as a constraint on preemptive attacks against those who have a culpable intention to harm, but have not yet done it. Against innocent threats, I believe, we may permissibly use means that have a direct causal relation to harm, indeed perhaps the same means that we may permissibly use against guilty aggressors.

The PPH may be further limited by considerations raised in the Tree-Trolley Case (pp. 160–162). Even if greater good (or what is intimately related to it) would cause the death of only one at the second level of the tree, it may be that one should refuse to be responsible for someone's being eligible for a permissible threat.

Next, the PPH is limited by what I call the *Principle of Secondary Permissibility*: If something we are permitted by the PPH to do to someone is something we physically can do (even if it is not something we would do) and if this act would cause the victim more harm than something that we physically could do but that is *otherwise prohibited* by the PPH, then we may substitute the less harmful act for the more harmful one. That is, we may do secondarily, as a substitute for what we may permissibly do and could do, something that we would not be permitted to do if it were our only option, when doing this is in the best interests of the person who will be harmed. So, for example, suppose redirecting the trolley from the five to Joe is permissible and we could do it, but it would cause Joe to die in a particularly painful way. It may then be permissible to explode the grenade to stop the trolley, if Joe's death as a side effect of the grenade is less painful. If there is no initially permissible act we could perform, there is nothing to replace with the initially impermissible act. The fact that avoiding only a small difference in pain will justify our doing something in the second place that we are prohibited from doing in the first place does not, therefore, mean that there is no really significant moral difference between the two acts. Something may be done to a person for his own sake that we may not do to one person for the sake of another. This then is a further example of the different role of the PPH in intra- and interpersonal cases.

Let us consider this issue in more detail. Suppose we direct scarce resources to helping save the lives of the greater number, thereby leaving the lesser number to die. For example, suppose we allocate health research dollars to develop a cure for a deadly disease that affects a great many people, leaving those few who suffer from a different deadly disease to die. One reason we might find ourselves doing this is that it is agreed to be impermissible to take organs from a few living people against their will to make a serum that will save the lives of the great many people from their deadly disease. This would be true even when the donors would not die from the loss of their organs (e.g., a spare kidney is used). There are various theories as to why it might be impermissible to take organs, for example the PPH and the DDE. Because it is impermissible to sacrifice some for others in this way, we have to do research and find a manmade cure to save the greater number, and must leave the lesser number to die.

But it would certainly be in the best interests of those few who have the rare deadly disease to have research done on their disease instead of on the other more prevalent disease. If they sacrificed their kidneys to make a serum for the greater number (assuming their disease does not affect the serviceability of their organs) we would not have to spend money searching for a man-made cure to the prevalent disease. We could then spend our money on saving those few stricken with the rare deadly disease.

So, it is, in the first place, impermissible to take without his consent, an organ from someone to save others. But this leads us, quite permissibly, to spending money on research to cure the prevalent disease rather than the rare one. This, however, leads to the deaths of those with the rare disease who are potential kidney donors. Thus it becomes in the interest of those with the rare disease to have their spare kidneys removed in order to have their lives saved by our doing the research on their disease.

But, in the circumstances, may we take an organ from those with the rare disease even without their consent? It seems not, if what was said above (p. 197) is true; consent is needed when we interfere with someone's body, even for his own good. But now we should add a proviso to this. When is consent not needed in order to intrude on someone for his own good? When the alternative, permissible course of conduct does not require consent, is worse for the victim, and also intrudes on him. So, for example, it is impermissible to intentionally kill civilians to stop a war, but we may (supposedly) drop bombs on munitions plants with the side effect that children are killed. Suppose we will do this. Then, if we can stop the war by intentionally killing fewer of those very same children who would otherwise die as a side effect, we may intentionally kill them, even without their consent. This is because, given what we could permissibly have done, (a) it is now in the interests of the children (by increasing the probability of each to survive) that we intentionally kill a few of those we would otherwise have killed as a side effect, *and* (b) the alternative permissible conduct was already intrusive as well as permissible in the absence of consent. The Principle of Secondary Permissibility endorses the permissibility our doing just this.

Is there a comparable case in the medical context? Suppose, as a matter of public health, it is permissible to redirect dangerously polluted air away from a large population center toward a small population area without consent of people in the small area. We foresee that this will cause severe sickness in the small population. An alternative is to impose less severely but still intrusively on the bodies of the members of the small population without their consent so that we can make a successful antidote for the severe illness caused to the large population center by the undeflected pollution. The Principle of Secondary Permissibility suggests that this would be permissible.

The Principle of Secondary Permissibility may not always apply. For example, unlike setting off the grenade or intentionally terror bombing, demeaning someone (e.g., making a prostitute of him) seems to be the sort of act that we may not secondarily engage in even for the victim's own benefit (e.g., to save his life). Perhaps this is because it is not to his overall benefit. Furthermore, if paternalistic acts are not always correct, we may not necessarily violate someone's right to noninterference simply because we will otherwise act rightfully in a way that has worse consequences for him but does not involve intrusion without permission. (Though it is interesting to note that ordinary cases of paternalism involve the impermissibility of violating someone's right for the sake of his own interest when the alternative is *his* doing what will be against his interests, rather than *our* doing (permissibly) what will be against his interest. In our cases, the beneficiary of nonpaternalism does not act to make his own mistakes.)

In connection with the nonabsoluteness of the PPH, it is worth mentioning the possibility that the violation of different parts of it may have different moral significance. For suppose it is less serious to cause harm as the effect of a mere means, than to harm someone solely as the means to a better state. Then we should expect that the achievement of a certain degree of utility might permissibly override the first transgression of the PPH when it would fail to override the second transgression.

Furthermore, I emphasize again that the PPH applies only when killing involves (as it does not always) depriving someone of life he would have had independently of imposition on the person who kills him or those to be saved. When we kill someone whom we are aiding, the PPH constraint may not apply; that is, his dying as the means to a greater good may be permissible. So, suppose that in the original Trolley Case, I was already providing Joe with life support in me but I had a stronger duty to help the five than to help Joe. It would then be permissible to set the grenade that stops the fatal trolley headed to the five, though it kills Joe as a direct effect, for this is my way of stopping my aid to Joe, bringing about the condition he would have been in but for my aid, and helping the five instead.

Or suppose a trolley is headed to a surgeon who can save seven but it can be redirected to five. If I was already providing life support to the five and decide the other eight deserve help more, I may switch my allegiance to the eight. If I then send the trolley from the surgeon to five, this is, in effect, a way to mimic the consequences of my stopping aid to the five, by depriving them of life they would only have had via my help (assuming no one else would have helped them instead of me). This creates the situation as it would have been if I had never started to aid the five; they would have been dying and it would have been permissible for me to turn a trolley from the surgeon onto people who would have died shortly anyway in order to help save the eight. The rules that govern letting die, rather than the PPH, govern such killings by contrast to killings of those who exist independently of imposition on us for life support. (Again, this case must be distinguished from not helping the five because we have a primary intention to use their deaths as a means to save the eight, e.g., by using their organs to save the eight. In this case, unlike the previous cases, our aid to the eight does not essentially take the form of turning the trolley, but rather of using the organs of the five. Morally, it has the same structure as letting someone die in order to use his organs to save the eight.)

Finally, the PPH may also be overridden to make someone a victim who would not otherwise be one. For example, in the Transplant III Case discussed at the beginning of chapter 6, the PPH prohibits killing Smith when (1) Jones will die in two hours unless we chop up Smith to get his heart and transplant it into Jones, and (2) Smith will die in four hours if not killed and can then use the heart from dead Jones to survive. Yet I have argued that fairness may be a reason for tossing a coin and killing if necessary, in part since Smith would lose little that he could have independently of Jones.

NOTES

1. This proposal is different from, though related to, one I presented previously [in "Harming Some to Save Others," in *Philosophical Studies* 57(3) (November, 1989): 227–260.] That previous proposal, somewhat modified, was as follows: It is permissible to cause harm to some in the course of achieving the greater good of saving a greater number of others from comparable harm, if events that produce the greater good are not more intimately causally related to the production of harm or to other intrusion onto the person or what is his which leads to such harm, than they are to the production of the greater good (or its structurally equivalent component). Put another way, events that produce the greater good must be at least as intimately causally related to the production of the greater good (or its structurally equivalent component) as they are to the production of the lesser harm or to the other intrusion onto the person or what is his which leads to such harm.

This is a comparative principle. For example, it claims that the degree of causal intimacy to the greater good must be at least as great as the degree of causal intimacy to the lesser harm. This does not imply the view that acts that produce harm by way of longer causal chains are less bad than acts that produce harm by shorter causal chains, when there is no aim in the act but to produce harm. For example, it does not claim that it is less bad to kill someone by using a complicated Rube Goldberg device that we foresee with certainty will hit its target than to kill someone by deliberately firing a gun which we foresee will certainly hit its target.

Spelled out in yet more detail the principle claimed that (1) greater good (or its structural equivalent) would be permitted to produce lesser harm; (2) a means to greater good would be permitted that had lesser harm as an indirect effect if it had greater good at least as a direct or indirect effect (but not by means of the harm); (3) a means to greater good would be permitted that had lesser harm as a direct effect if it had greater good at least as a direct effect; and (4) a means to greater good would be permitted that had lesser harm as its aspect if it had greater good as its aspect as well.

Another possible principle permits lesser harm to come from greater good, but only permits lesser harm to be an indirect effect of a means that directly produces a greater good; for example, if the trolley being moved is the greater good, the grenade that moves the trolley may cause death by a rockslide. This alternative principle in essence, requires that one's action have a *more* intimate causal relation to the greater good than to the lesser evil.

2. I owe the emphasis on the fact that the PPH may be overridden to Keith Lehrer.

3. There are cases that raise the question of when the trolley would cause the death of the greater number of people and hence the question of when redirecting it does have an intimate relation to the greater good. For it seems that we might say the trolley presents a threat to the greater number without this implying that it would cause their deaths, and the latter is necessary for the permissibility of redirecting. For example, suppose Joe is a surgeon who is needed to save the lives of twenty who will otherwise die and the trolley is headed toward him. It could be redirected to five. Should we do so because this will save twenty-one people from death (Surgeon Trolley Case)? I suggest that we may not because the trolley would not be the cause of death of the twenty who need the surgeon, even though it might be correct to say that it is a threat to them, since it does away with someone they need. Its hitting the surgeon will make them worse off than they would otherwise have been, since he would help them if he lives, but it would not be the cause of their death, given that it interferes with his performance of an act of aid that is not yet occurring. Alternatively, we could say it is not a threat to them. If we turned the trolley, the lesser harm would not be the consequence of what we take to be the greater good of a diminished threat.

Things would be different in the following cases. (1) Suppose the twenty were hooked up to a life-support machine toward which the trolley is headed. We can redirect the trolley toward five people. In this case, we may redirect, I believe, because the trolley would destroy a machine that is already providing aid to the five (Machine Case). (2) Suppose the trolley is headed toward Joe, the surgeon, who stands on a ledge. If it knocks him over, he will fall on twenty people below, crushing them. [Alternatively, he could fall on the life-support machine that is saving their lives (Ledge Cases).] Here also, I believe, it is permissible to turn the trolley away from Joe and toward the five, for the trolley is a threat to the five that will cause their deaths if it causes Joe to fall on them.

It might be suggested that the reason we should not turn the trolley away from the surgeon and toward the five in the Surgeon Trolley Case, when the trolley would not cause the deaths of the twenty, is that this would give greater weight to the surgeon than to any other single person, by virtue of the surgeon's ability to save other lives, and this would be wrong. But this, in fact, does not always seem to be a wrong reason for acting. For example, suppose the trolley is headed toward the five and can be redirected to a surgeon who will save twenty (Surgeon Trolley Case II). I believe it would be wrong to aid the five by redirecting the trolley toward the surgeon, thereby depriving the twenty of the person who would save them. We should not *save* the surgeon in the Surgeon Trolley Case, but we should not *harm* him to save five. The impermissibility of saving the surgeon in the Surgeon Trolley Case is, furthermore, in keeping with how we should behave when distributing a scarce resource. For, in the Trolley Case, we must not increase the *direct* harm that the trolley will cause (and so we do not turn from the surgeon to the five), and when we have a drug that can save lives we should put it to its best *direct* use, that is, use it to treat as many of those it is useful for treating as we can. We should not merely distribute it to save one who will then save others who do not suffer from a condition curable by our drug. We may, however, give it to one person rather than to others because he has an ability, which they lack, of delivering the drug to others who can benefit from it. But we need not turn the trolley from the five to the surgeon who will save twenty, because we are not here distributing a scarce resource that has a specific function to which we must attend. It is permitted for us to save someone because he will use his skills to save others from a different threat than he himself faces. Indeed, this case is an instance of the general fact that we could refuse to help save five from a threat because we are busy helping save one who will save twenty. (For more on these issues see *Morality, Mortality*, Vol. I [New York: Oxford University Press, 1993].)

4. In "Harming Some to Save Others," *Philosophical Studies* 57(3) (November 1989): 227–260, I dealt with this case differently. I thought of the safety of the five as the direct effect of the grenade, and, under the PPH proposed in that paper, it was permissible for the lesser harm to be as intimately related as the greater good to the means used.

5. This case should also be distinguished from one in which our doing what we must do to turn the trolley from the five *will* kill the one person, but we must do something *not* causally necessary for turning the trolley in order to get it to stick to the *already dead* bystander. In this case, doing the separate act that gets the trolley to stick *is permissible*. This is because the separate act or separate component does not increase the damage to the one person, whose death is the result of the parts of our act necessary for merely turning the trolley away from the five. This is true even though if this separate act or component were not permissible, it would not be permitted to turn the trolley away from the five (because it would be a waste of six lives), and then the bystander would not be harmed at all.

6. I believe Thomas Nagel's conception of intention, as exhibited in the cases he discusses in which one pursues the harm by various means, involves these four factors. See *The View from Nowhere* (New York: Oxford University Press, 1986). For more on Nagel's view of intention, see pp. 239, 247–8.

7. Might it be that *once we make efforts to turn the trolley* because we believe someone will be hit, though we do nothing extra that we would not have done to turn the trolley from the five in order to ensure his death, we will be committed to hoping that the trolley kills and sticks to the one person, for the sake of its effect? But this is not true. If the one person should escape, the worst that happens is that the trolley goes back and kills the five as it would have originally. This we should accept. On the other hand, there seems to be nothing morally wrong with hoping that if and only if the trolley has already killed the one person, that it stick to him. This does him no further damage. However, if it is wrong to be hoping for the death of the one, then we should not turn a trolley from five toward one when, if it does not kill and stick to him, it will proceed around a loop and kill seven. We would here have to hope that the trolley did kill and stick to the one, since matters would be worse than they had originally been if

the one escaped. (Even here, it is possible that our turning the trolley would be justified if the subjective probability of the one's being hit by our doing no more than turning the trolley from the five was high enough, even if he escapes. Then we need not hope for it to hit him.)

8. In the morality of character, an analogous thesis is present in the view that someone is allowed the (lesser) vices of his (greater) virtues, even if he may not cultivate lesser vices in order to achieve greater virtues.

9. Warren Quinn, "Actions, Intentions, and Consequences: The Doctrine of Double Effect," *Philosophy & Public Affairs* 18 (Fall 1989): 334–351.

10. Warren Quinn, "Actions, Intentions, and Consequences: The Doctrine of Double Effect."

11. For further discussion of abortion, see my *Creation and Abortion* (New York: Oxford University Press, 1992).

12. See J. Boyle, "Who Is Entitled to Double Effect?" *The Journal of Medicine and Philosophy* 16 (1991): 475–94, and my article "The Doctrine of Double Effect: Reflections on Theoretical and Practical Issues," *The Journal of Medicine and Philosophy* 16 (1991): 571. Most of the material that follows is reprinted from that article.

13. See A. Donagan, "Moral Absolutism and the Double-Effect Exception: Reflections on Joseph Boyle's 'Who Is Entitled to Double Effect?'" *The Journal of Medicine and Philosophy* 16 (1991): 511–514, and my article "The Doctrine of Double Effect: Reflections on Theoretical and Practical Issues," p. 571.

14. W. Quinn also makes this point in "Actions, Intentions, and Consequences: The Doctrine of Double Effect."

15. A lie need only involve the liar's belief that the information he passes on is not true, even if in fact it is true.

16. I. Kant, *The Groundwork of the Metaphysics of Morals* trans. T. K. Abbott (Buffalo, N.Y.: Prometheus Books, 1987).

III

8

Prerogatives and Restrictions

The Principle of Permissible Harm discussed in chapter 7 provides an account of certain restrictions on killing. This amounts to a description of when victims have rights not to be killed that restrict agents' conduct. These restrictions, it has been suggested, underlie the impermissibility (for example, in the Transplant Case) of killing one person in order to save the lives of five persons from natural disasters. These restrictions also imply, somewhat more indirectly, that we may not kill one person even to save the lives of five who will die unjustly, killed in violation of their PPH-given rights. For convenience, we may refer to the first class of rights as rights-as-restrictions and to the second class of rights as rights-as-constraints (or constraints, for short), a subclass of restrictions in general. For example, suppose five agents threaten to kill five innocent people in a manner violating the PPH unless we kill one other innocent person (call this the Constraint Case). Concern for certain aspects of the PPH, I believe, implies that we may not kill the one, at least since (we suppose) the single person would not die shortly anyway and the five were not being killed to save the one to begin with. (If they were being killed in order to save him, it would be permissible, I believe, to kill the one to save the five. This is because the single person would be losing nothing he had a right to have, given that he had no right to be alive if the only way to keep him alive was by sacrificing the lives of five others in a way that violated the PPH.)

On the other hand, if we could *redirect* the agents, who will violate the PPH-given rights of the five, toward killing the single person instead, this would be permissible according to the PPH. This all means that it is not always permissible to minimize occurrences of violations of comparable rights.

The detailed examination of why it is sometimes impermissible to minimize violations of comparable rights is a central concern of this and the next three chapters. The non-minimization thesis is controversial, since some might wish to argue that an individual has rights that prohibit us from killing him merely to maximize overall welfare, but that these rights do *not* prohibit us from killing him in order to minimize violation of comparable rights as in the

Constraint Case. If this is so, the PPH would not apply when the greater good we seek is to reduce rights violations. Furthermore, some who agree that we may *not* kill in order to minimize comparable rights violations, do not think this prohibition is based upon a fundamental concern with rights; they think that an agent is prohibited from doing certain acts for reasons not totally derived from the rights of his victim, but derived rather from some property of agents or victim-agent relations.[1] (This is the distinction between the victim-focused and the agent-relativized behaviors that we will discuss.) The agent-relativized account of restrictions can be thought of as a revisionist view. Another non-rights-based view is the duty-based view, which I shall refer to as agent-focused, but not agent-relative, since it is the content of what the agent does, rather than his special relation to an act, that is at issue.

In addition, some have argued that we may defend some components of a non-consequentialist morality, in particular agent prerogatives not to maximize overall good (taken to include not minimizing bad)[2] without justifying the existence of rights that stand in the way of utility maximizing in general or rights against minimizing violation of rights, in particular. This is the view for which Samuel Scheffler has argued.[3]

In this chapter we consider the position Scheffler argues for, which provides an agent with the prerogative (a permission, sometimes also referred to as an option) not to maximize overall good, but which denies the existence of any restrictions on the agent's maximizing overall good if she wishes to. (Scheffler calls this a "hybrid" theory, somewhere between Consequentialist and Deontological theories. Unlike a consequentialist theory, it acknowledges no obligation to maximize overall good, but, unlike deontological theories, it acknowledges no rights or duties that stand in the way of maximizing. Strictly speaking it is a form of nonconsequentialism, since it does not claim that only consequences matter.) We will also consider the views of Bernard Williams, which predate and bear a significant relation to Scheffler's. We follow with criticisms of Scheffler's theory and then discussion of possible ways of justifying restrictions and constraints on agents, using the premises of Scheffler's own system. Finally, we reconsider the grounds for thinking that there are prerogatives not to maximize overall good.

Before beginning the discussion of Scheffler we should say a bit more about the Constraint Case. It might have been that the one to be killed was someone who would soon die or be killed by someone else anyway. He might also be (a) someone who never had any chance of being one of the greater number who are threatened, or (b) someone who had a chance of being among the greater number. It is possible that objections to killing someone who would die anyway are fundamentally agent-focused rather than victim-focused, although, even here, it may be that the one power remaining to someone who will be killed by a particular person is to exercise his right to limit everyone else's violent behavior toward him. We focus in this chapter and in the following chapters on cases involving someone who would not die anyway and that also fall under (a) or (b).

I

Scheffler on Constraints and Restrictions

According to Scheffler, regardless of how we characterize the right that the single person in the Constraint Case has that is supposed to make it impermissible to kill him, the following objection can still be raised: Any type of right the single person has that would be transgressed by my killing him is the type of right that will be transgressed five times over if the five are killed instead of him. If we care about rights, it only makes sense to minimize their violation. Therefore, the rights of the single person should not constrain us in situations where there is already imperfect compliance with respect to the comparable rights of others. There may, therefore, be rights that should never be violated in the first place (e.g., to prevent greater natural disasters) but there are no rights that constrain our preventing the attempted violations of such rights. Further, any relation that exists between the agent and her victim (e.g, intending death) can be duplicated five times over with five other agents and their victims. If these relations are bad, should we not minimize their occurrence?

We might also add that it could be argued that no relation which would exist between that single person *and the five* if the single person is to be killed to save the five, can be pointed to as a definitive reason for not killing the single person. This is because the right of the victim or characteristic of the relation between the one and the five can (by hypothesis) be present five times over when the five agents kill their five victims for the sake, perhaps, of saving yet other people. For example, if the five are to be killed to save twenty from having their rights violated, the same relation will exist between the five and the twenty as between the one and the five. If we point to any right of the victim or any relationship as a reason not to kill, we will want to know why we should not minimize the presence of that rights violation or that wrong relation.[4]

However, Scheffler then asks, insofar as rights are thought of as "trumps" (to use Ronald Dworkin's term) against utility, the argument for minimizing violation of rights can be extended to show that there should be no such trumps (i.e., rights-as-restrictions) at all. The extended argument is as follows: We do not care more about rights violations than about the loss of the same utility without a rights violation. For example, if someone were drowning from natural causes and someone else were drowning because a villain had thrown him into the water (a rights violation), other things equal, we would not necessarily choose to save the victim of injustice first.[5] [In fact, with respect to this last argument, I believe it is a mistake to think that incurring a loss by rights violation is no worse than incurring the same loss by natural causes, and a mistake to so conclude from this example. Even if we would not save the victims of injustice before those of natural disaster—and this is not clear to me—we might well act to prevent the *act of injustice* before acting to prevent a natural disaster. That is, we might rush to prevent the *act* of killing (not merely its consequence, the death of the person) before we saved someone from natural disaster. Would spending public funds on a police force before we spend on a health service to stop natural disease support this claim? On the other hand, if we would not prevent the killings first, it might be because preventing them involves helping the *killer*, rather than helping his victim more than we would help another who dies of natural disaster: we would be stopping the killer's wrong act, and, some might ask, why should we help the killer?]

Scheffler on Prerogatives

Though Scheffler objects to right-based or duty-based restrictions, he does present reasons in support of agents' *prerogative* not to minimize rights violations or to maximize utility. However, he believes, these reasons cannot also support restrictions on agents' behavior. This is because the argument for a morally justified prerogative begins by noting that, typically, an agent values his own ends from his personal point of view, both independently of, and possibly out of proportion to, the impartial value of those ends, and agents are typically motivated to act from this personal (rather than impartial) point of view. [The personal point of view is not necessarily egoistic; one's projects may include the (magnified) good of others. The projects may also have, and be adopted because they are seen as having, some impersonal value.] Prerogatives are justified, Scheffler thinks, because moral theory should endorse, to some degree, our natural tendency to be motivated to act *directly* from the personal point of view, rather than consider it wrong to act from the personal point of view unless our action also promotes what is valuable from the impartial point of view.[6] Moral theory should endorse the permissibility of acting from the personal point of view, at least sometimes, because, Scheffler claims, moral theory must reflect the nature of the creature it is designed for, and it is an important component of our nature that we are motivated to act from the personal point of view. Furthermore, he thinks moral theory should reflect these facts in the form of a prerogative sometimes to act contrary to utility maximization, even if this does not maximize the ability or opportunity of agents to act from their personal points of view. [This is the Liberation Strategy. It changes the structure of a theory of the right away from maximizing consequentialism. That is, "the right" (as in "doing the right thing") is no longer a function of maximizing "the good," even if acting according to the personal point of view is considered a good. The Maximization Strategy, by contrast, would take acting from the personal point of view to be a good and seek to maximize it or seek to minimize interference with its presence.]

According to Scheffler, permitting an agent to act from his personal point of view increases the agent's freedom to act from his personal point of view, but restrictions of all sorts interfere with his freedom. Therefore restrictions cannot have the same ground as prerogatives. Scheffler also thinks that permission to act from the personal point of view may help to preserve the integrity of the agent, at least insofar as it respects an important characteristic of his identity—his strong tendency to act from a personal point of view, as a matter of natural fact. Scheffler here makes reference to Bernard Williams's integrity-based criticism of consequentialism (though he claims his view differs from Williams's).[7] It is worth considering Williams's view in more detail at this point.

Williams on Integrity

Williams (it seems to me) uses "integrity" in at least three different ways. He first argues that utilitarians might deal with the negative feelings someone has at the idea of killing one person to save others by counting it as merely a negative feeling in a utility calculation. This utilitarian view fails to recognize, he says, that the feeling is a moral feeling, a reflection of one's belief that utilitarianism is wrong. Not permitting us to act on these feelings, but merely counting them in a utility calculation, therefore robs us of our *moral integrity*; for we feel we are doing what is morally wrong. But, we may ask Williams, how can we prove that what we feel is wrong is really wrong? It is only if we do what is really wrong that we really lose moral integrity. In response, the idea of loss of *personal* (rather than moral) *integrity* may be used by Williams: If we would have to give up a personal commitment not to kill (or some other basic project), treating the feelings associated with killing as no more than hangovers from outmoded views, we then destroy our personal integrity in at least *two senses*. First, we become dissociated and divided against ourselves, lacking *integrity-as-wholeness*. (Scheffler's concern that we not be asked to act against our natural proclivity to the personal point of view comes closest to concern for this sort of integrity.) Second, we lose personal integrity insofar as personal integrity involves *continuing commitment* to projects. A moral theory (utilitarian or otherwise), Williams thinks, asks too much of us, if it asks us to detach ourselves in action from such an important part of ourself. If it asks too much, it cannot be the correct moral theory. If it is not the correct theory, then if we do as it says, we may really lose *moral* integrity. [Williams goes so far as to say[8] that strenuous moralities cannot have a claim on us since, if they require us to give up the projects that make us want to go on living (what Williams has called "categorical projects"), it could make sense to commit suicide and thereby escape the claims of morality. He contrasts categorical with "hypothetical projects" which we have *if* we go on living.]

Williams's arguments can be faulted. First, for someone whose most important commitment is to utilitarian morality, giving up other projects will not involve a destruction of wholeness or a loss of integrity understood as commitment to projects. A utilitarian can wish us to be intensely involved with our projects—for the more we care for them, the more happiness will be produced by our succeeding in them—and still believe that there is a highest project, the project of morality, to maximize overall happiness. A Kantian (whose strict deontological requirements Williams also criticizes) does not see morality as a project to produce good. Morality is held to be a set of background standards to which we must conform any projects we have. But, even *if*, therefore, as a devoted Kantian, one would not be intensely involved with morality *as a goal-oriented project*, morality could still have a dominant regulative function in one's life, and so giving up projects in order to abide by morality will again not involve destruction of personal wholeness. [To deny this in the Kantian case, would be to fail to note (as a Humean might) that the *intensity* of feeling for, or involvement with, ways of acting—which may not be as strong for the regulative as for a goal-oriented morality—is not necessarily the only factor in determining strength of motivation to act.]

In general, the argument that the correct morality cannot require a great deal of us seems wrong. Sometimes, morality does require great losses from us. For example, we may be obligated to give up a project that is at the core of our identity rather than kill someone to help complete it (even if we need not save someone's life at the cost of our project). The fact that someone would give up a categorical project rather than kill for it—indeed the fact that someone would commit suicide rather than kill someone else to complete a categorical project—shows that he believes morality's commands are supreme. Contrary to what Williams suggests, therefore, the willingness to commit suicide (as opposed to the willingness to kill another) if we cannot engage in our categorical projects does not show that a strenuous morality's claim on us is not dominant. Why commit suicide if one can escape morality simply by living in defiance of it? (Of course, if morality forbade suicide, someone might have to go on living even if he were deprived of the opportunity for categorical projects).

Finally, suppose that a consequentialist theory would be *wrong to demand* some act because doing it imposes more of a sacrifice than is required to help promote the greater good. This does not yet show that *the act* it demands *is wrong* (i.e., prohibited), as well as non-obligatory. Williams has not given a proof that the original negative feeling against doing an act shows that the act is morally wrong if his argument is based on the severity of the sacrifice required in doing it. The contrast in question can be further brought out as follows: If I sacrifice a personal project when I am not required to, I may behave in a morally exemplary (or supererogatory) way rather than in a way that violates my moral integrity by involving me in doing something wrong. This can be true even if I sacrifice a project at the core of my personal identity.[9]

This problem in Williams's discussion arises because he presents cases, for example, killing one to save others, that a non-utilitarian would say might involve restrictions on conduct, but he discusses them as though they were cases involving an agent's refusal to give up commitments and projects.[10] If they involved only giving up projects and commitments, performing these acts might be strenuous but not necessarily morally wrong, for suffering loss of *personal* integrity (in the senses discussed above) is not always to lose *moral* integrity. Preserving an agent's autonomy, his freedom from requirements to give up projects, is different from requiring him to abstain from certain conduct. However, note that the example Williams discusses to illustrate his views is a case (known as "Jim and the Indians") in which an agent is asked to kill someone who would otherwise be killed anyway. These cases, I believe, more than those in which we must kill someone who would not have died anyway yield to an analysis based on an agent's concern for his own projects and commitments. This is one reason why this case — which has been much discussed — is not a good enough example for purposes of discussing deontological restrictions and constraints.

Scheffler on Prerogatives versus Restrictions

To return to Scheffler's views, we recall that he claims that prerogatives give more choice and freedom to the agent, allowing her to do what she most wants to do from her own personal point of view. They do this at least on the occasion when they are used. But acting on one's prerogatives now may not maximize one's ability to act on such prerogatives over one's entire life nor maximize others' abilities to act on such prerogatives. The prerogative directly gives more choice and freedom; it may not do so indirectly, in one's own life or in the lives of others.

Restrictions (such as arise from the PPH) limit the agent's possible actions, making it morally impermissible for him to promote the greatest good if this happens to be his project. On these grounds, Scheffler claims, they cannot be motivated by the same considerations as motivate the prerogative.

Now we can see that Scheffler's system, with prerogatives but no restrictions, amounts to a system with liberties for agents to try to do certain nonoptimific acts, but it gives them no guarantee of noninterference by others with such acts. That is, it does not give them a *right* to exercise the prerogative. Interference is allowed, because taking something away from someone, without requiring him to give it up as a matter of duty, is not considered a violation of someone's integrity in Scheffler's scheme. The prerogative is intended to protect only *active* choices, reflecting a person's strong tendency to act (or omit to act) from the personal point of view. It does not provide protection from *passively* suffering a loss. Scheffler claims that it is only requiring certain active choices that interferes with integrity (understood as commitment to one's projects, or as being true to human nature) since this denies that a natural form of motivation is morally acceptable.

Objections

One thing to notice about Scheffler's joint argument for prerogatives and against restrictions is how totally it *seems* to eliminate restrictions, even when it is not a question of their standing in the way of maximizing overall good. If a prerogative means that my pursuit of projects that do not produce the best state of affairs may sometimes take precedence over producing the best state of affairs, and if producing the best state of affairs may take precedence over not violating the PPH (since, according to Scheffler there are no restrictions), may we conclude (by transitivity) that pursuing my own non-optimific projects may take precedence over not violating the PPH? For example, may I kill someone to complete my non-optimific project? (In shorthand, where "P" stands for "personal project," "G" stands for "greater good," "R" stands for "restrictions," and "≥" stands for "may take precedence over," if P ≥ G and G ≥ R, in a way that eliminates restrictions does P ≥ R in a way that eliminates restrictions?).[11] This problem can be derived even more directly if the best state of affairs (G) just *is* one that requires that we abide by restrictions. If it is not to be an implication of a hybrid system that we are permitted to kill another in order to pursue a nonoptimific project—and I assume this is an undesirable conclusion even to those who believe that we need not always sacrifice personal projects to promote overall good—and yet restrictions on optimizing are not to be reintroduced, a supporter of hybrid systems must explain why "may take precedence over" is not transitive. This Scheffler does not do.

Another (less "tight") way to make this point is to wonder why, if we need not make large sacrifices for the greater good (i.e., we have prerogatives), we do have to make large sacrifices to abide by restrictions or constraints. That is, if P ≥ G, why can P not take precedence over R in a way which amounts to there being no R? (This is a less tight way to make the point, because it leaves out the explicit claim that G ≥ R—but this may make it more attractive to those who think that impersonal good doesn't trump restrictions but the needs of individuals acting from their personal points of view do.)

Even if we block these arguments however, there is another route in Scheffler's system to the permissibility of killing in order to pursue what is only one's non-optimific personal project. Scheffler's discussion of prerogatives implies that he thinks that we are not obliged always to make big sacrifices to help others. But he also questions whether there is a morally difference between killing and letting die or between harming and not aiding in general. This implies that if we would have to suffer a large personal loss unless we did an act that killed someone, doing the fatal act would be no less permissible than not saving someone's life rather than suffer the same loss.

Notice that reintroducing the moral significance of the killing/letting-die, harming/not-aiding distinctions to solve the problem of killing for non-optimific personal projects, may also lead to a restriction on killing for the sake of optimific projects. If there is a distinction to be drawn between killing and letting die that motivates a greater limitation on the freedom of the individual when he needs to kill in order to pursue his non-optimific projects, perhaps there will also be such a limitation on killing when he has an optimific project.

It remains possible, of course, that one could argue for a restriction on killing for non-optimific projects and at the same time argue that any significance to a killing/letting-die distinction pales in the face of an optimific project. (I suggest how this might be done in chapter 12.) Furthermore, a bargaining model could be introduced to generate some limits on killing for non-optimific projects (and also for optimific projects not involving the maximizing of lives saved).[12] For example, one could be willing to give up the pursuit of one's own non-optimific projects that require the killing of others, in exchange for freedom from this threat to oneself. In particular, one might give up the freedom to kill others in pursuit of a project one would not be willing to sacrifice one's own life for, in order to avoid being killed for the sake of others' non-optimific personal projects.

The bargaining model could be extended: So long as one cares less for one's optimific projects as well as for one's non-optimific projects than for one's own life, one might strike a bargain for restrictions on anyone's being killed for the sake of any projects. Whether or not we accept such bargaining models as adequate justification for restrictions,[13] it is important to notice that they depend on weighing the passive loss of something (by someone else taking it away) as much as one weighs actively giving up something. This equivalence (as we have seen) Scheffler denies.

Scheffler's view has been that prerogatives and restrictions are separate matters, but I have been suggesting a connection: the retention of reasonable limits on the former may require introduction of some version of the latter.[14]

The Point of View of the Victim: Passive and Active Loss

The link so far suggested between prerogatives and restrictions is indirect. I turn now to the possibility of a more *direct* link between prerogatives and restrictions on projects that maximize utility, maximize lives saved, or minimize rights violated, assuming for the time being Scheffler's view that prerogatives are grounded in concern for a personal point of view. To separate the issue of the prerogative from that of the restriction (and its subclass, constraints on minimizing rights violations), Scheffler argues that prerogatives increase the freedom of an agent to pursue his projects, restrictions limit it. Therefore, restrictions cannot share the rationale of freeing someone to pursue his personal point of view. However, it might be suggested that the connection between prerogatives and restrictions need not be based on viewing the same person as an agent in two different situations, with prerogatives freeing him in one situation, restrictions restraining him in the other. That connection can be based instead on viewing the same person as an agent with a prerogative in one situation and as a potential *victim* of another agent in a different situation, and, hence, as the beneficiary of a restriction. The restriction provides the same person whose freedom is increased by the prerogative when he is an agent, with protection of his freedom and the special value he places on his own life from his personal point of view, when he is the potential victim. So, it might be argued, contrary to Scheffler, that both prerogatives and restrictions free and support the personal point of view, and hence that both derive from concern for the personal point of view.[15]

This anti-Schefflerian argument connecting prerogatives with restrictions also depends on de-emphasizing the significance of the distinction between actively sacrificing something and passive loss (i.e., having the same thing taken from one by someone else). Scheffler specifically distinguishes between active sacrifice and passive loss, arguing that when we take away from someone what he does not actively give, we do not interfere with his integrity, since we do not require him to act contrary to his own important projects and his personal point of view.

Emphasizing this distinction can help Scheffler out of what others might find an embarrassing theoretical position. Scheffler represents the agent who wishes to kill one to save five as someone whose personal project it is to produce the best outcome. This might ordinarily be taken to imply that he should be willing to sacrifice himself as readily as someone else to save the five. But perhaps it is possible on Scheffler's view to combine (a) giving greater weight to one's own life than to others' (via the personal point of view) and (b) having as one's project producing the (impersonally or impartially) best outcome. Then we might be confronted with an agent who exercised his prerogative not to sacrifice his own life to produce the best outcome, but wanted to sacrifice someone else's life to produce the best outcome.

I think our initial response to such an agent is contempt, on the grounds that we think the agent expects others *to do* what he himself is unwilling to do that is, give up one's life. But here emphasizing the distinction between active and passive loss becomes important. The agent might argue that he doesn't expect his potential victim to do what he wouldn't do, that is, sacrifice his own life for the greater good. He doesn't even expect the potential victim not to resist being killed. He only believes that it is permissible for him to try to impose the loss of life. Adherence to minimal standards of universalization requires only that the agent be willing to grant that others are similarly at liberty to try to impose such a loss on him.

To support the rejection of such a strong active/passive loss distinction, we might again emphasize two different notions of integrity already distinguished above. First, there is traditional moral integrity, which involves a commitment not to do what one thinks is morally wrong. Second, there is integrity in the sense Scheffler (and Williams) uses it, of commitment to one's most important projects whether or not that commitment is a matter of morality as ordinarily understood. As noted above, it seems that, at least sometimes, if one gives up a project in order to produce the best overall outcome, one does not lose moral standing. A sign of this is that voluntarily giving up some basic projects is often thought to be supererogatory, rather than forbidden, to a person with moral integrity.

As noted above, Williams believes that a sacrifice may not be morally required if it involves giving up an important life project. Again as noted above, even if this were true, this is not the same as saying that the sacrifice of one's project is morally wrong. Showing that a theory is wrong to demand a big sacrifice of us is not the same as showing that the particular act it demands (whose performance will demand this sacrifice of us) is itself wrong and should be prohibited.

To elaborate on what was said above, giving up one's life or one's work is often such a supererogatory loss — the sacrifice of what Williams would characterize as a categorical, in contrast to a hypothetical, project. It is permissible to abandon even a categorical project by sacrificing one's life to save five others. Indeed, this sacrifice of one's life — the sacrifice of what makes any categorical projects possible — or categorical projects does not strike us as the same sort of (quasi)-moral violation of integrity as is involved when, for example, someone sacrifices his pacifist principles by taking up arms in order to produce the best overall outcome. There are, therefore, many important, self-defining projects, for example, an artist's work, which one could actively give up for the sake of saving a life, without this indicating some moral or quasi-moral fault.

Now the anti-Schefflerian might argue that, in the case of goods whose abandonment does *not* indicate a moral fault, a passive loss imposed by others is as bad (or almost as bad) for the person who suffers it as actively giving up the same goods under the (mis)apprehension that it is one's duty to do so. So having one's career interrupted would be almost as bad for the person as giving it up. It is only when the good that is lost involves moral or quasi-moral integrity that an agent's actively (rather than passively) losing the good makes a big difference, since it is *only* by his acting that such integrity can be lost at all.

It is true, however, that, even in the area of projects whose voluntary interruption does not connote a lack of moral integrity, the corresponding passive loss (imposed by others), as bad as it is, is not as *difficult for the victim to bring about*. Perhaps it is the difficulty of bringing about a loss rather than any quasi-moral failure involved in it or badness of suffering it, that underlies the distinction between active and passive loss with which Scheffler is concerned.[16] Even if we take this difference into account, however, it seems to me to be a mistake to draw *too* great a distinction between active and passive loss. Each person desires to avoid either kind of loss. As agents with freedom to pursue optimific or non-optimific projects, all persons pose a threat of passive loss to one another.

If they are agents who combine a personal and an impartial perspective and, therefore (at least sometimes), place greater weight on their own lives than on even any optimific projects they pursue, each may want to strike a bargain with all. We here rereach our earlier conclusions about the possible role of bargains, though we should now emphasize that personal freedom is the point of these bargains. The bargain is that one will not impose passive loss on others in order to produce a given outcome, if they will not impose such losses on one; that is, one will impose no losses greater than what one would be willing to suffer actively (or risk suffering) for that outcome.[17] Such a bargain, however, could not be struck to avoid being killed (among other reasons) when there is some project for which the agent who wants to kill *would* be willing to give up his own life. If we think, nevertheless, that other victims should be protected even in this circumstance, then this way of generating restrictions could not be complete.

Among other major problems I identify with the bargaining approach are (1) how those who are too weak to threaten other persons with passive losses ever wind up getting protected from such losses, and (2) how those who are too strong ever to need protection wind up having to restrain themselves.

Bargains Fail to Minimize Interference

This attempt to generate the restriction from the same ground as the prerogative, by bringing the disvalue of losses actively and passively brought about
closer together, also faces problems from another direction. The restrictions
derived from bargaining would not necessarily *minimize* the interference from
being killed that is important to each person from his personal point of view.
For example, if someone who had the project of saving five people from being
killed would not give up his own life to save them, the bargaining model just
described says he should not kill an unwilling other to save them. If the single
person is not killed, five people will be killed and so lose the freedom from
interference that is important from their personal points of view.

Furthermore, when considered from the point of view of a single person
who did not know whether he would be among the group of five potential
victims or instead be the single potential victim who can be used to save the
five others, restrictions of this kind do not minimize his *own* chances of being
killed (given that he was five times more likely to be in the group of five). It is
one thing to strike a bargain not to kill or be killed for the sake of things worth
less to each individual than his life; it is another thing to bargain away a higher
chance of survival.

So, as already indicated in the beginning of this chapter, there are two
types of scenarios worth separating. There is one scenario in which the one
person to be sacrificed never himself ran any risk of being in the group that
will benefit from the sacrifice. We can imagine that the person is totally
invulnerable except to the attack that would sacrifice him to save the five. In
this case the restrictions (merely) prevent the optimal outcome, that is, overall
minimizing of lives lost or minimizing of rights violated. The second scenario
involves someone who might himself have been in the group needing aid. In
this case the restrictions prevent minimizing chances of interference for each
person. As noted above, it may seem that, if there is a restriction on being
killed in this latter case it could not be generated by the bargaining described
above, since absence of restrictions would provide a lower risk of death for
each. For now, let us consider only the loss of *overall* minimization of lives
lost or rights violated, rather than the failure of restrictions to minimize the
chances of interference even of the single victim who had faced the possibility
of being in the group of five. We shall return to the latter scenario in chapter 11.

Prerogatives and Non-minimization

Does the restriction, since it does not minimize certain types of interference
overall, face an objection to it that the prerogative does not? According to
Scheffler, a prerogative also does not maximize the instances in which people
may act from their personal point of view, or, perhaps more accurately, it
does not minimize the incidence of people's being required to act contrary to
their personal point of view. (Not maximizing might suggest that people are
not supported in their efforts to develop and carry out personal projects; not
minimizing emphasizes their actively going against established projects.)[18]

Scheffler specifically distinguishes his system with a prerogative from a system that minimizes instances of people acting against their personal points of view. How can such non-minimization come about in Scheffler's system, given the emphasis on active versus passive loss? Might one think that Scheffler's system makes it possible for no one ever to actively sacrifice anything of great importance to him, though the system might result—given no restrictions or constraints—in much passive loss? The non-minimization of action against the personal point of view can come about if individuals sometimes exercising their prerogative makes for such bad states of affairs that somewhere down the road individuals will be obligated to make big sacrifices.[19] This seems correct, since Scheffler does not think one can pursue one's personal projects in all circumstances. One is, rather, permitted to assign somewhat greater weight to one's project than it is given from the impartial point of view. Even multiplied by an additional factor, however, one's own projects may be outweighed by a great enough impartial good.

Given all this, Scheffler must explain why he thinks that if there were restrictions, then minimizing interference with them is clearly a more rational strategy than constraints, or why loss of lives should be minimized rather than have restrictions, though he does *not* think minimizing acts that are contrary to the personal point of view is clearly a more rational strategy than a prerogative. Since the prerogative does not minimize instances of acting against the personal point of view, a defense of prerogatives that will be separate from any justification of restrictions cannot be based merely on the idea that it is worse to actively give up, by one's own decision, something personally valuable than to have it taken away by someone else. This is because minimization would also do more than a prerogative would do to help us avoid having to actively give up something personally valuable.

One possible reason—which (is all) Scheffler himself suggests for tolerating non-minimizing in the form of a prerogative—is that having a prerogative incorporates acting from the personal point of view directly into a moral system's basic structure by altering the theory of the right. Unmediated by maximization/minimization, promoting the personal point of view becomes more than just a new part of the theory of the good, that is, another value we should maximize or whose disruption we should minimize. The personal is totally unmediated by the impersonal, as it occurs naturally. This may be a way to take acting from the personal point of view more seriously. (In that sense it introduces a new impersonal value, I would say.) But could not something comparable be said about having restrictions and constraints? If a defense of restrictions is being based on the significance of the personal point of view of the victim as well as that of the agent, why should interference with acting from the personal point of view be treated not merely as a disvalue, yet interference with victims should be treated merely as a disvalue to be minimized?

The Selection and Value Problems

Perhaps there are other reasons for tolerating non-minimization in the form of a prerogative but not in the form of a restriction or constraint. When an agent must decide about his own fate (in acting on personal projects) rather than about the fate of others, there is one personal point of view (his own) that bears a different relation to him than do all the others. In this way, concern for the personal point of view easily picks out the individual whose personal perspective is protected by the prerogative. By contrast, while it is true that the loss of his own life may mean more to the single person who would be killed to save five others than the loss of the five other lives means *to him*, to each of the other five the loss of his life will mean more to *him* than the loss of the one. How can concern for the personal point of view, even concern to incorporate it at the basis of the moral system unmediated by impersonal considerations, tell an agent which of the six personal points of view to protect? Could it be said that, from the point of view of the agent who must decide whether to kill the single person, none of the six personal points of view he confronts stand out as special, as does his own point of view when he exercises his prerogative?

Furthermore, while the prerogative is not minimizing, it does introduce at a foundational level a new value, the agent's special concern for his own projects. Restrictions fail to minimize losses, it is said, without explaining what value is served by highlighting with a restriction the personal point of view of the single potential victim (rather than the personal points of view of each of the five). It is not that this one person is *always* favored, since we might go to help the five rather than save the one from someone else's attack. And, it might be asked, how can it be the value of noninterference that we are highlighting, when five will be interfered with if the one is not?

This attempt to connect a prerogative, said to be motivated by concern for the personal point of view, with the restriction, therefore, seems to end with two queries: Why do we select one victim's personal point of view to protect rather than another's? (Call this the Selection Problem.) What value does such a selection introduce into morality? (Call this the Value Problem.)

We shall return to the Selection and Value Problems later. At present I wish to consider another possible hypothesis as to the connection between a prerogative and a restriction (or constraint), one that will also involve a more detailed look at one approach to the Selection Problem.

Personal Sovereignty

The single potential victim who would be killed to save the five has, according to Scheffler, the prerogative not to (actively) sacrifice his own life to save the five. It is attractive to think that if someone (at least sometimes) is not obliged to give up his life to save others, this should imply that no one may take it for the sake of others. It may seem that if we want to protect the prerogative of a person not to sacrifice himself and if we think that the sacrifice involved in actively giving up one's life is not markedly greater than the (passive) loss of one's life per se, we should also want to ensure that certain personal losses be brought about only by the choice of the person who will suffer them, that is, that there are certain things a person should *control* insofar as anyone does.

(On Scheffler's account of the prerogative, with which we have been working, it derives from our having a personal point of view insofar as this means having concern for things independent of and out of proportion to their importance from the impartial point of view. If the appropriateness of control had the same source, it might seem that we ought to control whatever we care about from the personal point of view out of proportion to its impartially considered value. I will return to this problematic view below.)

This proposal attempts to derive restrictions *directly* from prerogatives themselves, arguing that if someone has a choice whether to give something up, this must be connected with its being his choice whether that thing is taken. It derives *sovereignty* by the individual over something directly from the prerogative, or rather it derives the prerogative and restriction from sovereignty by the individual over something, where the sovereignty is derived from the concern that the individual has for something independent of and out of proportion to its value from an impartial point of view.

Evidence for this proposed relation between the prerogative and the limits on extracting sacrifices could come from considering how much easier it is to legitimate imposing a loss on someone if he also has a duty to make the sacrifice and so has no prerogative not to make the sacrifice.

If active choice is protected in a non-minimizing manner by a prerogative (i.e., in a manner that does not minimize instances in which someone must act contrary to his personal point of view), and if the present suggested connection between one's protected active choice and what may permissibly be done to one were correct, then the protection against certain things being done to one should also be distributed in a non-minimizing manner (i.e., as restrictions that do not necessarily minimize occurrences of interference).

Objections

The most obvious objection to this view is that it is generally agreed, even by non-consequentialists, that a victim's prerogative to (try to) avoid a loss is *not* always accompanied by a restriction on imposing that loss. The following are cases in which this seems clearly true: (1) I have a prerogative not to go into the army, but it is permissible to draft me. (In this case it is not even permissible for me to resist the call to arms, except on conscientious grounds that are not necessary to justify my refusal to volunteer); (2) A person has the prerogative *not* to tell me to let him drown, yet it is permissible for me to leave him to save a larger group. (He has the prerogative not to give up aid, but not the right to control it.) (3) It is sometimes permissible to redirect a threat away from a larger group of people to a smaller group. However, the smaller group has the prerogative of not volunteering their lives, and even of turning the threat away from themselves and back onto the larger group.

Furthermore, even non-consequentialists believe that sometimes it is impermissible to take something from someone (there *is* a restriction on us), even though he has a duty to give it up (no prerogative not to). It is not always permissible for us to enforce someone else's duty.

So the first objection to deriving a restriction directly from a prerogative is that it is not always true that the permissibility of choosing whether to sacrifice something implies the right to have final say over whether that thing will be sacrificed. This should be kept in mind even if we manage to show that there is some connection between a prerogative and a restriction.

The second objection to deriving restrictions directly from prerogatives in this way brings us back to the problem of selecting among victims. The five who will be killed if the one is not, like the one, had prerogatives not to volunteer their lives to save others, and if prerogatives *do* give rise to restrictions, they would each have a right not to be so used by an agent. If they die because the one is not killed to save them, and if they would not have chosen to give up their lives so that others might live, isn't the supposed link between their prerogative and the permissibility of their controlling their lives put in jeopardy? Would not the one and the five be in the same positions even if prerogatives *were* morally connected to a right to control whether one's life will be taken? That is, the Selection Problem appears again: How would one choose whose sovereignty to protect? Is there some difference between the one and the five, especially when the five will be violated to help twenty others?

The Selection Problem: Solutions?

Several types of answers might be offered to the Selection Question. I will here briefly summarize some approaches (without endorsing them). One approach, which is, in a way, *victim-focused*, would try to discover differences in what will happen to the victims or in their relationship to each other if one is selected for protection rather than another. This might be a basis for picking out one victim's personal point of view to be reflected directly in the moral system without regard to minimization.

A second approach, which is *agent-relative*, tells each agent that there is no difference between potential victims aside from the fact that one of them will be *your* victim whereas the others will be someone else's. My intended victim will stand in a different relation to me than will other victims: I intend his death but only foresee those of others, and I kill him but only let the others die. Note that this answer to the Selection Problem does not make the restriction so fundamentally depend on the significance of the victim's greater concern (for what affects his projects) from the personal point of view. It returns us once again to the importance of the agent's point of view. But, it can also be said, I will stand in a different relation to my victim *from his own personal point of view*, than I will stand in relation to the other victims from their personal points of view. The one will have a greater complaint against *me*, it is said, even if each of the five has the same complaint against the one who kills him. This assumes that killing or intending death is more to be complained against than foreseen abandonment. What is emphasized here is the different contents of the personal points of view of the victims toward one agent, which the agent in turn takes into account from his point of view. This is different from emphasizing the differences in what will happen to the single potential victim rather than to the five.[20]

But if intending deaths is bad or wrong, why shouldn't the agent minimize the bad intentions, or acts stemming from them, of other agents, rather than attend only to his own intention? One answer in keeping with highlighting the personal point of view of the agent is that, from an agent's perspective, his intention will weigh more heavily with him than those of others, and he will prefer what has personal value from his perspective to what has value from other perspectives. This account of why the single person is selected for protection does not appeal directly to the value of that person's freedom from interference as the basis for the restrictions, but appeals rather to something about the agent's personal perspective (though not his concern for personal autonomy). (The idea of an agent-relative approach should be distinguished from the idea of an agent-focused approach, which points to the prohibitive quality of the content of the agent's act or intent, not necessarily its greater significance for him because it is his.[21])

Asymmetry

At this point let us consider in more detail that particular victim-focused approach to answering the Selection Problem which tells us to look for differences between what will happen to the one if he is killed and what will happen to the five if they are killed. (This is not the only possible victim-focused approach.) One possible difference is that while the single person's death is arranged to serve as a means to save the five from a fatal threat already in existence, if the five are killed because the one is not so used, they will not have been used to save *his* life from a threat he faced independently of being used to save them. So the one, if killed, would stand in a relation to the five different from that in which the five, if they die, would stand to the one. The single person would have lost control over his life and freedom from interference *for the sake of* the five in a way that they would not lose control *for his sake* if they are killed. The restriction, it may be suggested, is based on the importance of not putting the single individual into this position vis-à-vis the five when the five would not be in this position vis-à-vis him. We do not really take the lives of the five for the one, and they are not in a position to give or not give their lives for him, as he is for them.

The value represented by a restriction so justified, and hence a solution to the Value Problem, would be "preserving appropriate relations among potential victims who are moral equals." Each person of the six has his personal point of view, but the value specifically represented by the restriction (described in detail by a principle like the PPH) would be treating individuals, each of whom has his own personal point of view, so as to relate them properly to each other.

Objection

Is this the sort of asymmetry that is embedded in the structure of morality to block our minimizing rights violations? For suppose (as we also did above) that the five are being threatened with death in order to save twenty other people and the five will die unless the one is killed to save them? Then while the five and the one will stand in a particular asymmetrical relation to each other (i.e., the same thing will not happen to the five vis-à-vis the one if they are killed as will happen to the one vis-à-vis the five if he is killed), the five will stand in the same relation to the twenty as the one would stand to the five. Hence if we were concerned with freedom from interference whose justification is derived from concern for the personal point of view, or with personal sovereignty, or with avoiding morally relevant asymmetries between persons, we should have to ask, whose freedom, sovereignty, and position in asymmetrical relations do we highlight? Do we highlight those of the one or those of the five who will die for the twenty? Is there some asymmetry between the asymmetries?

The following is a possible answer: Suppose someone need not volunteer to save five other people who need not have volunteered to save yet other people. Suppose also that there is an implication relation between the prerogative (freedom to act) and the right not to have a sacrifice extracted (freedom from interference). Then a restriction should protect that individual whose prerogative would *in fact* have determined the outcome in a given situation if we (who have to choose now) had been totally incapable of affecting the outcome. This will constitute the asymmetry between potential victims, the way of honing in on the person (or people) whose personal point of view should determine the outcome.

There are problems with this proposal, however. For example, suppose some third party has offered to kill the one person to save the five. The five might have exercised their prerogative by not refusing this offer, so *their* prerogative would have determined the outcome. This would imply that we should not interfere with a third party killing the single person. By contrast, if we allowed the restriction to be determined by the prerogative that would have determined the outcome *had no third parties (or any of the five themselves) interfered* with anyone, then we would locate the restriction with the single person. However, we would have to explain the motivation for picking just these circumstances as yielding the preferred outcome. Presumably the reason we would emphasize these circumstances has something to do with the view that it would be *wrong* for third parties (or the five) to interfere with the single person for the sake of saving the five to begin with. But what we are searching for is a reason to believe that this is true.

Summary

Scheffler thinks that having a prerogative instead of minimizing instances where people are morally required to act against their personal point of view, takes the personal point of view more seriously by making it basic to morality, unmediated by minimization of disvalue which serves the impartial point of view. Each agent knows whose personal point of view to promote because he stands in a special relation to one, his own. Indeed, if rather than pursue overall good, he acted promote to someone else's personal point of view (when this other person's personal point of view is not of special personal concern to him), he would not be instantiating the special role of the personal point of view. Therefore, he would not achieve at least one point of giving the personal point of view independent standing—namely having an actor's act express what he holds valuable. If we want a comparable analysis of restrictions and constraints grounded in the value of the personal point of view, to which we pay homage by not minimizing rights violations, an agent must pick out one personal point of view to protect by not acting contrary to it. The problem is how to do this, and also what value is represented by the choice of one personal point of view rather than another. Suppose we think we can solve the problem of selection by choosing on the basis of some asymmetry between the one and five—that is, the five would be saved by harming the one but the one would not be saved by harming the five—and this protects the value of maintaining appropriate relations between equals. We then face the problem of deciding why we do not minimize instances in which this value is violated, if we locate the same asymmetry between the five and those for whom they would be sacrificed.

II

Is the Prerogative Really Based on the Personal Point of View?

So far we have tried to see whether a restriction and constraint can be generated either from the same ground as Scheffler's prerogative (the importance of personal point of view) or directly from the prerogative itself. We have continued to assume that Scheffler correctly identifies the ground of the prerogative as the importance of the personal point of view. Now let us examine whether this assumption is correct. If it is not, then this will affect whether prerogatives, restrictions, and constraints—all of which together amount to strong sovereignty of the person over herself—could stem from the existence of the personal point of view.

Scheffler characterizes the personal point of view as the tendency to care about things independently of, and out of proportion to, the value they have from an impersonal point of view. "Independently of," means "not because of" its importance from the impersonal view. "Out of proportion to" implies "not in the same way" as the impersonal view. These are two separate characteristics. The question is whether either one, or both together, can, or need, ground a prerogative. Let us consider the second characteristic first. (I have already explained that I believe that the idea of impartiality rather than that of impersonality better captures the point of view Scheffler means to contrast with the personal point of view. Assuming this to be true, I will use these terms interchangeably in this section.)

There are two sorts of questions here: Does the existence of the sort of sovereignty that includes prerogatives, restrictions, and constraints—or any of these components, and in particular, the prerogative—depend on people's *in fact* giving weight to their own projects out of proportion to their weight from an impersonal (or impartial) point of view? Does the existence of this sort of sovereignty depend on people's *having the capacity* to give weight to their own projects out of proportion to their weight from an impersonal (or impartial) point of view?

Capacity for versus Actual Concern

If individuals *in fact* had only projects that coincided with an impersonal point of view, it might seem that there would be no need for the prerogative to choose not to act for optimal outcomes, since no one would want to do so. There would also be no need for restrictions or constraints. So it might seem that the existence of prerogatives and restrictions would depend on the nature of *actual* projects or preferences. But suppose individuals who in fact had no projects that conflicted with the impersonal point of view have the capacity for *different* projects and preferences, that do not coincide with the impersonal point of view. Suppose, further, that the foundation of prerogatives and restrictions and constraints is in the personal point of view. Then, if people changed projects they would want to have permission not to act for optimal good, and they would need restricting rights, which would protect them from being used by others for optimal good or minimization of rights violations. (Would they need prerogatives and restrictions in order for it even to be permissible for them to change their projects from optimific to non-optimific ones? Not necessarily, only to act on their projects when they conflicted with optimific ones.) I think, therefore, that if the prerogatives and constraints have anything basically to do with caring differently from a personal point of view, it is the capacity to do so, rather than the actuality of doing so, that matters. Prerogatives, restrictions, and constraints can and will be waived when all projects are in fact for optimal good, and if they are in place all along they protect individuals who may change to nonoptimific projects.

Concerns versus Entitlements

Still, given that it is preferable to make prerogatives depend on *capacities* for projects and preferences not in accord with the impersonal view, is it correct to do so? One point to make in this connection is that *what we have a prerogative, or rights amounting to sovereignty, over should not morally be determined by what we can care about most from the personal point of view*, but independently of this. What we have a claim to control via prerogatives and restrictions should not be determined by the nature of our projects and our preferences or by what projects and preferences we have the capacity to have. If what I wanted most to control via prerogatives (and restrictions) was some x, the fact that I had a capacity for projects that were best implemented by control of x would not be sufficient to legitimate my having the control. For example, if my projects involved concern for someone else's welfare out of proportion to the value it had from the impersonal point of view, I should not necessarily have the paternalistic prerogative to try to interfere with his decisions about his own life, or prevent him from being used for optimific ends by himself or others. This is true even if he cares about himself much less from his personal point of view than I do. There should not even be some compromise between my desires for him and his desires for himself. At the very least, accompanying the generation of prerogatives (not to act for the greater good) from concern for the personal point of view there must be some prior idea of entitlements, which function as constraints on the scope of the prerogative and also help generate prerogatives. These entitlements are prior in the sense that they stem from some source other than the strongest concerns people have from their personal points of view. So, your body is yours to control even if I care about it more than you do and more than the weight it has from an impartial point of view. It is permissible to act on the basis of one's personal point of view because there are things over which one has legitimate control, but this does not mean that one acquires legitimate control over things because one cares about them from one's personal point of view.

Ordinarily, one thing that a person is thought to have a right to control is (the person) himself. Yet the control someone has over what makes him a separate person seems to be limited in many ways; for example, morally by his duties. It also seems true that the person's control over what makes him a separate person, relative to another agent, extends only over what he retains independently of the (nonrequired/nonvoluntarily maintained) imposition on that other agent.

Such entitlements, of course, could be nothing more than restrictions of some sort, and so this argument against deriving prerogatives from the contents of the personal point of view might depend on (or be support for) the existence of restrictions. As such, it can be compared to the point made above, that if prerogatives to pursue one's projects are not limited by some restrictions, we will be permitted to harm others as a means to our nonoptimific pursuits. The present point is concerned with interfering paternalistically (rather than harmfully) with others, not simply as a means to fulfillment of our projects, but as the very point of these projects.

Likewise, if God owned me, the fact that I cared more about my projects than about optimific ones wouldn't necessarily mean that I would have a prerogative (or constraining right) over matters concerning only myself. The fact, if it is one, that God cannot own me must, therefore, depend on some other fact than what sort of valuing I am capable of, that I can care so much about myself. It is only if what it is permissible for me to control by a prerogative, restriction, or constraint, for example, myself, were always what I care most about controlling, that what we should be allowed to control and what we most wanted to control would not differ.

Another objection to deriving prerogatives, restrictions and constraints from the contents of the personal point of view stems from my sometimes being protected in pursuits that are of no great importance to me.[22] I may have a prerogative to clap my hands all day though it doesn't really mean very much to me at all to do so, and you may have no right to interfere with my doing this (even if it means a great deal to you to do so). The prerogative and right that protect this activity cannot arise because I care a great deal about the activity, out of proportion to its objective value from the impersonal point of view. I might have a protected sphere of choice: whether to engage in an activity, rather than act optimifically, though I do not care about the activity out of proportion to its true value, and its true value does not make doing it the optimific choice. I may do what is unimportant to me, though I could do something better, presumably because I am entitled to the time and means with which to do it, even if I do not care about *these* out of proportion to their value from the impartial point of view.

It is true that sometimes only personal concerns that are themselves recognized from an impartial point of view as weighty play a role in grounding prerogatives when these conflict with the possibility of helping someone avoid a serious loss. For example, one's concern to avoid the loss of an arm may count against the good of someone's life, but not one's concern to avoid the loss of one of one's ordinary hairs. However, even in these cases it is the objective importance of what we would lose, not our degree of concern, that matters most.

Suppose that my having control over something, as expressed by prerogatives and restrictions, is not totally determined by the types of projects for which I have a capacity to care much about from the personal point of view, but rather by some entitlement over the item generated in a different way. Then it may be that even if I had the capacity only for projects that coincided with the objective point of view, it would still make sense to think that there are prerogatives, restrictions, and constraints, though they would never be used and were constantly waived. This would be true, I believe, in a community of saints who would always act supererogatorily (e.g., volunteering their lives to save others), so the need to violate rights did not arise.[23] This implies that these saints could still recognize that each other's optimific acts were supererogatory, not duties. Furthermore, if this community had to live without either the prerogative or the restrictions, it is more likely that they would live without the prerogative. It would be exchanged for duties which others should not enforce.

Autonomy and Entitlements

Conceiving of the existence of restrictions, constraints, and prerogatives in such a world of saints prompts us to consider the other characteristic of the personal point of view, its independence from the impartial point of view. This means that one can be concerned about something for some reason other than that it is optimific from the impartial point of view. Is this true of the saints? It might be true that they care about what is optimific but not because it is. Is this why they should have a prerogative? Suppose they cared for what was optimific because it is optimific, and it is their nature to do so. Still, they would have reached their concerns by rational reflection. If we think they should decide in this way for themselves, this suggests that the deepest function of such devices as prerogatives is to protect areas of free choice, rather than the pursuit of projects not in accord with the impersonal point of view. One way of describing a concern for free choice is that it is a concern that individuals live (in the sense of direct) their own lives. It is a concern for autonomy, most often where significant personal concerns are at stake. (But note that autonomy may itself be one of those significant concerns.) Living one's own life may have nothing to do with one's project's not being in accord with what is best from the impersonal point of view. It does imply that one is not to be treated as if one's existence were "for" the goal of optimizing good. Rather one exists as an *end-in-itself*, even if one does not always serve the greatest good when it could be served.

If a person has a personal point of view there are possible alternatives to acting for the greatest good, even if these possibilities do not ground prerogatives and restrictions. So given constraining rights, one may not be permitted to act on a project which seeks outcomes endorsed by the impersonal point of view, unless these outcomes are chosen by those who must be sacrificed to bring them about. Freedom of choice must be limited to doing things to what one has a right to control in the absence of permission from others. That one has a rightful claim decided independently of what one happens to care about most from the personal point of view would be at the root of prerogatives and restrictions.

Reasons and Persons

To say that a prerogative is (in part) one way of expressing the view that the person is an end-in-itself, whose existence is not for serving greater good when he could serve the greater good, is very different from saying that the prerogative is justified by the fact that people are typically motivated to act from personal concerns. The latter is a natural psychological property of persons; the former is a non-natural, moral characteristic of persons, and so the former offers an immediate deduction of an "ought" from an "is." But, we may ask, what characteristics make persons ends-in-themselves and not merely "for" the greatest good even when they could be? Is it having a personal concern? But animals have this and yet may not have strong prerogatives, nor be ends-in-themselves. Is it having a rational will, that is, being able to act for the sake of reasons? But if people often act from personal concerns that do not coincide with impersonal concerns, and this is consistent with having a rational will, does someone's being an end-in-itself imply the existence of both personal and impersonal *reasons*? One way of taking Scheffler's derivation of the prerogative is that it validates as reasons the factors, and their weight, which are significant from the personal point of view. There are personal as well as impersonal reasons. The prerogative can then be understood not only for an endorsement of a natural tendency in persons, but as a way of generating a certain class of reasons, reasons that are possible because persons are rated as ends-in-themselves. But do we really want to say that people being ends-in-themselves implies that personal projects are valid reasons? What of cases where the reasons for which people act really are invalid (e.g., excessively risky behavior), and yet we think they should be allowed to act in this way because they are owed respect as ends-in-themselves? It is because I am the sort of creature who is an end-in-itself that my personal point of view can provide valid reasons and that I also have a permission to act on invalid ones. Of course, this leaves it open that being able to conceive of concerns as *reasons to act* (rather than to act as an animal might, on sufficiently pressing impulses) is what makes someone an end-in-itself, and this in turn makes certain personal projects one sort of valid reason. But then respect for the personal point of view or personal reasons that do not coincide with an impersonal judgement would be derived from respect for a person who conceives of considerations as reasons.

Kagan on Prerogatives

Shelly Kagan argues[24] that to try to justify prerogatives (which he calls options) by concern for autonomy is merely to assert again what they are by definition; that is, it is to argue that we should give people a choice (prerogative) because then they have choice (autonomy). But such an argument is not without merit if it draws attention to the intrinsic significance of being able to choose, especially when other significant concerns besides autonomy itself are at stake. Ultimately, however, as I have said, I believe prerogatives are justified by the view that persons are not essentially means to the end of the best state of affairs, but ends-in-themselves. This idea of a person as an end-in-itself goes beyond and helps justify autonomy understood as choice or control. It is this idea of persons as ends-in-themselves who deserve autonomy in action that prerogatives help capture.

The Pro Tanto Reason

The idea of the person as an end-in-itself is also relevant to another component of Kagan's views. Kagan refers to the "moral moderate" as someone who believes in both personal prerogatives and constraints on what may be done to others in pursuing both the greatest good and personal interests. Yet the moderate also believes there is some reason to promote the greatest good. Indeed, Kagan thinks the moderate also believes in a pro tanto reason to promote the greatest good (i.e., one that is always present to be acted on unless a stronger reason outweighs it). This seems hard to believe, since most moderates want to assign no moral weight to producing minimal goods, and may even want to argue that one is under no obligation to present a reason for not bringing about a significant good. They may, for example, think that having done a great deal of good already, someone might simply be uninterested in doing more good, even though it would not be burdensome to do so. The only reason for not doing more good would be that one had already done some, and this is not the sort of reason Kagan thinks of as a decisive countervailing reason. Why might the moderate think this? Because he thinks it understandable that a person resist the idea that he is a means for achieving the greater good; that he assert his independence from that goal and so recognizes that his own existence is an end-in-itself.

This leaves it open that promoting the good can always justify one's conduct, if one chooses to make that one's reason. In this sense, it is always a reason, but (to use Kagan's language) a non-insistent reason. It is only sometimes that it is an insistent reason. Thomas Nagel has pointed out[25] that a prerogative amounts to the view that there are non-insistent reasons for action, that is, reasons for action that do not mandate action. To use his example, if I buy a book because it is cheap, that is a reason for buying it, but it did not have to be my reason. In other words, prerogatives permit us to determine the amount of weight to give to factors of a certain type. Only certain factors may be able to serve as reasons, but these factors do not have to come assigned with a predetermined weight, or even any weight.

Non-minimization

Suppose choice is important because it is tied to the view of the person as an end-in-itself. Would we not express greater concern for this conception of the person if we minimized the number of occasions on which people may not choose, even if this means occasionally depriving someone of control by placing her under a moral obligation to make a big sacrifice to ensure that others may continue to choose? Here, then, the issue of whether to have a real prerogative, which makes the theory of the right non-consequentialist, arises, as it did for Scheffler. My view is that *permitting* this means to minimization, though it involved no physical coercion by others and no one in reality ever had to make the obligatory sacrifice, would defeat the very ideal we were supposedly trying to protect. This is because individuals would no longer be persons who are not to be treated as if they were "for" the greater good, since they would be permissibly available for minimizing interference with (the value of) choice. All individuals would lose a certain status. [I shall have more to say about this type of argument in connection with constraints. Note that it is a very different argument for anti-minimization and for grounding a prerogative than Scheffler gives. We have already described his view: Having a prerogative takes more seriously the personal point of view by making it independent of the impartial point of view. This part of his argument, of course, follows his initial claim that a natural tendency to act from a personal point of view should be given recognition. I have also disputed that part of his argument].

The Negative Argument for Prerogatives

Kagan suggests two other arguments that might be put forward to support prerogatives, and argues against them both. The first is the Negative Argument: We must have prerogatives since, given our regrettable nature, we cannot be motivated to act for the greatest good consistently enough, and nothing (e.g., the greatest good) can be a reason for our acting if it cannot motivate sufficiently (the internalist hypothesis). Against this argument (but without rejecting the internalist hypothesis), Kagan presents the *Argument from Vividness*:

1. If we had vivid (not mere pale propositional) knowledge of the fates of all other beings, we would act for the greatest good. (An example of pale propositional knowledge in another area: the idea of a billion dollars before we try to make it vivid through imagination.)

2. Our lacking such vivid knowledge is a cognitive defect in us (even if it has certain protective functions).

3. Therefore, we should be motivated now, even in the absence of vivid knowledge, to act as we would if we had it, because we recognize the lack as a defect.

The idea here is that once we recognize that lack of vivid knowledge is a cognitive defect with respect to truly understanding the content of beliefs, and that it is only this defect that prevents us from acting for greater good, we can be motivated to act as those who have perfect (vivid) knowledge would act. Analogously, we go to experts on the stock market and listen to what they say, even if they do not successfully communicate their knowledge to us so that we actually share it. If the cognitively perfect are motivated by the greatest good, we, too, while still cognitively imperfect, should be capable of being motivated by it, since we are motivated away from our defects. Hence, the Negative Argument is wrong.

Questions

My first question about the Argument from Vividness concerns *premise (1)*: the lack of vivid knowledge may not be the only thing that prevents action for the greatest good. If someone lies at your feet dying, you have vivid knowledge of his fate. Yet you are not motivated to give up your arm to save his life, though you recognize this would be for the best. Those with vivid knowledge are not necessarily motivated to act for the greatest good and against their own self-interest. Furthermore, this need not be because you are vividly aware of your own fate, for you have non-vivid knowledge of your own future, and (as Kagan himself notes) often find it hard to be motivated by the thought of your future when it conflicts with satisfying present desires. Yet you may refuse your spare kidney to save the life of the person dying before you simply because there is a danger you will need it in the future. Indeed, if you are tempted to give your organ, you may restrain yourself with the thought that it's *you* versus him. A strong bias toward the self survives vividness; therefore, the bias toward the self does not stem primarily from relative degrees of vividness in our knowledge of the self versus others.

Presumably those who resist the effect of vividness may do so because they believe they have a right not to sacrifice themselves. They do not believe that consequentialism without prerogatives (or any moral theory without prerogatives) is the correct moral theory. This is important for the proper understanding of Kagan's Vividness Argument. He does not intend it to suffice as a proof of the correctness of consequentialism. It is, given the internalist hypothesis, only one part of the proof for the correctness of consequentialism, the part that shows we could be motivated to act as consequentialism says we should if we had superior acquaintance with facts. If we have positive grounds for rejecting arguments for consequentialism besides the one from vividness (or other theories without prerogatives), there is no reason to think we will be motivated to act on even a full panoply of vivid knowledge.

In addition, suppose vivid knowledge did cause us to act when pale propositional knowledge alone did not. It might not be better appreciation of the reasons that there are for acting that would then be the cause of our acting. Rather, it might be psychological pressure resulting from the vividness: this is something we should also often resist, especially if other components of the argument for consequentialism are not right. If vividness did not give us new facts or make us better aware of facts we already know in propositional form, but only placed psychological pressure on us, it would not lead us to act for the reasons that give rise to a requirement to act. And, indeed, exposure to vivid knowledge, for example, via pictures and on-site visits, often gives us the sense that we are being psychologically manipulated, that reason is being overridden by feeling. Suppose this were how vivid knowledge affected us. Then even if we were cognitively imperfect in not having vivid knowledge but only complete propositional knowledge, it would not follow that we had imperfect knowledge for purposes of action. Therefore, contrary to *premise (2)*, we may now be cognitively adequate for purposes of deciding how to act.

Still, it is true that I tend to do more for the needy person who lies at my feet than for the one at a distance. It is also true that I am usually more vividly aware of the person at my feet. But the reason I respond may have nothing to do with vividness. Rather, the person is near at hand rather than far, and my obligations may therefore be greater because of this, not greater merely because I have vivid awareness. I should have this reason to be motivated to act even if I were not vividly aware of the near person, but just had propositional knowledge that he was near. But if nearness were the reason for my being obligated, I would not be obligated if I had vivid knowledge of those at a distance. Similarly, Kagan argues that the best explanation of why we help friends or relations is that we are more vividly aware of their problems. But we may help them because they are friends or relations (or because they have built up expectations that we will help), even if we are not vividly aware of their problems.

Alternatively, it may be because I actually have vivid knowledge that I have reason to act. It might be morally monstrous to be able to ignore such knowledge, whereas it might not be monstrous to be able to ignore the pale (even complete) propositional knowledge. But this does not show that I am obligated to obtain more vivid knowledge so that I will become obligated to serve the greatest good or behave as a person with such vivid knowledge should behave. Indeed, it may give me reason to avoid obtaining vivid knowledge, so that I will not then have new obligations.[26]

The Positive Argument for Prerogatives

Kagan constructs a second argument in defense of prerogatives. On the assumption that prerogatives have something to do with the possibility of satisfying the aims of the personal point of view, he attempts to identify positively good things that result from acting from the personal point of view, things that cannot be achieved in acting from the impartial point of view. This is a Positive Argument for prerogatives. But then, he asks, if there are such values to be achieved only in acting from the personal point of view — and he doubts this is true — would they not make action from the personal point of view obligatory rather than optional? Would they not be _insistent reasons_, and so fail to generate prerogatives?

I also believe that this argument fails to justify prerogatives. It is the wrong type of defense to put into the mouth of the defender of prerogatives: To provide a positive justification of prerogatives, we do not want just a defense of acting from the personal point of view via an enumeration of values achievable only by so acting. Rather, we also want a defense of having the _choice_ whether to act from the personal point of view or from the impartial point of view. This is a defense at the second rather than the first level, so to speak, where the first level is the choice of any given prong of the choice tree (personal or impartial point of view) and the reasons for choosing one way versus the other, and the second level is the presence of prerogatives (which allow the choice) versus only requirements in one's moral system. We want a defense not of the decision to pursue the personal point of view, but a defense of the prerogative to do so. [Pointing to the positive factors in acting from the personal point of view might yield a prerogative if these values weigh just (or almost) as much as those gained by acting from the impartial point of view. But this is too narrow a justification.] Further, the defense of the possibility of choice represented by prerogatives does consist of insistent reasons, in the sense that they should prove that any correct moral system must have prerogatives, any moral system without prerogatives is wrong. We have suggested that emphasizing the idea of the person as an end-in-itself provides such a defense since such a person may sometimes decide whether to work for the greater good.

Conclusions

Two conclusions that might be ventured at this point, then, are that some idea of rights and some conception of what there are rights to (entitlements) must be in place before we can have any reasonable conception of prerogatives, and that these prerogatives are themselves more likely to be derived from concern for autonomy and for the person who is an end-in-itself than merely from concern for the capacity and tendency to act from a personal point of view that has concerns different from, and generated independently of, the impersonal view. There are things people should control and decide on the use of, even if they would always decide in accord with and because of optimific outcome.

We still have the problem of justifying a constraint that stands in the way of minimizing violations of a PPH-right, and even, according to Scheffler (see pp. 209–210), the problem of justifying a PPH-restriction. If a prerogative, rather than minimizing the occasions on which people's choices are interfered with, preserves the identity of persons as ends-in-themselves, as was argued above, restrictions and constraints may do the same. Proving this would involve, in part, dealing with the minimization problem and showing that what is done if we permit minimizing does involve treating persons as other than ends-in-themselves. Before considering this possibility in detail, let us examine some revisionist approaches to the problems of justifying restrictions and constraints which emphasize the agent's special relation to her act.

NOTES

1. Jeremy Waldron takes this view in *Theories of Rights* (Oxford: Oxford University Press, 1984), Introduction.

2. These permissions not to maximize are understood as including permissions to act in ways that do not even conform to *rules* that maximize overall good.

3. In *The Rejection of Consequentialism* (Oxford: Oxford University Press, 1982).

4. I am imagining this as a case in which if I do kill the one person the five will be saved and the twenty will, therefore, die. A consequentialist who is concerned with utility would not kill the one in this case, since more people would die if he did. A consequentialist who cares especially about rights violations might kill the one if the twenty will die of natural causes. The traditional rights theorist would not kill the one, but not because the twenty would die if he did. We could imagine the case differently: killing the one to save the five will also save the twenty (from natural causes or from killings).

5. Scheffler attributes this example to Thomas Scanlon.

6. In *Morality, Mortality*, Vol. 1 (New York: Oxford University Press, 1993), I adopt Rawls' distinction between impersonal and impartial points of view. The latter permits us to recognize the separateness of persons in a way the former does not without permitting bias. An impersonal theory, like utilitarianism, does not care how goods are distributed among persons so long as there are more goods; an impartial theory does care about how goods are distributed among persons. Scheffler, I believe, means to focus on the contrast between impartial and partial points of view. Both impersonal and partial points of view are part of the objective point of view.

7. Which appears in J. J. C. Smart and Bernard Williams, *Utilitarianism: For and Against* (Cambridge: Cambridge University Press, 1973).

8. In his "Persons, Character, and Morality," *Moral Luck* (Cambridge: Cambridge University Press, 1981.)

9. For more on this point, see pp. 216–217.

10. Thomas Nagel made this point.

11. I made this point in "Supererogation and Obligation," *Journal of Philosophy*

(March 1985): 118–238. Shelly Kagan also criticizes Scheffler on the grounds that his system seems to permit us to violate rights rather than sacrifice personal projects in "Does Consequentialism Demand Too Much?" *Philosophy & Public Affairs* 13(Summer 84): 239–254, and in *The Limits of Morality* (Oxford: Oxford University Press, 1989). I discuss a possible answer Scheffler might give in chapter 12.

12. Chris McMahon suggested this model to me for use in this context.

13. They are probably inadequate since they do not explain how those who never had the ability to threaten death come to bargain for restrictions on their being killed.

14. Scheffler himself now realizes the need for some restrictions on nonoptimific projects. He calls a system that includes these a "modified hybrid theory." (Personal communication.) I offered the suggestions I make in chapter 12 as a way of constructing such a modified hybrid.

15. Kagan makes a similar argument in *The Limits of Morality*.

16. This suggestion about difficulty was made to me by Derek Parfit. Parfit also suggested that the difficulty of actively giving up rather than having a loss imposed may be what underlies John Rawls's concern about the "strains of commitment" to an agreement. Agreements involving coerced compliance rather than autonomous carrying out of a bargain would not, then, involve strains of commitment.

17. I present this as a possible scenario, but I do not wish to endorse such a bargaining model for the origin of moral restrictions.

18. This distinction was emphasized to me by Derek Parfit.

19. Derek Parfit's point.

20. This approach seems to be exemplified in the work of Thomas Nagel.

21. The distinction between agent-relative and agent-focused should become clearer in Chapter 9.

22. Michael Slote makes this point.

23. Saint-like behavior isn't always optimific, nor necessarily self-sacrificial. For example, it may promote the interests of one other person, not universal good.

24. In *The Limits of Morality*. The following discussion is included in my "Nonconsequentialism, the Person-as-an-End-in-Itself, and the Significance of Status," *Philosophy & Public Affairs* 21(4) (Fall 1992): 354–89.

25. In conversation

26. I owe this point to Lisa Warenski.

9

Constraints and You

Some attempts to justify restrictions and constraints, including answers to the Selection and Value Problems, have grounded the impermissibility of killing the single person in the Constraint Case in some property of the agent who would kill or in the victim-agent relationship. I shall call these "revisionist explanations," since I believe they remove the focus from the victim, *his* rights and properties, as the source of restrictions and constraints.

The aim of this chapter is to to see how closely revisionist recommendations for action match those which the traditional (victim-focused) explanation is supposed to have. I consider it traditional to explain restrictions and constraints in terms of properties of victims. To this explanation, I have argued in chapter 7, should be added victims' rights not to stand in certain relationships to those who would be benefited by their loss.[1]

It is important to recall, given our discussion of Scheffler, that there are two questions at issue. First, what are the traditional and revisionist explanations of restrictions? and, second, what are the traditional and revisionist explanations of constraints? These are two different questions. For example, one version of the first question is: What is the explanation of the impermissibility of killing someone in order to save five in the Transplant Case (but the permissibility of killing in the Trolley Case)? This concerns the explanation of traditional rights which restrict maximizing utility. The second question is: What is the explanation of the impermissibility of transgressing a right not to be killed in order to minimize comparable rights violations, as in the Constraint Case? This concerns the explanation of constraints on minimizing rights violations. Agent- or victim-focused factors that explain the impermissibility of one act may not explain the impermissibility of the other. In this discussion we shall *first* consider the second issue of the constraint.

I

All the revisionist explanations that I will describe accept the claim that a right cannot be a constraint to minimizing violations of comparable rights.

237

Furthermore, they agree that in the Constraint Case no right of the single person (or property in virtue of which he has the right), and no relation that would exist between that single person and the five should the single person be killed to save the five, can be pointed to as a definitive reason for not killing the single person. This is because, it is said, each right of the victim or characteristic of the relation between the five and the one can (by hypothesis) be present five times over when the agent(s) kill their five victims for the sake, perhaps, of saving yet other people. If we point to any right of the victim or relationship as a reason not to kill, we will want to know why we should not minimize the presence of the rights violation or wrong relationship.

All the revisionist views to be canvassed now, therefore, emphasize that there is nothing about any of the six people, per se, that makes it morally wrong to substitute the death of the one for that of the others. They also emphasize that there is nothing distinctive about any of the *victim-agent* relationships per se when viewed from an impersonal point of view that makes it impossible to substitute one such relationship for the others. For example, there will either be one intentional killing or five.

All revisionists agree that the only thing that makes the single victim, his right, and the agent-victim relationship involving him, different from the other victims, their rights, and the agent-victim relationships in which they are involved is that *I*, the agent who would have to kill him, stand in a different relation to him, his right, and the components of the agent-victim relationship than *I* stand to the other victims, their rights and the components of their agent-victim relationships, including the act that kills them. If I kill the single person, I will intend his death, and transgress his right, but if I don't I will only foresee the intentions of other agents and let the transgression of other victims happen. They will be transgressed but not relative to me.

So on these views, at least at first glance, it seems that substituting one victim for another in the Constraint Case is wrong only because it means that an agent has to substitute himself for other agents. Substituting himself is wrong because it means *he* will have to stand in a certain relation to a victim and an act, for example, intend his death, transgress his right.

On the traditional view, the victim's right or the inappropriateness of the relation in which he would stand to those for whom he would be sacrificed, constrain and make it wrong for the agent to kill. This view agrees that in virtue of the victim's right it is wrong to relate to the victim in a certain way (e.g., do the transgression), and not as wrong to relate in another way (e.g., let him die). This does not mean the view is fundamentally *agent-relative*, i.e., gives each agent a different *basic* aim not derivable from an aim each agent has (e.g., gives Joe a duty that other agents do not have to see to it that Joe not kill). It is also not *agent-focused*, meaning that some quality of agency not primarily concerned with the victim's properties and rights gives the agent a duty not to act. Nor is it *agent-concerned*, meaning that the agent is controlled by his perception of himself and his life.

II

Revisionist Views

Given this general characterization of the revisionist view (henceforth, RV), I wish to describe several possible varieties in more detail. The first two alternatives are consequentialist in form, the second two deontological. They are based on views described by several prominent moral philosophers, though not necessarily identical with their views.

RV1 tells *you* to attach infinite negative weight to *your* killing (in a particular way). Then any state of affairs that includes your killing in this particular way will be worse than one without your killing. Therefore, it will be wrong for you to kill in the Constraint Case.[2] Call this the personal-goal-maximizing view.

RV2 is close to RV1, and has been called "position-relative consequentialism."[3] In this system, protection of rights is included in the evaluation of states of affairs. This would seem to permit us to treat rights as entities whose protection is a goal, rather than as constraints, and to minimize the violation of comparable rights. However, the acts that produce states of affairs are also included in the evaluation of states of affairs, and these acts can be evaluated differently depending on the position one occupies relative to them. Sometimes, it is claimed, any agent should evaluate an outcome in which he kills as worse than one in which others kill more people. If the outcome in which he is the killer is worse relative to his position than the outcome in which he is not the killer, it would be wrong, on consequentialist grounds, for him to kill.

RV3, the first of these views with a deontological flavor, emphasizes responsibility: *My* not being responsible for deaths must take priority for me over there not being killings by others. The refusal to be responsible for deaths constrains me. There are different proposals as to how I become responsible. On one account I would be responsible for the death of the single person I kill, but not for the five I let die, because someone else's act caused their deaths.[4] On another account I am responsible for the death I intend, not for those I merely foresee.[5]

RV4 is related to RV3 in that it attempts to explain why I must not intend someone's death (where death is not in his interests). It is claimed that intending death (as an end or means) involves *pursuing* evil; that is, if the evil does not occur at first, I reinforce my efforts to bring it about. When I merely foresee a death, it is said, I will not reinforce my efforts to bring it about if it fails to come about. But pursuing evil, being guided by evil, runs contrary to the moral grain.[6] Further, for an agent, from his personal perspective, his intentions loom larger than those of others. (I shall argue that RV4 really splits into two views; one is agent-focused and agent-concerned while the other is agent-relative and agent-focused but not agent-concerned.)

It is important to emphasize that this account of why intending harm is wrong focuses on the agent's attitude or state of mind as well as how this causes him to interact with the world. It is to be contrasted with a different — and not as agent-focused — account of why intending harm is wrong: On this second account, the focus is once again on the victim and how we treat him inappropriately given his characteristics; it is more in line (I believe) with the Kantian prohibition on treating people solely as means.[7]

Contrasts

There are two major differences between the consequentialist and deontological revisionist views. First, in the deontological view, an agent can concede that the state in which five people are killed by others is worse than the state in which the agent kills one person, and still claim that it is wrong for him to kill. This cannot be done in the consequentialist views.

Second, the consequentialist views conclude that an act is wrong by having an agent contemplate himself doing the act, seeing that outcome as worse than the outcome in which he doesn't do the act, and, on the basis of this, declaring that his doing it would be wrong. The deontological alternatives can be construed along the same lines — and doing this will be most in keeping with the way I have described the revisionist views in general. Such things as intending someone's death are seen as negative factors, but factors that are also present when others kill. An agent chooses not to intend a death because he sees that intending the death would make him be responsible for something bad, that is, an intending of death. It is finding himself responsible for some negative factor that constrains him from killing. He has himself and his act within his field of vision, one might say. This is agent concern.

However, there is another construal of the deontological view. (This is the agent-focused, but not agent-concerned, split in RV4.) It agrees that we must shift our focus from victim to agent, but, within the agent realm, it locates the constraint on the agent's killing in, for example, the nature of intending death itself, *considered independently of who will have the intention*, and then tells an agent to avoid engaging in this forbidden — rather than merely bad — activity. It is my view that, once one accepts this second construal of the deontological revisionist views, one might as well reject its criticism of the traditional view of constraints and question the emphasis on agent-relativity.

III

Objections

I now wish to point out a few possible problems for the revisionist views. The problems bear on both their adequacy as moral views and on their ability to yield results coextensive with those that a traditional rights-as-constraint view is supposed to have.

Whose Complaint?

One implication of *all* revisionist views is that it is not permissible for one agent to stop another agent from killing the single person in the Constraint Case on the ground that there is a basic injustice being done to the single person. This is because the single person's right is not what constrains an agent; it is supposedly only something about acting against the nonconstraining right which constrains the agent. The reason for stopping another agent might still be to stop the agent from doing a wrong act, but the single person who is saved if we intervene becomes merely a foreseen beneficiary of this intervention.

A further implication is that the single person in the Constraint Case would have no direct grounds for complaint if he were killed, since he has no right that makes it overall wrong for him to be killed to save the five. If an agent kills him when he shouldn't kill him, the single person can at most bemoan the fact that he must suffer, when he could have avoided suffering had the agent acted correctly.[8] The revisionist accounts also fail to explain why one agent should stop another agent from killing one to save five. Suppose we decided to stop another agent from killing the one. Why place so much weight on saving an agent from performing a wrong act, when five lives will be lost as a result and five other agents will affect the world through their wrong acts? If one does not believe an injustice is being done to the single victim and the world would be better (at least from one's own position) if someone else killed one to save five, why stop him? It is a mistake to think that one is required to prevent another's killing on the ground that otherwise one would actually be intending that the single person be killed. If one believes there is no overriding injustice to the single person in his being killed (i.e., his right is not a constraint), one may give less weight to his being killed than to other things. Therefore, one may engage in other activities, only *foreseeing* that the single person will be killed. (Perhaps when corrupt agency is only present in the agent who would kill the one (e.g., a device has been set to kill the five), stopping corrupt agency outweighs loss of the five? Doubtful.)

This result contrasts with the following implication of the traditional view: We may save the five by innocuous means rather than prevent someone else's killing the single person. The need for doing this might arise because the killer does not know that killing the one person has only a low probability of saving the five, and so we must still save the five while he persists in killing the one. However, if one cannot save the five by permissible means, the injustice of what is happening to the single person gives one a reason to save him, even if this means that the five will then certainly die. One can indeed have a sense of the bizarre here – one minute one could be saving the five, and when permissible avenues to doing this close down, proceed to do what will ensure their death. Nevertheless, this is an implication of the traditional view that one must not refrain from saving the single person because one intends his death as a means to saving others, and yet the single person need not be saved if we have something more important to do.[9]

Minimizing and Nonpersons

RV4 says we should not kill the one because we should not pursue evil. However, in some non-moral realms of value it seems permissible to pursue an evil, which one would otherwise be prohibited from pursuing, for the sake of minimizing that type of evil. For example, if someone else will burn five valuable paintings unless I burn one equally valuable painting, I do not think it is inconsistent with my caring for paintings or even with the view that it is, in general, wrong to destroy paintings, that I intend the destruction of one in order to prevent the foreseen destruction of five. Further, all the revisionist views tell us that what constrains my destroying one type of thing in order to preserve more things of the same type cannot be concern for some characteristic of the single thing, since all the other things have the same characteristics. Rather, the constraint stems from the quality of *my* agency. But if this agency were the source of the constraint, it seems that it should make it wrong to destroy the single painting, as well as the person in the Constraint Case. If it is permissible to destroy the painting, but not to kill the person in the Constraint Case, might this not indicate that it is some characteristic of the person (e.g, his constraining right and whatever gives rise to it), a characteristic that the painting lacks, that constrains us?[10]

My Own Victims

A most crucial and interesting problem for the revisionist views is presented by the case in which the agent who would have to kill the single person to save the five is the very same agent who set the threat to the five to begin with. For example, imagine the Guilty Agent Case, like the Constraint Case in all respects but with the background fact that an agent has set a bomb that will kill five people unless he himself now shoots one other person and places that person's body over the bomb.[11]

The traditional view prohibits killing the single person in this case.[12] Unless the revisionist views do so also, they will not yield coextensive results. If we assume that my killing five is worse than my killing one, the idea that my killing one person has infinite negative weight, suggested by RV1, seems wrong. If it is wrong for me to give infinite negative weight to my killing one, should RV1 recommend killing in the Guilty Agent Case? Further, if the outcome in which I am the killer of five is worse than the outcome in which I am the killer of one—whether worse relative to my position or position-neutrally—should not RV2 also endorse my killing in the Guilty Agent Case? And since it seems that I would be equally responsible for the deaths of the five and the one, shouldn't RV3 also endorse my killing the one in this case? There is no other agent besides me who will be responsible for the deaths of the five, given that I intentionally planned their deaths. (For what RV4 would recommend, see pp. 245-47.)

Insofar as the revisionist views tell us not to kill in the Constraint Case only because *we* would then stand in a particular relationship to someone's death (e.g., responsibility for it via intent), a relationship in which we would *not* stand to the deaths of the five, then these views should permit us to kill in the Guilty Agent Case. For in this case, it seems, the agent *will* stand in that same problematic relationship to the five people, if he does not kill the single person.

The Guilty Agent Case thus seems to undermine one of the most popular defenses in the literature for the *impermissibility* of killing one to save others, namely that *I* must not kill to save *someone else's* victims. (It is interesting to note that the emphasis in the revisionist views on the difference between agents has led critics who do not carefully distinguish the traditional from revisionist views to claim that explanations of refusing to kill the single victim rest on a desire to "keep one's hands clean." Any way of explaining the Constraint Case, like the traditional view, which *refuses* to permit killing in the Guilty Agent Case, is less likely to attract the charge of mere concern with dirtying one's hands, since it does not permit certain killings to minimize deaths one causes.)

If it were permissible for an agent to kill in the Guilty Agent Case, this would imply that people who had done wrong acts would not only have greater responsibilities than others to correct their wrongs, but would have greater liberties to do so. Though I believe this may be true sometimes — for example, someone who has revealed a damaging secret might be required to lie to prevent the damage when others ought not to lie — I do not think it is generally true.

Several interesting escape routes from the conclusion that an agent may kill in the Guilty Agent Case present themselves to the revisionist. All, for diverse reasons, lead to the conclusion that one may not kill *now* even to prevent certain other of one's own (or "one's own") killings.[13]

Views of the Self

The *first* escape route involves joining a concept of the self as *noncontinuing* with either consequentialist or deontological revisionist views. Then injunctions, such as RV2's to minimize the killings *you* do (because more of your killings make a worst state of affairs from your position), are directed to you *now*, and this will be a different "you" than existed in the past when the bomb was set to kill the five. So you may not minimize the wrongs *you* do by minimizing the wrongs a past "you" has done. Likewise, on a deontological RV3 there could be less responsibility for the acts of a past self than for those of the present self. (This reduced responsibility, however, would have to be reduced just enough to rule out killing the one in the Guilty Agent Case, but not enough to rule out your having to sacrifice yourself to save the victims of the "past you." The latter is a responsibility that traditional deontological views would no doubt enforce.) It might be that this RV assimilates taking responsibility for one's past (or future) acts to taking responsibility for the acts of a relative: We must do more of what is *ordinarily permissible* (or to a minor degree violative) in order to help our relative reduce his burden of guilt, but we cannot violate the directive "Avoid *your* being responsible for killings" for *his* sake.

This first escape route's role in RV3 is particularly interesting, since it has been suggested that a noncontinuing view of the self is most appropriately associated with utilitarianism.[14] This is because it makes it possible for me to have equal concern for "my" future welfare and for the welfare of other people, there not being a much stronger connection between (1) *me* (now) and the future "me" than between (2) *me* and others. Yet, in our discussion, the noncontinuing view of the self has generated both what might be called a "deontology of the moment" and a consequentialist view that mimics traditional deontological rights theory in its consequences by prohibiting killing in the Guilty Agent Case.

A *second* escape route for the revisionist views involves the idea of a *continuing* self. It agrees that past sins are as much one's own as present sins, and that one should minimize one's transgressions over the course of one's whole lifetime, as conventionally understood. It would be possible to minimize the number of rights violations by preventing the consequences of a previous act — after all, if the five do not die, their right not to be killed is intact. In order for this second escape route to yield results that coincide with the traditional view, it would have to minimize something other than actually violated rights. For example, it could count the negative weight of performing an action (whether it succeeds or not), rather than the negative weight of actually violating a right. It could identify the transgressions that one must minimize as acts or intentions, independent of their actual consequences. So one could not minimize transgressions in the past by acting or intending in the present; the past acts or intentions cannot be undone. This view goes along with the division of time into what could be called "act-scenes." Within a given *act-scene* one may choose between fewer and more transgressions, but once one has chosen, one enters a new act-scene, and it becomes both impossible and morally impermissible to do an ordinarily forbidden act in the new act-scene in order to prevent the consequences of the wrong acts in past act-scenes. So, in the Guilty Agent Case one will be choosing not between killing one and killing five, but rather between killing one on the one hand and, on the other hand, letting five die as a consequence of a past choice. The latter makes one the killer of five, but this does not imply that one now kills them.

Among the problems that this second escape route faces is coping with the crucial case of one's own *future* transgressions. Since it is often not impossible to prevent my future acts or intentions, why may I not kill one person now to prevent *my* intentions or acts that will kill even more in the future (Future Case)?[15] Another problem is to distinguish killings (e.g., redirections) that are standardly permissible in a new act scene, in order to undo the effects of acts in another act scene, from killings that may not be done. So, if I have already sent a bomb toward five, it is permissible for me later to redirect it toward the one.

One may also feel, whether one accepts a continuous *or* a discontinuous view of the self, that what one is doing now is more important than what one has done in the past. In the past, perhaps I had the psychological make-up of a killer of five. Now I have changed for the better and would like to undo the past. But if I cannot undo the past because I have improved so much that killing of any sort is now impossible for me, then, in fact, the killing of the five *finally* occurs because I *am* so good, rather than because I *was* so bad. This response, however, fails to account for why some killings, for example, redirections, would be permissible. Killing now in the Guilty Agent Case cannot be impermissible *merely* because I will now not do any killings, since I will do redirections.

Furthermore, it might be suggested, if we take seriously such changes in character, is what matters most how I turn out in the end? If this is so, why isn't the future more important than the present? Why should I not kill now if that would (somehow) prevent not only my future killings, but even my future capacity to form the intention to kill? If there are compulsive killings in my future, they may not mean I have become a morally worse person. But suppose the future killings will be under my control and so will reflect badly on my character, and suppose it is possible actually to alter my character for the better in the future by killing now, then should we kill now according to the revisionist views?

The Present Intention

The *third* escape route for revisionism from the conclusion that we should kill in the Guilty Agent Case and in the Future Case may already be embodied in the substance of RV4, insofar as it focuses on *intending* not merely because it makes one be responsible (as in RV3), but in order to focus on an activity (mental or physical) at the time it occurs: not intending or not acting in certain ways *now* will then quite naturally take precedence over earlier or later acts or intentions. We might try to understand this emphasis on present intention or act in an agent concerned way. As some revisionist views emphasize the agent's different relationships to different victims, so we might try emphasizing the agent's different relationships to his *own* different intentional killings. Instead of dealing with six victims, all of whom have the same characteristics, we deal with six intentions, each of which has the same characteristic: they are all intentions *of the same agent*. One intention/act, however, is a present intention/act, and five are, for example, future intentions/acts. It might be said that the agent sees himself in a different relationship to the present (single) intention if he has it, than to the other five: he actually has the former, whereas from his position now he is only foreseeing himself having other intentions. The claim would then be that at no time is one morally obliged actually to intend a certain type of act, when the alternative is merely to foresee intending it in the future.[16] It may be said that the present intention looms larger, is magnified, and this stops the agent from acting.

This last escape route for revisionism from the problem presented by the Guilty Agent and Future Cases raises a new question about RV4: Does it split into two views, one (just described) that emphasizes the agent's awareness of himself in relation to a present intention that is magnified because he has it now ($RV4^1$), and a second ($RV4^2$) that simply emphasizes the character of intending harm whose characteristics should repel us? This second type, $RV4^2$, is agent-focused in emphasizing an agent's duty not to do something (rather than a victim's characteristics which give rise to rights). If one holds this type of view, how much sense does it make to flee to revisionism as a haven from the traditional view that the rights of the individual are constraints? For it seems that this revisionist view makes use of essentially the same move as the traditional view which says that each person has a constraining right; we as agents are simply constrained by the first such right we come up against. But the analogous way of viewing things is applied by RV4^2 to an individual's intention to kill: Each such intention is constraining (i.e., it has a property that makes having that intention prohibited). I am constrained by the first such intention I come up against (i.e., the one I would confront if I intended now). The fact that it is *me, now* is not important per se; it does not magnify the intention relative to other intentions. *Me, now* is important only because the intention that I am prohibited from having, the first I come up against, will, necessarily, be *mine, now*. (Likewise, the first victim I come up against will be *mine, now*, but it is his constraining right, not *me* or *now* that is driving the cart. So why call it agent-relativity?)

As we have seen, the revisionist views reject the traditional view on victims: There is nothing about a single potential victim, per se, that constrains us from substituting him for others, it is said. Rather, each agent is constrained from killing his victim by the type of agency he would have to exercise in relation with the victim's nonconstraining right rather than with other people's victims. Analogously, some proponents of revisionist views may reject the idea of a *constraining intention*. They see the intention as having some negative feature, but not as in itself settling the question of whether it may be engaged in. What may settle the question is the particular relationship that exists between *me, now* and *the intention*; it is the triplet that is constraining. One imagery which may capture RV4^1 is that the agent has *himself*, *now*, and the *intention*, inside his "visual" field. Because he sees himself, now, in the picture, he is repelled as another would not be. In RV4^2, by contrast, I, now, see the *intention* which is the sole content of my visual field. An alternative image of RV4^1 suggested by the idea of magnification has the intention as the sole content of the visual field but *my intending it now* magnifies it relative to other intentions. If I care first and foremost about me and about now, I will not associate them with the bad intention even in order to minimize bad intentions of others or of my own self at other times.

The view in RV4^2 that the intention or act *in itself* has features that give rise to a prohibition, and reflection on *oneself now* is *two* thoughts too many, seems close to the view that Thomas Nagel (at times) and Bernard Williams wish to argue for.[17] If so, then why would *they*, in particular, find incomprehensible the traditional focus on the rights of the first person one comes up against? At least, their embracing the criticism of this view, that is, that the position of the one and of the many is the same and therefore nothing about the one per se constrains us, seems misguided. There may, of course, be reasons for focusing on intentions rather than on victims' rights, but those reasons have nothing to do with the general *form* of the criticism lodged against the traditional view, i.e., that if we care about rights, minimizing violations of comparable rights should be permitted because there is no reason to protect the single person, located in him. (It is possible that Williams and

Nagel want to retain the other image, of magnification of the intention when I am intending it now. This would bring them closer to RV4[1].)

Nagel's View

It may be useful at this point to examine in more detail Nagel's views as described in *The View from Nowhere*. They present a mix of positions, though I believe what he is really after is best captured by the idea of an agent-focused constraint, where the emphasis is on what one is doing in intending harm.

Nagel begins by saying "The dilemma [of abiding by restrictions and constraints] must be due to a special reason against *doing* such a thing (twisting a child's arm)" (p. 176). He describes what is being done if we violate a constraint, and why it is wrong, that is, we intend harm, and this involves our being guided by the harm to another which is evil (pp. 181–183). (That is, we follow it and try to increase it if it diminishes.) When we merely foresee harm from our acts or omissions, we are not guided by it.

All this is consistent with the idea that the character of what I am doing gives rise to a constraint. It is a separate question whether Nagel has analyzed correctly why intending evil gives rise to a constraint, i.e., whether it is true that we are guided by what we intend only. Indeed, what he thinks differentiates intending from foreseeing doesn't, in fact, do so; that is, I may be guided by foreseen evil as a sign that my intended means or end is present. For example, suppose I try to bomb a munitions dump and if I succeed the children next door will die. If a cloud covers the dump, I can be sure that it is bombed only if the children are dead. So I go back and bomb the dump until I see the children dead.

But Nagel also says things that suggest somewhat different views. For example, he also speaks about the *special responsibility* (p. 180) that we have for harm if we intend it rather than foresee it, thinking of the distinction between our intending harm and our foreseeing the harm that others do. But this view—like RV3—will not help us to deal with the Guilty Agent Case and the Future Case, in which we will be responsible for the harm we now foresee, whereas the agent-focused constraint account will help us. Nagel also believes that we must give an *agent-relative* account of a constraint, where this means that the constraint arises because an agent stands in a special relation to his own act of intentionally killing by comparison to the acts of other agents who will intentionally kill. The constraint arises, he says, because there is a *collision between the subjective and the objective points of view*. From his subjective point of view there is magnification for the agent of his own victim and the harming he intends, in comparison to the victim and intentional harmings of others, which he merely understands from an objective point of view. (Nagel does not deal with cases where victims and intentional killings we foresee are our own.) He claims there would be no constraint if we acted merely from an objective point of view, because it would *be* a better state of affairs and a better thing would *happen* if we *did* the worse act, insofar as more victims would be saved. Perhaps also it is because fewer intentions to kill would occur, if we imagine that my killing would actually alter for the better the character of other potential killers and reduce the number of intentional killings. This emphasis on magnification is not in keeping with the idea that there is no magnification as a result of any special relation, but only the repellent features of the intentional killing that an agent comes up against. The latter is what an agent-focused reduced agent-relative interpretation of RV4 amounts to.

Nagel also discusses the victim's point of view. My victim sees me as someone who assaults his value when I guide my conduct by harm to him. Though my victim realizes that other agents do the same to other victims, he has a subjective point of view from which my act to him is magnified, and I know this. There is the special *relation between us*.

On Nagel's account, therefore, the single victim says: "Do not do *this* (intentional killing) to me, even though if you did you could prevent *this* from happening to the other people." For him to take an *objective* view, according to Nagel, would be for him to endorse being killed to save the others.

Note that this view of Nagel's contrasts with the following view.[18] The single person says: "You may not do this (intentional killing) to me since if it were permissible to do it to me, this would mean I had no right not to be killed. You may prevent the deaths of others if you kill me, but if it were right to do this, this would mean that no one was inviolable. Furthermore, my objection is based on an *objective* (not subjective/personal) evaluation of the nature and status of all persons equally. It is impermissible to treat people in certain ways and so it is not permissible to treat me in this way; I am simply the first person with this status that you came up against." You do not come up against the right not to be killed in those you let die.[19]

The Doomed Victim

Another problem case for both the traditional and revisionist views involves my killing a potential victim who is doomed to die anyway, in particular, someone whose right not to be killed will be violated by someone else anyway. On the traditional view, this individual may still have a right *against me* that I not kill him, even if others will surely violate his right. The fundamental issue here is first locating the fact that accounts for the prohibition on my killing someone who would *not* otherwise die. If most of the strength of that prohibition stems from the aim of ensuring that the victim not have certain things done to him, then if those things would be done to him anyway, it would be permissible for me to kill him. If most of the strength of the prohibition stems from an effort to ensure that the victim not suffer certain effects (death), regardless of how the death comes about, then if he would die anyway (even if not by another's hand) it would also be permissible for me to kill him. In other words, if the prohibition on killing essentially protects someone's autonomy and welfare, and he would lose these anyway, I could kill him. On the other hand, if at least some of the strength of the prohibition stems from the victim's right to control the behavior of every other person with respect to his life, then even if he failed to control *one* person's behavior he could still control mine, and I ought not kill him.

Suppose the doomed victim waives his right against me, will not be any worse off if I kill him than he would otherwise have been, and his being killed will save five others from being killed. Then the traditional view is hard pressed to resist the conclusion that killing is quite permissible. Do the revisionist views reach the same conclusion given their primary concern with agents' not doing certain things? It will still be me killing rather than others killing, and according to revisionism the person's right was not supposed to have been a constraint to begin with, so why should his waiving it change matters? However, revisionist views are surely sensitive to whether someone does or does not object to being killed (whether or not his objection has constraining force). Therefore, someone's dropping his objection to being killed, and his not losing more utility if I kill him than if others do, could lead to a switch from a position against killing to one in favor of killing.

Of course, it may be that we do think that, even in the case of the doomed victim who has waived his right not to be killed by me, especially when he is doomed because of injustice by another, that the correct answer is for me *not* to kill him. Here it may be that revisionism comes out better than the traditional view, sensitive as it is to the agent's point of view. If this is what is meant by a focus on the agent in morality then I agree that this agent-focused and even agent-relative concern — since there may be a basic duty that I not kill him — may be a component of non-consequentialist thought.

Self-indulgence

A problem that the revisionist views might seem to face as moral views, which the traditional view escapes, is the charge that it directs the agent to be self-indulgent. This is because the traditional view's concern is with a victim's right as a constraint on killing, even to save a greater number of one's *own* victims. This view is concerned with someone else and his rights as a *barrier* to my action. According to this view, I simply cannot march through a barrier to stop myself (or others) from violating more barriers, even if I could minimize the barriers I go through by going through one now. Further, this is not because going through one barrier (a right) involves violating another prohibition (e.g., don't use yourself solely as a means). So even if there were a continuing self, and it were possible to minimize the wrong it does over a lifetime by violating a right now, and there were no additional barrier, it would still be wrong to pass through *this* barrier of the person's right. The fact that the traditional view says you may not kill one bystander in order to prevent *someone else* from killing five people does not show that it tells you to care more for *your* not killing than for *his* not killing. After all the same moral view says that *you* may not kill to minimize those *you* would kill. The fact that one may not kill to save *other's* victims shows concern for self only if it is already *assumed* that the bystander's right not to be killed cannot be an impassable, constraining barrier, even for those who *would* be willing to join their fate to that of another potential killer.

By contrast, even if the revisionist views recognize the right of the one person (and the five others) not to be killed to maximize utility (i.e., ordinary restrictions), any reasons they give for the impermissibility of killing the single person to save the five from being killed do not ultimately depend on the barrier that the one person presents. Revisionism's concern is in good part with the agent.

However, if an agent ought not act because he perceives that it is wrong to enter into a certain relation (e.g., intending a death), he is motivated by concern with something other than himself or his character; he is morally repelled by the type of act. We have noted that this is at least a possible construal of RV4 (i.e., $RV4^2$). But other revisionist views that decide an act is wrong only after placing the agent himself in the picture, that is, views that ask each agent to see himself as engaging in an activity or having a certain attitude, rather than looking at the activity or attitude itself unmagnified by the fact that he is doing it, do seem more susceptible to the charge of self-indulgence.

Further, if one does certain acts for one's own sake but not for the sake of others, one is ordinarily thought to show greater concern for oneself than for others. (This does not necessarily mean that one is self-indulgent.) If some revisionist views permit killing in the Guilty Agent Case, but not in the Constraint Case, could they not at least be accused of this self-preference? Perhaps not, since doing otherwise forbidden acts for the sake of meeting one's *responsibilities* to one's own victims is not the same as doing such acts for one's own sake.

I believe there are two ways in which the charge of self-indulgence is more appropriately leveled against revisionism than against the traditional views. First, consequentialist alternatives (e.g., RV2) that tell one to decide that an act is wrong by giving added negative weight to an outcome that involves one's doing the killing seem to exhibit a self-indulgent attitude. This is so even if they require every agent to do the same. There is a difference between horror at what I would be doing, and horror at the fact that it is I who would do it, even if I expect each person to feel horrified at the fact that she would do it. Second, there are cases in which concern that one not do a wrong act could lead some revisionist views to recommend self-indulgent behavior. For example, if voting for a certain distribution of police patrols which diminished overall deaths actually made it more likely that I would kill, RVs 1, 2, and 3 might recommend my voting against it. Such a recommendation to see to it that all the world is arranged so as to help me fulfill my duties does smack of self-indulgence. The traditional view and $RV4^2$, by contrast, both seem to focus on not performing a particular act rather than on doing everything necessary to prevent oneself from performing it, and so they may escape this criticism.

Another illustration of this point is provided by considering whether it would be in keeping with the mindset of the traditional and revisionist views for you to prefer your *having* broken barriers to others' having done so. For example, suppose you are an amnesiac. The person filling in the gaps for you is unsure of a piece of your history. He knows that in the past either (1) *you*, in a responsible frame of mind, killed one person in order to save five, or (2) someone else, in a responsible frame of mind, killed the *same* person *plus two others* to save five. [20] You will not be punished if it was you who killed the one, and you also know that you would not now kill anyone to save others.

Would it be in keeping with the spirit of a nonconsequentialist theory that you now prefer to learn that you have killed the one over learning that some-one else has killed three, even if it was wrong to kill the one to save the five and you would not do it now? [Notice that this is *not* a case in which any preference you have for its having been you who killed can be based on your having reduced the number killed by killing someone who would have been killed *anyway* (e.g., a doomed victim). What one must imagine is the differ-ence between the state of affairs in which you kill someone who would *not* otherwise have died, and the state of affairs in which someone else kills that same person who would *not* otherwise have died, plus two others.]

It seems to me that, as a supporter of the traditional view, I should prefer that I have done the killing. It is rather striking that this result is consistent with not being willing to kill the one person now. If so, does this not indicate that the mental set associated with the traditional view directs one to be con-cerned with the barrier that one would have to go through at the time of action, and not essentially with oneself? The Amnesiac Case highlights the concern that the traditional view has for victims (i.e., whether they will be worse off than they might be in *another world*) rather than for the agent's moral record. By contrast, a proponent of revisionism should, I believe, prefer it to be true that he (the proponent) did not kill the one, at least if he has a view of the self as continuous. It would be a mark of self-indulgence to prefer to be someone who has not killed rather than that there have been fewer un-just deaths, when the killing is over and done with. (It would not be better to prefer that I now be someone who *will* kill one who would not otherwise soon die, rather than that someone else will kill one who would not otherwise soon die plus two others, since having this preference means I would now kill the person who would not otherwise soon die.)

The strongest ground for accusing the traditional view as well as revision-ism of self-indulgence, I believe, is that the traditional view does not require (though it also does not forbid) an agent to save others' victims even when only innocent means would be necessary to do this, at least not at the great cost required to prevent his harming someone. An important question to raise in deciding whether a theory's emphasis is on *your* moral record rather than on the barrier that resides outside you is whether the theory distinguishes between your preventing others from breaking barriers by breaking a barrier yourself, and your preventing others from breaking barriers without breaking a barrier yourself. Suppose that you, in fact, do more to avoid harming a bystander than to prevent someone else from harming him, when you could do both by innocent means. In that case you do, in fact, care more about not harming than about someone not being harmed. It may support a charge of self-indulgence if you do not harm because you do not care about another agent's victim as much as about not having your own victim. (Consider what this would imply about the Amnesia Case.) Suppose you do not care about another's agency as much as about your own agency. Self-respect may be crucially tied to responsibility for one's own acts, and this rather than self-indulgence could justify leaving other agent's behavior in their own hands. If there is a moral difference between harming and not aiding in equalized cases, and someone would not relate as agent to harm if he lets die, this could justify making a larger effort not to harm than to aid without one's being self indulgent.

An important question, in addition, is whether the traditional view says that you *must* do more to avoid *your* harming someone than to prevent others from harming, once you have done what is required of you not to harm. Suppose it were permissible for you to do more to prevent others from breaking barriers than to prevent your breaking them, *so long as* doing the former did not involve your failing to do what was required to avoid breaking barriers. You would not be *required* to care more for *your* not breaking barriers than for others' not doing so or for their victims. Then the significance of barriers for you would not be based on self concern.

Duties

The Case of the Doomed Victim reminds us again—and it is worth reemphasizing—that there may be nonconsequentialist constraint-type theories that do not focus essentially on rights. If the *nondoomed* bystander in the Constraint Case waives his right not to be killed by you, may you then kill him to save the five?

If you still may not kill, then how could the constraint on you stem from his right? Of course, someone may not be at liberty to waive his right. (An unwaivable right is different from, but a close cousin to, an inalienable right.) Then *both* his right and your duty not to kill would depend on something else about his nature which constrains you both. But we can imagine that someone may waive his right, and yet we still have a duty not to act as he requests or permits. (For example, suppose someone waives his right not to be killed, but it is against his interests to be killed. We may have a duty based on charity not to kill him, but not because he has a *right* that we treat him in a way that is to his advantage.)[21] This could still be a victim-focused theory, if the duty was, essentially, a response to something about the victim. By contrast, RV4[2] attempts to yield a constraint-like *duty* that is agent-focused, hence revisionist. As noted above, like other forms of revisionism, it focuses on an agent's mental state (intending) or on how he is relating to others. The type of mental state or relation is the source of the wrong. The theory is not agent-concerned in the sense that it asks an agent to see, in addition to this, that *he* will be the one having the state of mind or relation, and judge this a worse state of affairs than when others have it. Nor does it require magnification or basically agent-relative duties.

So, the fact that you could have a duty to someone even if he waives his right, need not mean that a theory emphasizes *you* essentially—that is, each person being concerned with his own moral record—as suggested by some forms of revisionism. Emphasis can still be on the *barrier of duty* (existing independently of a right), at each point at which one is confronted with it. What one sees is act or state of mind and that avoiding it is a duty. Certainly, one is doing the seeing, but one does not see oneself in this picture; one is outside it, even though it is one's own duty. (This is analogous to being able to visualize a world without oneself in it, even though one is doing the visualizing.) Furthermore, it needn't be the fact that the duty becomes magnified from the subjective point of view that makes for its constraining force. One can simply understand that that sort of behavior is in itself impermissible and each instance of it is impermissible; if we were permitted, for example, to intentionally harm one person now, that would mean that intentionally harming is not something it really is impermissible for agents to do.

It might be suggested that the *true* revisionist alternative to rights-based objections to killing in the Guilty Agent Case just is one that emphasizes duty as a constraint, whether or not someone waives a waivable right (or alienates an alienable right). This may be so. But the point is that this form of revisionism has *nothing* to do with the claim that a right that is not waived (or alienated) cannot, for logical reasons, be a constraint on minimizing rights violations. It is only if one focuses on the significance of oneself versus other agents that one connects oneself to that claim. Therefore, there is this deep sense in which rights- and duty-based nonconsequentialism can share a common structure.[22]

IV

We have considered agent-focused, agent-relative and agent-concerned reasons that might be offered to justify a *constraint*. To use the same or other agent-focused, agent-relative or agent-concerned reasons to justify a restriction on killing to promote utility (e.g., to save other lives from natural disaster) would be to use such reasons to justify a principle like the Principle of Permissible Harm (PPH). Let us consider some revisionist proposals, comparable to those we have already examined, for justifying such a restriction: (1) The PPH is justified because I should give infinite negative weight to an outcome in which I kill. This cannot be right, since I may kill in the Trolley Case, but not in Transplant. (2) The PPH is justified because, relative to my own position, it is a worse outcome if I kill than if others do. This cannot be correct, since it is permitted for me to turn the trolley. (3) The PPH is justified because I must avoid being responsible for a death, and I will not be responsible for deaths I allow to occur (or do not intend to occur) if I do not kill to prevent them. This cannot be right, since I may kill in the trolley case, being responsible for a death, rather than letting five die, even in Prevented Return. (4) The PPH is justified because an agent should not intend a death when he could instead merely foresee deaths. This is probably not right since, according to the PPH, intending death is neither a necessary nor a sufficient condition for the impermissibility of conduct. For example, it is not sufficient since it is permissible to do what seems like intending to kill someone in Prevented Return, and it is not necessary because it is impermissible to set off a grenade to stop the trolley when we foresee that it will kill a bystander.

All these criticisms could as well have been made of the use of these revisionist proposals to justify constraints. All these criticisms focus on the fact that the revisionist proposals are phrased too broadly to distinguish cases where we may kill from those where we may not kill. For example, we might permissibly turn the trolley (which would not violate a PPH right) to prevent the violation of rights. The broadness of the four RVs could be remedied for purposes of the discussion of constraints by substituting "violate the PPH" for "killing" or "death", but this would not help the RVs avoid criticism on grounds they do not focus on the significance of the victims' characteristics as giving rise to a type of barrier, and they overemphasize *me, now*.

In the next chapter we shall consider other possible agent-focused and victim-focused accounts of restrictions and constraints.

NOTES

1. Suggestions for revisionist explanations are to be found in Thomas Nagel, "Limits of Objectivity," *The Tanner Lecture on Human Values*, Volume I (Salt Lake City: University of Utah Press, 1980), *The View From Nowhere* (N.Y.: Oxford University Press, 1986), and Jeremy Waldron, *Theories of Rights* (Oxford: Oxford University Press, 1984), Introduction. As we shall see, it may be that those who claim to be offering revisionist explanations of rights as constraints are in fact replacing rights as constraints with an alternative device that has close to the same results. We considered such revisionist views on p. 222. We offered a victim-focused account of the PPH(1) (a restriction) on pp. 184–88.

2. Such a view is described by Robert Nozick in *Anarchy, State and Utopia* (New York: Basic Books, 1974), p. 29. Nozick does not like this view because he thinks it is "gimmicky," and should not be countenanced as a real teleological view because of its use of indexicals. But he does not reject it on the grounds that it yields incorrect results. That is, Nozick seems to present this goal-maximizing version of the rights-as-constraints morality as though the two were *extensionally* equivalent in the decisions they yield in particular cases. I wish to treat RV1 as a legitimate view and consider whether it always yields the same results as the traditional view.

3. Such a view is described by Amartya Sen in "Rights & Agency," *Philosophy & Public Affairs* 1 (Winter 1982): 3–39.

4. See Alan Gewirth, "Are There Any Absolute Rights?", in *Theories of Rights*.

5. See Charles Fried, *Right and Wrong* (Cambridge, Mass.: Harvard University Press, 1978).

6. See Nagel, "Limits of Objectivity" and *The View from Nowhere* (New York: Oxford University Press, 1986). This view of intending contrasts with our description offered in Chapter 7 (p. 181).

7. Though there are those who describe the Kantian view as primarily concerned with the agent as a rational chooser, rather than with rational beings who can be victims of those choosers.

8. Nagel, however, does believe the victim can complain at his treatment to the person who acts against him, but each victim can complain against his aggressor. I should be inhibited by my victim's complaint because his complaint is coming to me. The emphasis seems to be on agent-relative magnification: it is again because it's happening to me, versus to other agents, that something is (supposedly) enough to stop my act. This may contrast with the traditional view that the ground each victim has for complaint constitute the constraint on the agent and that the complaint's being directed to me is only an indication that I have come up against the factors that make the victim's complaint valid. We shall expand below on this understanding of the traditional view, which we here only mention in passing.

9. Suppose that if another agent does not kill his one victim, X, I would be in the position of killing Y to save the five. It might be suggested, since RVs 1 and 2 say that, from my position someone else's killing is a better outcome than my killing, that it should not be wrong to bring about that better outcome. For example, I might encourage the other person to shoot. Yet it does seem wrong for me to do so, and if RVs 1 and 2 imply that it is right, they must be wrong. Two possible responses to this objection come to mind. First, RVs 1 and 2 may find the outcome in which *I intend* that someone kill an innocent as bad as the outcome in which I actually kill the innocent. It might also be asked: if I need not shoot Y, even if X is not shot, why must I encourage someone to shoot X? (It might be answered: To save the five from dying and, possibly, to save the five agents from wrong acts.)

10. The idea that one pursues evil only when one intends it is also wrong; it is possible to pursue evil that one only foresees, if one takes it as a sign of what one does intend. For example, suppose I wish to bomb munitions plants, but a cloud cover makes it impossible to tell whether I have reached my target. If the plants blow up, children next door will certainly be killed; they will be alive only if the plants are not blown up. I can decide how many times to return to drop bombs on the munitions location by being guided by the death of the children: If they are not dead, I go back and bomb some more; if they are dead, my mission is complete. Guidance by evil does not make bombing the munitions plant wrong. Yet not all unintended killing is permitted. The example of the art works also, I believe, tells against the account of constraints given by the so-called expressive theory of rationality, as described by Elizabeth Anderson (in *Value in Ethics and Economics*, Cambridge, Mass.: Harvard University Press, 1993). Anderson, I believe, wants to argue that if, for example, our rationally justified attitude toward people is benevolence, rationality further commits us to expressing this attitude to each person (distributively) rather than merely to the aggregate of persons. She argues (p. 29) that harming one person for the benefit of others is not to act benevolently to the one (obviously) and is, hence, inconsistent with benevolence as an attitude toward people. Anderson's point here seems to be to derive a constraint on harming one to help others from the (supposed) logic of having the benevolent attitude. We might say that this logic is represented by a duct model. That is, the distributive aspect of the attitude (i.e., the requirement to express it to each person) is a function of the attitude "running" through all individual ducts, rather than through some pipelines and not others. But now consider the art works case again. Someone who is a lover of

beauty expresses this attitude by preserving and not destroying works of art. What does such a person do when confronted with the need to destroy one work of art if several equally good ones are to survive? The duct model suggests he should be unable to destroy the one for the many. His act of destroying one *does not itself express* the attitude of preserving beauty, even if it is done to save many art works. (This must be true on Anderson's account, otherwise, her view would license consequentialist reasoning.) Yet it is permissible to destroy the one painting to save the five. Perhaps Anderson need not deny this. Although this is not a case where values other than the appropriate attitude to beauty are at stake, she might still say that her nonconsequentialist point is made if there is regret at destroying the one painting—a recognition that something wrong has been done in the course of doing the overall right act. But to the extent that one can still be said to have the attitude of love of beauty even if one destroys the painting with regret, to that extent the argument that the *logic of the attitude* entails distributive concern fails. Hence, the constraint on killing one person to save others from being killed will also not be derivable from the (supposed) logic of the attitude. This all suggests, I believe, that the distributive component of the attitude is not derived from within it but from *outside* it, by consideration of the nature of the entity one would act against and the demands it, not the attitude, makes on us. The attitude will be the source of the distributive component only trivially, in cases where our attitude is to treat people as inviolable (in a certain way) because they are inviolable (in a certain way). But then the constraint on harming the one to save a greater number from being killed stems from its being logically inconsistent with the idea of the inviolability of each person that we be permitted to violate one to minimize violation of the inviolability of others. Here all the work ensuring distribution of respect is being done by the idea of the status of each person, not by the logic of an attitude. The constraints seem to be justified from the outside in, not from the inside out, as Anderson (and Darwall, whom she cites) claims (p. 7). (Note that Anderson comes closest to this way of arguing—though she does not believe it is distinguishable from her view on the logic of expressing attitudes—when she says (p. 76) that consequentialism, by requiring that we minimize violations of X by violating X, fails to preserve part of what is valued in X. My understanding of this is that if, for example, only friendship in which one never abandons a friend had great worth, one could not act in accord with that ideal of friendship—I would say one could not give the friend what is his due (*if* it were his due)—by abandoning one friend to minimize abandonment of friends. For this to be permissible, it would have to be true that friends are, after all, not owed absolute nonabandonment.) For more on this see chapter 10.

11. I believe Alan Zaitchik first discussed cases in which the person who needs to act is the person who tried to kill in "Trammel on Positive and Negative Duties," *Personalist 58*, Ja 1977:93–96. I first discussed the case in "Constraints and You" at the APA, Pacific Division Meeting, 1984. Judith Thomson has also discussed such cases in "The Trolley Problem," *Yale Law Journal* 94 (Spring 1985):1395–1415, and in *The Realm of Rights* (Cambridge, Mass.: Harvard University Press, 1990).

12. It might be thought that the traditional view *permits* killing in this case, as it does in cases of redirected threats. That is, the agent redirects himself. This is a mistake: What is done to the single person, and the relationship he is put into vis-à-vis the five that he would be used to save, is not what it would be in a Redirected Threat Case, and these factors are crucial on the traditional view. In a case where we redirect, the death of the single person does not play the role that the death of the one would if the agent killed him to stop the deaths of five.

13. The use of quotes here should become clear after the following discussion. The

material that follows was also first presented in the lecture "Constraints and You" (1984).

14. By Derek Parfit in *Reasons and Persons* (New York: Oxford University Press, 1985), and earlier in "Later Salves and Moral Principles," in *Philosophy and Personal Relations* (ed. Alan Montefiore). Montreal: McGill-Queen's University Press, 1993.

15. One possible answer, at least for the supporter of RV3, is that I am always free at the future time to kill or not to kill, and no present act is needed to prevent my future killing. Therefore, there is no good reason to undertake that present act. On the other hand, if I will be psychologically compelled to kill in the future, and a present killing would make that impossible, I should not kill now because a compulsive act would not be one for which I would be morally responsible. In response one might note that ordinarily, if I could do something now, but choose not to, to prevent a compulsive and dangerous act of mine at a later point, I would become morally responsible for that dangerous act. If we cannot *assume* there *is* a prohibition on killing now to stop future acts, then how can we generate the constraint by saying that we would not be responsible for a future compulsive act?

16. This idea that one must act well as long as one can despite what one sees in store in the future may also be connected to the Kantian notion of not using oneself as a means; for to perform an act one wouldn't otherwise perform for the sake of past or future acts is to use oneself as a means. Kant of course claimed that one should not use oneself *solely* as a means, and if one kills someone now to prevent one's own future killings it seems that one is also thereby promoting one's own ends, insofar as one thinks being a killer of many is a bad life for me to have. It may be that use of the revisionist views to defend a constraint on minimizing killings from one's past or future acts could be combined with the value of not using oneself as a means only if it involved an even stronger prohibition on not using oneself than Kant (at least seems to) endorse. (I suspect, however, that the strong prohibition actually is the Kantian one, since Kant rules out suicide or prostitution undertaken for one's own interests.) Alternatively, we might see the strong prohibition on using oneself as a means as reason for linking revisionist deontological views (RV3 and RV4) with a noncontinuous view of the self, since there is less reason to use oneself as a means for a future "self" who is not really identical with oneself now. Notice that in a consequentialist revisionism, if it has the sort of problems dealing with the Guilty Agent Case and the Future Case that I have described, using oneself as a means (even very strictly construed) should itself be subject to minimization. We should be allowed to use ourselves on a given occasion in order to minimize occurrences of using ourselves as a means over our whole lifetime. Would such a view yield different results from those of the traditional view? For example, would it recommend killing one person, in order to defuse a bomb that one had set in order to kill two people when these two people were to die *in order* to stop another of one's bombs from killing five people? It may depend on whether "using oneself as a means" is an act that can ever be undone by an act in another act-scene: If one has irrevocably used oneself as a means in setting out to kill the two to stop the five from dying, one will not minimize the using of oneself by any further act.

17. Williams, "Utilitarianism and Moral Self-indulgence," in *Moral Luck* (Cambridge: Cambridge University Press, 1981); Nagel, "The Limits of Objectivity." In that article Williams remarks on the lover who is absorbed not with his beloved, but rather with *his* being a great lover. He does not love Isolde so much as he loves being Tristan. Williams says this involves one thought too many.

18. Which I have presented in "Harming Some to Save Others," "Nonconsequen-

tialism, The Person as an End-in-Itself, and the Significance of Status," and which will be discussed in Chapter 10.

19. In a more recent paper, "The Value of Inviolability." *Revere de Metaphysique et Morale*, No. 2/1994, Nagel seems to alter his position, accepting my views on inviolability as previously presented in, e.g., "Harming Some to Save Others," in *Philosophical Studies* 57(3) (November 1989):227–60 and in "Nonconsequentialism, the Person as an End-in-Itself, and the Significance of Status," *Philosophy and Public Affairs*, 21(4) (Fall 1992):354–89. However, he does not note that this new position seems inconsistent with his former position.

20. The device of the amnesiac derives from Derek Parfit's use of it in a different context. See *Reasons and Persons* (Oxford: Oxford U. Press, 1985).

21. Foot suggests such an analysis in "Euthanasia," *Philosophy and Public Affairs* 6(2) (Winter 1977):85–112.

22. This is a point missed by those, such as Waldron, who accept the logical criticism of rights as constraints in the Constraint Case, and see duty-based morality as a possible solution. See his Introduction to *Theories of Rights*, p. 16.

10

Constraining Rights and
the Value of Status

> . . . from the fulfillment of this wish he can expect no gratification of his
> sensuous desires and consequently no state which would satisfy any of his
> . . . inclinations, . . . all he can expect is a greater inner worth of his own
> person.   Immanuel Kant, *Groundwork of the Metaphysics of Morals*

I

Common Foundation for Prerogatives, Restrictions, and Constraints

In the two previous chapters we described some attempts to decide which
potential victim(s) should be protected in the Constraint Case in which one
person could be killed to stop five from being killed to save yet others. We
have also considered ways in which to justify the rights as restrictions presented by the Principle of Permissible Harm itself. We did this in order to deal
with Scheffler's argument that, if it is no more important to prevent the violation of a right than to prevent a comparable harm brought about by natural
causes, then if we may violate a right to minimize violations of comparable
rights, we may violate that right in order to minimize disutility. This is essentially an attack on the correctness of the PPH or any form of restriction. We
dealt with these issues primarily on the temporary assumption that the single
potential victim who will lose life he would otherwise retain independently of imposition on us or other potential victims ran no risk of being one
among the greater number of victims.

The ways to justify constraints when this assumption holds according to
the strategies discussed in chapters 8 and 9, are (1) to show that some person
differs from all the other potential victims either in himself or in the relationship in which he stands to other potential victims (this is a victim-focused
approach), or (2) to show that the relation in which the agent stands to his
victim is different from his relation to other victims as an agent-relative approach, or (3) to show that the content of agency is immoral (an agent-
focused approach), or (4) to show that the agent's awareness of himself limits
his conduct. Option (4) was taken to include the agent's noting that his victim
cares more for his own survival than he does for the survival of others, or

cares more that harm to him should not motivate action than that harm to others not do so. This consideration was included in an agent-concerned view because, although each potential victim may, according to this theory, think the same, it is the agent's own victim whose concern looms largest to him.

My suggestion is that these approaches to selecting the potential victim who is protected are incorrect. Let us summarize briefly the alternative position that will be presented in detail below. To understand why we may not kill the single person, we need not look for a distinguishing asymmetry that makes that person different from all other potential victims. He may have the same characteristics and stand in the same relations as the others, but these properties and relations nonetheless constitute an impassable barrier — a restricting and constraining right — which we come up against when we would have to harm him for the sake of others. Each one of the potential victims has this same property, but this does not mean there is any problem in choosing whether to kill the one for the sake of the five. Further, this property need not be connected to the victim's caring more that he not be violated than that others not be. When I say that the constraining right does not rest on an asymmetry, I mean that there is not necessarily an asymmetry between the position the single person will be put in vis-à-vis the five for whom he would be sacrificed, and the position those five will be placed in vis-à-vis the persons they are sacrificed for. The constraining right may, however, be crucially tied to asymmetries in the relations *between* the one and the five for whom he would be sacrificed, as described by the PPH. For example, the single person would be used for the sake of the five as they would not be for his. These asymmetries give rise to a restriction, that is, a right against ordinary welfare maximization. A strengthened restriction gives rise to a constraint against minimizing violations of the restriction by violating the restriction itself.[1] The point here is that if it were not for this strengthened restriction, the victim would be treated in the same inappropriate way that is proscribed by the PPH, only for a different goal, that is, to protect other people from rights violations. He ought not be so treated.

Notice that there is a difference between saying on the one hand that each person has a personal point of view, leading him to care more for his projects than for those of others, incorporating this fact (in some way) into a defense of the person's right not to be used for others, and claiming on the other hand that this right truly constrains, when others' rights are also at stake, because the person we confront cares more about his rights than about the rights of others. The former use of the personal point of view could be correct and the latter still be incorrect.

If it is true that the single person has no distinguishing features that protect him but not the others, and if, nonetheless, it is wrong to harm him for the sake of others, then *all* the potential victims have a property that gives rise to a constraining right, a right that would not exist in any of them if it were permissible to kill the one to minimize rights violations in the others. The constraining right each has, furthermore, expresses a new value, the conception of the person as inviolable in a way he would not be without it. It is even a sublime and elevated conception of the person. This value can be the basis of a *non-agent relative* rights-based account of the protection afforded the person against being used to minimize rights violations. That is, there seem to be two different routes to take when one sees that the single individual has a right. In both routes I come up against his right if I try to kill him, and this stops me. The five will also be killed but not relative to me; I let them die. The agent-relative route interprets all this to mean that my *basic* duty is that I not kill. According to the second route when I see that the one has a right not to be killed, I should see that if it were permissible to kill him, this would mean that each of the five is also killable to save others from being killed (even though they wouldn't be killed if I saved them). By contrast, if the five are killed because it is impermissible to kill the one, this does not mean that morality endorses the permissibility of their being killed. Now suppose we care about the status of persons as inviolable (we care about nonkillability, not only not being killed), and each of us has a duty to promote this value. Suppose we are tempted to kill the one to promote this value. When we realize that we cannot promote the value by doing this—indeed the permissibility of doing it would deny the existence of the valuable status in everyone—we realize it is impermissible to kill the first person we come up against. Here concern for a victim-focused, agent-neutral value that all have a duty to promote, leads to a *derivative* (versus basic) duty that I not kill even if others do. (Notice that this implies a non-agent relative reason why permissible killing could be more serious than permissible letting die (of harm): the former endorses violability, and expresses a different conception of the status of persons, the latter does not endorse violability. The factors pointed to in chapters one through four do suggest why what we do and what happens to someone is morally different if we kill rather than let die. But even if someone will have been killed by someone else if we let him die, there is a difference in what is true of the victim if killing him is permissible from what is true of him if letting him die is permissible. This may justify doing more to avoid killing than to avoid letting die of harm.) The first, agent-relative, route begins by assuming that the one person has some right not to be killed that I come up against, but it is only the fact that I would have to kill that makes it true that the single person should not be killed even when preventing five from being killed is at issue. The second route (via concern for a certain status) gives an account of why the one person has the right not to be killed even when the five would be killed, a constraint that I then come up against. We can see the right of the single person not to be killed to save others as an expression of a certain status he and all persons have; the impermissibility of my killing him is implied by the requirement that I respect this right by doing what it tells me to do when I come up against it.[2] This is a victim-focused approach, which provides an answer to the Selection and Value Problems.

Are restrictions and constraints connected with a prerogative? It seems wrong to break the connection between prerogative, restriction, and constraint altogether, even though, as noted earlier, sometimes the prerogative is not present when the others are and vice versa. This may be because, although the restriction and the constraint do not stem directly from the prerogative, in some cases they all stem from the same source, namely, a person's entitlement to control something, because he is not merely a means to the greater good. The prerogative does not, I have argued, derive only from the fact that persons have a personal point of view and are motivated to act from it. It derives from the fact that persons, that is, rational beings, who are capable of a personal point of view, are not to be always used as mere tools to the greater good if they do not choose that as their goal. They are ends-in-themselves. (Nonrational beings with a personal point of view are not necessarily accorded such treatment.)

Contrary to Scheffler, this same ground is available for restraints and constraints. In those cases in which there is no restriction on taking what someone may refuse to give, but still a prerogative, the prerogative may be based solely on the greater strain of being the cause of one's own loss rather than suffering the loss at someone else's hands. In cases where there is no prerogative (i.e., there are obligations), but there are restrictions and constraints, some extra value is seen to come from an individual's fulfilling his own responsibility to act.

Let us grant that, from a formal point of view, having a constraining right strengthens a right and shows deeper commitment to avoiding the inappropriate relationship between persons and other ends proscribed by the PPH. Let us also suppose that it expresses a more elevated status of the person it protects. (We will need separate discussion to show these things.) Could it be a characteristic of morality itself, rather than of persons, that unavoidably implies a system with such a strengthening mechanism, so that a constraint, for example, is in this way not merely an optional feature of a moral system, but a requirement? Arguing that there is a characteristic of morality itself that requires a certain view of people, where this does *not* just mean that morality *recognizes* certain characteristics of people as giving rise to prerogatives, restricting rights and constraints, involves the claim that we could not carry out the demands of morality (be moral agents) unless we had certain rights, constraints, and prerogatives.[3] So to the extent that we must be moral, we must have these. I do not believe that this way of arguing for the existence of rights and prerogatives will succeed. It seems much more likely that it is the characteristics of people that give rise to the rights, constraints, and prerogatives to begin with.

II

Irrational Ways to Show Concern

Let us now consider in more detail whether rights-as-constraints are rationally possible or whether caring about rights and the persons they protect commits us to minimizing their violation, that is, commits us to having a utilitarianism of rights (as Nozick calls it),[4] or making of rights violations an agent-neutral disvalue (as Kagan puts it). This constraint could be analyzed as having two components—a core, which is an ordinary right not to be killed to save other lives as the PPH describes, plus a strengthening component, which prohibits killing to prevent violations of the same or a less significant right. Together these two components make the constraint a sort of *super right*. I will first discuss this issue in cases that are to be imagined as involving a single potential victim of whom it is known that it is impossible that he should ever himself have faced the threat of death that the five now face, or even have been in any other life-threatening position aside from our threat to kill him now. The aim is to deal most straightforwardly with the case in which someone's sacrifice would have to be justified solely in terms of protecting rights of others, rather than minimizing the chances of his own rights' being violated.

The basic thrust of the rights-as-constraints view is some sort of non-substitutability that is ascribed to each of the individual would-be victims. If in the Constraint Case the five who will be killed if the one is not have *their* non-substitutability ignored by being killed in order to save others, this would not alter the fact that the single person should not be substituted for them by any agent.

One strategy for defending the coherence of such a view is to describe a possible right whose violation it would be irrational to permit us to minimize by violating a comparable right. Such permission for minimization would be irrational because what would motivate it would be concern for the right, and this concern could not rationally be served by violation of that right.

One point this strategy emphasizes is that if caring about a right and the status of the person it expresses involves *heeding* what it demands, then minimization-by-violation does not show concern for that right since it will *not heed* the right. A second point is that if morality sought and permitted minimization of the violations of a certain right by transgression of that very right, it would essentially eliminate that right and the concept of the person it expresses from the moral system. Minimization-by-violation would be futile as a way of showing concern for rights; it would be a "futilitarianism" of rights.

Before proceeding, however, notice that one might respond to the question "If you care about rights, why don't you minimize their violation?" by stopping the "caring" approach in its tracks. One might simply say that it is not because one cares about rights that one does not transgress the right of one person in order to minimize rights violations. Rather, it is because one *respects* rights. As noted above (p. 261), I have chosen to see whether the notions of caring and respecting can be interwoven, to see whether, for example, respecting the single person's right could be seen as the best way to *care* about a right, and a certain view of the person with which the right expresses. I will distinguish this sense of caring from other, more common senses, below. One might also respond to the question "If you care about rights, why don't you minimize their violation?" by emphasizing that it is persons as ends-in-themselves, not their rights per se, that one should care about, and any answer to the question must be consistent with this second concern. We shall try to remain conscious of this point.

An Argument for the Irrationality of Minimization

Let us begin by supposing (for the sake of argument) that there is a PPH right. Now consider the idea of *a specified right*, by which I mean a right that implicitly or explicitly tells us to what extent the individual is protected from transgressions against her, a right that does not leave this matter of extent entirely vague. The PPH itself is, in a sense, already a specified right: it specifies *how* someone may and may not be treated. This is *manner specification*. By specified right here I mean the further specification of the numbers of lives we forgo in order not to treat people in violation of the PPH. This is *numerical threshold specification*. Suppose the right not to be killed in violation of the PPH were absolute, and that this meant that we had a right not to be killed for utility maximizing, for example, in the Transplant Case, no matter how many other people could be saved from being killed by our being killed. It might be suggested that to say it is permissible to violate one person's absolute right not to be killed for the sake of utility maximizing, in order to prevent the violation of other people's comparable absolute rights, is just to deny that people have such an absolute right. If it were permissible to minimize violations, fewer people might in fact die of violations of this absolute right, but people would no longer really have the absolute right not to be killed for utility maximizing. This further implies that they would not have the status of persons who had this degree of inviolability. (Or at least so the argument we are examining claims.)

Suppose the right not to be killed in transgression of the PPH is not absolute. For example, suppose (just for the sake of argument) that the PPH right specifically forbids killing one person as a means to saving up to ten others, but permits such a killing when more could be saved. Given a situation in which five people will be killed in violation of their nonabsolute PPH right unless we kill one, the decision to minimize the violation of the PPH right, out of concern for the PPH, by killing the one would, it is suggested, be confused. This is because the PPH right *specifically* excludes this as a correct course. If we care about the right, and the degree of inviolability of the person it represents, why should we act against its clear demands? (This is the first point about not heeding a right.)

Furthermore (this is the second point), for morality to endorse an act against the clear demand of the right seems to involve eliminating this version of the PPH from morality, and recognizing a concept of the person that makes it permissible for a person to be used in this way. Not minimizing violations is, therefore, in a sense to minimize violations (and show maximal concern for the right and the inviolability of the person it expresses) *consistent with* the right and that degree of inviolability being a part of morality at all.

Objections

Something seems to be wrong with this argument. We wish to distinguish between the restriction, as represented by the PPH, and the constraint. The PPH insists only on not doing certain things to maximize lives saved (or utility, in general). Suppose we kill one person to prevent two others from being killed in violation of their PPH right. This means the two might otherwise be killed to maximize lives saved, but the one person we kill would be killed in order to prevent the violation of two rights. It might also be true that we do save two lives at the expense of only one, but that is not our aim in acting. We aim to protect rights, it is said.[5] Therefore, if intention is relevant, we do not aim to violate the PPH (which is concerned with not killing to maximize utility), and we may not actually violate it, since we do not act against its stricture. Hence, if what morality endorsed (permitted) was not a transgression of the PPH, it would not, in permitting the killing of the one to minimize rights violations, eliminate the PPH-right from morality. It would not say it was, after all, sometimes all right to kill one as a means of saving simply more lives.

Suppose it is true that the PPH is not transgressed, strictly speaking, when we kill the one in the Constraint Case, because it explicitly makes reference to utility or saving lives. Then, killing the one to prevent transgressions of the PPH will not involve minimizing PPH-rights violations by violating *the same right*, that is, a right that forbids killing people (in a certain way) to minimize lives lost.

A Constraint Already

If the PPH were already an absolute constraint (i.e., if its *subject matter* dealt specifically with forbidding the killing of people to minimize rights violations), we could tell a different story. Then it *would be* self-contradictory to say that it is morally permissible to minimize violations of the constraint for the sake of showing concern and respect for it, or because one cared about it and the concept of the person as inviolable in the way the constraint expresses. For example, suppose there is a constraint not to be treated in the *manner* prohibited by the PPH (e.g., to be harmed as a means) in order to prevent violations of rights. To endorse minimizing violations of the constraint by permitting transgression of that constraint, would amount to the rejection of the constraint.[6] Indeed, if the constraint did not prohibit using people to maximize utility but only prohibited using people to minimize rights violations, it would make more sense as a *formal* matter to permit transgressing such a constraint for the sake of maximizing utility than to permit transgressing it for the sake of showing respect for the constraint or the degrees of inviolability it represents.[7] But we were trying to *argue from* the (hypothesized) existence of a restraining right to the existence of a constraint that would prevent killing one to minimize violations of the restraining right, and we will have failed to do so by this "inconsistency" argument if we have to assume what we were trying to prove, namely the constraint.

Another Argument

Suppose that, strictly speaking, killing one to save others from being killed (to save yet others) is not minimization of PPH-rights violations *by violation of the PPH*. There will still be other rights whose violation we could try minimizing by violating an instance of the right. These will be either absolute rights not to be killed or rights that specifically direct us not to kill to prevent violations of rights. To permit violating such rights in order to minimize violations of the right as a sign of concern and respect for the right will be irrational, since such permissibility will go against what the right itself directs. It will also make impossible the existence of a certain value, that is, whatever degree of inviolability of the person the right represents. However, the reason to endorse such rights—which are already constraining rights—is not that without them mere PPH-restraining rights cannot exist (as the first argument claimed), but rather that without them the status of a highly inviolable person, represented by the constraining right, and whatever value this has, cannot exist.

This has been a brief summary of an argument that I shall now describe in more detail. We can begin by restating all that was said (mistakenly) in connection with the PPH. Let us begin by considering the idea of a specified right. By a specified right, I here mean a right that implicitly or explicitly tells us to what numerical extent the individual is protected from transgressions against him, a right that does not leave this matter of extent entirely vague. This could be an absolute right or one with a numerical threshold. Suppose we had such a right not to be killed in certain ways, as suggested by the PPH, but it was not limited to a prohibition on killing in these ways for greater utility. This right has the same formal structure as the PPH—that is, the manner in which one is killed, the relation between victim and beneficiaries that are thought significant are the same—but it protects us against being killed in violation of the PPH's formal structure for the additional end of minimizing rights violations. This right has the manner requirement of the PPH at its core, but not necessarily the whole PPH where this implies the prohibition on utility maximizing. Why might we think there is such a right? Because, if the *way* of harming people prohibited by the PPH is objectionable, then we show just how objectionable it is by excluding that way of harming *for other goals*, utility or minimizing rights violation. This would also make people more inviolable. Suppose this right which is a constraint were absolute, and that we had a right not to be killed in the way we would have to be killed in the Transplant Case, no matter how many other people could be saved from being killed by our being killed. To say it is permissible to violate one person's absolute constraint not to be killed in order to prevent the violation of other people's rights (one of which is a constraint) eliminates from morality that absolute constraint. This is because, if that killing were permissible, it would no longer be true that morality insists that it is absolutely wrong to kill a person who would otherwise live, in order to minimize rights violations. Under such an interpretation, if we minimized violations of the absolute constraint, fewer people might in fact die of violations of this constraint, but people would no longer really be protected by the absolute constraint on being killed. This further implies that they would not have the status of persons who had this degree of inviolability.

Suppose the constraint on being killed (with the formal structure of the PPH but ruling out killing for ends besides utility) is not absolute, but specified numerically. For example, suppose (just for the sake of argument) that it specifically forbids killing one person as a means of preventing the constraint on being killed from being violated in up to ten others, even when they would be killed as a means of saving less than ten others. However, it permits such a killing when more comparable rights violations could be prevented. Given a situation in which five people will be killed in violation of this nonabsolute constraint unless we kill one, the decision to minimize the violations by killing the one would, it is suggested, be confused. This is because the constraint *specifically* excludes this as a correct course. If we care about the constraint, why should we act against its clear demands? This is the first point about the irrationality of trying to show concern for the constraint by not heeding it.

Furthermore, it is suggested, for it to be permissible to act in this way seems to involve eliminating this constraint and the status of the person it expresses from morality. Not permitting minimizing violations is, therefore, to show maximal concern for the right and the status, *consistent with* the right and the status existing at all.

Unspecified Rights

What if the right is not specified with a threshold nor specified as absolute? That is, what if there is a right not to be killed that focuses on the same formal properties of the PPH (i.e., the manner in which one is killed, the relation between victim and beneficiaries, etc.) and that prohibits killing for the sake of rights in addition to prohibiting killing for utility. This constraint, however, does not include any explicit specifications of how many rights violations can be tolerated out of respect for the constraint. Suppose that, on a given occasion, we decide that in order to save a thousand people from having their constraints violated, we will transgress this constraint of one person, and it is permissible to do so. One understanding of this decision is that we have now specified the strength of the constraint, and so removed the vagueness that existed before. Since there was no specification to begin with, however, granting permission to minimize violations of the right does not eliminate the right from morality. If it wasn't specified to begin with, there is no elimination by, in essence, specifying for the first time.

Infringing versus Eliminating

However, notice the following complication. Consider, first, an unspecified right not to be killed. Suppose we decide it is permissible to kill someone as a means of saving one thousand people from being killed. It may be said that the right of the one not to be so used still exists and is recognized even in the breach. That is, without thinking that we act impermissibly, if we kill the one we may think that there is a negative residue produced by our acting, for which we would owe compensation to the victim. The claim is that there would be no such negative residue unless the victim still had a right not to be so used. [8] Deciding that it is permissible to kill the person in this case does *not* conflict with the claim that he has a right not to be used to save a thousand people from having their rights transgressed, though we may permissibly infringe the right. Permission, or moral endorsement need not imply that people do not truly have the right and the accompanying status (and whatever properties it stems from or is associated with).

On this view, we have not, in fact, specified that the victim's right is not absolute (or we have not specified his right at a lower threshold than it is truly specified at) by granting the permissibility of killing. But, if all this is true, why, in the case of a *specified* right not to be used in a certain manner to save one thousand people who will otherwise themselves be so used, might it not also be said that the permissibility of killing the one to save the thousand from such killing would *not* — contrary to what was asserted above — involve a denial of the right not to be killed to save the thousand from such killing? Can we not here also use the language of permissibly infringing a right and owing compensation for infringing a right that we recognize is still in force? Such infringeable rights will be weaker than non-infringeable ones, reflecting a concept of the person as more violable; this could be a reason to think they don't exist. But with an infringeable right, there will still be some right. In fact, having an infringeable right not to be used to minimize the violation of the comparable rights of 1,001 people reflects a concept of the person as more inviolable than having no right at all not to be sacrificed when preventing 1,001 rights violations is at stake. (The latter is the implication of having a non-infringeable right not to be violated for up to a thousand rights.)

I believe that the crucial question about this proposal, so far as the present topic is concerned, is whether it is permissible to infringe the constraint that is specified only for protecting rights for some reason other than concern for rights violations, for example, utility, or whether concern for one thousand rights violations qua one thousand rights violations may permissibly prompt the infringement of the specified constraint as well. Similarly, the claim that permitting transgression of an absolute right not to be killed for minimizing rights violations in order to minimize rights violations eliminates the absolute right is consistent with the view that utility (or saving lives) is a permissible reason for infringing the right. It is also true that, if grounds offered for the infringement are the very factors that a specified right excludes as grounds for its infringement, that is, if it specifically says or implies "that we ought not kill one to save one thousand from being improperly killed," then the infringement cannot be done out of respect and concern for the right itself or the status of people which it expresses. Disregarding the instructions of the right shows disrespect for the right, not respect for it.

To make this issue clearer, let us consider in greater detail the relation between specification, elimination, and infringement. Suppose someone, A, has a right which is described as the "right to her house," without any explicit specification of threshold in the content of the right. It is also agreed that if someone, B, would die of exposure unless he breaks into the house in the absence of the owner, it is permissible for him to do so, although he may then be liable for compensating the owner. The favored way of describing this is that A's right to her house is infringeable; the fact that she is owed compensation shows that she had a right and that she was done some wrong in the course of someone's doing the overall right act. Suppose this is the correct description of the case. May we at least conclude from its being permissible for B to enter the house in A's absence that, whatever right the owner had, she had no right to exclude the person in dire circumstances when she was not using her house? If so, then it is not true that the reason compensation is owed is that the *right to exclude the person in dire circumstances* was infringed. We can also conclude that the fact that helping the person in dire circumstances is sufficient reason for infringing A's right to her house is just what implies that there is no right to exclude the person in dire circumstances. That is, more generally, if reason x overrides the right to y, there is no right to y even if x. If a reason is grounds for permissibly infringing the right, then a right that was specified to include in its content the denial of the reason would be an invalid right. That is, this right must be eliminated from morality.

If this is all true, what can we say about the claim that it is permissible to infringe a right that says someone is not to be killed, when it would be "infringed" for the sake of preventing a thousand (or fewer) from being killed? If a reason allows us to permissibly infringe a right, then the denial of the reason cannot be part of the content of a valid right. So if it is permissible to kill one for the sake of saving a thousand from being killed, we must eliminate, not merely infringe, a right that says someone is not to be killed even to save a thousand being killed.

There would, however, be a difference between our case in which someone's right to her house is permissibly infringed and cases in which someone would (by hypothesis) be permissibly killed to save a greater number from being killed. This difference might suggest a counterargument. In the house case, I believe, we think there is no right on the owner's part to resist the imposition. (This does not necessarily imply that there is a duty on her part to donate her residence.) In the killing case, even if we thought it was permissible to kill someone to prevent a certain number of killings, we would, I believe, think it permissible for the person to try to resist. Would the permissibility of resistance signify that he has after all a valid, specified right not to be killed to prevent a thousand killings, though it is permissible to kill him solely to prevent a thousand killings? I think it only signifies that he has a valid right to resist. It does not signify that he has a specified right not to be killed to prevent a thousand from being killed, and that we only infringe the right if we kill him to save a thousand from being killed.

Nevertheless, I repeat, that the right specifically prohibits killing to save one thousand from rights violations does not mean that one could not permissibly infringe the right for the sake of saving the one thousand lives, that is, out of concern for life rather than for rights. This would, however, violate a specified PPH. We shall consider this further below (p. 282).

Notice that if there truly are numerically specified (rather than absolute) rights, this could be consistent with the existence of a negative residue in cases where violating a person is specified (explicitly or implicitly) as permissible. The negative residue can express the sense that "it's a shame" people do *not* have a right to greater inviolability, and if they do not have a right to such greater degrees of inviolability, at least they have a right to be compensated for *this sad truth*. Put somewhat differently, suppose the list of reasons that make infringing a completely non-specified right permissible implies a set of invalid would-be specified rights (which is what has been argued above). Nevertheless, suppose trying to compensate is required even where infringement of a non-specified right is permissible (though this does not mean infringement is not permissible if compensation is impossible). Then it could be said that what someone has a right to is that there be transgression for a certain reason only if there is an attempt to provide compensation.

This analysis of when permissible infringement is consistent with continued endorsement of a right shows that this topic is related to the criticism of views (e.g., Sen's) that say that we may permissibly transgress rights to minimize rights violations but not for the sake of utility.

A Hierarchical System

A prohibition on minimizing rights violations by violating the right in question produces what might be called a hierarchy effect among rights violations. If someone is interested in minimizing, he counts violations of comparable rights. But when the absolute or specified right tells us that in this situation all things considered it would be wrong to transgress a right in order to save other people from comparable rights violations, we are not at liberty to say to ourselves, "The violation of this one person's right would be one wrong, but the violation of the rights of five others would be five wrongs, so better one wrong than five." When the wrong involves doing what *all things considered* the right says we must not do, not doing it dominates, if we are to show respect and concern for the right and for the idea of the person it expresses.[9] It is because of their specific exclusion of these other killings as justified reasons for infringing the right that in deciding whether to kill the one to save the greater number from having their rights infringed, we are not faced with a dilemmatic situation. So far as concern over rights (even when utility is associated with the transgression of rights) there is no dilemma, where dilemma is defined as a choice situation in which whatever we do, we do something wrong. (There may also be no dilemma because the duty not to harm is stronger than the duty to aid.)

Selection Problem

Once we understand why minimization of violations of a particular right by violating a comparable right is wrong, the additional supposed problem of how one selects, among all the individuals who have rights, the one who will not be killed—the Selection Problem—seems straightforwardly answerable: we select not to kill anyone we would have to kill in violation of the constraint. This is so, not because *we*, standing in a special relation to the person's right, generate a constraint for the first time. Rather, it is because we come up against the constraint of the right and the properties of a person that give rise both to his being inviolable in this way and to such a constraint. Analogously, we need not think that the power of a brick wall to constrain us is a new physical-chemical output of the interaction between intrinsically weak building materials and our body. Rather, whichever intrinsically constraining brick wall I meet first will constrain me. I will be there when it constrains me, but not because I help produce the constraint.

The Significance of Permission and Status

It is important to see that it is the permission to kill, the endorsement of killing, not any actual killing, that can eliminate certain rights not to be killed and a status of high inviolability from the moral system. If the comparable right is violated many times over, this does not involve morality endorsing such violation; though many people may be killed, we do not say that it was correct that any of them were killed, which is what permission would involve. More people may die, but the conception of each person that is morally endorsed involves a higher degree of inviolability. We have already noted two different reasons that might be given for endorsing a transgression of the one. The first is misguided concern for the right and the inviolability of persons it expresses, that would produce a system that eliminates the right and the inviolable status of the person. A second reason for endorsing transgression of the one is greater concern for saving lives than for rights. In this second case, it has been suggested that the permissibility of the killing may not involve a denial of the constraint. To repeat: this is because infringing the right for the sake of some competing value, for example, utility, can leave the right still existing, if the right itself excluded only minimizing rights violations. Permitting violation of the constraint for the sake of utility is not as formally irrational as endorsing violation for the sake of respect and concern for the right. (This does not mean that endorsing violation for the sake of utility is correct. It will, of course conflict with the PPH right which says we should not kill persons to maximize utility and it denies a highly inviolable status to persons. We discuss formal irrationality again at p. 282.) Suppose that right, unspecified or specified, were not eliminated by permitting its transgression for the sake of minimizing rights violations; it was only permissibly infringed. This would still reveal that the person had a less inviolable status. In this case the right would no longer be the sole expression of the status of the person; the degree of infringeability would express this as well.

On some views, non-consequentialist constraints are best characterized as concerned with the distinction between what I as an agent *do* and what *happens*; I must not do something, even if this means that something else happens. Without denying that, in a non–agent-relative sense, this is true, the view being presented here emphasizes a different distinction, that between what it is *permissible to do to people* (i.e., *their status*), and what *happens to people* (their fate, which may involve more rights violated). What I do, rather than what happens, is important when it reveals what it is permissible to do, that is, what the status of a person is. The realm of status is *not* what happens to people. If many are killed in violation of their rights because we may not kill one to save them, their status as individuals who should not be killed does not change. If it were permitted to kill the one to save them, their status would change. We may be concerned about what happens, but be unwilling to prevent it in a way that is only consistent with a change in status. It is a mistake to see an opposition between the rights of the one person and the rights of all others, since the status of everyone is affected by the way it is permissible to treat one person.

The Significance and Type of Inviolability

Suppose the correct constraint prohibits many types of killing even for very good causes. If we are inviolable in this way, we are more important creatures than more violable ones; this higher status is in itself a benefit *to us*. In consequence, we are creatures whose interests as recipients of such ordinary benefits as utility may be more worth serving. (It is having the status itself which is a benefit, not just its being respected. If only actual appropriate respect were a benefit, then one would be better off in a world in which one had a low status but this was fully respected than in a world in which one had a higher status, though it was not fully respected. If having a higher status were not a good to the person who has it, we should be indifferent between having a lower status but being treated better than we deserved (to level x) and having a higher status fully respected (to level x). Having the status is a benefit, in part, because it makes one worthy of respect, owed respect. Without this, respect becomes merely a psychological attitude others take toward one.) Furthermore, the world is, in a sense, a better place for having more important creatures in it. Our having higher status is a benefit to *the world*. In this sense, the inviolable status (against being harmed in a certain way) of any potential victim can be taken to be an agent-neutral value, and as providing a solution to the Value Problem. This is, however, a nonconsequential value. It does not follow (causally or noncausally) upon any act of ours, it is not something we must aim to bring about as a consequence of our acts. It is already present in the status that persons have. Respecting it provides the background against which we may then seek the welfare of persons or pursue other values. It is not our duty to bring about the existence of such valuable persons, but only to respect the constraints that express the presence of value. Kagan claims that the only sense in which we can show disrespect for people is by using them in an *unjustified* way. [10] Hence, if it is justified to kill one to save five, we will not be showing disrespect for the one if we so use him. But there is another sense of disrespect tied to the fact that we owe people more respect than we owe to other creatures, even though we also should not treat these other creatures in an unjustified way. And this other sense of disrespect reflects, I believe, a failure to heed the greater inviolability of persons. [11]

Individuals whose rights stand as a barrier to action are more potent individuals than they would be otherwise. There being rights and constraints with high thresholds is a mark that the person who has them is a stronger, more valuable type of thing, even if they prevent us from stopping more transgressions. It is true of all those who die because we cannot save them as well as of those who are not violated, that they have these rights. By analogy, a stronger, more impressive wall is one that we will not be able to pass through, even to prevent the destruction of comparable walls behind it. One would *expect* that the highest values or rights are intrinsically such that it would be wrong to minimize even a great many violations of them, either for the sake of rights or the sake of utility, by transgressing them; they would not be so almighty if they could be transgressed.

Suppose such a conception of persons involving a sort of inviolability, if true, would give persons great worth. What reason do we have to believe such a conception of persons is true? That is, why should we believe that the best is true, or even that what it would be best for us to believe about ourselves is true? Is it possible that in this area we can bootstrap ourselves into significance: If someone thinks he is inviolable, then he is? But thinking may make it so only because our capacity for such a self-conception indicates something else about us — for example, that we are rational beings — which itself renders us worthy of certain sorts of protections, even if we do not believe ourselves worthy.

In any case, it is certain properties (here not enumerated) that we have as individuals that would account for our status. (I mean to emphasize "as individuals" quite independent of any relations we are, or are not, part of.) Further, it need not be that having a personal point of view alone makes one inviolable, for those whose reasons are never out of synchrony with the impartial point of view could be inviolable (in a certain way) in virtue of, for example, being creatures who act for reasons. They would just waive their right not to be violated for the greatest good. If creatures who act for reasons happen to have a personal point of view, the factors seen from that point of view can be legitimate reasons as well, meriting noninterference. Even if they are not legitimate as reasons, actions prompted by them, in such a creature, could give one a reason for abiding by a constraint.

But recall that all this talk about inviolability is only rough. It is inviolability in a certain way that is at issue. Consider the right not to be harmed in order to produce greater utility (rather than the constraint on harming someone to reduce violation of rights). This right is not absolute. This does not mean only that there might be some number of lives (threatened by natural disease) such that we could kill one to save them, *in the way* the Transplant Case requires. It also means that we may kill one even to save two in the way the Trolley Case requires. Now the conception of the person could contain a higher degree of inviolability if it were not even permissible to bring about death in the way we do it in the Trolley Case (or in self-defense cases, etc.). Yet we think, presumably, that it is morally permissible to do these things. Persons are not absolutely inviolable, and so the fact that the constraint protects their inviolability does not show that it does so to the correct or to the highest degree. Indeed, if killing were impermissible in the Trolley Case, but there were no constraint on killing the one to minimize violations of the rights of others, then quantitatively it could be that the same degree of inviolability might be expressed. Simple talk about inviolability is not enough. Restrictions and constraints are better explained by inviolability against impositions that create inappropriate relations between victim and beneficiaries.

Suppose the right (against being used to maximize utility) whose violation we contemplate minimizing has its content given by what I have referred to as the PPH. Then if we treat people in the manner ruled out by the PPH right in order to minimize violations of it, we will be harming someone *in the very way* it rules out, even if *we do this for* the sake of something other than utility maximization. (We do it to minimize rights violations.) If this way of harming certain persons is wrong, then we should not do it even to minimize occurrences of this way of harming them. It is not inviolability against harm per se that is represented by the constraint; it is the person's inviolability against this way of being harmed.

The Inviolability of Persons and the Inviolability of Rights

I must emphasize that a component of the argument against *minimizing* rights violations that I have given is so *formal* that it itself does little to answer the questions of why the manner restriction at the core of the constraint has the specific content it does have and what the numerical threshold is on the constraint. This formal argument is merely concerned with the elimination of a specified constraint (of any sort) by the permissibility of minimizing violations of it by transgressing it. This formal component does only a little to directly support the view that persons have a high degree of inviolability. Our argument for a high degree of inviolability comes in part in deciding that the PPH is correct, since the constraint just has the manner restriction of the PPH extended to deal with protection against minimizing rights violations. The correctness of this extension itself contributes to higher inviolability. The high degree of inviolability also results from it being correct to set a high threshold for permissible transgressions. Once the constraint with this content is in place on these grounds, we can argue that trying to minimize violations of such constraints by violating them fails to show respect and concern for the constraint. This last step is mostly an argument for the inviolability of the right rather than the person. [12] A person can only have the status that the constraint expresses if it is irrational to violate the constraint to minimize violations but this irrationality is not the foundation of the constraint. One might reject the PPH I have suggested and have a more consequentialist description of a core right allowing killing in the Transplant Case and setting a low threshold for utility maximizing, and use this to generate a constraint. Whatever PPH right is generated, it could be said that we show greater concern for its manner restrictions if we do not engage in behavior it prohibits for the goal of minimizing rights violations. This generates the constraint. Once a specified constraint is in place it will make no sense to permit us to violate the constraint to minimize violations of it. This is the formal part of the argument. If it is permissible to violate the constraint people will not have the same status it expresses — even if this is low inviolability — and the right will be eliminated, even if fewer violations of people occur.

Indeed, because respecting a right and respecting a person can differ, by minimizing we might show more respect for a right that expresses lower inviolability of the person and show less respect for a right that expresses higher inviolability of the person. For example, suppose R1 tells us that someone has a right not to be killed to save up to ten other people from being killed. R2 tells us that someone else has a right not to be killed to save up to a million people from being killed. If we would kill the person covered by R1 to save nine people, we show only minimal disrespect for the right, but the inviolability of the person is quite low. If we would kill the person covered by R2 to save five hundred thousand people but not fewer, we show great disrespect for the right, but the status of the person is highly inviolable.

In sum, the account of the constraint as an expression of a new value, namely a person with great significance, because highly inviolable, should be distinguished from the futility (irrationality) argument. That argument is concerned with self-defeatingness, that is, the futility of trying to show respect for a specified constraining right by violating it, even to minimize violations. The irrationality argument claimed that utilitarianism of rights is a futilitarianism of rights. The argument which points to the value of the status of inviolability independent of what happens provides a deeper, more fundamental reason for not violating a right to minimize rights violations. It alone explains why there is a strong constraining right in the first place, by pointing to the significance of the status of inviolability.

Measures of Significance

There are at least two possible questions that can be raised about the view that higher inviolability is connected to the greater significance of persons. [13] Why is one not a more significant type of creature if one is less inviolable but more free to violate, and why is one not a less significant creature because one is not the sort for whose sake one may permissibly violate others? Being free to violate and having high saveability are both statuses that can hold even if they are not reflected in what happens. Indeed, we must be careful to separate the concern that (1) people have either of these two statuses to a greater degree than inviolability, from the concern that (2) what happens to people (whether they are actually saved) is more important than the status people have (e.g., inviolability). (We might imagine, for example, that as one's saveability went up, the actual numbers of people helped when in need went down.) Notice also that every degree of inviolability has its complementary degree of saveability; the question is what sort of combination of the two represents high status. Consider the first question. My sense is that if the person who gains legitimate liberty to violate is one of those who loses inviolability as well, he has come down on the ladder of significance. One does not gain anything in the way of status by being at liberty to violate a creature whose inviolability is less, and one will have lost inviolability oneself. Furthermore, the liberty one gains is not even a power that must be respected; that is, it is not greater authority. It can be resisted and for this reason also does not elevate its owner. If one is not of the same type as the creature whose inviolability is less, one's status still does not go up intrinsically merely because the status of another creature goes down so that one may violate it. It is only if one's status increases intrinsically to the point that one could permissibly violate someone, himself unchanged, whom one was not formerly permitted to violate, that one might seem to gain in importance. But even here one must be careful. If a creature is truly inviolable, how can one's own importance be less if one is not permitted to violate it than if one is? To say that one's importance is less and could still be increased is like saying that God's power is limited because he cannot change the laws of mathematics.

The second question is more difficult, I believe, since it does seem that if a creature is significant, it is wrong to abandon it and that some costs should be imposed on others to help it. Am I even more significant if I must be aided but I may leave others unaided? If we are all the same type of creature, universalization would apply; there could be no such comparative difference in significance: if I may leave others unaided, they may leave me unaided. One crucial issue in the use of constraints is whether we may impose a loss of a certain significant size on someone for the sake of stopping a comparable loss, only to each of several others. But sometimes constraints protect individuals from suffering losses that are significant, but still less than the losses others will suffer. Even in these cases, we need a good justification for why—as I believe is true—our own status as a person goes down rather than up if a great deal may permissibly be done to persons in order to save us. If our status is connected to being inviolable in a certain way, then it would be no wonder that the status of those saved would be decreased if everyone, including those saved, were violable in order to save persons. Suppose the high status of persons, making it important to save them, was held to stem from some other property than their inviolability. Then, to say that their status would go down if they were violable (in certain ways) even if they were more saveable is to claim that the properties that underlie one's inviolability are more important than those that give rise to any other significance one has. Might it be to claim that having a rational will, whose consent we must seek when interfering with what a person has independently of imposition on us, will give a person higher status than being a complex, feeling creature who cares about whether it lives or dies? But what if it is only a question of the saveability of individuals whose rational wills are being interfered with? If these people are highly saveable, they have a claim on what others have independently of imposition on them. This denies a high degree of personal sovereignty and also denies the significance of its ground — which is also the ground of the moral difference between harming and not aiding: the existence of separate persons with rational wills.

A Better World, the Status of Persons, and Non-consequential Value

What further values does the sort of high inviolability represented by the constraint built on the PPH express? It may be said that if the single person is not killed to save the five in the Constraint Case, the world will be a worse place (at least in some ways) from the point of view of the rights theory itself — a world in which more rights violations occur, and for worse reasons, than would occur if one agent, trying to correct a bad outcome, killed one person. As an indication of this it might be said that we would punish an agent who kills a single person to save five others from being killed less severely than an agent who maliciously (or non-maliciously) kills five (even to save yet others). Furthermore, it might be said, if we compare a world in which a morally deluded person, trying to do his best, kills one person to save others, with a world in which five people are maliciously killed or killed to save others, we must conclude the first world is better. The motivation of the killer is not bad, and we have a delusion leading to a rights violation. This contrasts with either maliciousness leading to five such violations, or five people dying as a result of a moral delusion.

We must be careful in doing this comparison. We are comparing a world in which one person, morally deluded and trying to do the right thing, kills one person, with a world in which five are killed, through a similarly morally deluded act or through a maliciously motivated one. This way of putting the comparison may be deceptive, in part because it suggests that we have a situation structurally analogous to a redirected-threat case: we are offered a choice between outcome A in which someone kills one and outcome B in which someone kills five. In the redirected-threat case, the failure of outcome B to come about is not a causal effect of outcome A's coming about. Outcome A is merely a substitute for outcome B. What the redirected-threat picture omits about our comparison is that the prevention of the outcome in which five are killed is a causal effect of the one being killed in a way, which is a violation of the constraint form of the PPH. In comparing the outcomes we must not omit the causal connection from the picture.

One response to the claim that it is a worse world is just to say that doing what is right in not killing the one does not necessarily produce the best state of affairs, even from the perspective of concern for rights. [14]

A second response, however, is that, at the very least, the world will *not* be a worse place if a constraint is in fact merited because a constraining right that expresses the right sort of inviolability produces a status for a person that is more sublime and elevated than a status that lacks it. This is an additional value that enters the world if people are worthy of inviolability. As was said earlier, this is a *non-consequential* value. Its presence does not follow from any act, but is already present in the status that persons have. The tendency to say that the world would be a better place if, for good motives, an agent killed one person to save others from killing five, arises most clearly when we think of the agent who kills the one person as doing what is nevertheless *wrong*, and *violating* the constraining right. This is because it is compatible with a highly inviolable status of persons. The killing occurs against a background in which it is the wrong thing to do. By contrast, if he did the right thing, morality would endorse and permit the act. To say that the agent did the right (not merely excusable) thing in killing the single person is either to say that there is no constraining right and so people have a lower degree of inviolability, or to say that the right exists, but is too weak to stand up to much and hence that people do not deserve to have their inviolability taken too seriously. A world in which these things were in fact true could, in fact, be a worse world.

There is an additional point: If we also believe that the agent who would kill the one person does the wrong thing, *we* are not deluded about the truth. This may also play a role in our thinking the world better if he acts: for if we were *all* deluded in thinking he did the right thing, then our living with an *incorrect* as well as intrinsically less elevated conception of ourselves might make it a worse world. So if it is better that he kill the one — and it is not clear that it is — this is so because it remains wrong for him to do this and we don't believe it is right. (We shall discuss the issue of wrong and worse beliefs further later.)

Note that the points we have been making here are different from, though related to those on p. 272 and to a point that Thomas Nagel emphasizes:[15] it is a better world if it is possible for wrongs to be done to us. For if it were not possible for the wrong of violation of the constraint to occur because we were not worthy of a constraint, then, although no wrong would occur if we were to minimize rights violations, it would be a worse world because we would have a lower status. (In other words, a world with only lions is worse than one with people in it, even if the people are improperly attacked and the lions couldn't be.) This is, I believe, analogous to Mill's claim that it is better to be Socrates unhappy than a pig satisfied, and even more to Kant's point that it is more important to be — i.e., have the status of a creature who is — worthy of happiness than to actually be happy, even, we might add, if having the higher status were the only thing that gave rise to the possibility of unhappiness. You can be subject to certain evils only if you have a high status.

In these remarks we have emphasized the good of inviolability and, perhaps, general belief in this truth. We have still to consider further whether, in a world with such entitlements and beliefs, it is better if one person acts in deluded fashion. Before doing this, however, we should make some additional points about value.

Agent-neutral Value

The analysis I have offered suggests that a nonconsequentialist, agent-neutral analysis of a constraining right based on the PPH could be given. That is, the constraint need not be based on an agent's perception that harm to the potential victim of his current act has a magnified value; nor is it based fundamentally on the agent-relative fact that I would kill my victim but only let die someone else's. Rather, the constraint may be based on the fact that if the agent were permitted to harm the one, this would defeat the agent-neutral value (i.e., a value all should promote and protect) of a certain sort of inviolability of any of the potential victims. Being let die of a killing does not threaten this value. The agent's victim is special only in that he will be there when the agent makes his decision. The agent's own act is special only in that it makes him come up against the constraining right. As already noted, this makes the constraint victim-focused rather than agent-focused or merely agent-relative; it is fundamentally about the potential victim and the fact that he is objectively an end-in-itself. The victim himself need only say that no one should be treated in a way that transgresses such a right; he need not say that his own fate is magnified for him.

Another way to emphasize that we offer a victim-focused, not an agent-relative, account of the constraint, and a proposal for agent-neutral value is to note that we should morally object to a consequentialist *natural order* with no human agent in it that proceeded as follows: whenever several people were to have their PPH-rights violated, another fell ill *solely in order* that his organs be available to save them. (The natural order here imagined is sensitive to moral wrongs; several people dying of natural causes would not trigger this odd illness.)

We can, therefore, think of the constraint as a way of expressing an agent-neutral value: not the number of lives saved, but the maintenance of a conception of the person as strongly inviolable. As noted earlier, this is non-consequential value. Its presence does not follow from any act, but it is already present in the status that persons have that provides the fixed background against which we may then seek their welfare or pursue other values. It is because of the constraints, or limits, morality places on us that the depths of morality, that is, the representation of the significance of persons, is possible. These limits, therefore, make possible the depths.

This way of explaining the constraint reduces the distinction between consequentialist and non-consequentialist ethical theories in at least one way. The non-consequentialists are identified as putting "the right before the good"; that is, the theory of right acts before the theory of value. Our way of explaining the constraint locates some new value which is such that its maximal presence is achieved only if there are constraints expressing high inviolability and it is not always permissible to act so as to violate rights to minimize rights violations. However, consequentialism is concerned with bringing about what some theory of value determines to be the best state of affairs. If the high status of persons is a good whose existence is reflected in constraints, then, in this sense, constraints are connected with a good and a good state of affairs, but this good state of affairs is not brought about causally by any act that seeks to maximize the value (or even by its being true that people are protected by constraints). It is rational to act for the reasons that there are, and if persons are inviolable (in a certain way) this gives us a reason, which we may recognize, to act in accord with this truth, even if we do not thereby produce anything of value as a consequence. The agent-neutral value I have emphasized can also reduce the gap between theories that are phrased in terms of respect for persons or rights (leading us to heed them) as opposed to those that emphasize caring for a value. If we care about this new value (whose existence can be expressed by the constraint), we act by heeding the rights of persons. [16]

Belief, Truth, and Action

We have been imagining how a certain value is present in the world if it is true that there are moral constraints, making it a better world. We have also assumed that we believe that there are such constraints. But these two conditions can pull apart. [17] What we have said above argues for the view that it would be a worse world if there were, in reality, no constraints. The hypothesis is that no world can be the best unless it is impermissible in that world to kill one person to save five even from being impermissibly killed. But we also considered the view — and here we return to deal with the question that prompted it — that so long as it is true that there is a constraint, it might be a better world if one morally deluded person killed one person to save the five. (If we are not consequentialists, we do not have to believe that it is *permissible* to kill the one if it will be a better world if he is killed.) What of a world in which not just one person, but none of us believe the truth that people have constraining rights? Would the world in which the one is killed to save the five be worse than the alternative in which he is not killed?

To help us consider these issues it will be useful to outline some of the possible relevant configurations of the world.

A. (1) In reality, there is no constraint; and
    (2) We don't believe there is a constraint, and either
       (a) his belief leads someone to kill the one, or
       (b) his belief leads someone not to kill the one.
B. (1) In reality there is no constraint;
    (2) We believe there is a constraint, and either
       (a) his belief leads someone to kill the one, or
       (b) his belief leads someone not to kill the one.
C. (1) In reality, there is a constraint; and
    (2) We *don't* believe there is a constraint, and either
       (a) his delusion leads someone to kill the one, or
       (b) his delusion leads someone not to kill the one.

D. (1) In reality there is a constraint.
  (2) We believe there is a constraint; and either
    (a) his delusion leads someone to kill the one, or
    (b) his delusion leads someone not to kill the one.

In some sense the issue with which we are concerned would be more easily resolved if we did not believe in moral reality antecedent to our beliefs, for then our beliefs about what rights people have might be thought to be necessary for making people have what rights they have. Our beliefs would be crucial for constructing moral reality, bootstrapping ourselves to status. Then its being better for there actually to be people who have constraining rights would imply that it would be better if we believed that people had constraining rights.

Assuming there is a moral reality independent of our views about ourselves, what can we say about these alternatives? How do A and B compare? Here the question is, assuming that it would be better if we really were the sorts of creatures who deserved to be protected by a constraint, though we *are not* such creatures, would it be better if we had a pleasant illusion or if we knew the truth? If it is better to have the illusion, is it better for someone to act on it and treat people better than they deserve to be treated? Is it better to treat them better than they deserve to be treated by way of the illusory belief in a good reality (via some fluke or persistent error) or to treat them appropriately by way of a true belief in a worse reality? In C, if we just consider (1) and (2), we see that there is some negative value attached to not knowing the truth, being deluded about ourselves, *especially* since the truth is about a better world. Suppose, however, that C(1) and C(2) are combined with option (b). If not believing truth about a good world led someone (somehow) to *act in accord with the truth*, this might be acceptable, and preferable to a world in which someone did not act in accord with what was, indeed, the truth, even though he knew the truth. (In this case, truth is assumed to be "don't kill the one to save the five.") Therefore, whatever negative weight comes from having a false belief, especially one with a bad content, is tolerable if it (somehow) leads to or is compatible with the right acts.

The combination of C(1), C(2), and (a) is what would exist if we thought it permissible to kill when it wasn't in fact permissible, and someone did kill. Suppose it is true that the negative weight of having a false belief about a good truth does not outweigh the positive weight of doing the right act (of not killing the one). Could the negative weight of our all being deluded about the good truth, all by itself, be large enough to make a world in which the wrong act of killing the one is done, a worse world? We ask this question, because earlier it was suggested that *one* agent's being deluded and killing a person to save the five might not make for a worse world only *because* his behavior does *not* imply that there is general delusion about right and wrong. (An alternative interpretation is that it is not a worse world if he kills because, in fact, he shouldn't, that is, it is true people are inviolable and *this* makes the world better, not people's beliefs about it.) This implies that doing the wrong act by itself is not making the world worse, since it minimizes rights violations. Would not a general delusion (even unaccompanied by action) make the world worse? In a world of general delusion, we lose two goods: (1) an elevated conception of ourselves, and (2) having our beliefs track the truth. If general delusion, as embodied in the moral system in which we believed, did *not* make the world worse, how could everyone's *not* endorsing the killing be what accounts for the world *not* being worse if the one kills to save the five rather than if he doesn't? But suppose it would be a worse world in which everyone, not just one person, were deluded about a good truth, and a killing were done because of the one's delusion. This does not mean that the presence of mass delusion is the only thing that makes a world in which one deluded person kills to save five a worse world than one in which no one is deluded and no one kills, nor does it mean that a world without mass delusion but a killing to save five is a better world than one with mass delusion and no such killing.

So we might backtrack and say that it *is* a worse world even when only the one person is deluded and he kills to save the five, let alone when all are deluded and all kill in this way. It is worse because events are not in accord with the truths of moral reality (i.e., with the reasons there are for doing things). Morality says the one person should not be killed to prevent the five killings. His being killed by the deluded person, not the person's being deluded, makes the world worse. This makes the worseness of the world simply a function of a wrong act taking place in it. Indeed, I think it is true that we would not be disappointed if the deluded agent suddenly lost his delusions and respected the constraint. The improvement might be due, in part, to the fact that a person had come to appreciate moral reality, but more to the fact that his acts were in accord with moral reality. This is buttressed by its being better if everyone through delusion denied a good truth, but they acted in accord with it; right action can speak louder than general correct beliefs. Also note that knowledge of a truth about a good world combined with action against it, [D(a)], can be worse than a false belief about a good world combined with action against the good truth, [C(a)]. There is an interaction effect; we do not give high marks for knowing a truth that is good when one can act against it. A misguided mind that leads to wrong acts is in some ways less disturbing than a clear-seeing person whose acts go contrary to the truth.

III

"Futilitarianism" and Rights to be Aided

I suggested that it is more likely to be formally rational to transgress a specified constraint in order to maximize things different from it, such as utility, than in order to minimize violations of comparable constraints. This may be true even when suffering a constraint transgression is more serious for someone than suffering the loss of utility alone, and even though we would do more to prevent constraints being violated than to prevent loss of utility if we did not have to violate a comparable right to do so. A basis for nonformal, substantive rationality of this claim is that within a subset of values, tradeoffs between components of the subset may be prohibited, yet the subset may conflict with some other subset of values with which tradeoffs make more sense. Perhaps an analogy is that it could be better to violate a religious rule to save the life of a nonbeliever (that is, someone who does not participate in the religious subsystem) than to save the life of a believer. This is true even if the believer is considered, and actually is, more valuable than the nonbeliever. [18] Without endorsing the permissibility of violating such rights for the sake of maximizing utility, I suggested that violating a specified constraining right for the sake of comparable rights is a form of "futilitarianism." What of a nonspecified right? It will not be strictly irrational to transgress it for the sake of rights; we may have a case of permissible infringement. But if the strength of the right that each has is a measure of how inviolable the person is, then there may not be many permissible infringements. This might be even more true if we aimed to minimize rights violations than if we acted for other values.

Related to the "futilitarianism" point is another way of arguing for the conclusion that concern for constraining rights does not imply minimizing violations of them by transgressing comparable rights. The point here is that concern for rights per se, independent of their relation to utility, would never prompt such minimization.

For example, suppose people sometimes have a right to be aided by others. It is then necessary to explain why it is permissible to refuse to aid the first person we meet who has a strict right to our aid in order to aid the five people we see further down the road, each of whom also has such a right to our aid. [19] This looks like minimizing rights violations. (Might we also abandon the person to whom we are obligated in order to help five who will suffer because someone else broke her commitment to them? I believe so.) If the single person has a claim to something (our aid), why is it permissible to deprive him of it in order to satisfy the five's similarly valid claims? How is this consistent with the possibility that neither I nor the five have any right to use what belongs to the single person (e.g., his device) to save others?

In search of an answer to this question, let us consider the Priest Case, in which a positive right *is* constraining against minimization: I argue that if we meet one priest, we should bow to him even if it means not rescuing five priests who will not be bowed to by others. By contrast, we said that we could ignore the first person who needed lifesaving aid in order to save those down the road. In the Priest Case, utility considerations are absent, that is, the five priests lose no welfare respect in not being bowed to. This suggests that, in the absence of utility considerations, one would never think that respect for rights alone called for violating one right in order to minimize disrespect for rights. [20]

By contrast, the cases in which each person has a claim to be given aid but the aider cannot help everyone *and* significant welfare for each is at stake, are like cases in which too much stock gets sold in the same thing. Each person was meant to have the thing in question. I believe that one way to handle these cases which accounts for the permissibility of ignoring the first needy person in order to save the later five, is to pay attention to numbers.[21] Each person with a claim must confront every other person with a claim. This means either multiple tosses of a coin or the balancing of one claim by a confrontation with an equal and opposite claim. In such confrontations we do not take away from someone his claim to something. Rather, he uses it up in a confrontation with his equal and opposite number. (In cases in which everyone buys a chance to get something, but it was never intended that everyone get to have the thing, there is no loss to the losers of that to which they had a claim, so the problem is somewhat different.)

Having a claim to something (e.g., my aid) that conflicts with others' claims to it, generates this required confrontation. When one has the only right to something (e.g., one's own body), there is no reason to enter into the confrontation procedure with others. This is what distinguishes the case of positive rights from those of negative rights, at least when the positive rights involve significant welfare. So it seems that when no utility is at stake, the positive right may be a constraint in the way a negative right is, and less often otherwise.

It has been said that the solution to the Selection Problem is victim-focused rather than agent-focused and that it is possible to understand a constraint as arising from concern for the manner restriction in a PPH right and what it expresses about persons, recognizing that to permit certain transgressions is to concede that a right and the status it seems to signify do not really exist. Let us consider how the treatment of positive rights shows the limits of these points.

It has been argued that we must attend in some way to the non-derivative, non-substitutability of individual victims. This non-substitutability is said to be non-derivative because it does not *depend* on the non-substitutability of agents or agent's time slices. Still, in this victim-focused view, the agent is called upon to attend to the victim primarily by himself not violating a non-substitution requirement, rather than by preventing its violation by others *even when preventing it would involve no transgression of rights by him*. One way a rights-as-constraint view may justify this is to note that someone's *status* of inviolability is not affected by his being left to be violated. But not limiting someone's rights against an agent for help will affect the agent's status of inviolability, insofar as this involves his right to be (to a certain degree at least) free from others interfering with him for the sake of helping someone be better off than they would have been independently of his aid. This is another aspect of separateness of persons.

However, we noted previously that if inviolability is related to the idea of significance, there may have to be some balancing between the idea of inviolability and saveability which is concerned with promoting the ends of such significant beings. If this is so, does it imply that those who are ends-in-themselves may also, in part, be, on occasion, pure means-in-themselves: though their goals are in no way promoted by aiding, they must give aid?[22] That is, is it this elevated status that itself makes possible and also requires the role as pure means on occasion? If inviolability of a certain sort stems from someone's having a rational will, the duty to aid may come rather from the capacity for rational reflection, which gives rise to an objective view about the importance of others and the adoption of their goals as ours.

Any position on whether there is a duty to aid should be distinguished from a position that says that while it is impermissible for an agent to kill the single person to minimize violations of comparable rights, he may nevertheless allow others to behave in this way *with the intention* that they minimize rights violations. The latter is not permitted on the view I describe, since it involves intending that someone else kill (which may be tied to willing the loss of what the victim would have independently of imposition on us) and endorsing the killing as morally correct. However, it might be permissible to leave the one to be killed if this is a side effect of not wanting to make large efforts to aid, or the side effect of being busy doing something else significant. This is a matter of the moral relevance of (something like) the intention/foresight distinction.

How does all this connect with the issue of caring about rights? In the *ordinary* sense of caring about a right, a "caring analysis" should lead us to prevent by innocent means the rights violation of others. This conclusion is tempered by the fact that both requiring an agent not to kill and not requiring him to prevent others from killing (i.e., giving him a *prerogative* not to aid) seem susceptible to a similar interpretation. That is, suppose the conception of persons as separate is expressed by noninterference and by not enforcing association through duties to aid. Then, as suggested earlier, caring about *this* conception of the person will generate both rights not to be harmed and permissions not to aid in the moral system. There is no conflict between this and endorsing—caring that people have—strong negative rights, since letting die does not endorse the killability of the victim, even if it lets him be killed.

Furthermore, there is a minimization scenario that can be envisioned here as well: suppose more people will have *their* right not to give aid violated unless one person has his right not to give aid violated. Then it can be in the service of making possible the existence of a strengthened right not to aid and a strengthened conception of persons as separate, that morality does not permit minimization. That is, we do not oblige one person to aid, even in order to prevent others from being forced to aid. If we care about separateness, and its purest expression tells us not to violate the separateness of one to save the separateness of five, then we show concern for the ideal of separateness by acting as it says we should. As has already been noted, if prerogatives are related to the ideal of a person as an end-in-itself, having a point even if she does not serve the greater good when the greater good could be served, obliging someone to minimize occasions on which people do not get to exercise a prerogative defeats this ideal.

Notice that I am not concerned here with making the right not to aid absolute. The claim is only that the permission to transgress an absolute right *or* a specified right not to aid for the sake of preventing more violations of comparable rights would eliminate the right as part of morality. Neither the one whose right we transgress nor the greater number we save will have this moral right. The permission to infringe a general right also reduces the status of individuals as separate, even if it does not eliminate the general right.

Summary and Conclusion

I conclude that it is not unreasonable to think that there is a connection between prerogatives, restrictions, and constraints, though the prerogative may have to be grounded differently than Scheffler thinks. That is, the prerogative may not derive simply from the significance things have from the personal point of view and our tendency to act from the personal point of view. Rather, it derives from some other ground which entitles one to control certain things. In particular, I have focused on the idea that one has a prerogative because a person is not a tool for the greater good, but is an end-in-himself for reasons other than his having a tendency to act from a personal point of view.

Scheffler says about his version of the prerogative that in order to introduce the idea of the personal point of view at a basic level in the moral system, it is introduced unmediated by maximization (or minimization). We are not required to minimize acts contrary to the personal point of view. Another way of saying this is that someone's personal point of view is permitted to block out consideration of the personal perspective of others in the aggregate, at least sometimes. On Scheffler's view, we make the personal point of view more important by permitting the person to try to act on it regardless of maximization or minimization. Yet, we have argued, to the extent that the status expressed by the prerogative would not exist if minimization of violations were permitted, we do "maximize" the presence of some impersonal value (this status) by having a prerogative.

Likewise, if we are not permitted to violate certain rights in order to minimize occasions in which comparable rights will be violated, to the extent to which this super right is based on the PPH, it introduces the idea of a highly inviolable person. This too is an aspect of the conception of the person as an end-in-itself. In both cases, we could say we "maximize" the presence of an inviolable person and a person who may try to exercise control over something, since these types of persons would not exist if it were permissible to minimize interference with self-control or minimize rights violations by violating rights.

We can see that the problem of finding an asymmetry between potential victims in the case of rights (a problem thought not to exist for prerogatives) does not exist, once we understand the very idea of the constraining right. Each person is protected; so any person we would act against is protected. The five who are left to die do not have a claim to the use of the single person to save them; so if they can be saved only by using him, we do no wrong in not saving them. Nor does this behavior imply that their status is lower. The type of argument I have given for the existence of constraints on killing could be offered to account for other constraints. For example, it can be argued that permission to interfere with the free speech of one person for the sake of minimizing violations of comparable free speech is inconsistent with the status of persons as bearers of the strong forms of free speech rights.[23]

We have distinguished between two questions: Can we give a justification for a constraint on violating rights to prevent other rights violations? and Can we give a justification for a restriction on maximizing utility? The second question deals with whether we can justify a restriction on killing one when we could save more lives from natural disaster.

It may seem that we should have answered this second question first, since we can most sensibly generate a right that we should not transgress in order to minimize rights violations by building on a restriction on maximizing utility or lives saved. Nevertheless, we began in this chapter by trying to answer the first question, and even suggested that we might, as formal matter, violate the constraint for the sake of utility. We can deal with the second question, essentially by reminding the reader of our previous discussion. The PPH is defended by showing why bringing about good by harming people in a certain way is wrong. We tried to begin such a defense in chapter 7. Objecting most seriously to the inappropriate relation that violating the PPH involves gives rise to a prohibition on bringing the relation about for any good, utility or maximal rights protection. This is a constraint, and it expresses a certain sort of inviolability of the person.

NOTES

1. This way of putting the problem is not quite right, as we shall see in later discussion.

2. Notice that traditional Kantian universalization arguments claim that I would be deprived of value if it is true that others, who are like me, have no value. The argument I have presented claims that if it is true that the one person does not have a certain status, then others who are like him, do not have it either. Might a parallel analysis, speaking of the agent, be given for an agent's unwillingness to act in a certain way? What is meant by saying "I stand in a different relation to a victim or an act when they are mine, and therefore I won't kill to prevent others from killing" is neither "I care more about what is part of my life than about what is part of the lives of others," nor "Each person must be morally responsible for his own conduct (or intentions) and not for that of others." Rather, what is meant is that, because I am considering which will be my act and my victim, *I* will come up against the barrier-like content of the act (comparable to the barrier-like property of the victim). It being my act just tells me that I will be situated at the barrier rather than elsewhere. We have here a duty-based, agent-focused theory but not an agent-concerned one, since it does not make the content of the constraint depend on seeing oneself in the picture or on magnification. But how is this read in a way which is not just basically agent relative? What agent-neutral value is at stake? A certain type of agency is inappropriate. Recognizing this is inconsistent with endorsing engaging in the agency to minimize instances of this agency; if we allow others to engage in the agency, we do not thereby endorse such acts. Therefore, each has a derivative duty not to engage in this type of agency.

3. For such a view, see Diana Meyers, *Inalienable Rights: A Defense* (New York: Columbia University Press, 1985).

4. In *Anarchy, State and Utopia*.

5. Later, we shall examine whether we would in fact care about minimizing rights violations if utility were not attached to them at all. Then, the question arises whether, if utility plays some role in our decision to kill the one, killing him violates the PPH.

6. It would be a mistake to describe the constraint as telling us not to violate a right — rather than not to treat someone in a manner prohibited by the PPH — in order to prevent violations of rights. Still we can derive this (which we can call) *constraint'* from the constraint as follows: If someone should not be treated in the manner prohibited by the PPH for the sake of minimizing rights violations (this is the constraint), then they have a *right* this should not be done, and we must not violate this right in order to minimize rights violations (constraint').

7. The position developed here contrasts with that developed by Amartya Sen in "Rights and Agency," *Philosophy & Public Affairs* 11 (Winter 1982: 3–39), where he argues that we might violate rights to minimize rights violations, but not to maximize utility, if it were not for the fact that from a position-relative consequentialist point of view, the outcome is worse from an agent's position if he violates a right than if more rights are violated by others.

8. These views on infringing and compensation are owed to Judith Thomson and Joel Feinberg (whose exposure case we discuss on p. 268).

9. Of course, if it is all things considered wrong to kill the one to save the five from themselves being used to save others, it will still be all things considered a wrong for the five to be so used. So it will be all things considered right to permit to continue what is all things considered still a wrong. Is it a *worse* wrong? We shall discuss this later (pp. 276–78 and 279–82).

10. In *The Limits of Morality* (Oxford: Oxford U. Press, 1989).

11. Those who argue that a constraint arises only from the quality of agency might give a somewhat different reason why the world will be worse if morality permitted killing one to minimize rights violations: It would be a better world in which there are more deaths and more rights violations and no person is permitted to be a *killer*, at least in this way. The five are, in effect, exchanging their lives to retain a certain conception of persons as agents. I do not find this agent-focused explanation of value plausible.

12. Amy Guttman and especially Arthur Applebaum helped to make this clearer to me.

13. Kagan raises these points in his "Responses to My Critics," *Philosophy and Phenomenological Research* 51(4) (1991: 897–901).

14. Virginia Held has suggested that if there are going to be some unavoidable rights violations no matter what we do, we should see to it that the comparable violations are distributed fairly, and on these grounds kill one to prevent more violations to the greater number. But this position fails to recognize that if we take rights seriously it may not be permissible to bring about what may in fact be the fairer state of affairs by violating someone's right. The best end-state of affairs — from the point of view of fairness — cannot be brought about by violating the rights of one person, if to take the right, which is everyone's right, and the status it expresses, which is everyone's status, seriously involves its being constraining. In the same way, an agent may refuse to do an act that produces a fairer state of the world, or someone may have a prerogative not to make a big sacrifice to produce a fairer state of the world. However, if someone receives the benefits of an unfair state of the world, it may be permissible to take that benefit away to undo the unfairness.

15. In his discussion of my views in "The Values of Inviolability" Revue de Metaphysique et de Morale No. 2/1994.

16. At this point, I believe it is worth repeating some remarks made earlier, so as to contrast the account of constraints given by the so-called expressive theory of rationality, as described by Elizabeth Anderson (in *Value in Ethics and Economics*, Cambridge, Mass.: Harvard University Press, 1993). See note 10, pp. 255–56.

17. This section was prompted by questions raised by Derek Parfit on the difference between belief in constraints and their objective reality.

18. Admittedly it is hard, substantively, to argue that we can transgress rights for something less, rather than more, important. It will often show respect for persons to just respecify the constraint so that it represents a lower degree of inviolability when minimization of rights violations is at stake.

19. Notice that this is a different case from one in which we are first involved in helping one person and must decide whether to abandon him to help five. It is also different from one in which we confront the one and five simultaneously. The latter case involves direction of our aid, which is different from breaking a tie of aid already established to one person. It also differs from doing nothing when one could do something to aid for the sake of helping others *much* later on. (On these other types of cases, see *Morality, Mortality*, Vol. 1. [New York, Oxford University Press, 1993].)

20. Still, this is consistent with utility loss *triggered by* rights violations being considered more serious than utility loss alone.

21. For more on this, see "Equal Treatment and Equal Chances," *Philosophy & Public Affairs* 14(2) (Spring 1985: 177–194), and *Morality, Mortality*, Vol. 1.

22. Is there a real moral difference between saying, as Kant does, that one has *a duty to make the ends of other persons one's own ends*, and saying that on occasion one has a duty to be a means to others' ends? Here are cases which highlight the difference: (1) I am opposed to A's goals but because I promised B, I let A use me. (2) I understand and approve of A's goals and hope he achieves them, and so lend him my services.

23. We might even see in a common argument against capital punishment a version of my argument for constraints: If the State kills a killer in order to prevent more killings by others, it endorses killing and this endorsement implies that people are less inviolable; if it does not prevent many killings the State nevertheless does not endorse them. (Of course, in this context the argument may be wrong, since guilty persons may not be as inviolable as innocent bystanders.)

11

Agreements

Self-interested Bargains

An account has been offered of why minimizing rights violations by transgressing comparable rights is not the proper way to show maximal concern for rights or for the concept of the person that they express. Although the permissibility of transgressing a right that protects against utility maximizing (the PPH) for the sake of minimizing violations of such a right does not, strictly speaking, deny the right, it does deny the force of not treating people in the manner prohibited by the right for the sake of *any* good (utility or minimization of rights violations). It also fails to reflect a strong conception of the person as inviolable to such treatment. If a specified constraint is justified, permitting transgression of it so as to minimize violations of it is straightforwardly to deny its existence. Hence, concern for persons as rights bearers is not a good reason for permitting the violation of specified rights in order to minimize violations of comparable rights.

However, there is another, more straightforward reason that could be offered for minimizing rights violations by violating comparable rights. It might be argued that minimization, rather than being the way to show maximal respect and concern for rights and the inviolability of persons, is a policy that ignores rights in order to maximize lives saved. Furthermore, when the person sacrificed seemed to be at risk of being one among the larger number whom he might be used to save, and the policy is adopted at a time when he did not know he would, in fact, not be among the larger number, this policy also maximizes each person's own chance of survival. The question then becomes, why should there be constraining *or* PPH rights rather than an agreement to waive such rights in order to achieve these alternative goals in all sorts of cases?

If we can make sense of a conception of rights and prerogatives that prohibits our being used to benefit *others*, can we make sense of a conception that prohibits our being used for the sake of others when, by a policy that permits it we might benefit *ourselves*? We have been assuming in the Constraint Case that the single person who would be sacrificed could not have been in the larger group that would benefit. But suppose we change that assumption, and now assume that we do not know whether we will be a single person who can be used to save five or one among the five. Restrictions and constraints would then seem to increase each individual's chances of being killed or dying. Let us imagine the following case—the Soup Case— so as to make this problem imaginatively more real. All six of us have eaten dinner. We discover that five dishes of soup were lethally poisoned, and one had an antidote in it. We do not know who ate what, and will find out only in an hour when the symptoms appear. We do know that using the organs of the one who ate the antidote is the only way to make a serum to save the other five. Is it permissible to make an agreement now to use one person in this way later?[1]

Why may not an agent who is entitled to control over his own life (via prerogatives, restrictions, and constraints) even in the face of others' welfare and rights, not *now* agree that in the future he will simply not have that kind of control over himself? If he could permissibly agree to this, then it would be permissible to kill him later, even though at that later time he will not want to allow himself to be killed. That is, it will not be a case of his waiving his constraining right at that future time of actual sacrifice, supererogatorily sacrificing himself, knowing he has the antidote.

In this revised type of case, there is no question of the individual's never having had a right to control over himself to begin with in the face of maximizing for the good of others, or of its being inconceivable why someone who cared about rights would choose a constraint rather than maximize protection from rights violations. It is a question of an individual's exercising his control in a certain way now, in making an agreement, so that at a later point in time, if he loses a gamble and is confronted with the prospect of being killed, he has ceded either his right not to be killed or his prerogative not to sacrifice his life.[2]

If we take Rawlsian-type veil-of-ignorance reasoning seriously, it is possible that dealing with this question is crucial for *any* account of the rationality of restrictions or constraints. The distinction I have drawn between cases in which the single person would never be at risk of being one of the five, and cases in which he was at equal risk with others, may collapse if we move behind a veil of ignorance. Even if he knows, once outside the veil, that he is not at risk, the right thing to do may be determined by what he would have done if he had been ignorant of this.

I

Frequency and Alternative Agreements

I would like to make several preliminary points. First, it might be suggested that if cases in which we could save five at the expense of one (who might himself have been in the more numerous group) arose frequently, we *would* all agree at t_1 to the permissibility of our being killed at t_2 (a time at which we would rather not be killed) to save the greater number. The emphasis on frequency, however, seems misleading. However infrequently the issue comes up, having a maximizing policy still maximizes lives saved and maximizes each person's chance for survival. So why be concerned about frequency? Does the strain of having such a policy outweigh the number of lives saved and the provision of a maximal chance for life to each individual if the issue arises only infrequently but not if it arises frequently? If the agreement is otherwise rational, such a consideration of strain would introduce into our reasoning a non-ideal-world factor. That is, a rational being would not feel strain at a rational policy. (Another non-ideal reason for refusing such agreements is that any increase in the type of occasions when killing is held to be legitimate may increase the number of *illegitimate* killings by weakening people's resistance to killing.)

The second preliminary point is that I believe there are at least three different ways to conceive of the agreement to maximize lives saved when all are believed to be at equal risk: (1) as a purely *hypothetical* agreement that would have been made from behind a *veil of ignorance*; (2) as a purely *hypothetical* agreement rational individuals would have made in conditions of *full knowledge* of everything that could have been known except who would be the one to be sacrificed and who would be among the five needing the sacrifice; (3) as an *actual* agreement under the same conditions as in (2). The strongest attack on the moral validity of a maximizing agreement would exist if it was not valid *even* when made in situation (3), I believe. (Some might attack the validity of a hypothetical agreement in the first situation on the grounds that there is no actual agreement and that requiring agreements to be made in ignorance of actually available information is a sign of disrespect for persons. The validity of a hypothetical agreement in the second situation might be attacked simply on the grounds that there was no actual agreement.)[3] Are there any reasons to think that if the single person in our Soup Case had been a party to an actual agreement, ex ante ceding his right not to be killed, it would still not be permissible to kill him because his right was inalienable?[4]

The third preliminary point to emphasize is that in the Soup Case someone will die who would not otherwise have died. This makes it different from cases in which *all six* would die unless one was chosen to make a serum for the others (the Serum Case). In the Serum Case, each maximizes his chances of survival by agreeing to such an arrangement, but the person who dies is no worse off than he would otherwise have been. He does not have anything taken from him that he would otherwise have had. It is this factor, rather than that the agreement would be in everyone's material interest, that may make this agreement permissible.

An interesting borderline case[5] involves six people who will soon die of the radiation in room A unless one of them goes into room B to push the button that turns off the radiation in room A. The person who leaves room A will escape death by radiation, and may escape death altogether if he then exits the house, but if he goes into room B, he quickly dies of his exposure to the gases in that room. Would an agreement among the six be permissible if it obligates the one person to go into room B, or sets up a machine that forces him into the room? In this case the person who would lose a life he could continue to have would have died without the agreement, and so he would lose only the life he has gotten as a result of the agreement. This may make the agreement and its enforcement permissible. In the Soup Case, the person who dies loses life he would have had independently of the agreement.

Finally, it is important to emphasize that discussion of the permissibility of agreements in the Soup Case has nothing to do with whether rights and constraints are absolute no matter how many lives or rights are at stake. For we are discussing cases where the number of lives at stake is five, not a hundred thousand.

Agent-focused Objections

It might be suggested that each of us would reject such an agreement, even though it increased our chances of living, because we would rather die than kill an innocent, non-aggressive person at a time when he did not volunteer to have his life taken. (This assumes that one of us would have to do the killing.) This is an agent-focused reason for not agreeing. In an effort to eliminate an agent-focused reason for objecting to an agreement, we might imagine that, once an agreement is reached, the loss of life will be imposed on the victim automatically; that is, a Doomsday machine will bring about the death. Here, too, however, the machine waits for the ex ante agreement; so each person would be partially responsible for triggering the machine and for the death. However, it is also true that, in agreeing, any victim would be helping to pull the trigger on himself, and a fatal event that was (in a sense) self-imposed — albeit not willed at the time the death was caused — might not be as objectionable as one person killing another.[6]

Another way of dealing with the agent-focused objection depends on distinguishing morally between the following two cases. In the first, the Disease Case, a deadly disease threatens a community. The only thing that an individual can do to significantly decrease his chance of getting the disease is take a drug which, if it doesn't help him, will kill him *if* he is one of the *few* who are not susceptible to the illness, the death occurring some time after he learns that he is not susceptible. My sense is that taking the drug is permissible in the Disease Case. Admittedly, there is a negative consideration here: one might die when one didn't have to, as a result of one's own attempt to outwit nature. Nevertheless, there seems to be no moral impermissibility in taking the drug, which increases one's chances of living.

Compare the Disease Case now with the Disease' Case, in which again, a deadly disease threatens a community and there is a drug that will kill those few who were not susceptible to the disease. In the Disease' Case, however, the drug itself never directly helps anyone who takes it. Here, if you take the drug and die because you were not susceptible to the illness after all, your body parts can be used to make a serum to save others from the disease. If no one takes the drug, those who fall ill will simply die. In the Disease' Case, but not in the Disease Case, a person's death is a source of benefit to others. However, ex ante in both cases the victim takes the drug from self-interest. Though, in the Disease' Case, the only thing that made it *be* in his interest to take the drug was that this was the only way to insure that others also take the drug. Then someone will die for the benefit of others when this person need not otherwise have died, but his chances of survival were increased. The Disease' Case also overcomes some interpersonal agent-focused objections insofar as the person himself, rather than anyone else, causes his death. A difference between this case and the Doomsday Machine Case is that here the final intervention which causes death occurs at a time when the person still has reason to believe that the agreement may actually save his life. My sense is that it is wrong for everyone to take the drug in the Disease' Case, unless it is part of a willing act of self-sacrifice to help others. That is, each might take the drug hoping it is he who will die and so be available to save the others.[7]

Victim-focused Objections

Let us consider some victim-focused objections to such agreements, reasons that, for example, might make it wrong for the agent to help set in motion a Doomsday machine for use on someone later, or to take the drug in Disease', because the agreement fails to respect the victim. This contrasts with the failure to respect an agent who makes an agreement or carries out the killing.

One victim-focused answer that might explain why taking the drug in the Disease' Case or agreeing (or carrying out the agreement) in the Soup Case is impermissible is that it is more important that the concept of the person expressed by a constraining right (built around PPH-factor considerations) be true of people inalienably, and that events accord with the existence of such a right, than it is to maximize chances of survival. This is because while more people may be harmed, and so the chances of each of us being harmed may be greater, the conception of each person that is endorsed involves a high degree of inviolability. We may all lead harder lives, but our dignity is greater.

What do we mean by "more important that the concept of the person . . . inalienably . . . "? We may mean that the good to each person in having a status of a certain sort inalienably, thereby increasing inviolability, outweighs the good to her of living a longer life as an individual with a different status. On the other hand, we may mean that it is simply true of people that they have this status inalienably and it is immoral to treat people as though they do not have this status, even for the sake of their material self-interest (which I take to include mere survival). The first interpretation suggests that we are appealing only to the self interest, broadly construed, of those who contemplate an agreement. We are just insisting that the goods they are allowed to consider in deciding upon an agreement be broad enough to include the good of such a status. The second interpretation implies that there is more to morality than that to which they choose to agree from self-interest. They may actually prefer this trade-off, but that need not be the ground of its being correct. What makes it correct, and what makes us as inviolable as we in fact are, is simply certain properties that we have as individuals, and this is a benefit to us.[8]

Assuming for now that one of the accounts is correct, can we say any more to characterize that status which is more important than maximizing one's chances of remaining alive? Suppose the conception of the person that is retained if the agreement is impermissible in the Soup or Disease' Case is that people are ends-in-themselves — that is, they are not to be used as mere means for achieving the good of others. How then does a maximizing policy treat people as other than ends-in-themselves, if that policy also serves the interests of the very person who is sacrificed, albeit not at the time he is sacrificed?

Ends-In-Themselves

The Kantian response might be that killing someone, even as the fulfillment of the condition (to which he agreed) that made possible greater security for him, contemplates using rational humanity as *a mere means at one time* in order to promote its continuation. But, the Kantian may say, we must first avoid intentionally acting against (our) rational humanity (this is a perfect duty) before we seek to promote it (an imperfect duty). (This is not a temporal order.) Is this answer clear, since it is permissible to intentionally inflict pain on ourselves for our own greater good at a later time? Why then are we not allowed to do what may result in our being used unwillingly for others' sake at a later time if this increases our chances of survival at an earlier time? It is also permissible for someone at the time of sacrifice to donate his life superogatorily. Is she then willing that she be treated as a mere means, or is she rather adopting ends of others (to survive) as her own end? (It is not clear that another person may do the killing, even of a willing victim, when it is against the interests of the victim that it be done.) Kant himself does not rule out intentionally acting against rational humanity for (what he saw as) noble ends: a woman may kill herself as a way to avoid being raped or if she believes she will reveal important secrets under torture. Note that, in our cases, it is not always clear whose rational nature an agent acts against — his own or another's. For even while each agent in Disease' will undertake any harmful act against himself, he hopes that it is another who will harm himself, so he can benefit. Ensuring an agreement, by agreeing to participate in it, may therefore, involve "acting" against *another's* humanity even in Disease'.

Limits on Agreements

A point associated with the view that the agreement treats people as means inappropriately is that one cannot tell what is right by seeing what rational egoists would agree to for their mutual material interest. This might be because it is not permissible to will treatment that is intrinsically wrong, even if it is in everyone's material interest. But, of course, that claim presumes that we have some idea of what is intrinsically right or wrong prior to this agreement and do not need the agreement to generate our knowledge of right and wrong. (It is possible that there is another type of agreement, one not concerned solely with mutual *material* interests, in which there is agreement that some status of the person is worth more than survival.)

In general, so long as there is any sense that right and wrong are independent of establishment by agreement for material self-interest, such agreements will not always be able to make acts permissible by overriding the influence of situational factors (such as characteristics of victims or agents) that would make the acts impermissible. Consider an example, the Case of the Disturbed Visitor. Suppose I wish to avoid helping someone with his severe emotional problems, and so arrange (permissibly) to leave town when he comes to visit. He will be totally lost in all respects in my absence, and I will be inconvenienced by leaving. It is in both our interests to agree to my staying in town to provide him with travel directions but also to agree to my being relieved of the obligation to help him with other problems—my being relieved, that is, of the ordinary obligation that anyone has to help someone nearby with severe problems. If I stay, and I alone am present when he is in trouble, does the agreement make it all right for me to ignore his plight?

I think not. The situation and the obligation it would ordinarily give rise to dominate any agreement. If it is nevertheless permissible for me to avoid the situation entirely by leaving town, then, although it will not maximize our self-interests should I do this, the agreement that I not help cannot be binding. If it were binding, some other value would fail to be represented. This is a case in which morality stands in the way of individuals' maximizing the promotion of their individual material interests.

It is possible that the limits on choice in the Disturbed Visitor Case are the result of another choice, that is, to value certain sorts of relations between people more than material self-interest narrowly construed. But it is also possible that a person's choice cannot override his nature or the nature of a situation, and those "natures" may demand certain behavior. Indeed, his choices may be morally sufficient to alter the character of other situations only because he has a certain nature that demands certain limits on the power of his choice in *this* sort of situation, on this sort of topic.

An Objection

In the Case of the Disturbed Visitor, the individuals know to begin with who the disturbed person is and who the potential aider is, and any agreement between them would not be made from an initial position of equality. It might be suggested, therefore, that what makes the agreement immoral is not the limits presented by the situation or by the nature of people, but rather that the agreement could not have been made by people in a position of equality. On the other hand, in the Soup and Disease' Cases in which one person is to be killed to save a greater number, the agreement is made in a condition of equality and also would not violate maximin conditions, insofar as the one sacrificed would not be made worse off than any of the greater number would have been without the agreement. Note that this insistence on equality as a precondition for an agreement is an unlikely objection to the Disturbed Visitor Case if made by someone who thinks it is permissible for me to exercise the option to leave town, an option I have only in virtue of my superior position.[9]

An Aside: Agreements and the Law

These general considerations concerning whether antecedent notions of right and wrong place limits on what are otherwise taken to be valid voluntary agreements bear on a problem in the law raised by Richard Abel.[10] Abel notes the apparent conflict between tort law, which presumes the right to contract to accept any risk, and statute law, which makes liability for damages independent of the assumption of risk by the victim. Abel asks whether statute law does not, therefore, fail to respect the free individual who should be allowed to contract for risk (thereby freeing someone else from liability) if that risk brings with it lower costs.

I suggest the following three-pronged solution to this problem: (1) The liability of parties who create risks is based on a *duty* they have not to behave in a risk-creating fashion. (2) The fact that the potential victims waive their rights not to be put at risk does not release the risk-creating parties from their duty not to put those others at risk. (Admittedly, it then becomes unclear what the potential victims are doing in waiving their rights.) (3) Not recognizing the validity of such agreements does not imply diminished respect for the freedom of the potential victim, though it does involve a view of the limits of his *powers* to release others from their duties. That is, there is a distinction between liberties and powers.

Indeed, this analysis helps explain a fact which Abel notes but is unable to explain: namely, although victims may have a much larger causal role than other agents in bringing about risk of harm (and actual harm) to themselves, by exposing themselves to the slightly risky items which other agents introduce into the environment, it is the agents who are held liable and not the victims. This shows nonpaternalistic respect for the victim's free choice; that is, the victim is *allowed* to assume risks without being penalized for doing so. Instead, a duty-based penalty is placed on the agents.

Nonwaivable at Certain Times Only: The Constant Agent

It was suggested that the conception of the person as an end-in-itself might be a constraint on making certain agreements. It might now be suggested that there is another conception of the person which we are trying to retain in refusing to recognize the validity of the agreement in the Soup Case. In this conception, a person may not alienate at one time the decision-making power over his own death which will occur at a later time in violation of PPH-manner restrictions, when it would be physically possible for him to exercise the power at a later time. His status as an agent with this power is nonwaivable and inalienable. A person may, however, waive his right to life supererogatorily, thereby deciding to give up his life, at the same time as the sacrifice is to be made, or if earlier, when there is no time intervening between the making of the agreement and the imposition of the loss such that during that time the individual could decide that he does not want to suffer the loss.

Notice that this account might have different consequences from those of the Kantian account above, in that it would allow us to give up something very significant for reasons of material self interest, even though it involved our being treated as a mere means. This assumes that giving consent at the time of sacrifice does not always imply that one is not being treated as a mere means. The example of prostitution speaks in favor of this assumption. A Kantian might find something intrinsically wrong with prostitution, and think that one ought not decide to engage in it even at the time one had to engage in it, let alone commit oneself at t_1 to prostitution at t_2. But giving up one's life is not like prostitution; that is, one might not be permitted to commit oneself now to its disposal at a later time, but one might permissibly (even in the Kantian view) give it up voluntarily at that time. So taking a life in a manner not in accord with the PPH is not permitted unless it is volunteered at the time it is taken, or at the closest time when one's desires have not changed. The PPH represents a restriction on nonvoluntary losses rather than a description of an intrinsically morally objectionable manner of treating people; even voluntary donation could not make the latter permissible.

According to this proposal, the conception of the person that morality endorses in rendering invalid agreement in the Soup Case or the Disease' Case is not the conception of "a person controlling his fate," since the person *would* be controlling his fate if he made the agreements in question. The conception would have to be something like that of "a person constantly in control." Commitment to this conception of personal sovereignty would be especially strong if it were not transgressable for the sake of minimizing the number of times agents lose such control.

So, according to this proposal, we are taken to be *constant agents*, whose fates must be continuously determined by ourselves. The proposal is not saying that our chances of living must be reduced (1) for the sake of not becoming intentional killers of the innocent (the agent-focused argument), or (2) for the sake of not being mere means, or even (3) for the sake of inviolability. It says rather that our chances of living must be reduced when only this is consistent with our being the sort of people (some of) whose constraining rights are under their own control at such time as losses are to be imposed upon them (or the nearest competent conscious period to it).[11]

Objections: Losing Control

One problem with this proposal may be that it does not account for the problem with Disease' Case. That is, in Disease', the last intervention which leads to death is undertaken willingly by the person himself, though, of course, he does not willingly give up his life. Another problem is that we do not, in general, believe in the constant-agent conception of the person. We commonly adhere to agreements that it would prohibit, that is, agreements made at a given time to lose control later over something of ours that would otherwise be protected by a constraining right. There are the type of cases where, pursuant to an agreement at t_1, we interfere with someone at t_2 when his refusal at t_2

to allow interference is considered to be the product of mental incompetence at t_2. (The classic example is in the tale of Ulysses and the Sirens.) In these cases, however, the imposition is for the sake of a future greater good for the very person who suffers the imposition at t_2, *and* he is considered incompetent at t_2. In the Soup Case at the time we kill, the person is interfered with against his current desires (not to be killed), [12] the person is competent, and it is against his interest that it be done.

Nevertheless, there are many cases in which we *do* enforce at t_2 an agreement made at t_1 to suffer a loss, when the person has not become incompetent to change his mind at t_2 and the only benefit the person got from the agreement was an increase in his probability of avoiding a *larger* loss than the one we impose. We do this even though it is known at t_2 that he would not have faced the large loss after all.

As an example of the permissibility of ceding at t_1 one's right at t_2 to control less significant items than one's life, one could agree to a policy that ensures the rebuilding of one's house if a storm that will arrive *this year* destroys it, and agree to be bound to pay for this policy at yearly installments of five dollars for many years. One will then be bound to pay — ceding one's right to the five dollars per year — for many years after the storm has hit the community, at a time when it is no longer in one's interest to pay, and even if the storm never did hit one's house. In this case, all one has bought is the increased probability, at an earlier time, of retaining one's house, and, perhaps, a significant amount of psychological security (if one agreed much before the storm). [13]

If the agreement occurs just before the storm, one cedes the right to decide whether to undergo a loss of five dollars at a later time, and one must suffer that loss at a time when it is no longer in one's interest to do so, when the *only* benefit was the increased probability of having avoided an even greater loss. If some schemes with these general features are acceptable, why would we insist on retaining the idea of the person as someone who cannot bind himself to a later *loss of life* for the sake of having had increased chances of living? Wherein lies the difference between the cases?

Insignificant or Fractional Losses?

One suggestion is that the size or the nature of the loss involved — five dollars versus the life of a rational being — is crucial; agreements about smaller losses are permitted, those about larger ones are not. One is a constant agent only for large losses. Whether this hypothesis is correct depends on whether the same type of moral dissatisfaction felt with an agreement involving loss of life can be generated in cases that involve small losses but which mirror the other formal characteristics of the seemingly unacceptable agreement.

So one alternative explanation is that, regardless of the size of the loss to be incurred, the agreement is *not* morally acceptable if the loss is not significantly less than what the individual was trying to protect himself from losing, if the loss is imposed in a manner not in accord with the PPH, if the loss is imposed at a time when it is no longer in the interest of the payer to pay, if the payer does not want to pay, if (almost) all he acquired was an increase in the subjective probability of keeping what he is now going to lose in payment, and if now, ex post facto, we know that he would not have suffered the loss even if he had not participated in the agreement.

Two crucial factors of this suggested explanation of the impermissibility of certain agreements are that (1) the loser loses either the very thing (x) that he was trying to protect by the agreement or something of nearly equal value, and that (2) he loses it at a time when it is known that the only benefit he has received was an increased probability of not losing x.

To take a particular case (the Five Dollar Case), suppose we know that a gust of wind will blow away the five-dollar bills of five of six people, but we do not know who will be the victims and who will be spared. We also know that if we take away the five dollars from the one person who winds up retaining his and invest it, we can gain just enough to return five dollars to each of the five who lost theirs. We are (by hypothesis) unable to distribute the sum so that the person who had his five dollars taken for investment is repaid.

It would maximize each person's chance of retaining five dollars if we agreed to take away the bill of the one whom nature leaves unharmed. Suppose that enforcement of such an agreement would be wrong and, hence, the agreement was morally improper to begin with. If this is so, it cannot be because the loss is especially large (let alone because anyone has an inalienable or unwaivable right to his five dollars). It might be because the loss to the loser here consists in the very thing the six people sought to diminish their chances of losing. By contrast, when we insure the house — by definition implying that we will not have to give *it* up — and then have to pay five dollars a year for the rest of our life, the value of the payment is only a small fraction of what it insured.

Let us return to conditions (1) and (2) of the proposed explanation of the impermissibility of certain agreements. They might account not only for the fact that the loss of $5.00 in the Five Dollar Case and the loss of a life in the Soup Case or the Disease' Case share a crucial objectionable feature, but also for the fact that taking someone's arms and legs (a large proportion of his capacity for a good life) in exchange for an increase in the probability of his being alive at all is unacceptable. Also objectionable is taking $4.98 from someone in exchange for an increase in his probability of keeping $5.00. By contrast, an agreement to take $.50 from someone, who thereby retains $4.50 and also increased his probability of keeping his $5.00, is acceptable. The most important part of what the person wanted to insure remains with the person. Even an actual (though not hypothetical) agreement to give an arm to save five lives, when one might have been among the five in danger of dying, seems acceptable (Arm-for-Life Case). If this is so, it implies that self-interested bargains can legitimate uses of people that violate formal concerns of the PPH (e.g., not to have simple harm be a cause of greater good), though mere concern for minimizing harm cannot legitimate such lesser harms. For example, we could not take the arm of someone who does not donate it if he did not himself ever run the subjective risk of being among five threatened with death, in order to save those five from death.

All this is consistent with the acceptability of an ex ante agreement to give up a very large part of what one wants to insure when *at the time that the loss is imposed* one will not yet know that the only benefit one will receive in exchange is the increased (subjective) probability of not losing what one wants to insure (i.e., one wouldn't yet know that one wouldn't, in fact, have lost what one is insuring). [14] For example, suppose we are told that unless one of us loses his arms and legs *now*, five of six of us will lose our lives tomorrow, but that if the one does lose his arms and legs, he will save *all five lives* and go on living himself. At the time when the single person's arms and legs come off, the loss to him can be seen as in his interest in that for all we know it might be saving his life. Also, in this case the person who loses his arms and legs is thereby assured of something larger, that is, his life. Even here, however, if he objected at the time of sacrifice, would it be permissible to force the loss simply because it is also in his interest to the best of our knowledge? Hardly, I think. There is no duty to maximize one's chance of living.

Notice that this Arm/Leg Case differs from the Disease′ Case, in which we would suffer a small chance of a big loss (life itself) in order to eliminate a bigger chance of developing a fatal disease, in the following ways: In the Disease′ Case, the actual sacrifice of a life cannot help the person whose life is lost. Rather, it is his *willingness* to risk the sacrifice, along with others' willingness, that might help someone and that does raise one's subjective probability of survival.

Objection: Losing What One Insures to Prevent a Larger Loss to Others

The emphasis on not losing what one insures fails to demarcate a moral distinction, I believe. There are several points to be made in this connection. First, in fact, we permit agreements in which individuals will be required to lose *more* than the worth of the object they are trying to insure. If one expects with a high probability to lose a jewel, an insurance company can cover its expected losses only by charging more for the policy than the object is worth. Theoretically, this payment could be due after it was clear that the insured jewel was no longer under a threat of being stolen. [15]

Second, consider a case, the Two Diseases Case, in which there are two diseases in a community. One, the Arm Disease, causes one and only one arm to fall off, and is very prevalent among a part of the population whose members we can identify beforehand. The second, the Death Disease, is very rare in a *different* part of the population that we can identify as susceptible to it. The only thing that cures the Arm Disease is a serum made from the finger of a person who was subject to the Death Disease but didn't get it, and the only cure for the Death Disease is a serum made from the arm of a person subject to the Arm Disease who did not get it.

I believe it would be in the interest, ex ante, of all involved to make an agreement to provide the resources necessary to make the serums needed at the time they are needed, and that enforcement of this agreement ex post (i.e., once one knows who will and who will not be getting the diseases) would *not* be morally wrong. There is a high incidence of the Arm Disease; so there is a high probability that the people once susceptible to the Death Disease will lose a finger in exchange for avoiding the small risk of a big loss to themselves, that is, death. There is a low incidence of the Death Disease; so there is a low probability that a person once susceptible to the Arm Disease will lose an arm, that is, a low probability of his making a larger sacrifice for others (than those susceptible to death make) in order to diminish his chances of losing an arm (i.e., in order to lower a high probability of his suffering the loss of an arm).

Yet this is also a case in which an Arm person would have to pay with the *very item* he had attempted to increase his probability of keeping (his arm), at a time when it is known to be no longer in his interest to do so (for he no longer faces the threat of the Arm Disease), having received only the benefit of that increased probability of protection from the Arm Disease. The significant difference between this case and cases considered before, however, is that here the arm would be sacrificed to prevent an even greater loss (death) to another person. What the person who is sacrificed loses is significantly less than what the person who is saved would lose if he were not saved. Note that the agreement is permissible even though the Arm Disease person stood no risk of getting the Death Disease.

Earlier I said that an actual agreement to give up an arm to reduce one's chance of death, even though the arm is taken when it is no longer in one's interest to have it taken, seems acceptable. (This was justified on the rationale that the loss was a relatively small fraction of what one was insuring.) What the Two Diseases Case helps us see is that an agreement to have an arm taken is acceptable *not* merely because the person does not lose the very thing he was trying to insure. These two examples present us with situations in which self-interested agreements could legitimize losses which could not be legitimized simply by the goal of maximizing lives saved.

Nonaggregation when Causing Harm

It might seem that what underlies the distinction exposed by the Two Diseases Case is a nonaggregative attitude toward losses that several people suffer when each one suffers no more of a loss than the person whom we would deprive for the sake of the others. It may seem wrong to enforce agreement to *cause a loss* to someone when no individual among the larger number to be protected stands to suffer any more than the person to be used would suffer, though it may be permissible to enforce agreement when someone to be protected stands to suffer a greater loss (as in the Two Diseases Case). An arm is less than life, and a finger is less than an arm; but a life that someone loses is not a lesser loss to him than the loss of his own life is *to each* of the five who would be saved.[16]

Suppose a basically nonaggregative outlook is required when we decide whether to enforce an agreement to take from the one to save the five, or when the one would be obliged to give something up. This would further imply that there is a big contrast between cases in which we harm one (or oblige one to give up something) to save five, and cases in which we refuse aid to one so as to give it instead to five. For it has been assumed[17] that aggregation of lives *is* permissible in the latter cases. Taking away from someone (or obliging him to give up) what he has a claim to, and what he would have had independently of us (or those he would save), makes a moral difference to the permissibility of aggregating. Of course, the agreement we have been discussing would have been undertaken not for the sake of saving the greater number but for each party's self-interest, this being the assumption emphasized in this chapter. Nevertheless the conclusion is that such an agreement to take a life is invalid.

Objection

We can raise an objection to the theory of the agent who is not permitted to precommit herself to losing what she is trying to insure where this benefits more people who would lose no more than she (an objection other than that it is an odd theory of sovereignty). Consider the Ambulance Case.[18] A community has to decide whether to have an ambulance. If it does, it will save many lives that would otherwise be lost, but a small number of people who otherwise would not have died prematurely will be hit by the ambulance as it races to the hospital. Indeed, we may imagine that (for some reason) it is known to be only people who would not need the ambulance to save their lives who will be hit by it. At the time of the agreement, no one knows whether he or she is such a person. Is it permissible to have the ambulance? Suppose it is. Then some people will lose the very thing (life) they are trying to insure. Furthermore, a person will not lose it to prevent others' losing something greater, in contrast to the Two Diseases Case. And he loses his life at a time when he knows the loss cannot be in his interest.

But the Ambulance Case should be contrasted with the Ambulance′ Case. The same community is deciding the rules for the performance of the ambulance. More lives overall will be saved if it is agreed that when the ambulance is on its way to the hospital with many people whose lives are to be saved, it will not stop — even though it could — to keep from running over someone in its way. Should the community agree to this? Another possibility is for the community to agree to install new brakes that make it impossible for the ambulance to stop before hitting someone whenever more dying people are in the ambulance than would be hit in the road.

If the agreements in Ambulance′ are impermissible, but agreement in Ambulance is permissible, we seem to be back to some form of the first Kantian suggestions for the Soup Case — namely, that certain *ways* of causing persons deaths cannot be made permissible by agreement because they are too inconsistent with the moral ideal of the person and interpersonal relations.

It might be suggested that the way we should not treat people involves merely violating the PPH. But such a suggestion ignores the Two Diseases

Case, for example, where an agreement can override the impermissibility of taking an arm. It also cannot be true that only *intending* harm to persons is what is always ruled out, even with agreements; for in Ambulance' we would not intend harm to the person who would be run over; we do not even intend an intrusion upon him which we foresee will lead to harm. We intend to go over the spot where he stands, as doing so is necessary to getting to the hospital. Still, it is true that we would *intend* that the driver not (be able to) stop before she hits the person on the road. This is to be contrasted with the case in which we do not install a device that will help a driver better detect a person on the road because the device is too expensive. Here we merely *foresee* that the driver will not (be able to) stop before she hits the person on the road. There is some moral distinction related to doing something (agreeing to a policy) while intending versus foreseeing an event that turns out to be harmful to a person. (This is neither the distinction between intending versus foreseeing harm nor the distinction between intending verus foreseeing an intrusion on a person that we foresee will cause him harm.) Nor can we say that the Ambulance' Cases show that agreements are invalid only when big losses are at stake, for it is possible that we would not allow a car to continue speeding if it could otherwise stop, when the speeding will merely dirty a bystander's clothes while the car is merely rushing other people's dirty clothes to the cleaners.

Agreements and Mutual Exploitation

It now seems to me that the most general way to identify cases in which self-interested agreements justify people's using themselves or others in ways ordinarily prohibited by the PPH can employ an analysis offered by Thomas Scanlon. In discussing the correct understanding of the veil of ignorance, Scanlon[19] argues that we must not imagine one person behind it deciding as if he had an equal chance of occupying any of the positions available in his society. Rather, we must think of the veil as forcing him to identify with each person who will occupy a position available in his society. I would extend this, saying that we must decide how to treat people by considering whether the final outcome—in which we do something to someone or something happens to him as a result of his own deed, with a resulting effect on others—treats each individual appropriately in relation to every other individual. We cannot decide this simply by seeing if each individual ex ante would find a certain risk of being in one position rather than another in his material self-interest. This is consistent, I believe, with the model of argument I have used (elsewhere) in trying to justify saving the greater number of people when we cannot save everyone who needs to be saved.[20] That is, I did not argue that we should save the greater number because ex ante this would be a policy in the interest of each, given that it would maximize each person's chances for survival to save the greater number. Rather, I considered the relation between the smaller and the larger number of people and argued that what we owed each person in the smaller group was that he be balanced off against someone who was an equal and opposing person in the larger group.

Similarly, we might try to account for the cases where agreements are permissible on the ground that the relationship established between those sacrificed and those benefited has *a character in itself* which, when combined with the fact that it is in each person's interest ex ante to have the agreement, permits an agreement to legitimate an action that would otherwise be impermissible. So, for example, in the Two Diseases Case, what helps make permissible the agreement to intentionally take away an arm when the person does not at the time it is taken away volunteer it, I believe, is the fact that the person who loses his arm will be suffering a loss which is less than any person he helps would suffer if he were not helped. In the case where an arm is taken to save lives, this same factor plays a role in making the agreement permissible.

But suppose we would have to intend, rather than merely foresee, that a car pass over a spot that it could avoid going over even though a bystander is seen to be at that spot (in Ambulance'), or intend the death of a person who would not otherwise die though he does not volunteer his life (in the Soup and Disease' Cases). In these cases, when we look at what finally happens—independent of its being motivated by each person's ex ante self-interest—we see that one person will suffer a loss in a morally prohibited manner that is no less than what any other individual who benefits from his sacrifice would suffer. In the Soup Case, the manner violates the PPH. But how does Disease' violate the PPH? Here each person agrees to do what might kill him, hoping that it will kill another who would not otherwise have died. The person who will die uses himself (doing what harms him when he needn't have died) to maximize his expected chances of living. The others encourage this behavior because they wish to use this person—whoever it is—to save themselves. This is a case, I believe, of mutual explotiation. It does not violate self-interest or equality, and even can be seen to undo the underserved luck of one person; but it is wrong nevertheless in the way persons are treated. Each takes the drug himself, so there is no violation of the PPH, given that the PPH is a principle of inter- rather than intra-personal relations. But it involves a violation of appropriate behavior toward oneself as an end-in-itself, and inappropriate attitudes to others who are ends-in-themselves, assuming we can understand how this happens when one treats oneself or others as a means even for the self-interest of each. This is mutual exploitation.

In Soup and Disease', a moral principal is violated with the conseqence that the *aggregated persons* benefit, even though no one of them would suffer a greater loss than the one sacrificed. We cannot make this upshot morally nonsalient simply by repeating that this all comes about not in order to benefit the aggregated persons but in order to give each individual his maximal chance to live. We are here presenting a modified antiaggregative position which still allows for an agreement in Two Diseases and the Ambulance Case. In the latter case, we are asked to override a form of conduct which is not as morally offensive as in Ambulance', that is, instituting a policy (not an act) which we foresee will harm some, and not as a result of the greater good or its structural equivalent.

Therefore, one conclusion to draw from this discussion is that of policies that lead to unchosen behavior which does not accord with the PPH may be legitimate if the policies result from self-interested bargains that result in benefit to mere aggregated persons, none of whom will suffer more than the person victimized. Policies that involve a choice now to make a choice over later behavior unavailable have not been shown to be permissible (witness the unacceptability of the special brake), perhaps because they involve intending an event which will lead to harm rather than merely foreseeing it. Another conclusion to draw is that there may be a difference in the appropriateness of our interfering with those who agree in Disease′ and Soup. Even if those who agree in Disease′ do what they shouldn't, each takes the drug himself, and it may be beyond our rights to interfere. But in Soup, when it comes time for a person (or Machine) to carry out the killing of the unwilling loser, it is permissible to interfere.

Some Remaining Questions

If we should enforce an *actual* agreement in the Two Diseases Case and in the Arm-for-Life Case, why should we not enforce the same policy if it would be the outcome of a *hypothetical* agreement? I assume we should not, and in fact we do not, in general, impose lesser sacrifices on some who were at greater risk originally in order to prevent greater but less frequent losses to others. Next, we can imagine fates worse than death, for example, being tortured to death, and, based on this fact, we could create a situation with the same formal structure as the Two Disease Cases: a bargain between those who more frequently face death and those who less frequently face the threat of being tortured to death. Would an agreement in this case be valid, that is, agree to have one's life taken to save some (or someone) who would be tortured? I suspect not. If not, this must be because there is some significant difference between intending the loss of everything one has (one's life) and the loss of, for example, an arm. It may be that we think that so long as one is alive, compensation for any other loss is possible, but with death the possibility of compensation is at an end.[21] So in some cases the nature of the loss seems to be crucial. Finally, are the sorts of distinctions needed to distinguish permissible from impermissible agreements agent- or victim-focused, and are they subject to an essentially agent-relative analysis, or can they be taken to express agent-neutral values? If policies (rather than acts) are permitted, though we foresee they will cause harm, this might be evidence for an agent-focused or at-base agent-relative interpretation, i.e., it is only something about being an agent or relating to a victim on an occasion when one could have then desisted that is objectionable. But the impermissibility of the "special brakes policy" does not seem to rest on agent-focused or at-base agent-relative factors, i.e., the policy is not disallowed because it involves any agent's causing harm when he could have desisted at the time he confronts his victim. (However, those agreeing to the policy do now arrange for an event, which someone could have prevented, to become inevitable.)

Conclusion

If we wish to maximize the good of lives saved in our cases, we would use the one to save the greater number. The individual-rationality answer for these cases tells us that ex ante each individual maximizes his chances of survival if we have a policy of using one to save the many. If we find cases where there is such an overlap between these two approaches and yet it is still impermissible to use the one to save the many, we may have a clue that we would do something that would violate a background, constitutive idea of the person, something that is part of the constraints that are necessary in order to make the goals of saving persons and respecting their self-interested choices morally right in other cases. Preserving this status — inviolability or personal sovereignty of a certain sort — may be more important than increasing each individual's chances of survival or giving him the freedom to make any binding agreements that he wishes to make to alienate such constraints. Alternatively, a concern for victim-agent relations and the impermissibility of limiting opportunities to avoid bad relations may constrain agreements.

NOTES

1. This charming version of the problem was offered to me by Douglas Husak in the midst of a *dinner* discussion about similar cases.

2. In case there is any remaining question that each individual does maximize his chances of surviving by such an agreement in our Soup Case, it should be obvious in the following Random Illness Case: If one person is killed, we will have organs enough from his body to save n people, each of whom would die of a disease^y attacking one of his body organs. Any person is much more likely to die of this disease^y than of being an organ donor, since the disease is prevalent and strikes at random. It is true, however, that to avoid a maximizing argument *against* such agreements, we must imagine that the agreement would not discourage people from, for example, keeping themselves healthy (so as to avoid the possibility of being an organ donor), and would not encourage villains to make large numbers ill in order to have handed over the one person they really want to kill. Agreements that had these effects would not maximize the number of lives saved over the long run nor involve an equal chance for everyone of getting ill.

3. The agreement in (1) would take place in a Rawlsian framework, though since there is nothing else to be known if we exclude knowledge of who is the one and who the five are, agreement in (1) would be the same as agreement in (2). Though I will emphasize agreements of type (3), I believe it is worth noting a conflict that seems to arise in dealing with our case in a Rawlsian framework. This conflict also seems to give rise to another possible conflict between the Rawlsian view and an interpretive extension of Rawls which Thomas Scanlon offers. The conflict within Rawls's system arises between (1) his concern that in constructing agreements we identify equally with each individual who will be affected by the outcome, and (2) his concern for maximum security which maximin provides. If we are tempted to improve the benefits associated with one position before seeing that other positions are at least equal to it, Rawls's two

concerns lead to the same conclusion: In identifying equally with each position one will maximin before improving any position further. But when we must distribute a scarce life-saving item either to one person or to a group of five, who are otherwise at the same level of primary goods, identifying with each position *may* seem to require giving each individual an equal chance to be selected to live. (I am now *not* discussing the case where we must kill one to save five.) By contrast, concern for maximining as many people as possible, via concern that each individual assure himself the safest possible outcome, might seem to lead us to save the greater number (at least when each individual has the same chance as others of falling into any position, and each individual, hence, has a greater chance of being in the group of five).

Scanlon (in "Rawls' Theory of Justice"), in trying to extend the Rawlsian view, argues that when there is a choice between social policies affecting two different groups who are equal in primary goods, that policy should be chosen which raises the *larger* group to a new level of greater primary goods. However, *if* the correct solution from behind a veil of ignorance were to give each individual an equal chance to achieve a certain higher level of primary goods, Scanlon's recommended extension would conflict with a true Rawlsian position. Furthermore, in a later article ["Contractualism and Utilitarianism," in A. Sen and B. Williams (eds.), *Utilitarianism and Beyond* (Cambridge: Cambridge University Press, 1982.)] Scanlon analyzes Rawlsian decision-making from behind the veil of ignorance and argues that the spirit of Rawls's enterprise does not involve *one person* considering the possibility that he might occupy any of the different positions available in society. (This approach could lead a person to recognize that he has a greater probability of being in the larger group and so, in general, be willing to risk a very bad fate for the sake of ensuring a better fate for the greater number, i.e., abandoning maximin.) Rather, Scanlon argues, reasoning behind the veil involves considering the several positions of people outside the veil as actually occupied by different people, rather than as positions that one person behind the veil has some probability of occupying. It is this, Scanlon claims, that accounts for Rawls's eliminating from the decision-making process information concerning the probability of falling into certain positions. Does this approach make one reluctant to abandon anyone for the sake of saving the greater number? Is it an approach that suggests equal chances? If it did, Scanlon's second analysis would conflict with the conclusion he reaches in his first discussion of Rawls.

However, it might be suggested that the requirement that we identify with each individual in society *is* fully satisfied when we seek to give each individual his greatest chance for a better outcome in a situation in which there is no way to completely eliminate someone's falling into a worse situation. The preference for maximin could still dominate a policy of giving each individual his greatest chance for a better outcome when the two conflict, that is, when *not* giving each person his best chance for a better outcome is the only way to eliminate a small chance of someone getting a worse outcome. As noted, Rawls rules out acting on the basis of probability calculations; he rules out making use of empirical data that tells us probabilities of being in one position rather than another. In our case, knowledge that someone would have a greater chance of being in the group containing more people would be a priori (given no reason to think that some individuals are more likely to fall into one slot than another). But this distinction is not crucial. What is important is whether concern for each individual is better expressed by giving him his greatest chance for a best outcome in a situation in which there is no way completely to eliminate a chance of someone's falling into a worse situation.

One problem with accepting that identification with each person is accomplished when we give each person his best chance for a better position is that we do not know whether it is true that the very individual who will occupy the position of the single person we contemplate killing had an equal chance to be in any of the six positions. But if we cannot assume this, then identification with each person in the actual, outside-the-veil world might lead us back to giving each an equal chance by tossing a six-sided die. A second problem with the proposed solution of giving each person his best chance is that it seems to involve identifying with each person *behind* the veil, rather than with each of the people actually occupying positions outside the veil.

The proposal I favor is that saving the greater number of those who will be equally badly off, at the expense of an equally badly off individual, must involve some idea of the legitimacy of substituting individuals who are seen as equivalent, rather than merely maximizing the chances of each individual in his own best interest. That is, when we identify with each individual outside the Veil, it is not equal chances but the balancing off of equal and opposite individuals that is mandated by a morality which respects each, at least when we must choose whether to save the smaller or greater number from the same fate. I discuss these issues and the specific question of not saving the single person (rather than killing him) to save the greater number in *Morality, Mortality*, Vol. 1. (New York: Oxford University Press, 1993). I will return to the issue of what is required by identification with the position of each person outside a Veil of Ignorance when I discuss the Soup Case later in the text.

4. Joel Feinberg says that if we arrange to kill ourselves, agreeing at the time of death, or at nearest competent time before death, to be killed, we are waiving our right to life, not alienating it. This is because if our assisted suicide does not succeed, we still have our right to life. (See his "Voluntary Euthanasia and the Inalienable Right to Life," *Philosophy and Public Affairs* 7 (Winter 1978): 93–123.) However, when one makes an agreement, as in the Soup Case, one aims, I think, to alienate one's right, because one will have no right to one's life at a later point when one does not want to die. When one donates one's life voluntarily to save others, one only waives one's rights, I believe, even if one dies as a consequence.

5. This case and its analysis were suggested by Tim Hall.

6. It is also possible to consider a bargain to reduce one's chances of being an agent (who was never himself at risk of being a victim) who has to kill one innocent to save others, and another bargain that is to reduce one's chances of having to act contrary to the personal point of view but requires that one take one's own life if one loses. It may be suggested that these agreements would be more difficult to carry out if one lost the gamble than an agreement to passively *be* killed. I have already suggested that I think the difference introduced by the strain of acting may be overemphasized. Let us suppose, however, that there is this difference. Will we still not minimize strain if we make such an agreement, since, it is assumed, there will be fewer occasions on which anyone will have to undergo the strain? It might be objected that acting on an obligation to give up one's life or to kill another, before the pressure of circumstances forces one to do so is, in fact, a greater strain than acting when circumstances force one to. (Analogously, it may be more irksome to store food when the need is far off, even if not storing it now means that one will have to work harder to store it when the pressure of circumstances is on.)

7. Both the Soup and Disease' Cases are to be contrasted with the Escape Case (suggested by Michael Bratman). In this case six people are told that five of six of them will be shot if they stay where they are. If they try to escape, someone standing outside

waiting (or a rock slide that their escape triggers) will kill one of them. It is quite permissible to try to escape. In this case, the form of the PPH is satisfied: the greater good of five out of danger results in one person's death.

8. An implication of this seems to be that one's status is higher if one has inalienable (but not unwaivable) rights than if one does not. One might dispute this. Since it may be a case where inviolability and personal sovereignty conflict, dignity might go with the latter. (On this, see p. 298.)

9. If people do make agreements in positions of initial equality, but what is agreed to is still immoral, there is one factor that might make us think the agreement should be kept anyway: Each person who agreed to do what ought not be done, did so in the hope that it would be done not to him but to someone else. Each person, therefore, was willing to treat others immorally or anxious to have them be treated immorally. One may think, therefore, that the individual who would be killed immorally deserves no better than what he gets in virtue of his willingness (in the sense of intention) to do it (or have it be done) to others. I do not believe, however, that a moral view can tolerate such grounds for doing what it would otherwise be wrong to do. We can also imagine that the resistant loser, after agreeing, reflects on what would have to be done to keep the agreement: He may honestly change his mind about the permissibility of the original agreement and not will that another be killed.

10. In Richard Abel's speech at New York University Law School, Spring 1989.

11. The right to this control is not intended to cover guilty aggressors, innocent threats, innocent beneficiaries of life via inappropriate means, etc.

12. Having a desire not to be killed, as I understand it here, is consistent with willingness to abide by a moral requirement to permit the killing, if agreements were morally valid.

13. William Reeves has reminded me that this is the scheme involved when we buy flight insurance and pay for it by credit card after the flight is already over. Furthermore, it might be argued that agreements can sometimes also succeed in eliminating our right to control something at a later point in time (when we do not wish to cede the item), if others who have been caused to rely on the agreements would be worse off if the agreement is not kept than they would rightfully have been had there been no agreement. ("Rightfully" is used to bar counting the effects of other *inappropriate* agreements that they might have made in lieu of this one.)

14. This point was made by Lewis Kornhauser.

15. Ronald Dworkin's example.

16. Judith Thomson, in *The Realm of Rights* (Cambridge, Mass.: Harvard University Press, 1990), makes a similar point about nonaggregation in cases of causing harm, but believes it can be overcome by agreement, and even by factors that would justify hypothetical agreement.

17. And has been argued for by me in *Morality, Mortality*, Vol. 1, and by others elsewhere. John Taurek argues against aggregation in all contexts in "Should the Numbers Count?" *Philosophy and Public Affairs* 6(4) (Summer 1977): 293–316.

18. I owe the case to Ronald Dworkin.

19. In "Contractualism and Utilitarianism." This point is previously cited and discussed in note 3 above.

20. In *Morality, Mortality*, Vol. 1.

21. David Wasserman suggested this.

12

Supererogation, Obligation, and Intransitivity

A story of Auschwitz was told to me by Helen . . . When the women were given the chance to go and work elsewhere in the work zones like Hamburg, mothers with children were, in fact, given the choice between their lives and their children's. Children could not be taken along. Many preferred to stay with their children and face certain death. Some decided to leave their children. But it got around amongst the 6-year-old children that if they were left there they would at once be gassed. There were terrible scenes between children and their mothers. One child was so angry that though the mother changed her mind and stayed and died, the child would not talk to her.

"Bergen-Belsen, April 24, 1945," *New York Times*, April 21, 1985

So far we have discussed the relative importance of harming and not aiding, negative and positive rights, and how they do and do not set up restrictions and constraints on what we may do. We have considered why there might be prerogatives not to promote the greater good, consistent with our having to make efforts not to harm others who are independent of us, whether harming them would be for the greater good or our own good. In this chapter we shall investigate another aspect of this problem: how it might be possible for rights, and the duties to which they give rise, sometimes to fail to restrict our pursuit of the greater good while still restricting the pursuit of our own projects, even though we still do not have strong positive duties to promote the greater good at the expense of our own projects. This adds another step to the problem we have considered above, of whether prerogatives for, and restrictions on, seeking personal goals are consistent. In the earlier discussions, we assumed that there were restrictions on actions taken in pursuing overall good. Now we weaken the strictness of these restrictions and constraints insofar as they apply to actions for the sake of greater good, and we also consider why it would be wrong to weaken them similarly as applied to actions for the sake of personal goals, even though there are prerogatives to pursue personal goals.

We shall also examine the bearing of this issue on the structure of nonconsequentialist morality, in view of the fact that if there is a prerogative not to promote the greatest good, that morality can have as one of its components supererogatory acts. These are acts whose performance has positive moral value, but which it is not morally wrong to omit. (It is not necessarily always clear which acts are obligatory and which supererogatory, as the introductory quote suggests. Ordinarily sacrificing one's chance for life, especially on behalf of a child who will die in any case, might seem supererogatory. Yet a mother's willingness to make such a sacrifice in order to postpone her child's death even slightly — perhaps merely in order to ensure that the child does not go to its death alone — is probably seen as obligatory by the child.)

I

Each of the following three propositions seems to be true; yet the three together may seem to be inconsistent:

> For some effort E, some duty D (which may be the correlative of someone's rights), and some beneficent act B (which promotes greater good or the greatest good),
>
> (1) The personal preference not to make effort E may permissibly take precedence over doing act B. That is, doing B at effort E becomes supererogatory.
>
> (2) Doing B at effort E may permissibly take precedence over doing duty D.
>
> (3) The personal preference not to make effort E may not permissibly take precedence over doing duty D.

There seems to be an intransitivity here. That is, where $\geq$ means "may permissibly take precedence over," $-$ means "not," S is some supererogatory act, D some duty, and P some personal interest, $P \geq S$, $S \geq D$, and yet $-(P \geq D)$.

This intransitivity involves the claim on the one hand that we may permissibly do a supererogatory act and as a foreseen consequence fail to do our duty and on the other hand the claim that we may not permissibly refuse to make some sacrifice of a personal interest with the foreseen consequence that we fail to do our duty. There is another, closely related intransitivity that involves the claims that we may deliberately violate our duty as a means to performing a supererogatory act, but may not deliberately violate our duty as a means to achieving our personal goals. The duties involved in the first intransitivity are primarily positive duties we omit to perform; those in the second are primarily negative duties not to violate negative rights. The second intransitivity is demonstrated by the following variants on Propositions 1, 2, and 3.

> For some personal goal G, some beneficent act B, and some duty D,
>
> (1′) Since the pursuit of G may permissibly take precedence over performing B, doing B rather than pursuing goal G becomes supererogatory. That is, $G \geq S$.

(2′) We may deliberately violate duty D in order to do supererogatory act S. That is, S ≥ D.

(3′) We are not permitted to deliberately violate our duty in order to achieve personal goal G. That is, −(G ≥ D).

In this chapter I will consider whether even within a basically nonconsequentialist ethical system, all six propositions can be true. This will involve trying to show how it is that "may permissibly take precedence over," as well as certain other relations (even "worse than" and "better than"), seem to be intransitive. It will also involve arguing that, although it is ordinarily thought that we are morally obliged to do what, all things considered, we have a duty to do, it is sometimes *permissible to do a supererogatory rather than a dutiful act.* I will also argue that there are at least *two different measures for the importance and stringency of duties to act.* The first is the amount of *effort* we are obligated to make to do an act; the second is whether *doing one act may permissibly override a requirement that we do another act.*[1] The fact that there are these two measures of stringency and importance raises the question of whether we may, in fact, permissibly refuse to make great efforts to do an act (e.g., our duty D) when that act may be superseded by another act (e.g., supererogatory act S) for the sake of which we need not make such efforts. I shall argue that we are obliged to make certain efforts to do our duty, though we need not make the same efforts to do a supererogatory act that we may nevertheless permissibly do instead of the duty. There are, however, more significant limits on the claim that we may not violate a duty for some personal goal, though we may pursue the same personal goal instead of doing a supererogatory act for the sake of which we may permissibly violate the duty. That is, the first and second "intransitivities" behave somewhat differently since there often are stricter limits on violating a negative right than on failing to satisfy a positive duty even when there is a correlative positive right.

II

The Supererogatory over Duty

It is commonly thought that we sometimes have a duty to help people, at least when the sacrifice to ourselves is not very great. It is also commonly thought that if the efforts required of us in order to help are great, helping is supererogatory, that is, beyond the call of duty. The personal preference not to make the large effort, or to pay the large cost, may permissibly outweigh considerations in favor of helping. (This is one aspect of the prerogative.) Therefore, proposition (1)—that personal preference not to make effort E may permissibly outrank the beneficent act B and make it supererogatory—is commonly accepted as true. Likewise, if I must sacrifice an important personal goal to help someone, helping is commonly considered supererogatory. Therefore, proposition 1′ is also commonly accepted as true.

Now consider the following case (the Lunch Case): I have promised to meet someone at 12 P.M. for lunch; so I have a duty to be there. I shall be using the notion of duty in such a way as to allow that there might be other duties of mine that conflict with my duty to go to lunch. In cases of conflict I would have to decide which was my strongest duty, and then *it* would be my duty all things considered. (Alternatively I might refer to my conflicting duties as "prima facie duties," and to the strongest one as "my duty.") Now imagine that on my way to the lunch appointment I come across a car crash. One of the victims has had his kidneys crushed, and he needs an immediate kidney transplant in order to survive. I am the only person available who has the right type of kidney. Given the size of the sacrifice to me, most people would say that it is not my duty to donate one of my kidneys. Therefore, in these circumstances (barring the existence of any other duties) the only duty I have is to keep my lunch appointment.

Suppose, however, that I am willing to give up a kidney, but this will cause me to miss my lunch appointment. It still seems that my only duty is to keep the lunch appointment. Nevertheless, if I want to give the kidney I may, and I need not do my duty. Indeed, it would be morally stupid of me to think that I had to do my duty. I would be a moral idiot (though not immoral) if I felt that I had to keep my lunch appointment.

Those who think that I have a duty to save lives when the cost to me is small, and also a duty to keep my lunch appointment, would, no doubt, think that the duty to save lives outranks the duty to keep lunch appointments. If they also maintain that I must always do my strongest duty before doing supererogatory acts, they will be committed to the view that I must keep my lunch appointment rather than give my kidney. They will also be committed to the view that if there is a choice, I am obliged to do what will save someone's life at minimal cost to myself (a duty), rather than make great sacrifices that I am willing to make in order to save a great number of lives. Thus, since it is my duty, for example, to give a penny to save the life of one person on an island, I should do this rather than give away a fortune I am willing to give away to save thousands of lives on another island, when I can reach only one of the islands in time to save any lives. This seems quite the wrong conclusion to reach.[2]

I conclude that if "I am obliged to do act *y*" implies that doing other acts instead of *y* would be wrong, then I am not always obliged to do my strongest duty. If "I am obliged to do act *y*" just means "*y* is my strongest duty," then I need not always do what I am obliged to do. Contrary to the views of many, there is no strict system of priorities linking duties and acts of supererogation, such that we may perform a supererogatory act only if it does not involve our failing to do our duty.[3] We cannot always claim that we are prohibited from doing something that would require much sacrifice on our part and produce a great good, because we are bound by our duties. Also, though supererogatory acts are beyond the call of duty, it should not be thought that doing them implies that we have first done our duty, and then gone beyond it. In doing a supererogatory act we may have permissibly failed to do our duty. As proposition (2) states, an act of supererogation may permissibly take precedence over a duty. Likewise, if I wish to save a life, I may deliberately violate my duty not to take someone's car without his permission, as a means to save the life, even though, because of the risk it will involve to me driving on a stormy night, this is not a life it is my duty to save. Therefore proposition (2′) is correct.

Objections

Is there a way of avoiding this conclusion, that duty does not take automatic precedence over supererogation? Objections might be made to the argument I have presented. The first objection might be that someone who is willing to make a large sacrifice is therefore obliged to make it, and so he does have a duty stronger than his luncheon appointment. But I do not think it is true that being willing to make a large sacrifice implies that one has a duty to make it.

A second possible objection is that since the friend I am to meet for the luncheon appointment would himself be obliged to release me from my duty to him, once he found out what I would be doing if I missed lunch, I do not have a duty to meet him that is overridden by a supererogatory act. I believe this objection is wrong, whether or not my friend would have a duty to release me. It is wrong because we can imagine cases in which releasing me is supererogatory for the person to whom I am duty-bound, and yet it would be permissible for me to fail him in order to do the supererogatory act. For example, suppose that I have a choice between giving up my own life to save a thousand people (which is not my duty), and saving one person at small cost to myself (which is my duty). The loss that the one person will suffer if I save the thousand instead of him is larger than he would be obliged to suffer in order to save the thousand people. Therefore, in this case, the one person would not be duty-bound to release me from my duty to him. Yet I think that I may permissibly decide in favor of the thousand, though it is supererogatory for me to do so. I believe I may permissibly save the thousand even if I have *promised* to save the one (or if I have promised to meet one person for lunch and know that he will die if I do not keep the appointment, though I did not promise to meet him in order to save his life).[4]

It is important to note a significant difference between these last three cases, in only one of which I have promised to save someone. When it is said that I have a duty to save a life at small cost to myself, the aiding is commonly referred to as an imperfect duty. That this duty is imperfect does not imply that I am at liberty to leave a person to die on an occasion when I see him in need, but it does imply that if I could save the thousand at small cost to myself, I would *completely* carry out my imperfect duty to save someone by saving the greater number. We could say that *though there is a conflict about whom to save, there is no conflict of duties.* (An alternative analysis would say I have a conflict between my duty to one person and my duty to many, but whichever I do, one of my duties is left undone.) But if the only way to save the greater number is for me to give up my life, I would not be carrying out an imperfect duty if I saved the many instead of the one. At the same time it seems clear that I would not have failed in any way to execute my imperfect duty to save a life if I saved the thousand instead of the one at great cost to myself (a supererogatory act). For when I do this, I have tried to save at small cost (the imperfect duty) and then gone beyond that; it seems that I have done my duty in the course of doing what it was not my duty to do. If so, then it also seems this is not a case that proves that S ≥ D.

By contrast, if I break my promise to save someone or to meet someone, I transgress a perfect (positive) duty: If I could save the thousand at little or great cost to myself, but at the expense of my promise to save or meet the one person, I would not have carried out my perfect duty, however permissible this failure may be. (I shall return later to the role these distinctions between perfect and imperfect duties play.) As noted previously, the person to whom I promised is not under an obligation to release me from my promise if he will thereby lose his life.

But notice an additional wrinkle in this analysis: We said that the imperfect duty to save at small cost seems to be stronger than the duty to keep a lunch appointment (even though the latter is a perfect duty). If our making a big effort to save lives involves our doing the stronger duty (i.e., making a small effort to save lives) in the course of doing the supererogatory act, then we will not have failed to do our strongest duty. The problem with this claim, however, is, first, that it is not our duty to make a small effort to try to save a life when we know with certainty that this will be insufficient to save the life, and anything less than the kidney transplant will be useless in our Lunch Case. It seems that making the small effort becomes our duty only if we are prepared to go beyond it. But this is not quite right either, for someone could get out of doing the large, supererogatory part of the effort by noting that something additional is still needed, and this intrinsically small addition is the straw that breaks the camel's back. That is, the willingness to make the supererogatory part of the effort does not make the small effort obligatory. Nevertheless, despite all this, if the person does the supererogatory act, we do think that he has in the course of it done what the strongest, albeit imperfect, duty in the context required as well. This is because he has done what could have been required of him if it alone had been necessary in order to save a life.

But what supports the truth of (2) and (2′) is that the part of our effort that is beyond the call of duty and is necessary to save the life *could* permissibly be avoided, leaving one free to completely fulfill the luncheon duty at little cost. Therefore, to say that the supererogatory may permissibly take precedence over a duty is to say that we are not morally obliged to avoid doing something that we could permissibly avoid, because it has as one of its components something that is beyond the call of duty, in order to do what requires nothing but the dutiful from us. To say that duty *always* takes precedence over supererogation would be to deny *this*.

Finally, we can reach an even stronger version of the claims in (2) and (2′) by considering cases where we may do a supererogatory act that does not involve as a component of doing it the fulfillment of what is considered to be the strongest duty in the context. For example, a father has a duty to take care of his son, when no one else can, and his son will lose his arm if he is not cared for. (The father's is a strict positive duty, I believe, in virtue of his having assumed responsibility for a child.) But outside, five strangers will lose their lives if the father does not offer assistance at minimal direct cost. Although helping the strangers is a duty at small cost, it is *not* the strongest duty in this case; that is, it is not something we would all recognize that the father must do even if it requires him to leave his son. Yet if he goes to save the strangers when this is directly very risky to himself, it is a supererogatory act that could override his helping his son (the Father Case). In this case, however, the supererogatory accomplishes what would, if sufficient on its own, have been a duty that was no weaker than any other duty in the context. An even stronger case would involve supererogation that contained no behavior that could have been a duty in the context. Perhaps the pursuit of artistic greatness is super-erogatory at any effort, but it could override a duty in some context.

There are therefore two interpretations of the claims in (2) and (2′), one weaker and one stronger. The weaker says there is a sense in which supereroga-tion may take precedence over duty when what would have been the strongest duty would be accomplished in the course of the supererogatory. The stronger claim says that the supererogatory may take precedence over the duty even when the supererogatory does not accomplish what would have been the stron-gest duty, or been any duty at all.

A third possible objection to the claim that supererogatory acts may take precedence over duties is that duties have escape clauses built into them, so you have a duty to keep your luncheon date except when . . . This view of duties as fully specified (like the comparable view about rights)[5] is problem-atic, since it implies that, given that we never plot out all the exceptions in advance, we never know what our duties are. Also, it has some difficulty accounting for compensation that we may owe for having failed to keep our appointment, since it implies that we have not failed in any duty if we acted on an escape clause. [Although it is possible to analyze the duty as "keep the appointment except when . . . and then pay compensation," it may be said that this does not capture the sense that the person we fail has been done a wrong, i.e., that the compensation is not just an equally preferable manner of treatment. But compensation could capture this idea if it expresses the view that it is a *shame* that someone's duties are correctly limited by exceptions. It is not wrong that they have to be specified, but it is a shame, it is regrettable. (This distinction between its being wrong and its being a shame can also be used when rights are infringed or overridden, but here the idea is that it's regrettable that we must impose on someone.)]

Most important, the doctrine of fully specified duties really seems to have all its work done for it by a prior weighing of a simple duty (e.g., to keep the lunch appointment) against other acts (e.g., supererogatory acts), and so it seems parasitic on the doctrine that a duty may be overridden by a supereroga-tory act.[6] The doctrine of full specification, I believe, makes the most sense, and does not confront the issue of compensation, *when we are dealing with a duty to aid that is uncontracted for and not dependent on a special status* (i.e., a true imperfect duty). For example, the specified duty might be: "Each person has a duty to save lives at moderate personal cost, except when he wishes to do a different greater good even at large personal cost." Here there is no compensation owed the person who is not aided. As noted earlier, in these cases, there is no failure to meet an imperfect duty (only a choice of whom to aid), and this accounts for compensation not being required. But, as was also noted, it is possible to violate a perfect duty as well, and to do the supererogatory act when it does not also fulfill what would have been the strongest duty in the circumstance.

Finally, it is possible to argue that supererogatory acts do not override duties, since our *general duty* is to do either one of our *particular duties* (e.g., keep the lunch appointment) or do a supererogatory act.[7] It may be objected to this view that there are other reasons for not doing one's particular duties, that this view, like the idea of fully specified duties, makes it difficult to account for a duty to compensate when one fails to do a particular duty (having done the supererogatory instead), and that it is overly consequentialist, implying that one may always abandon one's duties in order to do supererogatory acts.

The view is also problematic if it implies (and perhaps it does not) that if I fail to do my particular duty in order to do a supererogatory act, I am then obliged to do that supererogatory act. Although the pressure on me may increase to do the supererogatory act, I do not believe that failing my lunch date will necessarily leave me with a duty to give up my kidney to save someone. Two points may mislead us in this regard: First, suppose that in order to do a supererogatory act, someone fails to do a duty that we permissibly could have required that he do at a great effort to himself. Then he would be no worse off than he had a right to be if we did hold him to making the same large effort to do the supererogatory act. Second, suppose that at a given point in time, t_1, someone could do either his duty or a supererogatory act. If he fails to do his duty at that moment he should *then* be doing the supererogatory act, if (*suppose*) that is the only permissible alternative course of action. After all, if he is not doing the supererogatory act he should be doing his duty. However, when there is unavoidably a time gap between failing to do one's duty and the performance of the supererogatory act, then this same reason for doing the supererogatory act does not exist; that is, it is not the only permissible alternative to doing some act one is otherwise required to perform, assuming it is too late now to do one's duty. (Michael Stocker has pointed out to me that it also seems true that if I do a strenuous supererogatory act I may be relieved from performing my duty even if it is still possible to do it — if they are not mutually exclusive acts, *temporally* speaking. So if I have been into a *burning* building to save lives, I may go home and rest rather than continue on to a faculty meeting that I could still catch in progress. This need not conflict with my owing compensation for not performing the duty, I think. How much compensation will probably vary with the importance of what one did alternatively. This is a whole separate issue which I bypass.)

It would, however, be sufficient for my purposes just to argue that a supererogatory act may permissibly supersede a simple, unspecified duty or a particular duty (rather than a disjunctive meta-duty, which includes the supererogatory act as one alternative). Our having a disjunctive meta-duty, however, may be significant for the relation between the personal (P) and the supererogatory (S) *in the particular circumstance* where we do not do the supererogatory disjunct. That is, P will not take precedence over S, if D takes precedence over P, since we would have to be doing D (rather than indulging P), if we are not doing S. I discuss this later.

In sum, one bottom-line point is that if it would have been our duty in the circumstances to save a thousand people had the cost to ourselves been small, even when doing this would have meant that we could not fulfill a promise to save one person, then we may save the thousand people, even if the cost is great. This is true even when, because it involves a much greater cost to us, it is supererogatory to do so. We may also do the supererogatory when no component of what we do would have been the strongest duty in the circumstances had it been sufficient. [These are the weaker and stronger versions of (2) and (2′).] Furthermore, the fact that we may permissibly choose to do the supererogatory act does not mean that those whom we abandon are obliged to make the large sacrifice of releasing us from our duty to them.

Types of Supererogatory Acts

Most of the supererogatory acts I have discussed are of one sort: they involve acts it would have been an agent's duty to do, given a general duty of beneficence, if they did not require large efforts on the agent's part. One justification for not doing one's duty in these cases seems to derive from the ability of this duty of beneficence (sometimes) to dominate another duty. (However, this was not true in the Father Case, where a second type of act that did not dominate a duty was supererogatory.) Its ability to outrank the other duty becomes salient when the large sacrifices required to carry out the supererogatory act are voluntarily undertaken. But it is important to note that acts whose supererogatory nature does not depend on their requiring large efforts (e.g., acts of kindness, mercy, forgiveness), and do not involve as parts acts which would have been duties if sufficient on their own, might also permissibly be done instead of duties, even though the person to whom the agent owes a duty is not obliged to release him from it.

A case that would satisfy these conditions is one in which: (a) there is a noncrucial large gain to the recipient of the supererogatory act, (b) the act costs me nothing to do, and (c) the act leads me to fail in my duty to someone else, who thereby suffers a loss that is not crucial but is large enough so that he would not be obliged to release me from my duty to him, once he knew how I would otherwise act. Suppose, for example, that someone asks me to help him complete a contest application which he must submit this evening (Contest Case). I am very good at contests, and the middle-income man stands to win a lifetime secure income if I help him. I have, however, already promised to spend the evening with a sick friend who really does need the company. It seems to me that I may leave my friend to help the man earn his lifetime income even though it is a supererogatory act at any cost to me (and hence does not involve, as a part, fulfillment of what would have been a duty if sufficient on its own). I see that helping him win the contest does much more good than keeping my promise to the sick friend, yet I do not believe that my friend is obliged to release me from my promise to him, given the importance of my visit from his personal point of view. (If he does not release me he is not merely excused, but justified.)

It might be claimed about these cases in which no great effort is required by the supererogatory act that we are dealing with imperfect duties rather than true supererogatories; that is, that we need not do this particular act, but we are obliged to do something out of the class to which it belongs. It is not clear to me that this must be so, however.

III

The Efforts Required

I have argued that we may sometimes fail to do our duty in order to do a supererogatory act, that is, that proposition (2) is true. I believe that the truth of proposition (2) implies that it is sometimes the case that *we may fail to do an act (our duty), which we might ordinarily be obliged to make large sacrifices to do, in order to do another act (e.g., a beneficent act) which we would not be obliged to make those same sacrifices to do*. For example, if I am a contractor and have promised to give my construction plans to a business associate by a certain date, I may be obliged to spend a great deal of extra money (e.g., on special delivery, keeping my employees working overtime, etc.) in order to meet the promised deadline. (Call this the Contractor Case.) I am not obliged to make the same effort in order to save someone's life when I have not promised to. Yet it would be morally permissible for me to miss the business deadline (e.g, to skip the meeting at which I was to give the plans) in order to save someone's life. (When the effort to save the life is small, this may be an instance of an imperfect duty taking precedence over a perfect duty, but I am permitted to do it even if the effort is large.)

Notice that not all the duties discussed in Section II in connection with proving proposition (2) are duties that require great personal sacrifice. Obviously the duties for which $S \geq D$ but $P \geq D$, rather than $-(P \geq D)$, will not play a role in generating the apparent intransitivity of interest in this chapter. The duty to keep a lunch appointment in the Lunch Case which can be overridden if we decide to give up a kidney to save a life, is a duty we need not make big sacrifices to do; for example, we need not give up a kidney to fulfill it. Here $P \geq D$. But the duty to keep the business deal in the Contractor Case is a duty we are duty-bound to make a large effort to fulfill—the same effort we are not obliged to, but may, make to save a life.

In general, we seem to feel obliged to go to a great deal more trouble to keep our professional commitments or other comparable obligations than to aid people in need. Yet we feel that we may drop these professional commitments to save a life. Proposition (2), therefore, is true not only when what we fail to do is something that we would not have been obliged to make great efforts to do. Indeed, when the effort required to save a life is small, we may have a duty to save the life, rather than meet the business deadline, although, in general, we would have been obliged to make greater efforts to keep the business deadline than to save the life.

Furthermore (and most importantly), we may skip the business deadline to save the life, even if we would not be willing to make large efforts to save the life should this be necessary and if we would be willing to make the large efforts to keep the business meeting. That is, we cannot come to be required to make the large efforts to save a life just because the alternative to doing so is making the large efforts to take us to the business appointment. This is so even if we would be *required* (not merely permitted) to drop the business appointment to save the life at small cost.

Two Standards for Stringency

This Contractor Case shows that there are two possible standards for the stringency or importance of an obligation. (We can also think of these as two defeasibility tests, on the model of those discussed in chapter 4, tests for when the requirement to do an act is defeated.) One is the *efforts standard*. Keeping our business commitment seems to be a more stringent duty than saving lives in general, in the sense that we are required to make greater efforts to fulfill it than we are required to make to save a life. Some efforts that would be beyond the call of duty in order to save a life would not be beyond the call of duty in order to keep a business commitment. The efforts we have to make to keep commitments can be seen as subsidiary duties. Someone who promised to meet me, but went to no trouble at all to keep the promise, would be failing in his duty. Some duties may require a great deal of us. For example, if I have a duty not to kill someone, I may have the subsidiary duty to make a great effort to avoid killing him. [How much I am willing to do, both of what I am required to do (subsidiary duties) and of what I am not required to do, in order to fulfill my duty is a mark of how conscientious I am, how much I care about my duty.] Of course, not all duties require the same degree of effort for their associated subsidiary duties.

The second possible standard for the stringency or importance of two obligations determines which of these obligations may or must be met when it is impossible to meet both. Call this the *precedence standard*. (Understood as defeasibility tests, these two standards say that a duty may be defeated if more effort is needed than we owe, and a duty may be defeated by the need to perform another act.)[8]

Proposition (2) implies that sometimes it is permissible (or even required) that we do an act that is required of us *less* stringently when measured by the efforts standard, rather than an act required *more* stringently by the efforts standard. This may be true, for example, of life saving and promise keeping. Put more formally, where C = promise keeping, A = saving a life, > =

takes precedence over (dominates), and $-$ = not; the following might all be
true:

> (I) We are required to make effort E for the sake of doing C. That is, C
> $> -$ E, doing C takes precedence over avoiding the effort.

> (II) We are not required to make the effort E for the sake of A. That is,
> $-$ (A $> -$ E); it is permissible to avoid the effort to do A. And yet,

> (III) (a) We may permissibly do A rather than C; that is, $-$(C $>$ A).
> Therefore, we have the option of doing A or C, or

> (b) We must do A rather than C; that is, A $>$ C.

On the measure of efforts required, C seems to be more stringently required than A; yet, on the measure of which we must do if given a choice,
either A and C seem equal or in some cases (when we must do A) A seems
more stringently required. We have here generated the intransitivity described
at the beginning of this chapter. Indeed, we could say that the (so-called)
intransitivity represents nothing more than the fact that there are two sometimes conflicting standards (effort and precedence) for stringency. That is, D
(duty) and S (the supererogatory) differ in relation to P (the personal effort
or loss), with D taking precedence over P and P permissibly chosen over S,
and yet S can take precedence over D. Given a duty (D), personal interest
(P) in not doing E, supererogatory act (S), and given that $\geq$ means "may
permissibly take precedence over," (I) states that $-$(P $\geq$ D), (II) states that
P $\geq$ S, and (III) implies that S $\geq$ D; or equivalently, P $\geq$ S, S $\geq$ D, yet
$-$(P $\geq$ D).

Because an act that is less stringently required by one measure may permissibly take precedence over another act that is more stringently required by that
same measure, we cannot resolve the problem of whether we may violate a
negative duty to perform a positive duty simply by showing that negative
duties are more stringently required than positive duties. For example, Philippa Foot says that we may not kill one person to save others, because the
duty not to kill is more stringent than the duty to aid.[9] But if greater stringency
meant only that we would have to make a greater effort to avoid killing
someone than we would have to make to aid others, this would not show that
it is impermissible to violate a negative duty in order to aid, or even that we
might not be required morally to violate the negative duty in order to aid.
More has to be said to prove that it is impermissible to violate the negative for
the sake of the positive duty.

The following should make clear how the second version of the intransitivity described at the beginning of the paper arises. It has been argued that
we may sometimes violate a duty as a means of doing a supererogatory act
[proposition (2'), S $\geq$ D]. For example, we may take someone's car without
his permission in order to save a life at great cost to ourself. It has also been
said that it is commonly thought that we need not sacrifice goals that are
personally important to us in order to save life [proposition (1'), G $\geq$ S].
Yet, we may not violate duties for the sake of our personal goals; $-$(G $\geq$ D).

The Two Intransitivities

One objection to the way in which we have generated the apparent intransitivity is that, although aiding others at large cost to ourselves is, in general, supererogatory, making a large sacrifice in order to aid someone is not supererogatory in the specific context in which we have already failed to make an obligatory large sacrifice to perform our duty. So although, considered by themselves, it may be true that P ≥ S, where P means avoiding large effort E, it is no longer true when S, D, and P are options together, S ≥ D and someone has failed to do D in order to do S. If $-(P \geq S)$, it is said, it is not surprising that $-(P \geq D)$.[10]

I do not believe this objection is quite correct. Consider the first intransitivity, where P means avoiding large effort E. Even focusing on the particular situation in which we will do the supererogatory act rather than the duty, I believe we are not obliged to do as much to carry out that supererogatory act as we would have been obliged to do for the sake of our duty. So, if we drop a business commitment in order to save a life, I do not believe this means we must do as much as we would have done (or had to do) for the business in order to save the life. (I have already emphasized this point above.) That is, P still may take precedence over S to some degree though $-(P \geq D)$. Even at that very time, when we drop D for S, there are two separate measures of stringency. We still do not have to make the effort for S that we must make for D, though S may be more important than D, and so in this sense P may permissibly take precedence over S. What is true in the situation where S, D, and P are options is that we must either do D even by sacrificing P, or do S, though not necessarily at the cost of P. Another important possibility is that we might do S at cost of P, but only because we can thereby avoid having to sacrifice D to S. That is, we must do both D and S at P, because D takes precedence over P, not because S does directly.

However, the concern that while, in general, a given value for P may take precedence over S, it will not take precedence in the specific situation where S ≥ D and one drops D, may have more merit as an objection to the second form of the intransitivity. The second form is:

(1) The pursuit of some personally valued goal, G, may take precedence over S;

(2) We may violate D to do S;

(3) It is not permissible to violate D in order to achieve G.

Pursuing a goal instead of doing S is different from making an effort to do S. Although, in general, we may not have to give up G to do S, if we had to give up G in order to do D *and* if we then drop D to do S, it does indeed seem that we may not drop S to do G instead. (Nor is this true only if D is still a possibility.) Then, we have S ≥ D, $-(G \geq S)$, and $-(G \geq D)$. The significance of discussing our issue in the particular context in which S ≥ D and D is actually dropped can be emphasized by thinking of the steps in the following order: S ≥ D; $-(G \geq D)$, and hence $-(G \geq S)$. But, S ≥ D, $-(P_{(efforts)} \geq D)$ does *not* imply $-(P_{(efforts)} \geq S)$.

Nevertheless, we can distinguish between the fact that, in separate, pairwise comparisons of goals, duties, and supererogatory acts, $G \geq S$, $S \geq D$, $-(G \geq D)$, and the fact that in a context in which all three factors are present together, and $S \geq D$, D is dropped, and $D > G$, we are not at liberty to pursue G. I shall call the first fact the *pairwise* fact, and the second fact the *complete* fact. Should we attribute moral significance to the pairwise fact? What is this "pairwise fact"? Understanding it depends upon considering each of the premises independently of the others. The question then is whether it is morally significant that, so considered, all three are true. I suggest that it is morally significant; considering the premises independently allows us to see the relation between G and S on their own. After all, what does the work of making S permissibly dominant over G in the specific context where we would do S rather than D is the fact that we ought to be doing D, not G, if we are not doing S. It is really the significance of D that accounts for the dominance of S over G, nothing about the relation between G and S on their own. It, therefore, remains interesting that something which, on its own, cannot require us to give up G should have the power to override D, which on its own can require us to give up G.

Accordingly, we can conclude by saying that the first apparent intransitivity, concerning efforts, is stronger in the sense that it is present both in the pairwise and in the complete form. The second apparent intransitivity, concerning goals, is weaker in the sense that it is present in the pairwise form only. (Henceforth, where necessary, I shall distinguish between pairwise apparent intransitivity and complete apparent intransitivity.)

Objection: Duty Does Not Take Precedence over Personal Interests

Another way out of the intransitivity is to deny that we must make great efforts to do our duty. The fact that we may do the act required less stringently as measured by the efforts standard, rather than the act more stringently required by that standard, may even lead one to reason as follows: If one may, and sometimes should, permissibly break one's business promise in order to save a life $[-(C > A)]$ and if one may permissibly refuse to save a life in order to avoid large efforts E $[-(A > -E)]$, then, perhaps, one *may* break one's business promise in order to avoid large effort E $[-(B > -E)$ or $P \geq D]$. The idea here is that if I may or must do A rather than C, they must be essentially equal in significance, or else A must be even more significant than C; so, if I need not make effort E (sacrifice myself personally) to do A, I need not make the effort to do C. Another way to put the point is to ask: If we have a choice between doing our duty and doing the supererogatory act [proposition (2)], and a choice between doing the supererogatory act and conserving our effort [proposition (1)], why indeed don't we have a choice between doing our duty and conserving our effort [denial of proposition (3)]? Likewise, if we may violate duties to save lives, why may we not straightforwardly and always violate duties for the sake of what may take precedence over saving lives, our personal goals? Why may we not take someone's car without his permission to go on our long-planned vacation? That is, why is proposition (3'), $-(G \geq D)$ not false?

If we reject this suggested solution, as I think we should, we must explain the fact that the act that is less stringently required by the efforts measure may indeed take precedence, and we must also show that, even if we are not required to make great efforts to do it, we may still be required to make just such efforts to do the duty over which it may take precedence. (This amounts to showing that there are two different stringency measures which do not always yield the same results.) Similarly, how can we show that we may have leeway to violate duties for the sake of an act for which we need not sacrifice personal goals, but do not have such leeway to promote those personal goals?

Scheffler and the Intransitivity

As has already been noted in chapter 8, this problem comes to mind as possible criticism of the position for which Samuel Scheffler has argued.[11] Scheffler claims that we have the prerogative not to make great personal sacrifices to do what is best overall from the impartial point of view.[12] He also suggests that it may be permissible to kill one person in order to save the lives of five others. But if we may permissibly kill for the greatest good, and avoiding sacrifices may take precedence over the greatest good, perhaps we may kill a person to avoid personal sacrifices. We asked, would Scheffler permit this? Even more directly, if in a certain case abiding by the duty not to kill just *is* promoting the greater good, why may not personal interest permissibly take precedence?[13] Scheffler's position is especially radical insofar as it argues for the elimination of restrictions. It is possible, however, to understand someone who thought S $\geq$ D (where D is "abiding by restrictions on harm"), and P $\geq$ D, as arguing that although there are restrictions, P may override them, leaving a negative residue for which compensation is owed.

IV

Let us now begin by trying to explain the first intransitivity, since the explanation of it will also help explain the second. My strategy will be to consider possible explanations of the permissibility of doing the supererogatory instead of one's duty, and then see whether the correct explanation provides a basis for distinguishing between (1) doing the supererogatory act and (2) avoiding a personal sacrifice, as a ground for failing to do one's duty. That is, I examine why S $\geq$ D, but $-(P \geq D)$. [This is different from examining why, if P $\geq$ S, $-(P \geq D)$.]

Doing the Less Stringently Required Act

The first suggested explanation for the permissibility of doing the act less stringently required by the efforts standard is that saving-someone's-life-at-small-cost-to oneself is more stringently required by the precedence standard than keeping-the-business-appointment-at-great-cost-to-oneself (with the emphasis on the different costs involved for oneself). But this will not do as an explanation; for what if there is a great cost attached to saving someone's life but a person is willing to pay the cost? The willingness to make large sacrifices to save a life would not make it impermissible to save the life rather than keep the appointment. Second, there may be no great cost involved in keeping one's business appointment on some occasion, and one could nevertheless choose to save the life, even at great personal expense. Third, this explanation does not tell us why we *may* permissibly do a less stringently required act on the efforts standard at great expense; it will only tell us why we *must* do it at small expense. [14]

Fourth, to say that we may permissibly do what is less stringently required by the efforts standard just because it now involves less effort to ourselves suggests that acts that are in general less stringently required may be done when it is in our self-interest to do them, given the alternative. But this would imply that we may devote time to volunteer work whenever we can thereby escape some strenuous commitment, and this is wrong.

Furthermore, doing the act less stringently required by the efforts standard, instead of one's duty, may not release one from having to make great efforts to compensate the person to whom one had the duty; yet doing the less stringently required act on the efforts standard does not become impermissible just because efforts to oneself increase when one compensates.

(It is possible to consider this proposed explanation from an alternative perspective, however: We could say that, as long as the efforts involved are within the range of efforts that *can* be required for doing a great good, doing good is more important than some other duty that we could do instead. We shall later consider this explanation further below.)

Doing the Most Good?

A second explanation of the permissibility of choosing the act less stringently required by the efforts standard is that although, in general, the type of act more stringently required produces more good than the type less stringently required, this is not always so. On some occasions the reverse is true. In these situations it is permissible not to do the act more stringently required by the efforts standard.

However, it does not seem to be true, in general, that acts more stringently required by the efforts test do more good than acts not so required, or that if most people did the latter instead of the former things would be much worse. So, the more stringently required duty (by the efforts standard) may be doing its ordinary amount of good now, and *in general* the act less stringently required by the efforts standard might do more good.

Beyond the Required Minimum and What May Be Required

A third possible explanation of why the act less stringently required by the efforts standard is sometimes permissible is that the more stringently required act is a minimum, but minima are not necessary requirements. It is right to require people to make great efforts not to fall below a minimum. They may be permitted, however, to do something else that is better than the minimum, as a substitute for it, even though the substitute does not involve great efforts and even though the substitute does not include the minimum. By requiring great efforts to do it, we emphasize that a type of act is a rock bottom below which we may not fall. Other types of acts are beyond the minimum, and so we do not demand as much of people to do them even though they produce better overall consequences. But this does not mean that doing such an act is not an adequate substitute for doing the minimum, in some cases. To use an example from another area: We are required to work hard in school to learn to read and write, not so hard to compose great poetry. But composing great poetry (and dictating it to a machine) may, nevertheless, be more than a fair exchange for learning the minimum. In a sense, the fact that we do another act that produces much good means that we have not really fallen below the minimum, that it is only if we first fail to read and write and then also fail to do poetry that we are below the minimum. [15]

A *fourth explanation* of the phenomenon in question, which builds on the third, is that the difference in how stringently different types of acts are required as measured by the efforts standard is not a function of how important or good what they accomplish is. It is simply that only certain types of acts are of the sort that it is permissible to require of people at large expense to themselves. Other types of acts cannot permissibly be required of people, or cannot permissibly be required of them at great expense, even if these acts have good and important consequences. In other words, being this permissibly requirable type of act is not necessarily a function of having better or more important consequences than other types of acts would have. It is not necessarily preferable that you do one type of act rather than the other; it is just that it is permissible to require you to do only one type of act at great expense to yourself. Similarly, it is morally permissible to require a prisoner to serve his term; it is not morally permissible to require him to participate in drug research. However, if he is willing to participate, we may prefer that, and release him from his prison term. (I shall not here attempt to describe what makes it permissible for us to require an act at great expense, except to note that not harming those who are independent of imposition on us contrasts with helping those who would lose only what they would get via such imposition.) But it is important to note that there are at least two possible senses of "not requirable." One is that we are not morally entitled to require something of someone; the second is that it is not feasible to require something of someone, though, if it were, we would be morally entitled to. I am concerned with the first sense of "not requirable," but it might also be argued that when we do not require big efforts for acts with very good consequences it is only because it is not feasible to enforce the requirement. [16]

The concept of duty according to which we may permissibly be required to make great efforts for some duties seems to conflict with the theory of duty offered by Susan Wolf. [17] Wolf suggests that our duties are a compromise between promoting the good of the world and respecting a person's interest in his personal good, whereby we find ways in which the former can be achieved without violating the latter. This seems to imply that, by definition, duties cannot require great sacrifices from us and that if they do on occasion, this is an error generated by the benefits of having a system that has general categories of duties. Therefore, it seems that the problem that concerns me, why acts stringently required by the effort standard may be superseded by acts not stringently required in this way, cannot arise in a system like Wolf's, since she seems to think there are not duties of a general type stringently required by the effort standard. Furthermore, it may be that the duties that are stringently required do not, contrary to Wolf, represent a concern for the good of the world, whether compromised for personal interest or not. On the view for which I have argued in earlier chapters, there are at least two components of the nonpersonal perspective: concern for the greater good, which (as standardly understood) represents concern for the general well-being,[18] and respect for persons, which gives rise to constraints on action. (The constraints do not necessarily stem from concern for the personal point of view of agents.) There could be supererogatory acts on behalf of both components, but it would be morally permissible to require strenuous efforts, in general, only for directly respecting (that is, not violating) the constraints and for meeting positive rights brought about by consent or contract.

It seems that we are not morally permitted to require effort from an agent merely in accord with the goodness of the consequences of his making the effort. But it is worth noting again that it may be permissible for an agent to do a supererogatory act because it produces important consequences though the costs to those he lets down in failing to do his duty will be greater than they would have been obligated to pay. This indicates that there are at least two different types of costs requirable for doing acts: dutiful acts may justifiably impose costs on the agent who does them; some supererogatory acts may justify the agent in imposing costs on someone else. What might account for this is a view that sacrificing oneself is more difficult than sacrificing others. It may be, however, that the only *large* losses (versus taking someone's car) an agent may impose on others against their will are the consequences of the agent not doing something positive *for* them (even something that they had a contractual positive right that she do). It may be wrong to take from them something significant that is theirs by right and that they can have without her help.[19]

As noted, this fourth explanation really includes the third as a part, since the third explanation identifies "what it is morally permissible to require people to do" (even at large cost to themselves) as "the minimum." Both the third and fourth explanations, however, share the defect of being overly consequentialist. They imply that duties are minimal and requirable acts that never stand in the way of acting for the greater good. But the nonconsequentialist view is that it is not the case that just any greater good can serve as a reason for failing to do one's duty, and not every duty can be overridden by greater good.

*Costs of Not Doing the Supererogatory: The Unimportance
of What We Care About*[20]

A fifth suggestion[21] as to why it is permissible to do an act less stringently
required by the efforts standard rather than one more stringently required by
that standard focuses on the costs of not doing the supererogatory act. On the
efforts measure of stringency, I may be obligated to pay a high price to do a
duty. But this does not necessarily mean that I am morally obliged to pay
every price to do my duty. For example, I may have to make an unpleasant
trip to keep my business appointment, but not give up my life. If I am willing
to save lives, though it is not required that I do so, the cost to me of not saving
the lives (not doing what I want to do) must be included as part of the cost to me
of doing my duty. This may make the cost of doing my duty higher than can be
required of me, and I may be released from doing it. If I were not willing to save
the lives, the cost to me of doing my duty would not be so great.

This suggestion seems to remedy one of the defects of the third and fourth
suggestions, since it would explain why not every act that produces a great
good may override a duty. It is only if the loss *to me* of the good that would
come from the supererogatory act is greater than the cost I would be obliged
to bear to do my duty that I may permissibly abandon my duty.

The emphasis in the fifth explanation is on the cost to me that I would bear
if the many lives I am willing to save are lost.[22] The following points may help
to show that this proposed explanation is a mistake. First, it is quite possible
that someone has personal projects that he cares about just as much as he
cares about the greater good that will be accomplished by the supererogatory
act. Yet, there will be cases in which he would not be morally permitted to
drop his duty for the sake of such personal projects. This also indicates that
one's personal projects and the satisfaction they bring one are not being considered merely as part of the general good. For example, saving my own life
may not be a reason for abandoning my duty, whereas saving some innocent
bystander's life might be. One life is not being counted the same as another,
even if I care about myself as much as, or more than, I care about the innocent
bystander. Second, some duties may require a very great deal of us. For
example, I may be morally required to give up even my life to fulfill some
duties; for example, it may be that if someone threatens to kill me unless I kill
someone else, I ought to die rather than kill the other person. Suppose there
were a conflict between my carrying out a duty for which it could be right to
require me to sacrifice my life (e.g., going on a dangerous combat mission)
and my saving many lives. The fifth explanation could justify my doing the
supererogatory act of saving the many rather than the duty, when doing the
duty *in fact* costs me nothing other than the loss of the many lives, *only* if I
cared significantly more about the loss of the many lives than about the loss
of my own life alone. This is the only way those many deaths could raise the
cost to me of doing my duty beyond the cost I am already required to pay.
This means that I would have to be willing to give up my own life to save the

many people in order to be justified in abandoning a duty that I could be morally required to die for. (This is contrary to my earlier claim that I might have to make an effort for D that I did not have to make for S, even in the *specific* context where S ≥ D and I drop D to do S.)

I believe this implication of the fifth explanation is wrong. First, suppose I were required to give up everything I most care about, even those things that mean more to me than my life, in order to do some duty. Does this mean that I ought not abandon this duty in order to save many lives? I believe not, since it is possible for someone to be willing to meet his obligation to sacrifice anything he cares about in order to do his duty, and yet not be willing to allow other people to die just so that he do his duty. Indeed, he may care more about doing his duty (as measured by how much of what else he cares about he would be willing to sacrifice to do it) than about saving many lives, and yet still abandon his duty to save the lives. He may be willing to give up his life to do his duty and yet fail to do his duty in order supererogatorily to save many people, even though he would not be willing to give up his life just to save those other people. He would, however, give up his life to save those people, if by doing this he could avoid sacrificing his duty in order to save those people.[23]

How does such a person reason? I believe he compares the objective importance of the content of his duty with the objective importance of many lives being lost, and finds the loss of life to be much more important. Even though he would give up (and it is morally right to require him to do so) more of what has personal value to him (what he cares about) in order to do his duty than he would give in order to save the many lives, he cannot allow something of much greater objective value (many lives) to be lost just so that something of less objective value (the content of his duty) be achieved. In general, on all measures of how much a person cares for something, he may care more about the consequences of doing M than of doing N, and still reasonably do N. And not just because it is his duty to do N, since our discussion says that N could be supererogatory. So although someone might be morally justified if he failed to do his duty in order to do a supererogatory act because he cared more about its consequences (saving many lives) than about the duty, he might also be morally justified in doing one supererogatory act rather than another (e.g., saving a hundred strangers rather than ten friends) because it seems the objectively better thing to do, though he does not care as much about the outcome.

It is worth discussing this point a bit further, since there is a tendency among some philosophers to argue as follows: One cares more for one's loved ones than for millions of strangers. The evidence for this is that if one's loved ones were killed one might lose the will to live entirely, but if the strangers die, one could perfectly well go on. One even cares (these philosophers say) more for one's loved ones than for avoiding morally wrong behavior. For even if one would feel some guilt at doing the wrong act, this would soon pass, but one might kill oneself if one's loved ones died. From these premises (they hold) we can draw the conclusion that one ought to abandon the millions of strangers to save one's loved ones or even kill the millions of strangers to save one's loved ones.

My point is that this is quite the wrong conclusion to draw. That one cares most about an outcome in the sense of what one feels the most for, does not determine what one will do, what one ought to do, or what it is rational for one to do. If I can see that one thing is more important than another, it does not necessarily matter whether I *care* about the things in proportion to their importance in order for me to *act* in accord with their importance.

It might be that the lucky few are those who come to care (in the sense of *feel*) about the greater good they act for. However, a further puzzle about human beings seems to be that we cannot actually seem to believe that this would be a lucky transformation: It is as if certain things are meant to be cared about and other things are meant to be acted for (at least sometimes) independent of the sort of concern that motivates great personal sacrifice.

As has been said, when someone would sacrifice what he cares about more than his own life, or what he is required to do at the cost of his own life, in order to produce a good for whose sake alone he would not give up his life, he will still sacrifice his life to produce the good if this prevents the loss of what he cares about more than his life or what he is required to preserve at the cost of his life. What this shows, in part, is a compromise between the impartial and personal point of view. He is not willing to sacrifice his own life when he compares it directly with the great good. His sacrifice is mediated by its role in saving what has greater personal value to him or in what he is required to do, regardless of whether what is saved is objectively more important than he is. This account implies that an agent may refuse to weigh his own life on an impartial scale and yet weigh on that scale something he cares about more than his own life (for example, his duty). This is one of the most puzzling features of this analysis: how differently we treat what we care about other than ourselves versus the direct losses to ourselves. The existence of this difference argues against *simply* accepting—though it does not imply that we should reject—the view that the loss of what is personally important to us is to be treated straightforwardly like a cost in effort imposed on us. (This view would imply that it is permissible to choose to save one friend rather than ten strangers, because the cost to us of losing the friend is so great.[24])

It might be suggested that this puzzle is an indication of how closely being an agent is tied to not seeing oneself as just another creature in the world. Or it may be connected to the fact that an agent in sacrificing himself would be actively donating his life for the greater good but a person he abandons for the sake of the greater good would not actively give up her life. (This is the active/passive loss distinction we discussed earlier in connection with Scheffler.)

The type of cases I have in mind, however, divide into (at least) two: (1) cases in which what the agent cares about more than his life is "doing his duty," and (2) cases in which what the agent cares about is the state of affairs that will result if he does his duty. If someone is firmly committed to doing whatever he must (causally or morally) to carry out his duty, even giving up his life, and so cares about his duty, he may, permissibly as well as rationally, I believe, still weigh what would result if he did his duty against what would result if he did the supererogatory act, and decide to do the supererogatory act. This is good moral judgment and consistent with rationality, even though he would not give up his life (only suffer some other lesser though still sizeable loss) to do the supererogatory act. It may be more difficult to believe that an agent who *cares about the state of affairs that would result if he did his duty*, e.g., saving the life of a person he loves, would weigh that person's life against the greater good achievable by the supererogatory act, when he would give up his life to save the person but would not do so to perform the supererogatory act. That is, it is harder to make sense of the agent (1) not weighing his own life *directly* on a scale of impartial weights relative to the greater good, but (2) weighing on that same scale, the life of someone he cared about so much, and (3) sacrificing his own life, only if it could be given in place of the loved one. (Notice that it would not be morally wrong or irrational for this agent to weigh on the impartial scale the life of someone he cared about and the greater good in deciding what to do, just because there was the possibility of substituting himself as sacrifice.) In this second case, I believe, the detachment from what the agent cares about is different from, and more radical than, his detachment from his concern for doing his duty alone (when he does not care that much about the state of affairs that would result if he did his duty).

Possible Solutions

There are two puzzles then: Why is it morally acceptable and not irrational to put on a scale which objectively measures value what means more to one than one's own life, when one doesn't directly put one's own life on that scale? and why is it morally acceptable and not irrational to be willing then to give up one's life for the greater good, but only as a substitute for something one cares about more than one's own life? So, if $S \geq D$ and $D > P$, S can come to take precedence over P indirectly, sometimes, by way of concern for D. (Notice that how it does this here is different from how S comes to take precedence over G at the specific time when S was to be done instead of D, as discussed earlier, pp. 323–24.) S did not dominate G because not doing G meant that D did not have to be sacrificed to S. We earlier also noted that $-(S > P)$ whenever S is, in fact, substituted for D. But now we are dealing with a case in which $S > P$ when losing P can be the substitute for losing D (i.e., the substitute for either failing to do the duty or losing the state of affairs that would result if the duty were done.) To focus on a case in thinking about these matters, let us consider a case that involves many strangers on one island and my loved one on another. I would not give up my life to save the many, but I would do so to save my loved one. Yet I could decide that it is wrong to choose to save my loved one rather than the many (when the immediate cost of saving either is small, e.g., I press a button that sends a rescue mission), but I will give up *my* life if that will allow me to be sacrificed rather than my loved one (the Loved One Case).

There are several possible approaches to the first puzzle [which is part of the objection to the fifth explanation for why $S \geq D$ when $P \geq S$ and $-(P \geq D)$]. One approach notes that there is a moral difference between someone's own death and the death of his loved one, who means more than life itself to him. Being willing to give up one's life for a loved one does not imply that one will die (or even be forever after miserable in life) if his loved one dies. [25]

Accordingly, not everything that I care so much about that I would give up my life to save it, is something whose absence would literally rob me of life or even rob me of it metaphorically. This moral difference between my life and what I would give my life for, it might be said, accounts for my not weighing my life directly on an objective scale even though I would so weigh the loved one's in deciding what to do.

Suppose, however, that someone *would* die of heartbreak if he chose to save, at small immediate cost, the lives of many strangers instead of saving the life of his loved one. (We have already noted that in a different case someone would, in fact, sacrifice himself by placing himself in the position his loved one would be in if he, at small immediate cost, saw to it that the many strangers were saved instead of his loved one. In this case, he would also die if he chose the greater good over his loved one's.) If our agent really is in danger of dying of heartbreak, we cannot explain the first puzzle by emphasizing that the agent does not himself really die.

A second approach emphasizes that if I give up a state of affairs that involves the survival of someone I care about very much in order to do a supererogatory act, it seems that I pay a large personal price to do the super-erogatory act. From my point of view, however, the fact that the loved one will die does *not* constitute merely a personal cost to me. I see its coming about as bad because it is *bad for the person* I care about. This is why I prefer to substitute myself for him, though *I* will thereby suffer a greater loss than I would suffer if I survived the loss of him. It is a reflection of my personal concern for him that *I* do not see his loss as merely a loss to me. Indeed my seeing it this way, rather than as a loss to me, is part of what shows I do care for the loved one. Oddly enough, because I care so much for him that I see his loss as separate from mine, I can more easily place his loss on the impartial scale to be weighed against the greater good. That is, my caring so much for him that his loss is not merely a loss to me, may make it possible for me to sacrifice him for the greater number. If loss of him were just a loss to me (i.e., part of P) I would not sacrifice it for S. When I consider P versus the greater good, I may give P more than its impartial weight. But when I see the loved one and the larger number as separate from me, I may (though I need not) think of myself as taking an impartial perspective, and since I am called on to make a decision between people who are separate from me, I may do it as a god would, that is, impartially.

However, we must always remember that I would substitute a great loss *to me* for a like loss to him, since it seems worse to me that he suffer a loss than that I do. This means that I would lose my life; it would clearly be my loss that comes about. (This is the second puzzle.)

A third approach to both puzzles, however, is consistent with its being the agent himself who will lose his life. Essentially, this approach tries to argue that neither abandoning a loved one for the many, nor substituting oneself for one's loved one, involves "a loss to someone *for the sake of* the many" that would involve bringing about good *by means of* harm in the way ruled out by the PPH. Whether I abandon a loved one for the many or substitute myself for my loved one, I will be doing something significantly different from what I would do if I sacrificed myself directly for the many or had the many saved by causing harm to the one. If I must save many strangers at the expense of my own life, I am deciding whether they shall be saved by sacrifice of my life. I do not want this to happen, but I do want my loved one's life to be saved *by* sacrifice of mine, if this is necessary. Suppose I am not called on to save the strangers by giving my life, but only to choose whether to send my medicine to help the strangers or to my loved one; I begin to think about what is objectively good, about how a resource that is mine (whose use does not *intrinsically* cost me much) can be best used. If I give the resource to the strangers, I am not saving the greater number of strangers *by* using my loved one's life (e.g., I will not be chopping him up to make a serum to save the many). I save the strangers by means of the resource, so the loved one does not die *for* the strangers, they do not live *by* means of him.

Suppose the resource (a pill) is mine and it can save my life or the strangers'. If I am like the person whose conduct I am trying to explicate, I will keep the pill for myself, because otherwise the many would be saved *by* what was mine and this would result in grave harm to me. If I give my pill to the many rather than to the loved one, he will die as a consequence, but if I really care about him, this is not counted by me as a loss to me so much as a loss to him (as the second approach emphasized). The strangers will be saved *by* the loss to me of my friend, but this loss is not my life, it is his. Yet they are still not saved by his life. So they are not saved *by* my life, nor *by* his. [26]

Now if I wish to substitute myself for my loved one, I will die, but I still will not die *primarily for* the strangers, though it is true that they will be saved by my decision in their favor which leads to my sacrifice. So the direct reason I die is not so that the strangers should live, though the choice that they live rather than my loved one — made without any step involving their being saved *by* sacrifice of me or my loved one — led to the situation in which I die for the sake of my loved one.

In sum, if the situation is as imagined in the Loved One Case, it is possible that I am willing to give up my life so that good may come *by means of* this loss only if my action helps my loved one or serves my duty; other large losses to me or to my loved one should not be the direct route by which greater good comes about. When I leave my loved one, to help the greater number, it is not by the sacrifice of my loved one that the greater number are saved. If I sacrificed myself for the greater number, they would die by the sacrifice of my life. Is this why I would sacrifice what I care about more, for the sake of what I care about less and sacrifice myself for the former?

Objective Value

Regardless of how we explain these two puzzles, the objection to the fifth explanation of why $S \geq D$, shows that when I am willing to save lives supererogatorily, the cost of doing my duty instead should be understood to include the *objective* value of the lives that will be lost. By this I mean only that it is the objective value of those lives that counts, not merely their personal value to me, though the objective value may depend in part on the value of their lives *to* those who would die if I do not aid. We may call the fifth explanation so revised "the revised fifth explanation." It should take into account not merely the cost to me of those many deaths (i.e., how much I care about them) but the objective costs. However, if I were not willing to save the many lives supererogatorily, the cost of doing my duty would not include the value of those lives.

Including the objective value of what will be lost if I do my duty, not just the value of the loss to me, *reintroduces* the problem of utilitarian calculation. How can we account for the fact that doing much more good may override doing our duty, but doing only somewhat more good may not? We could have accounted for this fact if, as the fifth explanation suggested, we saw the cost of not doing the supererogatory act (and doing duty instead) as the cost-to-me, since the costs I am required to bear to do my duty are assumed to be fixed, and when the actual costs go higher I need not do my duty. But if it is not a question of the costs *to me* in not doing the supererogatory being too high, we shall need an independent measure of what objective losses may and may not be incurred in order to ensure that a duty be done. One way to stem straightforward utilitarian calculation is to include the weight of the constraint of duty, rather than just the good in the outcome that doing one's duty produces, as needing to be outweighed.[27] (In the case of imperfect duties, the calculation will not include any weight of a constraint, since whether I save one at small cost or many at large cost, my imperfect duty will be satisfied.) Furthermore, in deciding how much weight the constraint of duty should have when weighed against the greater good (i.e., when $S \geq D$), we might look at how much effort someone is obliged to make to perform his duty: The hypothesis is that the more effort, the higher the amount of greater good necessary to override the duty. (But for reasons against believing this, see p. 342.) The extra weight added by duty per se can be seen as a form of *objective* weight, not stemming from concern for maximizing the good but rather from deontological considerations. This is another type of objective consideration, based on the status of the person (as we have argued in chapter 10). I will not try to settle here the issue of how much good is necessary to override the duty.

The Duty that Overrides Duty

Suggested explanations 3, 4, and 5 for why S $\geq$ D all attempt to explain why it is sometimes permissible to do the type of act that is less stringently required by the efforts standard. None of them, however, explains why we sometimes *must* do the act that is less stringently required by the efforts standard. For example, none of them explains why it is obligatory to save a life at small cost to ourselves rather than keep an important business appointment.

To explain this, we may have to return to a version of the first proposed explanation and accept a view that combines an act with the effort necessary to do it, and weighs the stringency of the requirement to do this weighted act against that of other acts. We do this without implying, however, that the agent will therefore be morally obliged to do whichever act requires less of him *because* it requires less of him. So, saving-a-life-at-small-cost-to-ourselves may be as obligatory or more so than keeping business promises at even smaller costs, and the greater good produced by the former makes it dominate the latter.

Conclusion

It seems that we can explain, to some degree, how an act can be more stringently required as measured by personal efforts demandable to do it, and yet be dropped in favor of doing an act that is less stringently required by this measure. It may be morally justifiable to require us to make large sacrifices for some types of acts (e.g., minima) but not for others, even though the latter have more important consequences. However, if we are willing to make sacrifices in order to do the act that has the much better consequences, then it is permissible to abandon the more stringently required act (our duty), when either (a) the cost to us of not doing the supererogatory act is greater than we would have to pay to do our duty, or (b) the cost to the world (as opposed to cost to us) of our not doing the supererogatory act is greater than the cost that should be tolerated to enforce the duty. Furthermore, sometimes it is *obligatory* to abandon an act that is more stringently required as measured by the efforts standard in favor of an act less stringently required by the same standard. This is because relative stringency can also be measured by combining acts with the efforts necessary to do them, and it may be more stringently required that we do acts at small cost to ourselves that we need not do at large cost, than that we do acts that (considered by themselves) we must do even at large cost to ourselves. Again, this is connected with the possibility that certain types of acts (roughly, not harming those who are independent of us and not violating contracted positive rights) are requirable at large personal cost whereas others (aiding) that just promote general welfare are requirable only at smaller cost.

The exchange between D and S represents playoffs of one component of objective morality, rights and duties (representing the objective characteristics that make a person an end-in-itself) against another component of objective morality, which is more concerned with welfare considerations and related well-being values, but may also be derived from concern that persons who are ends-in-themselves succeed in pursuing their conceptions of the good. (We have argued in chapters 9 and 10 that it is a mistake to try to derive rights and duties from the personal concern an agent has for his own acts or from the personal concern a victim has for his own fate.) P (and G) represent sources of impositions on the person. This playoff between the personal (P) and each component of objective morality (D and S) may differ. That was the point in arguing (in chapter 10) that a system of constraints is compatible with a system of options (not to promote the greater good).

This explanation of why it is morally permissible to fail to do our duty in order to do the supererogatory act enables us to concede that (a) P, personal preference not to make effort E may permissibly take precedence over super-erogatory act S [proposition (1)] (b) doing supererogatory act S may permissibly take precedence over duty D [proposition (2)], and at the same time accept that (3) P, personal preference not to make effort E, may not permissibly take precedence over doing duty D [proposition (3)]. This will be explicable both in the pairwise and in the complete form (where S ≥ D and duty D is, in fact, dropped). The explanation of the intransitivity of "may permissibly take precedence over" depends on the difference between acts morally requirable at high personal cost and those not so requirable and also on the fact that we are not morally obliged to suffer every loss of objectively valuable consequences for the sake of doing an act stringently required by the efforts standard.

The Objective Worth of Goals

The second question we had to answer was whether the permissibility of intentionally violating a duty as a means of promoting the greater good, and the permissibility of pursuing personal goals instead of the greater good, implied that it might be permissible to intentionally violate a duty to promote one's personal goals. The answer we have just proposed in the previous pages to the first question, whether we may omit to make efforts for duty, also provides possible grounds for answering "no" to this second question, at least at the general level. (As already noted [p. 324], in the specific context where S ≥ D and we drop D, we claim that −[G ≥ S].) That is, it is morally permissible to require that someone sacrifice goals for certain types of acts and not for others, but if we choose, it is sometimes permissible to do what has greater objective worth.

There is, however, an additional point worth making that relates to both intransitivities, but which arises more naturally in considering what means we may use to achieve various goals. It involves focusing on the choice between personal goals and a supererogatory act, rather than on the choice between duty and a supererogatory act. As noted, our justification for believing that people ought to make large efforts or to forego personal goals in order to do their duty may not depend only on how much good results from their doing their duty. For example, we may be justified in expecting greater sacrifices to be made to keep a business promise than to save a life. Likewise the prerogative to avoid inconvenience and pursue one's own goals rather than pursue the greatest good is not based on the claim that our personal interests are objectively more important than the many lives we could save. But the permissibility of abandoning or violating a duty may well depend on the objective importance of what we hope to achieve by doing so.

It seems reasonable to think that the permissibility of supplanting one goal (great good) with another (personal projects), as a general matter, is more likely to lead to the permissibility of violating the same type of duty for either goal, if the goal of personal projects were as important as the goal of greater good for which we may permissibly violate the duty. (I will examine this seemingly reasonable belief further in a later discussion.) So long as the prerogative to choose the personal goal is not based on its being as important as or more important than the goal of greater good, its ability to replace the greater good does not license use of the same means to accomplish it.

One may be misled by thinking that the permissibility of avoiding a personal sacrifice (in complete and in pairwise contexts) or the permissibility of pursuing personal goals rather than saving many lives (in pairwise) is based on the dominance of the personal concerns, in virtue of their greater importance. But neither are they more important, nor do they dominate in the sense that we are morally obliged to pursue personal goals rather than the greater good. We have a choice whether to pursue personal good, not a requirement to pursue it.

In general, even if it is permissible to do x or y, and permissible to use a given means to achieve x, this will not mean that we may use the same means to achieve y. For example: I have a choice between going swimming and hiking. If I go swimming, I have a right to have a key to the pool, but this does not mean that I have a right to the key if I go hiking.

In this case, of course, the key to the pool would not help me to achieve my new goal (hiking). Would the general point hold even if the same means would do me good with either goal? Consider another example: I may do personal chores (personal goal) or go and do volunteer work (greater good). My neighbor will understand if I take his car to do the latter, but not to do my personal chores, though the car would be useful for that purpose too (Neighbor Case). Is my neighbor's position inconsistent? It certainly does not seem to be. Another way of putting this point is that, when P or G may take precedence over S, someone is allowed to decide how to put to use what is his, indeed our allowing that P or G may permissibly take precedence over S *just is* our allowing that certain things are his to control as he wishes, for he may decide how to spend his time and resources. But duties are, in a sense, a part of the world (as is the greater good achievable by S), and while it is permissible to use what is ours, personally to pursue our interests, it is not permissible to take a part of the world that is not ours to pursue our interests.

V

Equal Importance, Intransitivity, and the Principle of Contextual Interaction

I have claimed that the relation between the pursuit of personal goals (G) and avoidance of personal efforts (P) on the one hand and on the other hand, supererogatory acts, is neither a strict dominance relation of the personal over the supererogatory nor based on the greater objective importance of the personal. I have also suggested that it seems reasonable to think that if the pursuit of personal goals were equal in importance to the consequences of supererogatory acts, it would be easier to justify violating a duty to pursue the personal. But I believe it is important for understanding the intransitivities discussed in this chapter to examine further what would be true if, first, the relation between the personal and supererogatory *were* one of dominance, and, second, if the dominance were based on importance.

Suppose that there were a strict dominance relation between personal concerns and supererogation, and between supererogation and duty, in the sense that one was morally required to do the supererogatory act rather than one's duty and to put one's personal concerns ahead of the supererogatory act. To endorse such strict dominance is to take acts with the same content and effect as those currently considered supererogatory and, in part, forbid our doing them at large personal cost. This gives one a duty to pursue significant personal concerns, care for oneself or other projects important to one, rather than to do acts formerly beyond the call of duty. It also takes acts with the same content and effect as those currently considered supererogatory, and requires that they be done rather than a duty. This requirement turns the act currently considered supererogatory into a duty in some cases. (To be consistent with the prohibition on sacrificing one's projects, a "supererogatory" act could involve no large sacrifice of one's interest—it could be, say, an act of mercy.)

My claim is that even such a dominance relation would not imply that it was permissible to violate one's duty for the sake of personal concerns. (Recall that violating a duty to achieve a goal is somewhat different from not performing a duty because the effort to do it is so large. These accord with the second and first types of intransitivity, respectively. We are concerned with both in their pairwise form, and the first type in its complete form as well.) This is so even though it seems like a straightforward requirement of transitivity that personal concerns dominate duty. This means that "ought to do — — — rather than . . . " and "obliged to do — — — rather than . . . " at least give the appearance of being intransitive relations. If we let S* stand for the content of the act currently thought to be supererogatory, and > for dominates, one intransitivity we will be investigating is how P > S*, S* > D, and yet D > P. One explanation for this intransitivity is that there could be different reasons for each of the dominance relations.[28] The following is an analysis of how this could happen, in keeping with the explanation given in earlier sections for the intransitivity between P, S, and D, when ≥ stood for "may take precedence over." S* could dominate D because it produces very much better consequences, P could dominate S* because of the value of someone devoting himself to self-realization in comparison to the value of some better overall consequences, and D could dominate P because of the greater importance of accomplishing certain minimum requirements in comparison to the value of devotion to self-realization. The way in which we accounted for our original intransitivity (in Part IV) also involved pointing to different factors that accounted for the "may take precedence" relation between D and S, and between D and P. S may take precedence over D because of its greater objective importance. P may not take precedence over D because minima require big efforts or losses, but P may take precedence over S, because all objective good cannot force large efforts or losses. But it is also true that if the factors that made S ≥ D and −(P ≥ D) were the same, it is still possible that P ≥ S because of the particular relationship between those two factors.

The following is a somewhat different analysis of how strict dominance is compatible with intransitivity when duties involve personal *commitments*. S* could dominate D for one reason (much better overall consequences), P could dominate S* for a second reason (greater value of devotion to self-realization), and it could be that neither these reasons nor others lead to the dominance of P over D, because, for example, self-realization may not take precedence over keeping commitments that the self has voluntarily undertaken. In this second analysis what is emphasized is how, in the case of duty, one aspect of the self (its voluntary commitments) overrides another aspect of the self (its interests and potentials). It might be overall destructive to the self for its commitments to be sacrificed to its concerns and interests. The commitment aspect of the self, however, may be sacrificed to overall good without this damaging the internal relations between aspects of the self. Likewise, not doing supererogatory good when there has been no personal commitment to do it would not create a conflict between aspects of the self.

The possibility that there are different reasons for each of the dominance relations contrasts with the view that there is a single scale, for example, production of happiness, according to which we decide about each dominance relation.

Suppose we now describe the dominance relation explicitly in terms of one characteristic, importance: We must do S* instead of D since it is more important; we must do P rather than S* because it is more important. Still, it may be that D is more important than P. I believe the following way of explaining this intransitivity (with the help of the following diagram) is especially illuminating for understanding duty. Where > means "dominates," S* > D > P > S*.

The diagram emphasizes the special relationship holding between my duty and my personal concerns, how tightly they can be bound together in a dominance relation, while individually duty and personal concerns go their separate ways, so to speak, with respect to S*. It might be that the goal of devoting oneself to one's development is morally more important than S* at the pairwise level (or avoiding excessive personal efforts is morally more important at complete and pairwise levels). On the other hand the content of personal duties might make them unimportant morally in comparison with S* (e.g., great good of the world). Indeed, D might be sacrificed to S* on a strict utilitarian calculation. Yet the unimportant personal duty could make claims on me that override my personal concerns, self-development, or efforts. In virtue of its being my duty, something whose content is in itself not very important (D)—and it is its content alone that might be compared to S*—could "humble" something that is in itself very important (P). What is noteworthy is that D never be subordinated to P, whatever else it is subordinated to, and whatever else P subordinates.

An analogy may help to understand this point. It might be part of a theory of royalty that a king must never sacrifice his personal interests for the greater good of his country; he must be its single venerated subject. He may, however, have to fail in his duties to his parent and even sacrifice the parent for the greater good of his country. This goes further than our analysis of the "puzzles" allowed; i.e., there could be direct sacrifice of the parent to the greater good. The king may not care about his parent much; so her fate is not even among his personal concerns. Yet it may be absolutely wrong for him to sacrifice his parent to his own interests, in virtue of the special relationship between them. Suppose there were no prohibition on his being sacrificed to the greater good of the state when it is not his goal to do so. Then if he had to subordinate his own welfare to his parent's but not subordinate the interests of the state to her interests, he could be required to make the sacrifice-for-her of sacrificing himself rather then her to the state. But the state could not dominate his importance in any other unmediated way (Royalty Case).

In the same way D could dominate P though P dominates S* and S* dominates D. Likewise, if there were two duties, D_1 and D_2, it would be possible for $P > D_1$, $D_1 > D_2$, and yet $D_2 > P$, in virtue of the special relation between D_2 and P. There could be three duties, D_1, D_2, and D_3, and $D_1 > D_2$, $D_2 > D_3$, and yet $D_3 > D_1$ (the Dominating Duties Case). The following illustrates this. Suppose we have duties to give to charities A, B, and C. In conflicts, it may be that we are required to give to A rather than to B because it does better work and to B rather than to C because it does better work, but required to give to C rather than A, since A is the offspring of C, and it would be wrong to prefer the offspring to the parent, even when the offspring does better work (the Charities Case).

If P does not dominate S, but it is permissible for us to choose between P and S, the same strong prohibition on sacrificing D to P can hold, regardless of what else it is permissible to sacrifice D to and what else it is permissible to sacrifice to P.

The discussion of these analogies helps make clear that the intransitivity we have been examining is another example of the Principle of Contextual Interaction: A factor (P or D or S) behaves differently, unexpectedly, in one context from what one would expect given its behavior in other contexts. This helps us understand further the claim that the intransitivities are due to differ-

ent factors being responsible for dominance. This does not merely mean that
if A > B and B > C by virtue of different factors then we should not expect
A > C. Even if A > B and B > C by virtue of the same factor it may be that
−(A > C) because of a new factor that arises in their particular relationship.
(This is implied by the Charities Case.)[29]

Insular and Noninsular: Measure of a Duty's Strength

In an earlier discussion (p. 335), I claimed that a strict utilitarian overriding of
duty by the "good for the world" outcome is incorrect. I also suggested that,
consistent with the truth of the intransitivity I am describing, the personal efforts
(P) that duty may demand might be an indication of duty's significance *even
relative to the supererogatory good*: The more D dominates P, the harder it is for
S* to dominate D. I have now suggested that it is theoretically possible that the
relationship between D and P is between them alone, so to speak, and the efforts
demandable by D are no indication at all of the worth of its being done rather
than S*. The former is a *non-insular* understanding of D > P, the latter the
insular understanding of D > P. Insofar as D represents the component of morality that is concerned with respect between individual persons, and S represents
their greater good in the sense of individual happiness or development, *and* the
degree of personal sacrifice to D is a measure of the importance of duty even
relative to S (the non-insular understanding of D > P), then D could not be
truly insignificant relative to S. (That is, it might be insignificant in terms of the
promotion of good, but significant insofar as it is part of the respect-owed-
persons component of morality.)

Truly supererogatory acts, of course, do not fit neatly into the greater
good rather than the respect component of morality. Although their non-
performance will not exhibit lack of respect, their performance might be for
the sake of preventing disrespectful acts by others or one's own disrespectful
acts on other occasions. A conflict between a duty and a supererogatory act
concerned with respect might arise in the following case: Suppose a minor
obligation we had to meet in order to show respect weighed more than supererogatorily preventing others from violating more serious duties. Here, too, not
violating the duty may have superior weight within a system concerned with
respectful acts. Sometimes violating a duty—even one that is capable of demanding very little personal cost—to promote some aspect of the respect
system (whether by supererogatory effort or otherwise) simply makes no
sense, as when we are asked to violate a duty for the sake of preventing more
violations (other people's or our own) of the *same* type of duty (as discussed
in chapter 10).

The Less Important Supererogatory

What the discussion of cases of strict dominance has shown, in addition to the
explanation of intransitivities already given, is that sometimes it is permissible
for us to neglect our duty for the sake of supererogation, even though the
objective value of what will be lost if we omit the supererogatory is *not* greater
than the ordinary cost that can be required for doing our duty. In such cases,

objectively speaking, we lose more with the sacrifice of P to D than we would with the sacrifice of S to D. For example, in our Royalty Case, the state is worth less than the king, and yet the king is sacrificed to his parent, but the state cannot be. Any attempt to treat the cost of sacrificing P to D *as part of* the cost of sacrificing a greater good(s) to D, however, is excluded where the sacrifice of P is required by D. We must ignore the objective value of P, just as we ignored it in permitting $P \geq S$ though for different reasons, even though we weigh D and S on a scale of objective importance. We must focus on the special relationship induced by D onto P.

Intransitivity and Cycling

If there is an intransitive relation there may be cycling, that is, an endless movement from one option to another without a resting place. For example, if $P > S^*$, $S^* > D$, and $D > P$ and we are just engaging in pairwise comparisons, if we stop with D, we should then prefer S^* to D, but then move to P rather than S^*, and on and on. Or consider the Dinner Case, in which someone prefers steak to lobster, lobster to halibut, but halibut to steak. If three restaurants offer only the three different pairs of options, and this person must choose where to eat, he will circle around all night. For if he decides on the first restaurant, he should instead choose the third, but then he should go to the second, from whence he should go to the first, and so on endlessly.

But if there is cycling among pairwise comparisons in our cases, this does not imply that when all three options are presented together there will be cycling. We may always be able to find a resting point when there is a three-way comparison because one of the factors that accounts for the dominance of one item over another has lexical superiority over the factors that account for dominance relations between other items. For example, suppose a single restaurant that already serves steak and lobster adds halibut to its menu. If and only if it carries both lobster and halibut this may be a good sign that its lobster is really excellent and hence to be preferred to steak. Then $L > H$, $H > S$, and $L > S$. One should choose lobster.[30] In the complete case, where G, D, and S are all present, we can stop with S. In the complete case where P, D, and S are all present, we must stay with D (done at P), if P is necessary to achieve S but we are unwilling to do P for S. If there is some chance of achieving S without doing P, then we can try to achieve S.

In the Charities Case, though we would pick C1 over C2 and C2 over C3 if presented with the pairwise comparisons separately, it seems we must choose C2 when all three are presented as options. We can reach this conclusion if we interpret $C3 > C1$ as implying that C1 must never be selected when C3 *could* have been selected, and C3 is worse than C2. (However, $C3 > C1$ is ambiguous; it may only imply that C1 should never get a donation when C3 *would* get it instead, and C3 won't have it instead if C2 has it. If we further follow what was done in the Loved One and Royalty Cases, we might distinguish between selecting C1 directly over C3 and selecting C1 over C3 *indirectly*, because C2 is chosen and C1 dominates it. If this were a possible course of action, we would not then have to move on to favoring C3 over C1 if we chose C1 over

C2 and C2 over C3. This is because the reason for preferring C3 over C1 would not be present when C1 is chosen *indirectly* over C3. Whichever interpretation of "C3 > C1" we pick — and we must pick one to avoid equivocation — we find a resting pont.)

Notice that in the Dinner and Charities Cases, when all options are present, if we settle with lobster and C2, it will not be unreasonable to violate Arrow's Principle of the Independence of Irrelevant Alternatives. For when halibut is added to the menu at a formerly steak-and-lobster restaurant, though one does not choose halibut — in that sense, its addition is irrelevant — its availability makes me choose lobster. This is because it is not truly irrelevant, serving as it does as an indication that the lobster is truly excellent. Similarly, in the Charities Case, the addition of C3 to a field including only C1 and C2, does not make us choose C3, though it may change our choice from C1 to C2.[31]

I conclude that the fact that it is sometimes permissible to violate a duty in order to do overall good, and sometimes permissible to act for personal concerns rather than for overall good, does not show that it is permissible to violate a duty for personal concerns, and also that the fact that we need not make large efforts to pursue overall good, but are permitted to pursue overall good instead of duty, does not show that we need not make large efforts for the sake of duty. Furthermore, just because we are required to do A rather than B, and B rather than C, does not mean we must do A rather than C. We can say either that "may take precedence over" and "required rather than" are intransitive or that there is only apparent intransitivity (hence no cycling in a complete case), because the phenomena occur when different factors are responsible for the precedence relations between different items.

Let me emphasize that I have been concerned to argue that we cannot conclude that we may permissibly abandon duty for our personal interests merely as the conclusion of a transitivity argument. There are cases where transitivity is shown to fail because we are required to make efforts for duty's sake even though we need not and would not make the same efforts to bring about a great good, and the great good can trump the duty. Nevertheless, all this is consistent with the possibility that sometimes a morally decent person could fail to do his duty for personal reasons.

Dutiful Person's Intransitivity

Notice that the seeming intransitivities I have emphasized in this chapter depend on accepting the claim that supererogatory acts may sometimes permissibly take precedence over duties. But it is interesting to observe that those who do not accept this claim may get involved in an intransitivity of their own, at least when they also accept the view that one may sometimes make greater personal sacrifices in order to do a supererogatory act than one is required or willing to make to do one's duty. (We might refer to this as the Dutiful Person's Intransitivity.)

Suppose someone never fails to do his duty in order to do a supererogatory act, because he thinks it would be wrong to do so, and makes all efforts that are strictly required of him, but not more, in order to do his duty. Suppose this person also does a supererogatory act at great personal sacrifice when it does not interfere with duty. The question arises, If he is willing to make this great sacrifice to perform a beneficent act, why is it that consistency does not also require him to be willing to make the same sacrifice if it will help him to perform a duty that he thinks takes precedence over supererogation? Another question is, If one *is willing* to do more for S than D, how is it that $-(S \geq D)$? [The intransitivity discussed in the body of this chapter involved the different question: If one is morally obliged (as well as willing) to do more for D than for S, why is it that $S \geq D$?] A specific example: Someone will not leave work at his office to save a life, but he will not give up his life to finish his work at the office. In his spare time, he will cheerfully give up his life to save a life (the Office Boy Case). If he considers his office work more important than saving a life and if he will give up his life to save a life why won't he give up his life to do his office work?

Accepting the view that there is an inconsistency in the dutiful person's position would imply that one could not consistently do all that is generally required of one to do one's duty, as well as forego a supererogatory act, and then devote even greater energies to doing non-obligatory beneficent acts, at least not if making these greater efforts could help one succeed in doing one's duty. Can one consistently think that doing the duty is worth omitting the supererogatory, but that the supererogatory is worth more effort than the duty?

I believe the dutiful person's position is not inconsistent, and so we cannot undermine his commitment to duty over supererogation by charging him with inconsistency. (I also believe that this may be the position Kant would take on these matters.) At minimum we can say that once one has given duty what is owed it, one may do what one likes, without this implying that duty is owed more. But we can go beyond this (which suggests only that doing the supererogatory may be an object of free choice), and say that the supererogatory act is *worth* doing more for than is the duty, yet it is wrong to substitute the supererogatory for the duty. Duty may represent constraints that should never be overridden for a better state of affairs, and yet it would be foolish to think that individuals should sacrifice personally more than a certain amount to see that they are fulfilled. The important thing is to subordinate better states of affairs to duties; we do not allow *better states* to be the reason for failing the duties. But when it comes to the degree of personal effort that each is *worth* eliciting from *individuals*, the better state of affairs may take precedence. (This does not mean it is permissible to *require* efforts it could be personally worthwhile to make.) The factor that makes a duty take precedence over supererogation is different from the factor that makes it be worth while to make great personal sacrifices.[32]

VI

Modified Hybrid Theory

The results of this chapter, I believe, have implications for other important theoretical problems. One, which has already been mentioned in chapter 8, is

Samuel Scheffler's problem in explaining why in his hybrid theory it is permissible to kill to promote the greater good, but not to promote our own nonoptimific projects, even when such projects may take precedence over the greater good. (If we think of a person pursuing a project, she might kill as a means to or in the course of doing something to achieve her project. Alternatively, we can think of our personal concerns leading us to omit efforts to avoid an act that will kill.) The problem might be solved for Scheffler if he could motivate a moral distinction between different reasons for harming, so that there could be a constraint on harming for personal concerns, but no such a constraint on pursuing the greatest objective good. This is the basis for what Scheffler called a *modified* hybrid view. Essentially, the explanation I offer follows the form of argument presented earlier in this chapter.[33] I offer it only as a suggestion for someone who rejects constraints on harming for the greater good. Since I have argued for constraints on harming for the sake of greater good, I do not accept the modified hybrid theory as correct.

One needs some sort of account (call it X) of why a no-harm constraint ever matters — this is the basic issue Scheffler worries about. But suppose we had this account, and even suppose a consequentialist account were correct. Then, where " $\geq$ " means "may take precedence over" the formula is

(1) Prerogative $\geq$ GG (greatest good)

(2) GG $\geq$ No harm

(3) $-$(Prerogative $\geq$ No harm)

This intransitivity can occur, in part, because the personal point of view which motivates the prerogative (according to Scheffler) does not strictly dominate the GG in terms of objective importance. As Scheffler emphasizes, I do not have to be more important than the greater good to be entitled to exercise the prerogative. So the prerogative does not take precedence over that which may override the no-harm constraint in virtue of its importance [like the GG, assuming we accept (2)]. The factor (objective importance) that makes it permissible for the GG to take precedence over the no-harm constraint is not the factor that makes it permissible for the prerogative to take precedence over the GG. Therefore, there is no surprise in saying that No harm takes precedence over the prerogative. (It may take something of more importance to dominate that constraint.)

However, it can still be asked *why* it is that whatever makes it permissible for the prerogative to take precedence over the GG does not also make it permissible for the prerogative to take precedence over No harm. That is, it is one thing to isolate two properties (call them I(importance) and P(personal)) and say that precedence is in virtue of different properties in different steps, i.e., in virtue of P in (1), and in virtue of I(importance) in (2) and (3), but it is another thing to explain why, when I is present in both No harm and GG (though perhaps in a different way or degree), P may not take precedence over I *in both*, not just in GG.

Again, one way of answering this that has been explored earlier in this chapter is that if we understand the GG as the best, and the no-harm restriction as the minimum required of us, then we may be relieved of doing the best in order to exercise the prerogative and be relieved of the minimum if we do something better than it (on analogy of being relieved of ordinary school requirements if we write great poetry), yet still the objective minimum (e.g., No harm) may restrict the prerogative. This analysis (or something like it) should allow for a *modified* hybrid view, which escapes the problem of no restrictions on a prerogative if the greater good can overcome the restriction. Therefore, options and constraints are compatible, even if there are constraints only on personal projects and not on optimific ones.[34]

Final Words

In thinking about what has been said in this volume (and also in volume I of *Morality, Mortality*), it is possible to detect, I believe, a certain non-naturalistic spirit to the views presented. For example, we have emphasized entitlements generated independently of personal concerns of human beings in grounding a prerogative to control certain things (perhaps in the light of personal concerns). The entitlements played a big role in explaining restrictions as well as prerogatives. We have likewise highlighted the way in which it can be rational to act contrary to what one cares about most.

It has been said that "if considerations of what I may do, and the correlative claims of my victim against me, can outweigh the substantial impersonal value of what will happen that can only be because the perspective of the agent has an importance in practical reasoning that resists domination by a conception of the world as a place where good and bad things happen whose value is perspective free."[35] I have argued that there is a significant alternative to this view. I have rejected the primacy of views about personal perspectives and relations underlying a constraint by seeing the constraint as a way of expressing the view that persons' characteristics make them each inviolable in a certain way. An agent's own victim is special only in that he is the one whose constraining right the agent comes up against. The agent's own act is special only in that it makes him come up against the constraining right. This makes the constraint victim- rather than agent-focused and related to an agent-neutral value.

A strong role for the concerns generated by a personal point of view arose only when we presented arguments against taking an objective, aggregative view in deciding whom to aid when aiding one person rather than another would provide us with small additional utility. We said (in volume I) that the importance from the personal point of view of each potential victim that he not lose his equal chance to be helped was the basis for not deciding between them on the basis of the small additional utility.

A further example of the non-naturalistic spirit of these discussions is the concern for the status of persons, where this is contrasted with concern for what happens (in the flesh-and-blood) to persons. (A somewhat similar attraction to an abstract benefit is exhibited in the discussion of why death is bad, in volume I, where we presented the case of the Limbo Man. This is someone who prefers that it be true that his life is not over yet for as long as possible, even if extending his life does not add any more goods of life to the total that will happen to him as conscious or active being.) A final example of non-naturalism is the refusal to allow the weightiness of a loss to determine, by itself, that a person is not morally required to suffer the loss. Whether she has to suffer the loss depends on what the loss is to be suffered for, to save a life or to avoid taking a life, for example.

I do not take this non-naturalism to be a flaw; it may be a mistake to try to naturalize morality. [36]

NOTES

1. These two tests for stringency also can be used to distinguish stringency of rights (i.e., how much effort must be made to avoid violating a right versus whether one right may be overridden by another). The issues in this chapter first arose for me when I was considering tests to measure the relative stringency of positive and negative duties (discussed in chapter 4), since it seemed that acts less stringently required by an efforts standard (acts to aid) could take precedence by the override standard. A further question is whether the stringency of rights is a function only of how serious the effect of infringing the right could be. (We have considered this issue in discussing Thomson's views, pp. 122–124.)

2. I here assume that it is better to save the greater number (at minimum, when other things are equal). This is controversial, and I try to argue for the view in *Morality, Mortality*, Vol. 1 (New York: Oxford University Press, 1993).

3. The view that there is such a system of priorities is held by R. M. Hare, *Moral Thinking* (New York: Oxford University Press, 1981); David Heyd, *Supererogation* (New York: Cambridge University Press, 1982); and David A. J. Richards, *A Theory of Reasons for Action* (New York: Oxford University Press, 1971), among others.

4. However, if he put himself in a position where he faces a threat of death *because he relied on my promise*, it may no longer be permissible for me to save the thousand instead.

5. As discussed by, for example, Judith Thomson in "Self-Defense and Rights," *The Lindley Lecture* (Lawrence: University of Kansas, 1976). Thomas Scanlon suggests specified duties.

6. Amartya Sen made this point.

7. This point was suggested by Isaac Levi and Susan Wolf.

8. We have criticized (pp. 122–124) Judith Thomson's view that the stringency of a right (and its correlative duty) is a function of how badly off someone will be if we do not respect his right (essentially because it equates the stringency of not killing and not letting die). Her idea also fails to explain why efforts requirable to respect a right could be great and yet some other right or duty, less stringent by the efforts test, could take precedence.

9. In "The Problem of Abortion and the Doctrine of Double Effect," reprinted in Bonnie Steinbock, ed., *Killing and Letting Die* (Englewood Cliffs, N.J.: Prentice-Hall, 1980).

10. One of those who has emphasized this objection is Derek Parfit.

11. In his *The Rejection of Consequentialism* (Oxford: Oxford University Press, 1982).

12. I remind the reader that when discussing Scheffler's view in chapter 8, I noted that I believed that the best description of the contrast he had in mind was between the partial (or personal) and impartial view, since impersonal might imply disregard for the separateness of persons. Theories like utilitarianism add pleasures and pains without taking account of their distribution among individual lives, except insofar as there is diminishing marginal utility. Impartiality between persons does not do this. In this chapter I use "impartial" (as I did in *Morality, Mortality Vol. I*). Both impersonal and impartial views are parts of the objective point of view.

13. It was also noted in chapter 8 that even if the assumption of *transitivity*, on which this argument is based, is wrong, Scheffler's views may still lead to the same conclusion. This is because Scheffler rejects a moral distinction between harming and not aiding. The absence of such a distinction, combined with the permissibility of not suffering large losses in order to aid, would imply the permissibility of killing rather than suffer large losses. For example, if I may carry on my work rather than save a life, I might be permitted to run over someone as a side effect of doing something, not the result of a prior intention, that I will do voluntarily while I work, rather than give up my work. (Actually, if S represents aiding and if D is not killing, this is another way of considering why, if $P \geq S$, it is not also true that $P \geq D$. This, in turn, is the question why we have to do more to avoid killing than to avoid letting die.) The intransitivity we examine also bears on the question of whether it is rational to disobey moral requirements, a question Scheffler discusses in *Human Morality* (New York: Oxford University Press, 1992). It seems to present an argument *internal to morality* that self interest may permissibly take precedence over moral requirements. See "Reason and Morality," my discussion of Scheffler's book to appear in *NOUS* (1995).

14. I made a similar point earlier (in chapter 8) about the justification of prerogatives whether to act from personal or impartial point of view, rather than the justification of a requirement to act from the personal point of view.

15. This explanation is similar to the view that our general duty is to do some particular duty or a supererogatory act. A variation of the third explanation would insist that we may allow some people to fail to do the minimum and do the supererogatory act instead, so long as most people do the minimum.

16. Derek Parfit made this suggestion.

17. In "Above and Below the Line of Duty," *Philosophical Topics* 14(2) (Fall 1986: 131–145).

18. In chapter 10 we considered the possibility that the world is a better place if there are ends-in-themselves in it. This is definitely a *nonstandard* greater good.

19. This is the distinction between killing/letting die and harming/not aiding appearing again.

20. With all due respect to Harry Frankfurt's *The Importance of What We Care About* (Cambridge: Cambridge University Press, 1988).

21. Made to me by Thomas Nagel.

22. Perhaps also the cost to me if *I* am not the one to save them, when they could be saved by others. I shall ignore this possible cost.

23. I allow myself to speak about someone's caring about his duty and (later) about his caring about the state of affairs his doing his duty would bring about. Yet I do not thereby intend to blur the distinction between P (or G) and D. That is, P and G may involve things one cares about besides oneself, including duties. This does not mean that we cannot distinguish in a particular example between a duty one cares about (or the state that doing the duty would bring about) and other concerns designated by "P." But the fact that doing one's duty can be part of one's P does suggest that the seeming

intransitivity we are investigating has a form independent of D. That is, we might be *obliged* to lose P′ for the the sake of P″, i.e., (P″ > P′), not losing P′ may take precedence over S, (P′ ≥ S), and yet S may take precedence over P″ (S ≥ P″).

24. See Derek Parfit's "Innumerate Ethics," in *Philosophy & Public Affairs* 7(4) (Summer 1978: 285–301).

25. This is one reason why the egoists's argument (cf. e.g., Ayn Rand) that one gives up one's life to save someone only out of self-interest, to avoid the misery of one's life if he should die, indeed to avoid dying after he dies, is wrong. Most people who try to save their loved ones with their own lives and fail do not commit suicide, as they should if life becomes so continually miserable.

26. The permission to give extra weight to my preferences when it is a question of distributing what is mine to control and is of significance to me (e.g., my medicine) also comes into play here. If the resource does not belong to me, but is, for example, public, I might as easily place myself as my loved one on the impartial scale, to be weighed against the strangers, and send the resource to them.

27. I owe this point to Shelly Kagan.

28. I first suggested this explanation of intransitivities in 1985 in "Supererogation and Obligation." Larry Temkin subsequently made the same suggestion in "Intransitivity and the Mere Addition Paradox," *Philosophy & Public Affairs* 16(2) (Spring 1987): 138–187.

29. We will illustrate this point further below by considering how "overall better than" can yield intransitivities (pp. 351).

30. I owe this case to Steven Munzer.

31. A humorous example of the seeming illogicality of violating Arrow's Principle is the joke attributed to Sidney Morgenhesser. Waiter: "You can have your sandwich on white or rye. Patron: "I'll have white." Waiter: "I forgot, you can also have whole wheat." Patron: "In that case, I'll have rye."

32. After the article on which this chapter is based was written, Derek Parfit suggested to me that there is a connection between my claims that "may take precedence over," "dominates," and "is more important than" are seemingly not transitive, on the one hand, and, on the other hand, the claim made by Ronald Dworkin and Amartya Sen that the relation "worse than" is not transitive and allows for only partial comparability. Parfit discusses this Dworkin-Sen claim in *Reasons and Persons* (New York: Oxford, 1985), pp. 430–432. But note that the aims of those who use intransitivity to prove only partial comparability of items may be defeated by the analysis of intransitivity I have offered. That is, partial comparability involves at least a certain degree of incommensurability. (Complete incommensurability claims that A is not better than, worse than, or equal to B.) Joseph Raz, for example, has argued that if A > B, B > C, but −(A > C), this intransitivity must be due to the fact that A and B, or B and C, are not really comparable in the "better than relation." Hence, they are only partially comparable or totally incommensurable. I have offered a different explanation of intransitivity that does not depend on total or partial incommensurability; that is, contrary to Raz, we cannot argue from intransitivity to incommensurability. This is because the intransitivity is accounted for by a different factor appearing when A and C are compared that is absent when A and B, and B and C, are compared.

33. I first presented this proposed solution to Scheffler in conversation, March 1988.

34. A second theoretical problem to which the results of this chapter apply is the important one Derek Parfit raises, the problem of the Repugnant Conclusion. (In

Reasons and Persons (Oxford University Press, 1985).) Since this problem does not strictly deal with the structure of nonconsequentialism, I discuss it in a footnote.

Imagine a state of the world (real or even hypothetical) in which some people are very well off (A). Now imagine a second state (A+) in which these same people are just as well off but some others have lives worth living that are not as good as the lives of the first group. This state of affairs is not the result of any injustice and the second group lives at a distance so that it is impossible to make them better off. A third state (B) involves equality between the two groups at a lower level than that which the first group was originally imagined to occupy. Parfit argues that A+ is at least no worse than A (if not actually better), and B is better than A+. This implies, by transitivity, that B is better than A. But is it? Would we not think that a world with fewer (but enough) people living at a higher quality of life was better than one with more people living at a lower level?

Furthermore, Parfit argues, we can repeat this type of argument for the group of people in B so that we are driven to the conclusion that a yet larger population living at a yet lower level of quality of life is even better. This eventually leads us to what he calls the Repugnant Conclusion, that a vast population with people living lives just barely worth living is better than a smaller population having a high quality of life.

Parfit suggests that the solution to this problem is perfectionist, i.e., to emphasize that the things of great quality in human life will be lost when population increases, so that a larger population with a life without goods of great quality is worse than A for this reason; it may even be worse than A+, if A+ has quality items and B does not.

But there is an alternative explanation which makes it possible to accept the premises that (1) A+ is no worse (even better) than A; (2) B is better than A+, and also the conclusion (3) B is worse than A. That is, we can explain why the seeming intransitivity is acceptable, why "better than" and "no worse than" understandably may be intransitive. (Larry Temkin argues for this view in detail in "Intransitivity and the Mere Addition Paradox," *Philosophy & Public Affairs* 16(2) (Spring 1987): 138–187)

To explain the intransitivity in the argument for the Repugnant Conclusion, we should divide Parfit's case into two different versions. In one version the very people who are in A also exist in A+ and B. In another version there is no identity between any parts of the population in A, A+, and B. In this version it is clear that we can evaluate each state independently of assuming any of the other states actually existed.

As in explaining the intransitivity of "may take precedence over," or "required to choose," we focus on the different properties which explain the "no worse than" or "better than" relation in the first version: (1) A+ is no worse than and even better than A because it would be no worse for anyone who is in A and it has some additional good lives (a *utility consideration*); it does introduce inequality but even if this is a negative factor it does not weigh more than the additional good lives; (2) B is better than A+ because it helps the worse off (a morally compelling "rightness" reason for moving from A+ to B). However, it has the negative feature that it does this by making some people who (would have) existed in A+ worse off than they were. This negative can be outweighed by the factor of make the worse off better off, to make B *all things considered* better than A+. But B is not better than A is, indeed, it is worse all things considered because (a) it is worse for those who existed in A, and (b) unlike what is true of B relative to A+, no better for anyone. This is because the extra group of people who exist in A+ and for whose sake the move to B is undertaken would not exist in A. Put another way, B represents a worse state of life for the population with which we began in A, and the loss to them can not be compensated for by bringing into existence additional people who live at an equally low level with them. A+ is no worse than (and perhaps an improvement over) A since utility of more people overrides inequality, B is better than A+ since improving the worse off who already exist overrides a decrease in quality of life for some, but B is not better than A in terms of helping the worse off since in A (unlike A+) there were not people whose quality of life was worse and it is not overridingly better than A in terms of utility because the additional utility in B over that in A is not worth the loss to those in A of high quality of life.

Notice that we have described the negative factor in comparing B with A not as "the loss of high quality of life" but as "the loss to some people of a high quality of life." For A would also be preferable to B+ which I imagine to be like B except that there is an additional group of people (different from those in A) who live at an even higher level than those in A. B+ shows that Parfit's perfectionist solution is not neccesary in the first version of the argument, since we need not lose high quality of life in order for the intransitivity to arise.

Laying things out in steps: A+ > A because utility (U) > equality (E) when there is no large loss to already existent people (L); B > A+ because improving the worse off (W) > large loss to already existent people (L); −(B > A) because loss to already existent people (L) > utility (U) and W is not an issue. In other words, U > E where there is no L, W > L, and −(U > L) or L > U. Because U > E only when there is no L, and W > L, there is no reason to think that U > L when W (and producing E) are not issues. It is because B > A+ *overall* but not on every dimension [i.e., it is worse from the point of view of a loss to some who would already exist (L) and better in virtue of W], that the way in which B is worse makes it *overall* worse when the factor (W) is no longer present.

What about the second version of the argument? Here we compare A, A+, B (and B+ which I have added) as possible states of the world with no overlapping populations. A+ is still no worse (and maybe better) than A, if utility takes precedence over equality in this context. B is better than A+ overall since its worse off group is better off than the one in A+. This dominates a negative factor, that we lose the existence of a higher quality of life. Notice that this negative factor is different from the factor emphasized in the first version of the argument, namely that the population of A suffers a loss. This is not true in this second version of the argument. B is still not better than A, however, since the extra utility does not compensate for the loss of a high quality of life, and A is even better than B with respect to the status of its differentially worst off members, that is, it has none. Therefore, the negative factor (loss of high quality) that was trumped in B relative to A+ here remains undominated. But B+ in this version of the argument, by contrast to the first version, comes out no worse than and perhaps better than A; since it is merely a version of A+ whose worse off group includes more people at a higher level of well-being than the worse off group in A+.

I have argued that it is quite understandable that there is an intransitivity in Parfit's argument which lets us reject the Repugnant Conclusion, given that the "better than" or "no worse than" relations are based on different factors between A and A+ and between A+ and B. But what we have also argued for in this chapter implies that it is even (theoretically) possible for the relation between A and A+ and between A+ and B to depend on the *same factors* and yet B be worse than A, because some special interaction effect appears in the relation between A and B in particular which makes the latter worse than the former.

Another approach to solving these problems is worth exploring. We might be tempted to say that A+ is only *intrinsically* better than A. That is, if no further changes could occur after reaching A +, it would be better to move from A to A +. Yet, in a sense, A + is "instrumentally" worse than A, because once we reach A + an effect of this — though only via our acting on moral principles and if it is physically possible — is that we move to B. Hence we say, in effect, that *A + is instrumentally worse* than A. Thus, even though B is intrinsically better than A +, it cannot be concluded that it is better than A *because* it is in this way better than A +, since A + is not instrumentally better than A.

One problem with this analysis is that in comparing A with A + we consider intrinsic *and* instrumental features, but in comparing B with A + we focus only on intrinsic features, and so we may be accused of equivocation when we say that A + is worse than A though B is better than A +. But the most significant problem with this analysis is that if we say A + is instrumentally worse than A we must mean that it leads to a worse state of affairs, and how can it do so if it leads to B which is agreed to be *intrinsically better* than A +? To show how B is worse, we must move to the first argument against the Repugnant Conclusion anyway (i.e., show how B is worse relative to A).

35. Thomas Nagel, *The View From Nowhere* New York: Oxford University Press, 1986.

36. At this point, I would have liked to have directed the reader to the final fourth section of this book, in which we "applied" theoretical results to the problem of creating people and aborting them. What was originally a section of this book (and the two-volume work of which this book is a part) was, however, split off as a separate book, *Creation and Abortion* (New York: Oxford University Press, 1992). I invite readers who are interested in the "application" of theory, and the topic, to read that book.

BIBLIOGRAPHY

Anderson, Elizabeth. *Value in Ethics and Economics*. Cambridge, Mass: Harvard U. Press, 1993.

Bennett, Jonathan. "Morality and Consequences." *The Tanner Lectures on Human Values*, Vol. 2. Salt Lake City: University of Utah Press, 1981.

Boorse, Christopher, and Sorensen, Roy A. "Ducking Harm." *The Journal of Philosophy* 115(3) (1988): 115–134.

Boyle, J. "Who Is Entitled to Double Effect?" *The Journal of Medicine and Philosophy* 16 (1991): 475–94.

Costa, Michael. "Another Trip on the Trolley." In *Ethics: Problems and Principles*, edited by J. M. Fischer and Mark Ravizza. New York: Harcourt Brace Jovanovich, 1992.

——"The Trolley Problem Revisited." In *Ethics: Problems and Principles*, edited by J. M. Fischer and Mark Ravizza. New York: Harcourt Brace Jovanovich, 1992.

Dinello, Daniel. "On Killing and Letting Die." In *Killing and Letting Die*, edited by Bonnie Steinbock. Englewood Cliffs, N.J.: Prentice-Hall, 1979.

Donagan, A. "Moral Absolutism and the Double-Effect Exception: Reflections on Joseph Boyle's 'Who is Entitled to Double Effect?'" *The Journal of Medicine and Philosophy* 16 (1991): 495–509.

Feinberg, Joel. *Harm to Others*. Oxford: Oxford University Press, 1984.

——"Voluntary Euthanasia and the Inalienable Right to Life." *Philosophy & Public Affairs* 7(2) (Winter 1978): 93–123.

Fletcher, George. "Fairness and Utility in Tort Theory." 85 *Harvard Law Review* 537 (1972).

Foot, Philippa. "Euthanasia." *Philosophy & Public Affairs* 6(2) (Winter 1977): 85–112.

——"Killing and Letting Die," in *Abortion: Moral and Legal Perspectives*, edited by Jay Garfield and Patricia Hennessy. 1984 p. 182.

——"The Problem of Abortion and the Doctrine of Double Effect." Reprinted in *Killing and Letting Die*, edited by Bonnie Steinbock. Englewood Cliffs, N.J.: Prentice-Hall, 1979.

Frankfurt, Harry. *The Importance of What We Care About*. (Cambridge: Cambridge University Press, 1988).

Fried, Charles. *Right and Wrong*. Cambridge, Mass.: Harvard University Press, 1978.

Gewirth, Alan. "Are There Any Absolute Rights?" In *Theories of Rights*, edited by Jeremy Waldron. Oxford: Oxford University Press, 1984.

Hare, R. M. *Moral Thinking*. New York: Oxford University Press, 1981.

Harris, John. "The Survival Lottery." Reprinted in *Killing and Letting Die*, edited by Bonnie Steinbock. Englewood Cliffs, N.J.: Prentice-Hall, 1979.

Heyd, David. *Supererogation*. Cambridge: Cambridge University Press, 1982.

Isenberg, Arnold. "Critical Communication." Reprinted in *Art and Philosophy: Readings in Aesthetics*, edited by W. E. Kennick. New York: St. Martin's Press, 1964.

Kagan, Shelly. "The Additive Fallacy." *Ethics* 90 (1988): 5–31.

————"Does Consequentialism Demand Too Much?" *Philosophy & Public Affairs* 13 (Sum 84): 239–254.

————*The Limits of Morality*. Oxford: Oxford University Press, 1989.

————"Responses to My Critics." *Philosophy and Phenomenological Research* 51(4) (1991): 919–28.

Kamm, F. M. "Constraints and You." Paper presented to the American Philosophical Association, Pacific Division, Long Beach, California, 1984.

————*Creation and Abortion*. New York: Oxford University Press, 1992.

————"The Doctrine of Double Effect: Reflections on Theoretical and Practical Issues." *The Journal of Medicine and Philosophy* 16 (October 1991): 571–85.

————"Equal Treatment and Equal Chances." *Philosophy & Public Affairs* 14(2) (Spring 1985): 177–194.

————"Ethics, Applied Ethics, and Applying Applied Ethics," in *Applied Ethics and Ethical Theory*, edited by D. Rosenthal and F. Shehadi. Salt Lake City: University of Utah Press 1988.

————"Harming, Not Aiding, and Positive Rights." *Philosophy & Public Affairs* 15(1) (Winter 1986): 3–32.

————"Harming Some to Save Others." *Philosophical Studies* 57(3) (November 1989): 227–60.

————"High Theory, Low Theory, and the Demands of Morality," *Theory and Practice: NOMOS XXXVII*. New York: New York University Press, 1995.

————"The Insanity Defense, Innocent Threats, and Limited Alternatives." *Criminal Justice Ethics* (Summer 1987): 61–76.

————"Killing and Letting Die: Methodology and Substance." *Pacific Philosophical Quarterly* 64 (Winter 1983): 297–312.

————*Morality, Mortality*, Vol. I. New York: Oxford University Press, 1993.

————"Non-Consequentialism, The Person-as-an-End-in-Itself, and the Significance of Status." *Philosophy & Public Affairs* 21(4) (Fall 1992): 354–89.

————"Prerogatives and Restrictions." Paper presented at the American Philosophical Association, Pacific Division, San Francisco, 1985.

————"The Problem of Abortion." In *Ethics for Modern Life*, edited by R. Abelson and M. Friquenon. New York: St. Martin's Press, 1982.

————"Reason and Morality," *NOUS* (forthcoming).

————"Supererogation and Obligation." *The Journal of Philosophy* 82(3) (March 1985): 118–38.

Kant, Immanual. *The Groundwork of the Metaphysics of Morals*, Trans. T. K. Abbott. (Buffalo, N.Y.: Prometheus Books, 1987).

Meyers, Diana. *Inalienable Rights: A Defense*. (New York: Columbia University Press, 1985).

Montmarquet, James A. "On Doing Good: The Right and the Wrong Way." *The Journal of Philosophy* 79(8) (August 1982): 439–55.

Moore, G. E. *Principia Ethica*. Cambridge: Cambridge University Press, 1903.

Nagel, Thomas. *Mortal Questions* Cambridge: Cambridge U. Press, 1979.

————*The View from Nowhere*. New York: Oxford University Press, 1986.

————"Limits of Objectivity." *The Tanner Lectures on Human Values*, Vol. 1. Salt Lake City: University of Utah Press, 1980.

————"The Value of Inviolability," Revue de Metaphysique et de Morale, No. 2/1994.

Nozick, Robert. *Anarchy, State and Utopia*. New York: Basic Books, 1974.

Parfit, Derek. "Innumerate Ethics." *Philosophy & Public Affairs* 7(4) (Summer 1978): 285–301.

————"Later Selves and Moral Principles." In *Philosophy and Personal Relations*, edited by Alan Montefiore. Montreal: McGill-Queen's University Press, 1973.

————*Reasons and Persons*. New York: Oxford University Press, 1985.

Quinn, Warren. "Actions, Intentions, and Consequences: The Doctrine of Doing and Allowing." *Philosophical Review* 98 (1989): 287–312.

————"Actions, Intentions, and Consequences: The Doctrine of Double Effect," *Philosophy & Public Affairs* 18 (Fall 1989): 334–351.

————"Reply to Boyle's 'Who is Entitled to Double Effect?'" in W. Quinn, *Morality and Action*. Cambridge: Cambridge University Press, 1993.

Rachels, James. "Active and Passive Euthanasia." Reprinted in *Killing and Letting Die*, edited by Bonnie Steinbock. Englewood Cliffs, N.J.: Prentice-Hall, 1981.

Richards, David A. J. *A Theory of Reasons for Action*. New York: Oxford University Press, 1971.

Ross, W. D. *The Right and the Good*. Oxford: Oxford University Press, 1930.

Russell, Bruce. "On the Relative Strictness of Positive and Negative Duties." Reprinted in *Killing and Letting Die*, edited by Bonnie Steinbock. Englewood Cliffs, N.J.: Prentice-Hall, 1979.

————"Presumption, Intrinsic Relevance, and Equivalence." *Journal of Medicine and Philosophy* 4 (1979): 263–68.

Scanlon, Thomas. "Contractualism and Utilitarianism." *Utilitarianism and Beyond*, edited by A. Sen and B. Williams. Cambridge: Cambridge University Press, 1982.

————"Rawls' Theory of Justice." *University of Pennsylvania Law Review* 121 (1973): 1020–69.

Scheffler, Samuel. *The Rejection of Consequentialism*. Oxford: Oxford University Press, 1982.

Sen, Amartya. "Rights and Agency." *Philosophy & Public Affairs* 1 (Winter 1982): 3–39.

Smart, J. J., and Williams, Bernard. *Utilitarianism: For and Against*. Cambridge: Cambridge University Press, 1973.

Taurek, John M. "Should the Numbers Count?" *Philosophy & Public Affairs* 6(4) (Summer 1977): 293–316.

Temkin, Larry. "Intransitivity and the Mere Addition Paradox." *Philosophy & Public Affairs* 16(2) (Spring 1987): 138–187.

Thomson, Judith. "A Defense of Abortion." *Philosophy & Public Affairs* 1(1) (Fall 1971): 47–66.

————"Killing, Letting Die, and the Trolley Problem." *The Monist* 59 (1976): 204–17.

————*The Realm of Rights*. Cambridge, Mass.: Harvard University Press, 1990.

————"Rights and Deaths." *Philosophy & Public Affairs* 2(2) (Winter 1973): 146–59.

————"Self-Defense and Rights." *The Lindley Lecture*. Lawrence, Kan.: University of Kansas, 1976.

————"The Trolley Problem." *The Yale Law Journal* 94 (Spring 1985): 1395–1415. Reprinted in *Rights, Restitution and Risk*, edited by William Parent. Cambridge, Mass.: Harvard University Press, 1986.

Unger, Peter. "Causing and Preventing Serious Harm," *Philosophical Studies* 65 (1992): 227–255.

Waldron, Jeremy, ed. *Theories of Rights*. Oxford: Oxford University Press, 1984.

Williams, Bernard. "Moral Luck." *Moral Luck*. Cambridge: Cambridge University Press, 1981.

————"Persons, Character, and Morality." *Moral Luck*. Cambridge: Cambridge University Press, 1981.

————"Utilitarianism and Moral Self-Indulgence." *Moral Luck*. Cambridge: Cambridge University Press, 1981.

Wolf, Susan. "Above and Below the Line of Duty." *Philosophical Topics* 14(2) (Fall 1986): 131–148.

Zaitchik, Alan. "Trammel on Positive and Negative Duties," *Personalist* 58 (January 1977): 93–96.

INDEX

abandon 276, 288n18

Abel, Richard 297, 310

Abelson, Raziel 118n3,9

ability to change 276

abortion 42, 193
    death of the fetus in 193, 194
    fetus as morally innocent threat in 194
    loss of life-as-a-benefit from mother in 194
    and PPH 194

absolute restriction and DDE 150

accomplices to letting-die cases 93

achieving a good with a foreseen harmful effect of another good 175

act. *See also* action
    "act-scenes" 244, 257n16
    against knowledge of truth about good world 282
    as those who have vivid knowledge would act 232
    compulsive 257n15
    guided by the harm 247
    in accordance with moral reality 282
    in accordance with the truth 281
    more than once 161
    not in certain ways now 245
    vs. omission 29, 37, 39
    one must act well as long as one can 257n16
    for one's own sake 250
    prohibitive quality of the content of agent's 223
    for reasons 273
    that can ever be undone 257n16
    that produce state of affairs, evaluation of 239
    to show concern for ideal of persons as separate 285
    wrong act doesn't imply worse world 281

action. *See also* act
    innocuous 93
    probability of dangerousness of 94
    wrong 89

acting against reason 197–8

actively giving up something 215

advantage 167

aesthetics 83

agency 331
    corrupt 241
    negative 76, 85n11
    positive 76–9, 85n10, N11

agent 135, 297
    agent-concerned 238–40, 245, 253
    agent-focused 208, 223, 236n21, 238–40, 245, 247–49, 252–3, 284, 306
        arguments 293, 298, 306
        objections 293, 294
    agent-neutral 261, 279–80, 287n2
    agent-non-relative 261, 272
    agent-related 261
    agent-relative 208, 222, 223, 236n21, 238, 240, 246–9, 253, 255n8, 261–3, 279, 287n7, 306
    concern about something out of proportion to its value 210, 221, 225–6, 228
    constant 298
    contemplating his act 240, 250, 253
    content of what the agent does 208
    disvalue 263
    duty 245
    duty-based penalties 297
    freedom of 215
    Guilty Agent Case 242–5, 247, 253, 257n16
    has to substitute himself for other agents 238
    integrity of 210–11
    inviolability 279
    magnified value 279

359